Teaching Second Language Reading

Also published in
Oxford Handbooks for Language Teachers

Teaching American English Pronunciation
Peter Avery and Susan Ehrlich

Success in English Teaching
Paul Davies and Eric Pearse

Doing Second Language Research
James Dean Brown and Theodore S. Rodgers

Teaching Business English
Mark Ellis and Christine Johnson

Intercultural Business Communication
Robert Gibson

Teaching and Learning in the Language Classroom
Tricia Hedge

Teaching English Overseas: An Introduction
Sandra Lee McKay

Teaching English as an International Language
Sandra Lee McKay

How Languages are Learned 3rd edition
Patsy M. Lightbown and Nina Spada

Communication in the Language Classroom
Tony Lynch

Teaching Young Language Learners
Annamaria Pinter

Doing Task-based Teaching
Jane Willis and Dave Willis

Explaining English Grammar
George Yule

Teaching Second Language Reading

Thom Hudson

OXFORD
UNIVERSITY PRESS

OXFORD
UNIVERSITY PRESS

Great Clarendon Street, Oxford OX2 6DP

Oxford University Press is a department of the University of Oxford.
It furthers the University's objective of excellence in research, scholarship,
and education by publishing worldwide in

Oxford New York

Auckland Cape Town Dar es Salaam Hong Kong Karachi
Kuala Lumpur Madrid Melbourne Mexico City Nairobi
New Delhi Shanghai Taipei Toronto

With offices in

Argentina Austria Brazil Chile Czech Republic France Greece
Guatemala Hungary Italy Japan Poland Portugal Singapore
South Korea Switzerland Thailand Turkey Ukraine Vietnam

OXFORD and OXFORD ENGLISH are registered trade marks of
Oxford University Press in the UK and in certain other countries

ISBN-13: 978 0 19 442283 3

Printed in China

This book is printed on paper from certified and well managed sources.

To my mother, Patsy Hudson

CONTENTS

ACKNOWLEDGMENTS

I owe thanks to many people for helping to bring this text to fruition. I want to thank my graduate students who read and commented upon previous versions of the chapters. I also wish to thank Julia Sallabank of Oxford University Press. She patiently worked with me during the editing and production process. I want to thank Shira Smith for listening to me talk about the content over meals, in cars, on trains, and planes. And finally, I want to thank my mother for working with me so unwearyingly that reading summer during my youth.

The authors and publisher are grateful to those who have given permission to reproduce the following extracts and adaptations of copyright material:

The *Bakersfield Californian* for permission to reproduce 'AIDS test blocked' from the *Bakersfield Californian*, September 13, 1990.

Blackwell Publishing for permision to reproduce a diagram on cross-cultural differences from 'Cultural thought patterns in intercultural education' by R. B. Kaplan, from *Language Learning* Volume 16 (1996), pp 1–20.

The Copyright Clearance Center for permission to reproduce: 'Table of correlations of language by skill' from 'Reading–writing relationships in first and second language' by J. E. Carson et al. from *TESOL Quarterly* Volume 24 (1990), pp. 245–66; the table 'Means and standard deviations on L1 reading test' from 'The relative contributions of L2 language proficiency and L1 reading ability to L2 reading performance: A text of the threshold hypothesis in an EFL context' by J.-W. Lee and D. L. Schallert, from *TESOL Quarterly* Volume 31 (1997), pp. 713–49; and for permission to adapt the table 'The reading strategies identified by readers' from "The cognitive reading strategies of ESL students"' by S. Knight el al from *TESOL Quarterly* Volume 19 (1985), pp. 789–92, and the table 'A summary of the responses to interview questions' from "That's just how it was": the effect of issue-related emotional involvement on reading comprehension' by R. W. Gaskins, from *Reading Research Quarterly* Volume 31 (1996), pp. 386–405.

JP Donleavy for permission to reproduce a brief extract from *The Unexpurgated Code: A Complete Manual of Survival and Manners*. Reproduced by kind permission of the author.

The *Los Angeles Times* and Jim Mann for permission to reproduce ' Bush's Brother Linked to Firm in Panama Deal' by Douglas Frantz from *The Los Angeles Times* 20 December 1989.

The Nikkei Weekly for permission to reproduce the Table of Contents from 'Japan Economic Almanac 2002'.

The University of Hawaii for permission to reproduce a screenshot of the University of Hawaii webpage www.hawaii.edu.

University of Tornoto Press for permission to reproduce the figure 'The VKS elicitation scale self-report categories' from 'Assessing second language vocabulary knowledge: depth versus breadth' by M. Wesche and T. Paribakht, from *The Canadian Modern Language Review/La Revue canadienne des langues vivantes* Volume 53 (1996), pp. 13–40, published by University of Toronto Press.

INTRODUCTION

My interest in reading began at an early age through my own initial experiences of learning to read at school. Books and magazines were all around my house as I grew up. Everyone around me read with little apparent difficulty or noticeable effort. Yet when I began school, I initially found the task to be impenetrable. It made no sense to me that the letters that we practiced drawing endlessly came together to produce anything other than a collection of those letters. For a time I could hide my bewilderment and I did so because none of the rest of my diminutive classmates appeared to be confused, and indeed, much of the time I was not aware enough to know that I was confused. It often appeared to me that we were all doing the same thing. I looked at the page and drew the letters, and classmates looked at the page and drew the letters, though I did not seem to be having as much fun as the other kids were.

Finally, toward the end of second grade, my teacher contacted my mother and told her that I was having real trouble reading. She said that they were considering holding me back. That got everyone's attention. They conferenced and the teacher said that they would test me at the beginning of the next school year to decide what to do. That summer, my mother sat with me every day, helping me learn to read. My friends were outside, playing and going places, having fun, while I sat for what initially seemed like endless hours. Clock hands seemed not to move. However, gradually, the process began to make sense. As I read, the typefaces in the books began to get smaller, and the readings themselves more interesting. Over time, less and less cajoling or coercion on the part of my mother was required to get me to read. Eventually, at my urging, we would go to the public library to check out piles of books. The content in the books was fascinating. The books were about pirates, lost puppies, mysteries, sinister murderers, devious villains, wild horses chased by cowboys, and about how to do magic tricks that would amaze and astound your family and friends. There were wonderful descriptions of countries like Egypt and China and India. You could find out how to make a kite and stink bombs. Since that summer, I have rarely been without a book, magazine, newspaper, guide, list, or other reading material.

Those summer experiences have remained with me, and have in part been the stimulus for my interest in reading and learning to read as research areas. They have made me curious about how and why people have trouble learning to read, and how good readers will at times come across textual material that gives them momentary trouble.

This book is about how people read and learn to read in a second or foreign language. I use the term second language or foreign language much as Mitchell and Myles (1998) do when they state that 'the learning of the "second" language takes place sometime later than the acquisition of the first language' (1). Thus, the text does not directly address the simultaneous learning to read of bilinguals, although it does discuss some of the ancillary research that addresses the topic.

Teaching Second Language Reading addresses issues of second language reading from a combined psychological and social perspective. The book attempts to place reading within its contexts, placing relatively less emphasis on the decontextualized views of reading typical in texts that adopt a primarily psychological view. Additionally, it attempts to provide more detailed information about, and critiques of, the studies discussed in the literature. There are four tenets central to the themes in this book. First, reading takes place in a particular context with a particular purpose. That context and its familiarity will affect how the reader reads and interacts with the text. Second, becoming a successful second language reader involves overcoming both language problems and reading problems, and the extent to which language is a problem varies with the type of cognitive processing that is required by the particular reading task. In short, relatively low proficiency can be less problematic when the reader is engaged in a familiar and easy reading task. Third, the knowledge of the world that a reader possesses can assist in the reading process. This knowledge of the world is often reflected in the depth and breadth of the learner's vocabulary base. Finally, the extent to which the learner's reading experience is congruent with a meaningful literacy act will affect his or her motivation, interest, and engagement with the text. These are recurrent concepts throughout the text.

This book is designed to be both a textbook for teachers in training, and a reference for those teachers and researchers who wish additional information. It goes into many of the research studies in depth in order to provide the reader with a broad scope of knowledge of the types of research practices that are available. It also presents implications for instruction in response to the different research findings. The text is organized as follows:

- **Chapter 1: Issues in reading**, briefly presents an overview of issues particular to second language reading, including an examination of the process and a synthesis of requirements for successful reading. It discusses different types of text formats and functions and shows how each requires a different reading focus on the part of the reader.
- **Chapter 2: Theories and models of first language reading processes**, presents a historical overview of research on reading processes, including

many of the different models that have been developed to explain the reading process for first language readers.

- **Chapter 3: Second language reading issues**, looks into views that have been used to explain second language reading and instruction, discussing the relationships between first and second language reading and learning to read.
- **Chapter 4: Reading skills**, addresses the notions of reading skills in first and second language reading with an emphasis on the extent to which reading skills are separable and hierarchically ordered. It addresses the ubiquitous terminology that employs terms such as *lower-level* and *higher-level* skills.
- **Chapter 5: Strategies and metacognitive skills**, examines reading strategies and their implications for instruction. It addresses the question of how the reader tackles problems in the reading process as well as how he or she orients himself or herself to the reading task and process.
- **Chapter 6: Content schema and background knowledge in second language comprehension**, presents a discussion of the role that content and cultural schemata and background knowledge, play in the interpretation of texts. It is important to try to understand how the background of our students can influence their interpretation of the texts that they encounter.
- **Chapter 7: Formal schema and second language reading**, addresses the roles that can be played by orthographic and phonemic relationships, syntax and language structure, text cohesion, and knowledge of typical text structures such as narrative, cause-and-effect, and description. It then provides some discussion of the pedagogy involved in teaching text structure.
- **Chapter 8: Genre and contrastive rhetoric**, is in many ways an extension of the previous chapter but focuses on how the text structures used in different languages may differ, and how these differences can affect comprehension. It provides an overview of instructional approaches that have been used in addressing genres and rhetorical structure.
- **Chapter 9: Vocabulary in second language reading**, looks at work that has been carried out to improve our understanding of how vocabulary affects second language reading. It first addresses the very basic issue of what it means to know a word, and then examines various models for the relationships between vocabulary and reading comprehension. Finally, it focuses on second language vocabulary pedagogy.
- **Chapter 10: Reading and writing relationships**, is concerned with views of reading and writing relationships and with the connections between second language reading and second language writing. It focuses on ways to contextualize reading instruction rather than view reading as an isolated instructional subject.
- **Chapter 11:** The book then finishes with an overview of the discussions.

Each chapter in the book has discussion and study questions at the end. These are designed to promote further discussion about issues raised in the chapter. At the end of the text there is a glossary of terminology appearing in the text that might need clarification. Words which appear in the glossary are printed in small capitals in the text.

1 ISSUES IN READING

Introduction

The capacity to read is a truly wondrous human ability. Just the fact that over a billion and a half human brains distributed around the world can read or can learn to read, while no other animal or machine can accomplish this feat, is more than merely noteworthy. It is an amazing capacity that allows people in different physical locations and eras to communicate ideas, grand and mundane, to one another. Yet, on a day-to-day level, most people who can read do not normally think of the ability as being any kind of extraordinary activity. Those who cannot read, however, in most contemporary societies at any rate, think about reading frequently and devise many ways to cope with its absence.

If we reflect on the reading process as objective observers, reading appears to be at least as magic as pulling rabbits from hats, conjuring pigeons from coat sleeves, or producing dimes from behind someone's ear. It is a skill that has only been around for about five thousand years. Through script, writers are able to communicate with others at great distances. Readers are able to take arbitrarily determined shapes presented against some appropriate background and turn them into meaning. Whether the contrasting shapes and backgrounds happen to be letters on a page, skywriting against a blue sky, neon flashing an advertisement in a window, or letters on a computer screen, individuals in the process of reading create meaning on their own. As the reader becomes more proficient at reading, and uses the reading ability in more and different tasks, this process of interpreting letters and words becomes increasingly automatic. As will be seen throughout this book, there is a great deal of debate about the complexity of this process. For example, the process is affected by how much control the reader has over the sound-symbol relationship of the alphabet (Stanovich and Stanovich 1995). Also, there is a great deal of disagreement about just how 'autonomous', the processes are and how much they are 'context dependent' (Street 1993a). However, the skilled reader generally has little problem in the processing of these different media as long as they are clear and legible.

Furthermore, this process of identifying words from the visible letters is not the end of the reading process. The reader is able to interpret words that have different meanings in different sentences. There is an ability to be flexible in the interpretation of what particular combinations of words mean. As Rayner and Pollatsek (1989: 4) point out, a proficient reader can comprehend each of the following potentially ambiguous sentences with little trouble.

John knew the boxer was angry when he started barking at him.

John knew the boxer was angry when he started yelling at him.

The boxer hit John because he started yelling at him.

The boxer hit John and he started yelling at him.

John thought the billboard was a wart on the landscape.

John hit the nail on the head with his answer.

In addition to vocabulary knowledge that allows multiple meanings for any particular word, successful reading involves being actively involved in the process and understanding what types of possible interpretations can be made. This ability to evaluate possible outcomes and interpretations is based to a large extent on the prior knowledge that the reader brings to the text. That prior knowledge allows the reader to know what the possible events for any particular text type are. Skilled readers use a great deal of context to interpret words and sentences while processing text (Perfetti 1995). Consider the following extract referenced by Just and Carpenter (1987: 247):

Imagine yourself walking into a room; it is the master bedroom of a quiet Victorian house, in a slum of Bombay, which has just had a fire and been rebuilt in modern style, except for the master bedroom which is only half remodeled having its decorative paneling intact but barely visible because of the thick smoke.

(Feldman 1975: 93)

Our background knowledge of archetypical Victorian houses, concepts of Bombay, previous experience with house fires, and an understanding of home remodeling interact with our reading specific skills to supply and update meaning in real time as we proceed through the text, shifting and refining the image. Our interpretation is context sensitive and continually rearranged to reconcile newly incoming information that is inconsistent with internalized images and interpretations developed milliseconds before. We continually construct and reconstruct our interpretation of the passage and its meaning.

Further, even the proficient reader occasionally encounters troublesome text. Such uncooperative text may result from a perceived lack of coherence, from a temporary lapse of attention on the part of the reader, or from any number of other mismatches between the text and effective processing by the reader. In such instances, the reader brings strategies to bear to repair the problem (Bereiter and Bird 1985). The reader employs numerous monitoring strategies throughout the reading process as facilitating aids for a smooth and efficient reading activity. These strategies are goal driven (Garner 1990b) and vary across different contexts or settings. It is precisely this interaction of goals and strategies that makes it difficult to define a single construct for the reading process in isolation.

Finally, it is important to see that throughout the processing of text, applying background knowledge to the message, and monitoring and making repair processes, the reader in the real world is involved in a meaning-based activity that is purpose and comprehension driven. Reading is motivated by the reader's particular purpose and is propelled by increasing comprehension of the texts. Whether we are looking at children reading at school or at home, or at adults reading university-level course materials or a selection of popular fiction, it seems clear that most comprehension is linked to purpose, and it is important to consider reading within the context of that purpose (Ferdman and Weber 1994). Readers do something with the texts they read. They talk about them; they write about them; they summarize them; they synthesize different texts into something that represents their own ideas. They do many things with text, and the facility to do what they do with text is a large part of what constitutes 'reading proficiency'. Adler (1940: 14) alludes to how purpose affects reading in his passage:

> If we consider men and women generally, and apart from their professions or occupations, there is only one situation I can think of in which they almost pull themselves up by their bootstraps, making an effort to read better than they usually do. When they are in love and are reading a love letter, they read for all they are worth. They read every word three ways; they read between the lines and in the margins; they read the whole in terms of the parts and each part in terms of the whole; they grow sensitive to context and ambiguity, to insinuation and implication; they perceive the color of words, the odor of phrases, and the weight of sentences. They may even take the punctuation into account. Then, if never before or after, they read.

Thus, it is necessary to see the reading process as a series of literacy events or literacy acts. Throughout this text, we will be concerned both with the basic information processing the reader is involved with in reading a text, and with what the reader does with both the text and the information that has been gained.

This concept of literacy events or literacy acts in the second or foreign language context generally entails a concern with literacy as directed at some target language literacy practice. There is a concern, for example, with how well the student can read a second language and perform some act based on the text, such as summarization or SYNTHESIS. However, it is important to continually recognize that many second language readers also have a literacy in their first language that they use daily, simultaneously with the target language (Reder 1994). This first language literacy is an asset to the learners and should be seen in that light. Whether the second language reader is a recent immigrant engaged in filling out forms, a foreign student in a second language context reading an assigned text, or a secondary or tertiary student in a foreign language context, will affect the role that the first language literacy plays in different ways. However, the particular context is an important variable to examine in any analysis of which target language literacy skills are applied. In most cases, the second language learner/reader will be using multiple languages in daily discourse. With respect to second language learners/users of English, for example, our understanding of their English literacy practices must be viewed in terms of the ecology of their entire literacy experiences. Whether we are working with a foreign student attending a university in Australia or the United States, an immigrant working in a restaurant or computer store, or a high school student in Japan studying English for a university entrance exam, it is rare that English will be the only language that the person uses throughout his or her literacy experiences each day. As Cook (1992: 584) notes, 'The L1 is present in the L2 learners' minds, whether the teacher wants it to be there or not. The L2 knowledge that is being created in them is connected in all sorts of ways to their L1 knowledge'. Further, throughout their normal days, they will frequently be interacting only in the first language.

Investigations into literacy have their roots in a number of different disciplines, each with its own set of concerns and assumptions. Some views focus on the linguistic elements of reading, emphasizing the importance of LEXICON, syntax, and PHONEME–GRAPHEME CORRESPONDENCE. Other views concentrate on the cognitive processes of the reader encountering text and constructing meaning through strategy and skill activation. In addition, there are views that focus on sociocultural dimensions of literacy, emphasizing such factors as how literacy is defined through social practice and the attendant links to ideology and power (Kucer 2001). It is clear that all of these factors are important in understanding first and second language reading. Literate readers simultaneously control the linguistic, cognitive, and sociocultural aspects of written language. Without the cognitive process to inquire after and discover meaning, or a systematic linguistic text representation, or a social context, literacy events would not occur. Literacy is multidimensional in the way it incorporates multiple features and processes.

Reading involves the interaction of an array of processes and knowledges. It involves basic DECODING SKILLS such as letter recognition, higher-level cognitive skills, such as inferencing, and interactional skills, such as aligning (or not aligning) oneself with an author's point of view. So, throughout the discussions in this text, we will be looking at the relationships between: a) AUTOMATICITY; b) background knowledge; c) reading strategies and metacognitive skills; and d) purpose and context. Additionally, second language reading involves second and first language literacy interactions. All of these factors are important to any explanation of second language reading processes.

To the extent that we focus on reading as involving individual skills, we are taking an orientation referred to by Reder (1994: 33) as a 'dipstick' model of literacy instruction and assessment, 'in which the individual's head can be opened up, a linear instrument inserted (the dipstick), and a measurement taken (the individual's literacy "level")'. This measurement indicates whether there is a sufficient amount of literacy there, or whether we need to add some more through additional formal instruction. On the other hand, to the extent that we focus on literacy practices as a set of social, cultural, or academic practices in some particular discourse community, then literacy develops through social practices that are not clearly understood as products of formal instructional activities. Thus, while formal and structured instruction may be important, Reder notes that it may be seen as just another set of literacy practices.

When we consider how to assess the success or lack thereof of automaticity, background knowledge, etc., it is important to consider reading from a perspective linked to questions of literacy. What is literacy? How do we see the relationships between reading and writing? Do we see the two as interrelated or as separate skill areas? Do we see them as sharing the same underlying language processes or as being reinforcing? Second, we need to consider the nature of literacy acts. Each reader has a range of texts to read, and these texts represent a range of different writing genres. When we think of reading and literacy, do we proscribe some of these texts, or do we mean that a person is capable of reading all texts and GENRES encountered? Do we specify that reading involves texts from social and natural sciences, the Bible, paper and on-line computer manuals, email, cartoons, Internet homepages? Finally, we will have to come to terms with what explanations we have for the differences in reading ability that we see. What are the causes of the variables within the learners? How much of the difference in second language readers is due to background knowledge, the relationship of the first language to the target language, general language level, learner reading strategies, or the task expectations of the reader? All of these play an important role in the reading process, and consequently on how reading ability is assessed.

Second language reading

As we take the issues mentioned in the previous section into account specifically in second language reading, we are reflecting the various perspectives
mentioned by Ferdman and Weber (1994) that have been used to research
language and multilingualism. They reiterate that the approaches applied to
second or foreign language reading include linguistic, psycholinguistic, and
sociolinguistic approaches. Further, they note that these differing approaches have not traditionally been very successfully integrated. The first of these
traditions can be seen as seated in an autonomous language-based approach
to reading. This approach focuses on the form of the language and its
relationships to reading. The second approach to reading emerges from
psycholinguistics and focuses on cognitive aspects of reading: how people
acquire, organize, and use their bilingual abilities. Ferdman and Weber note
that the need for this focus goes beyond considerations of first language
interference with the second language, but rather concentrates on how
knowing more than one language is an asset in terms of overall cognitive
functioning. The third stream of research focuses on sociolinguistic
traditions that emphasize social-psychological factors in acquiring reading
ability. Here the concern is with the particular uses to which reading is put in
various social settings, such as home, business, or academic environments.
Each of these traditions contributes to areas that need to be addressed in
examining the variation among readers and within any particular reader.

In looking at second language reading, we will always be confronted with
several questions that can potentially help to explain the variability in second
language reading performance from one person to another. These are,
at least:

1 Is this a reading problem or a language problem?
2 How are lower-level learners different from higher-level learners?
3 How does research into reading processes translate into implications for
   reading pedagogy?
4 How uniform is the reading process within any particular individual,
   much less across individuals?
5 How similar is the role of PHONOLOGICAL CONTROL in the first and
   second language and how does that affect second language reading?
6 What roles do background and cultural differences play in reading and
   learning to read?
7 What roles do first language vocabulary and syntax play in second
   language reading ability?
8 What role does background knowledge play in second language reading
   ability?
9 What is the relationship between reading and writing, speaking and
   listening?

10 What are the differences between the cognitive and learning processes of children, adolescents, young adults, and adults learning to read?
11 What role does the way individual learners value various languages, the target and their own, play in the success or failure of learning to read the target language?

We will not always be able to answer these questions in all contexts. However, it is important to keep them consciously at the front of our attention as we examine how second language learners read and learn to read, two different processes, because how we view them will affect our interpretations.

Examining some of the processes

Given the complexity of the questions posed above, we need to take a close look at some of the features involved in the reading process. Look at the following extracts and decide what is necessary in order to read each of them, what categories of knowledge are needed for successful processing of the text. Which of the questions that follow the extracts can you answer and which can you not answer?

> Every Saturday night, four good friends got together. When Jerry, Mike, and Pat arrived, Karen was sitting in her living room writing some notes. She quickly gathered the cards and stood up to greet her friends at the door. They followed her into the living room but as usual, they couldn't agree on exactly what to play. Jerry eventually took a stand and set things up. Finally, they began to play. Karen's recorder filled the room with soft and pleasant music. Early in the evening, Mike noticed Pat's hand and the many diamonds. As the night progressed the tempo of play increased. Finally, a lull in the activities occurred. Taking advantage of this, Jerry pondered the arrangement in front of him. Mike interrupted Jerry's reverie and said, "Let's hear the score." They listened carefully and commented on the performance. When the comments were all heard, exhausted but happy, Karen's friends went home.
>
> 1 Where did the friends meet?
> 2 Who asked to hear the score?
> 3 How many people were involved?
> 4 What were the people doing?

Extract 1

The first three questions are not difficult to answer at all. The needed information is directly in the text and there is little need for inferencing. The fourth question, however, will involve a great deal more inferencing that utilizes background knowledge. This text was used in a study by Anderson et al. (1977) in which the passage was presented to two groups of college students:

music majors and physical education majors. The music majors tended to interpret the text as about a quartet coming together to play music, and the physical education majors tended to interpret the text as about a game of cards. In some instances, the participants did not see the other option at all. This passage helps to point out that background information and experiences are important in text interpretation. Background knowledge and expectations provide the initial set of possible interpretations of the text. Extract 2 below is another example of how information is used to process text.

> The procedure is actually quite simple. First, you arrange things into different groups. Of course, one pile may be sufficient depending on how much there is to do. If you go somewhere else due to lack of facilities, that is the next step, otherwise you are pretty well set. It is important not to overdo things. That is, it is better to do too few things at once than too many. In the short run this may not seem important but complications can easily arise. A mistake can be expensive as well. At first, the whole procedure may seem complicated. Soon, however, it will become just another facet of life. It is difficult to foresee any end to the necessity for this task in the immediate future, but then one can never tell. After the procedure is completed, one arranges the materials into different goups again. Then they can be put in their appropriate places. Eventually they will be used once more and the whole cycle will then have to be repeated. However, that is part of life.

> 1 What is the first step?
> 2 Is it better to do too many things or too few?
> 3 What is the passage describing?

Extract 2

As with the previous passage, it is fairly easy to answer the first two questions. The answers are stated directly in the text. However, the third question is often difficult. This text was used by Bransford and Johnson (1972) in a seminal study to examine text passage recall. Some of the participants in the study were given the title 'Washing Clothes' prior to reading the text, others were given the title only after they had read the text, and still others were not given the title at all. The recall of the ideas in the text was greater only for the group that received the title prior to reading. The conclusions drawn by Bransford and Johnson were that it was only when a reader has some pre-existing notion of what the text might be about that it is possible to determine what to do with the information that is being presented. Such research points to the need to consider the amounts of ambiguity that exist within a text. It further points to the extent to which it is the reader's job to pick out what is relevant in a text and assign importance. The reader makes assumptions and has default scripts. Extract 3, for example, indicates how prior assumptions color text interpretions.

Jack and Jill went up the hill to fetch a pail of water. Jack came down, and broke his crown, and Jill came tumbling after.

1 Jack and Jill were the only people to go up the hill.   True / False

2 Jack fell down the hill to the bottom.   True / False

3 Jack was either a prince or a king.   True / False

4 Jack carried the pail.   True / False

5 Jill was female.   True / False

Extract 3

Each reader will have some default image with which to answer the questions as either true or false. However, it is easily seen that those answers are not based upon information coming directly and unambiguously from the text. Perhaps the answers come from years of hearing the passage, seeing illustrations in children's books, or from social convention which says that typically 'Jill' is a female name and 'Jack' is a male name. Answering the questions,

Clones, you idiot...I said clones.

GENETIC RESEARCH

Printed by The Ohio Printing Company, Inc.

1 What are clones?

2 What do you have to know to get the point?

Extract 4

indeed simply processing the text, is an active process of inference and prediction, and determining what is a *correct* answer is not solely a process of recognizing the individual words. However, background knowledge and expectations are not all that is involved in reading. Extract 4 indicates how different levels of processing are involved.

This is a fairly clear instance of the need for the reader to be able to make phoneme–grapheme correspondences. Granted, this is a very particular type of reading, but without a recognition of the phonological relationship between *clone* and *clown*, humor is lost. At the same time, the reader is required to make several conceptual connections between the meanings of the two words and the visual information in the picture. In addition to such low-level processing as phoneme–grapheme correspondence, knowledge of vocabulary is also important.

Take a moment to read Extract 5 below. This passage was written by a long-time resident of Hawaii whose memories were often of a long past island period and frequently written with well-deserved nostalgia. In this passage the author assumes a particular audience with particular experiences and particular vocabulary associated with those memories.

Kalua turkey
a welcome
change for outings

MAILI YARDLEY

The Island Way

It might be a bit early to think about plans for Labor Day, which falls on Sept. 3, but not if you want something re-ally special. Lots of you smart ones may have your plans well laid already, and hope all goes well with you. But for those of you who are still vague about what to do, the following suggestion might be a worthy project for a congenial group of all ages.

Why not spend the day at a beach-house around an imu with kalua turkey instead of a pig? You really don't have to be an old pro at this, but it does help to have lots of extra hands and to dig the pit in sand rather than hard soil. Besides fire-wood, ti and banana stumps and leaves, the most important item is real imu stones special porous rock from a river bed that will not explode when heated.

Once the hard core of the troops is gathered, dig a puka about 5- by 6-feet and $2\frac{1}{2}$ feet deep. Place hardwood logs (kiawe is the best for this) criss-cross in the bottom of the imu, leaving enough room in the middle for kindling and kerosene oil; place the special imu stones all over the wood, and then light your fire. This should burn about $2\frac{1}{2}$ hours and give you time to prepare the *piece de resistance*.

Bring out those ancient Hawaiian aluminum-foil baking trays and place one to four 10 to 12-pound turkeys in the pans, stuff with one whole carrot, a stalk of celery, sprig of parsley and quartered onions. Season with Hawaiian salt and pepper and lather with softened oleo. Place foil tent-like over the turkey so the sides are open.

When all the wood is burnt up, flatten the imu down, rake out all smouldering wood and level the bed of stones. Place your foil pans on top of stones, surround with baking bananas, sweet potatoes and puolos of stripped and cleaned luau leaves dampened with coconut milk and pile on the shredded banana stumps and leaves and ti leaves. When all is covered, top with wet burlap bags or large dampened canvas and cover securely with sand. Be sure that no steam vents are left open.

Once this is all done, you're free to swim, sleep, play volleyball or whatever for the next 5 to 5½ hours . . . but just don't forget it! Gingerly open the imu, making sure no sand dribbles down into the pit and on top of the bird. Remove the burlap, the leaves, the vegetables and then lift the ancient pans on to serving tables.

Don't be dismayed at the sight of the "white, white bird," but quickly set about shredding the meat the way kalua pork is done and pour the hot pan juices over the prepared meat. Keep hot to serve. This should be sufficient for 50 servings.

The hard part has been done, so everyone should just relax and enjoy the kau-kau. Today, all and any Island favorites are served at a luau, and actually, some prefer rice or potato salad to poi, which is just as well, since poi is becoming scarcer, and the consistency hardly up to one-finger standards! However, somehow an imu calls for lomi salmon and some poi . . . just for old time's sake!

Watermelon is the easiest commodity to top off this meal, so be sure you have lots of cold melon available. Haupia is traditional, too.

Some malihinis refer to a salad course when they mean the lomi salmon. Actually the word lomi means to shred by hand.

1 What is an imu?
2 How do you shred the meat?
3 What is a puka 'about 5- by 6-feet'?

Extract 5: from The Honolulu Advertiser, *August 22, 1990*

Here it is assumed that newspaper readers will be familiar with such vocabulary as *imu* (a pit), *ti* (a leafy plant), *puka* (a hole), *kiawe* (a type of tree similar to mesquite), *puolos* (bundles), and *kau-kau* (food). It is also assumed that readers will be aware of what it means to be 'shredding the meat the way kalua pork is done'. Clearly, background information is essential if you are to actually carry out the instructions and have kalua turkey on Labor Day. As a relative newcomer to Hawaii when this article was published in the local newspaper, I found my own level of literacy to be challenged.

Although reading involves such processes as applying background knowledge and vocabulary knowledge, it also frequently involves close and detailed reading. Read Extract 6 below and track your understanding.

AIDS test blocked

SAN FRANCISCO—The state Supreme Court blocked mandatory AIDS tests for convicted prostitutes hours after the inaction of an appellate court allowed the resumption of such testing.

A Superior Court judge's order blocking enforcement of the 1989 city law allowing testing of prostitutes for the AIDS virus expired Tuesday morning when the 1st District Court of Appeal refused to extend the enforcement ban.

1   How many courts are involved?
2   What expired Tuesday morning?
3   What is going on here?

Extract 6: from The Bakersfield Californian, *Sept. 13, 1990*

This text requires close reading in order to keep track of the dense information. It requires processing the semantic directionality of such terms as *inaction*, *blocked*, *blocking*, *refusing*, and *ban*. It is necessary to keep track of whether the term encourages action or retards action by the actors. The message is very compact and may easily elude the inattentive reader. This passage is an example of text that requires careful attention to vocabulary and reference.

Extract 7 presents some of the same problems in processing the text. For most readers, a careful reading and questioning is needed to determine the various relationships and implications of this newspaper article.

The headline and text sentence following the bullet lead to conclusions regarding the first president George Bush's brother in relation to potential shady business dealings in Panama during the time that Manuel Noriega was president of that country. However, on close reading, the Bush brothers are actually shown to have had no direct connection to the Panama deal. The reader needs to attend to the relationship between a newspaper heading and the article itself, and recognize that they are both parts of the general newspaper genre. Here we see the need for the reader to be actively involved in questioning the text in a critical manner. Such reading skills are frequently the result of direct and explicit instruction in formal settings, rather than what would be viewed as traditional reading skills such as skimming, scanning, etc.

PANAMA: THE ROAD TO RECOVERY

Bush's Brother Linked
to Firm in Panama Deal

+Noriega: Prescott Bush is a partner in a venture with a Japanese firm accused of paying bribes to the ousted dictator.

By DOUGLAS FRANTZ and JIM MANN
Times Staff Writers

WASHINGTON – Prescott Bush, the President's brother, is a partner in a business venture in China with a Japanese company accused in Senate testimony of paying $4 million in bribes to Gen. Manuel A. Noriega, the ousted Panamanian strongman.

The deal between Bush and Tokyo-based Aoki Corp. involves construction of an $18-million golf course and resort outside the Chinese port city of Shanghai. Bush introduced Aoki to the Chinese officials participating in the development, according to a businessman involved in the deal.

The Shanghai project is unrelated to Aoki's dealings in Panama, and Prescott Bush is hardly the first presidential relative to engage in business ventures that could be affected by government policies.

1 Who was involved in the Panama deal?
2 What are the relationships here among Panama, China, and Japan?
3 What does the last sentence imply?
4 What does it say?

Extract 7: from the Los Angeles Times, *December 30, 1999*

The sign in Extract 8 appeared on the door of the entrance to the European Languages and Literature (ELL) Department at the University of Hawaii toward the end of 1989.

The air conditioner
will be ON tomorrow,
12/1/89.
The European
Languages and Literature office
WILL be OPEN.

---

1 Was the air conditioner off on November 30th?
2 Was the European Languages and Literature office closed on November 30th 1989?
3 What is the purpose of this notice?

Extract 8

Trott helps Otago home in a canter

Otago's South African import Jonathan Trott starred again as the southerners beat Central Districts by 24 runs yesterday to set up a tense four-way State Shield cricket play-off race this week.

Trott scored 72 and took two for 48 with his medium pace as Otago restricted Central to 226 for nine off their 50 overs.

It left a logjam of four teams within one point of each other at the top off the points table – Canterbury and Otago on 25 and Wellington and Central on 24.

The feature match in this Wednesday's final round will be between Central and Wellington in Palmerston North, with just three teams qualifying for the play-offs.

It was Otago's fifth win from seven completed matches this season and confirmed their status as genuine title contenders after being the perennial strugglers.

Otago posted what appeared just short of a par score on the friendly University Oval batting surface when they were dismissed for 250 in the 48th over.

But tight bowling from the Otago part-timers slammed the brakes on and despite the best efforts of New Zealand allrounder Jacob Oram, the hosts always had control.

Oram, returning in the past week from a heel injury as a batsman only, top scored with 60 off 64 balls including five fours and a six.

But wickets fell regularly and the run rate slumped in the middle stages, with Oram and Jarred Englefield adding a fifth wicket partnership of 44 off just 86 balls.

Aside from Warwickshire professional Trott, Otago captain Craig Cumming took an excellent two for 30 off 10 overs of medium pace while Bradley Scott chimed in with two for 48.

It was a good all-round match for Cumming, who scored 52 and with Trott gave Otago a solid batting platform.

Trott hit seven fours in his 72 off 82 balls, keeping his hefty Shield average in three figures with 421 runs at 105.25.

Wicketkeeper Gareth Hopkins boosted the total by cracking 40 off 28 deliveries.

Greg Hegglun took four wickets for Central but they came at a cost of 60 runs off eight overs, while allrounder Brendon Diamanti took three for 49.

In other final-round matches on Wednesday, Otago host Northern Districts and Canterbury host bottom-placed Auckland.

1   Did Otago or Central Districts win?
2   In the second paragraph, what did Trott take two of?
3   What did Greg Hegglun do with the four wickets?

Extract 9: from the New Zealand Herald, *January 30, 2006*

Simply seeing the sign without knowing the context might lead the reader to see several implications about the history of the department and its air conditioning. In order to understand this sign it is necessary to have a context. In November, one of the offices on campus announced that the air conditioning would be turned off in the building in order to conduct some repairs. A sign was placed on the door indicating this. Given the often-oppressive heat and humidity in office buildings without openable windows, the office staff became alarmed and put a sign on the same door to the effect that the ELL office would not be open during the repairs. After some negotiation with University and Department administrators, the scheduling of the repairs was changed and the office was kept open. The sign above is the sign that announced that, in essence, the previous signs were to be ignored. Someone coming upon this sign without that context could easily assume that the air conditioning had been off at some time and that the ELL office had been closed but was to reopen. Thus, being able to simply decode the text and make the appropriate phoneme–grapheme correspondences would not suffice to accurately understand the meaning of the literacy event. Context is essential in that this reading reveals how literacy can take place over time. A decontextualized view of reading is not sufficient to capture the intended meaning of the poster in relation to its intended audience, those who might expect the office to be closed. However, the poster would affirm to someone not of the intended audience that the office will be open for business at the specified time.

Comprehension of the information in Extract 9 requires the reader to understand the rules and scoring system in cricket competition.

Without such knowledge (knowledge which the author of this book does not have), it is almost impossible to understand what is meant in sentences such as 'Trott scored 72 and took two for 48 with his medium pace as Otago restricted Central to 226 for nine off their 50 overs' or 'But wickets fell regularly and the run rate slumped in the middle stages, with Oram and Jarrod Englefield adding a fifth wicket parternship of 44 off just 86 balls'. Passages such as this certainly point out the need to address the role of background information in the selection of texts for instruction or assessment. No amount of attention to low level processing of vocabulary and grammar will clarify the article if the reader is not familiar with the game and its conventions.

Extract 10 is an example of a relatively new type of reading.

The web page assumes knowledge of how to interact with the screen. Very little information is provided by way of instruction as to how the reader is to behave. A basic understanding of how to click on various parts of the screen is assumed. Also, it is assumed that the reader can determine when to click on words, and when to click on visuals or icons.

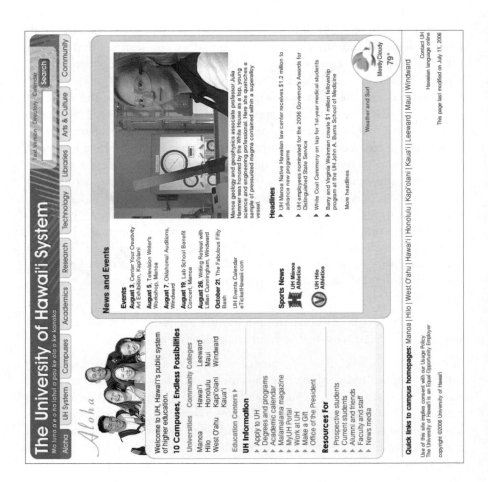

1   How will you discover what is happening on August 26th?

2   How will you locate information about the Maui campus?

Extract 11 again indicates how low-level processing is essential to reading and how prerequisite skills are necessary.

HAZ	— 182 —	HEA	
Hazy a.	ضَبَابِيٌّ . مُغبَرٌّ	Hear v. t.	سَمِعَ اصغَى . أَطَاعَ
He pron.	هُوَ	Hearing n.	سَمْع . مَسْمَع
Head n. or v. t.	رَأْس . قَادَ . تَرَأَّسَ	Hearken v. t.	أَصغَى . إِسْتَمَعَ
Headache n.	وَجَعُ الرَّأْس . صُدَاع	Hearsay n.	قَوْل . قَالَ وَقِيلَ
Head-dress n.	كِسَاءُ الرَّأْس	Hearse n.	مَرْكَبَة لِحَمْل المَوْتَى
Heading n.	أَوَّلُ الشَّيْءِ . عِنْوَان	Heart n.	قَلْب . لُبّ
Headland n.	رَأْس (فِي البَحْر)	Heart-felt a.	قَلْبِيٌّ . مُخْلِص
Headlong a. or ad.	الرَّأْسُ إِلَى أَسْفَل	Hearth n.	مَوْقِدَة
Head-quarters n.	مَرْكَزُ القَائِد أَو الحُكُومَة	Heartily a.	قَلْبًا . بِنَشَاط
Headship n.	رِئَاسَة	Heartiness n.	خُلُوص . هِمَّة
Headstrong a.	عَنِيد . صُلْبُ الرَّأْس	Heartless a.	قَاسٍ . بِلَا رَأْفَة
Heal v.t. or i.	شَفَى . تَعَافَى . إِنْدَمَلَ	Hearty a.	قَلْبِيٌّ . مُخْلِص . مُتَعَافٍ
Health n.	صِحَّة . عَافِيَة	Heat n. or v. t.	حَرَارَة . سَخَّنَ
Healthful a.	مُتَعَافٍ . مُفِيدٌ لِلصِّحَّة	Heathen n. } Heathenish a.}	وَثَنِيّ
Healthfulness } Healthiness } n.	صِحَّة . عَافِيَة	Heathenism n.	الدِّيَانَة الوَثَنِيَّة
Healthy a.	صَحِيح . نَافِعٌ لِلصِّحَّة	Heave v. t.	رَفَعَ . رَمَى
Heap n. or v. t.	كَوْمَة . عُرْمَة . كَوَّمَ	Heaven n.	السَّمَاء
		Heavenly a.	سَمَاوِيّ

1   What kind of text is this? What is its function?
2   What is the meaning of 'Health' in Arabic?

Extract 11: from Wortabet, J. and Porter, H. English-Arabic and Arabic-English Dictionary *(1954)*

In this extract, a knowledge of both the English and Arabic alphabets is essential. Without this knowledge, no amount of contextual knowledge will help the reader understand the meaning of the word that has been looked up in the dictionary. This is a clear example of the need for readers to activate those abilities that are traditionally termed low-level decoding skills. If the reader is unable to apply such skills, reading will not take place.

As with the web page above, Extract 12 assumes a familiarity on the part of the reader with how to *use* the particular text.

2 *Japan Economic Almanac 2002*

Table of Contents

1 What category contains "Video Games"?
2 What is the function of this page?

Extract 12: from Japan Economic Almanac *2002*

The text is closely aligned with the reader's purpose, and is a tool that acts as an interface between the reader's goals and information that is provided elsewhere about particular areas of interest to the reader. The reader must know how to process the particular text type in order for this genre to be meaningful at all.

Synthesis of reading requirements

The above passages point out several necessary variables to consider as we examine the reading processes of both first and second language readers. Some of the variables are necessary all the time, such as knowing the graphemes of a language. Others are variable in their importance. The information in Table 1.1 is a minimal list of variables that will differentially affect success in reading.

Differing models of the reading process tend to emphasize selected variables in the list and de-emphasize others. Arguments about the relative importance of the variables in the reading process have often been contentious. However, as we progress through this text and attempt to answer questions about the role each of these variables plays, we will see a need to distinguish between what Gough (1995) terms literacy[1] and literacy[2]. The first refers to the ability to read and write, while the second refers to the contextual application of that ability, in the sense of being educated and being a part of the literacy community that produced the text. We will also see that the two concepts are not always mutually exclusive or clearly dichotomous. The complexity of the relationships among variables in reading performance makes any strong statements of relative importance appear simplistic. In reading the extracts above, we have seen the need to take several types of variables into account as we discuss success or non-success in reading. The features identified in Table 1.2 will affect any interpretation of the reading act.

1 Grapheme recognition
2 Phonological representation (perhaps)
3 Syntactic structure
4 Background knowledge
5 Processing strategies
6 Text structure understanding
7 Vocabulary (mixed with background knowledge?)
8 Context of the reading act.

Table 1.1: Variables affecting success in reading

1   Reasons: The category of motivation a reader has for engaging in the reading activity
2   Media: The physical entity that contains text
3   Content: The content material of the reading text
4   Text structure and form: The cohesive structure and textual characteristics as well as text genre
5   Strategies and skills: The application of reading techniques used to fulfill the reader's purpose as well as the specific techniques or abilities possessed by the reader.

Table 1.2: Features affecting the reading act

The importance of the relationships between these can be seen as we view reading in its broadest applications. Although the reading extracts above reflect some of the differing texts and purposes a reader confronts, they give only a hint at how varied the reading process is. For example, look at the expansion in Table 1.3 of the areas just mentioned in Table 1.2.

Clearly, the possible combinations of these variables show how complex and varied the reading process is. This book assumes that all of the variables mentioned in this chapter need to be considered in a discussion of reading. Only by taking into account the many different variables can the richness of the reading process and the process of learning to read be appreciated. However, this view is not always taken by researchers in reading. For example, in discussing the role of the relationship of reading to such activities as proofreading, examining a computer program to locate a programming error, or scanning a newspaper for the latest stock market results, Rayner and Pollatsek (1989: 22–3) state that they take a conservative view and that:

> none of these activities are what we have in mind as reading … we will focus on the rather careful type of skilled reading that occurs when you read to comprehend a textbook, a newspaper article, or a narrative.

Such decisions regarding how to identify reading will inevitably have consequences for how the nature of the reading process is viewed, and for how instruction is determined to take place.

Some concerns about reading that motivate this text

Throughout the remainder of this text, we investigate models of reading in first and second language settings, reading skills and background knowledge, reading strategies, the effects of text structure and genre, selection and

The reasons
Information
Information/pleasure
Pure pleasure

The media

Books	Forms
Newspapers, magazines	Signs
Photocopies, articles	Handheld media devices
Notices	Computer screens
Correspondence	Multi-media carriers

The content

Fiction (long and short)	Poetry
Songs	(Auto)biography
Plays	Schedules
Current events feature articles and essays	Maps
Academic articles, reports, reviews	Menus
Warnings, directions	Advertisements
Letters, postcards, and notes	Announcements
Business letters, solicitations	Comics
T-shirt messages, bumper stickers	Workbook exercises
Raw data	Bibliographic information

The text structure and form

Charts, graphs, illustrations	Point and click images
Isolated lines of text	Expository
Free form	Narrative
Interlinear notes	Headings, subheadings

The strategies and skills
Skimming
Scanning
Extraction of specific information
In-depth (extensive) reading
Proofreading
Metacognition

Table 1.3: Expansion of features affecting the reading act

development of second language reading materials, instruction, assessment and research, reading context and purpose, as well as the wider role of literacy concerns in second or foreign language reading. Several assumptions about reading are made and serve as the bases for the discussion. It is important to understand these assumptions in order to evaluate the value of the information presented.

First, a primary assumption is that reading is meaning based. It is purpose and comprehension driven in that each reader is engaged in reading in order to achieve some goal. It is incumbent on instruction or materials to take this into account. It is clear that language is embedded in contexts, and it is the contextualized language that is of importance to most language users. Thus, second language reading methods, materials, and instruction should focus on contexts and purposes and deal with language specific problems as they emerge from context. Authentic reading is task-based and involves finding information in an active manner, not in a passive way.

Second, it is assumed that the active reader provides a lot of the information necessary to comprehend any text. In this way, the reader is approximating the original author's intentions. Sperber and Wilson (1988) point out that the degree to which a message is comprehended in alignment with the intended meaning is to some extent dependent upon the mutual knowledge shared by the participants. Many traditional models and frameworks for reading adopt an encoding/decoding model of communication which assumes that reading can be represented as the following schematic (after Sperber and Wilson 1988):

message → encoder → channel → decoder → message

This is a strong view entrenched in much Western thought. Here there is a message that is to be communicated. That message is encoded by an author and is presented through text to a recipient decoder who decodes the input and comes up with the author's original message. However, it cannot be true that any person can decode any properly constructed linguistic message. Take the following three sentences, as an example.

1 Beat the eggs until firm.
2 It is cold in here.
3 The air conditioner will be ON tomorrow.

In the first sentence, there must be some experience to interpret *beat the eggs* in a way different from *beat the carpet* or *Beat the Spurs!* Further, that experience will lead to interpreting *firm eggs* differently from a *firm mattress*. The second sentence will be understood in some contexts as a statement of fact, a warning, or a request to turn up the heat. Finally, the implications and meaning of the third sentence can only be accurately understood with knowledge of its historical context. In short, we have to account for what is decoded as well as what was encoded and we have to have some notion of how this takes place.

A third assumption relates to being clear about the relationships between reading and reading instruction in any discussions about reading and instructional planning. It is necessary to address the issue of what reading is not. Reading is not: 1) the reinforcement of oral skills; 2) grammatical or discourse analysis; 3) the acquisition of new vocabulary; 4) translation practice; 5) answering comprehension questions; or 6) practicing to improve reading ability. Certainly, these may aid in learning to read, but they are not reading. We need to be aware of that as we address issues of reading instruction and interpret what a teacher means when he or she says 'My students were reading in class today'. Indeed, they might have been reading, but they might also have just been practicing reading. Our long-term goal is to have students who do not stop reading when the reading class is over. In order to get there, they have to be allowed to read in a meaningful way.

Summary and conclusions

This introductory chapter has presented a number of concerns that will continue to be the meat of discussions throughout the remainder of the book. An attempt has been made to view reading as involving a large number of acts depending upon such features as the reader's purpose, the text type, and the reader's knowledge and skill. Additionally, it has tried to present' those areas within the reading literature that have been the key features of debates about reading and literacy. Reading is a complex activity that involves combinations of the factors in Tables 1.1 through 1.3. The factors vary in their relative importance depending upon the particular reading context. There are contexts in which basic grammatical parsing is of primary concern, while in others the reader's knowledge of the world factors heavily.

The next chapter will focus on key influential models of first language reading with a view toward examining their implications for the second lan-guage reading context. As we will see, most of the models address similar components; they just often value one component over the others. It is this relative emphasis that generally plays a dominant role in the conception of the reading model.

Discussion and study questions

1 Why and how can reading ability vary between readers of the same first language when reading in the first language? When reading in the same second or foreign language?

2 Why and how can reading ability vary within a single individual reader?

3 Table 1.1 lists the following variables as affecting success in reading

   1 Grapheme recognition
   2 Phonological representation
   3 Syntactic structure
   4 Background knowledge
   5 Processing strategies
   6 Text structure understanding
   7 Vocabulary
   8 Context of the reading act.

   How can each of these affect comprehension? Can you think of experiences you have had while reading that indicate the importance of these different variables? What factors will affect the importance of each variable in the comprehension process? In your view of reading, which do you think are most important?

4 Find a text in a book, magazine, or newspaper and discuss what reading characteristics are necessary in order to understand the passage.

5 Take five to ten minutes to reflect upon the types of texts you have read in the past week. List each of them, remembering to include such texts as forms, lists, schedules, etc. Categorize the purposes and contexts for each of these, including pleasure, study, work-related reading, etc.

6 The text notes Gough's (1995) notion of literacy[1] and literacy[2]. Do you feel that this distinction is useful in clarifying how reading instruction should be conceived?

2 THEORIES AND MODELS OF FIRST LANGUAGE READING PROCESSES

Introduction

Any examination of second language reading must address the historical development of theories, approaches, and models that have been developed to explain the processes involved in first language reading. Indeed, many of the concerns for second language reading have evolved from initial research into first language model building.

The first language models that have been developed are meant to describe one of at least two different processes: how a skill is acquired and what the processes of a skilled reader look like (Carr 1982). The models of each process represent overall frameworks that describe what facets of reading or learning to read are viewed as important by the researchers engaged in explaining the processes. As such, a model provides a set of criteria against which research findings can be evaluated. Historically, first language models have provided frameworks for help in explaining second language reading processes and the variables that may be involved. It is important to keep in mind that the models that have been developed in first language settings are tools and that there is a great deal of overlap in the models, particularly as one gets closer to teacher practice. As Stahl and Hayes (1997) point out, academically developed models tend to influence formal pre-service and in-service training, while each practicing teacher's own internalized models tend to mediate the information they get from this academic training and influence what actually takes place in the classroom. The various models that have been proposed tend to change over time and mutate into a hybrid of differing models. Further, as Barnett (1989) notes, there are general problems with the model building of reading processes and instruction. First, the models are limited to the knowledge, historical perspectives, and trends of the time in which each is embedded. Second, the implications of experimental data will change depending upon age, skill, tasks, materials, etc. Indeed, the notion that there can be a single model for reading across tasks, genre, and purpose is doubtful. A more specific problem for second language reading's reliance on first language research and models is the fact that in many second language contexts we are dealing with students who are already literate in a first language.

Additionally, second language learners may come from literacy in languages with a variety of different orthographies. Thus, it is important to distinguish between the processes involved in learning to read versus the process of reading by an accomplished reader in either the first or second language.

A brief overview of research on reading processes

Venezky (1984) notes that research into reading processes can be traced back to cognitive psychologists James Cattell and Wilhelm Wundt in Leipzig in the late 1870s. However, reading research was traditionally focused on reading primarily as a vehicle for examining perceptual processes such as eye movement, field of vision, perceptual span, and word recognition. A great deal of such research was carried out between the 1880s and the 1910s. During that time, most of the language processing issues that are viewed as important today, such as the relation of memory and text, whole word versus phonics approaches, breadth of eye span, subvocalization, and latency times between visual processing and vocalization, were identified and were the focus of research. However, soon after the publication of Huey's pivotal text, *Psychology and Pedagogy of Reading* (1908), psychological research turned its focus to behaviorist explanatory theories, and little cognitive processing research was pursued for quite some time until the 1960s. Although some research did take place, it did not form a cohesive body of knowledge and as such did not reach the critical mass needed to push an academic discipline forward. Venezky (1984) points out that the current emphasis on reading comprehension has only been of primary concern for thirty or forty years. He notes that though the term appears in early reading literature, it was generally associated with teaching methodology or testing. In the 1960s, in part as a response to Chomsky's critiques of Skinnerian psychology, attention to reading process research began to re-emerge with studies addressing speed of word recognition and comprehension (Tulving and Gold 1963; Morton 1964). Some of the cognitive approaches mentioned by Beck and Carpenter (1986) indicate a renewed emphasis on the reading process rather than product alone, with research into eye-fixation times, text structure processing, and word recognition speed.

As will be seen in what follows, a review of models and theories of first language reading can only loosely be viewed as reflecting chronological historical developments. Discussions of the relative importance and role played by visual word recognition, linguistic comprehension (visual or aural), comprehension processes, background knowledge, etc., cycle through time in a recursive fashion that thwarts clear statements that one view began at a particular time and ended at another. However, we can identify trends in the ways that reading has been viewed. This cyclic development in reading theory and models is yet another reason that second language reading researchers need to attend to developing issues in first language reading circles. As will be seen later, many of the approaches that are now ascribed to second and foreign language educators, approaches that were based on first language models, are now being re-evaluated in first language research and pedagogy.

The discussions regarding the nature of reading vary across a scale between the two most paradigmatic approaches termed *bottom-up approaches* and *top-down approaches*, with many current researchers adhering to what has been termed to be an *interactive approach*. Again, it should be kept in mind that there are few adherents to the strong form of either polar approach. Rather, the approaches represent the initial biases and default perspectives of the differing authors.

Bottom-up approaches, which correspond to the cognitive and information-processing psychological concerns mentioned in the last chapter, basically assume that a reader constructs meaning from letters, words, phrases, clauses, and sentences by processing the text into phonemic units that represent LEXICAL meaning, and then builds meaning in a linear manner. This approach assumes that the reading task can be understood by examining it as a series of stages that proceed in a fixed order, from sensory input to comprehension and appropriate response. In strong versions of this view, the process of text comprehension begins with a soon-to-be writer having some notion or idea. This person encodes the message into letters and words, and some soon-to-be reader decodes the letters and words linearly in order to reconstruct the original notion or idea of the writer. The basic difference between reading comprehension and listening comprehension lies in the visual rather than auditory processing of the language (Gough 1972; Hoover and Tunmer 1993). Generally, there is an assumption that information is gained in a rather passive manner, processing is rapid and efficient, and that the information that has been processed and stored in memory has little effect on how the processing occurs (Rayner and Pollatsek 1989).

The top-down approaches, on the other hand, which are generally more sympathetic with the psycholinguistic and sociological perspectives mentioned in the last chapter, assume that a reader approaches a text with conceptualizations above the textual level already in operation and then works down to the text itself. This approach views the information-processing circuit as being slower than assumed by the bottom-up approach as a result of memory capacity and mental limitations on the speed that information can be stored. Consequently, the reader makes continually changing hypotheses about the incoming information. This reader applies background knowledge, both formal and content, to the text in order to create meaning that is personally and contextually sensible. Strong forms of these models assume that the reader is not text-bound, but rather samples from the text in order to confirm predictions about the text message (Smith 1971, 1983, 1994). Consequently, according to these approaches, the reader does not necessarily read each word in the text as is assumed in the bottom-up approaches. Goodman (1968) popularized this approach labeling reading as a *psycholinguistic game*. For him, the key element was that reading was a psycholinguistic process that was an interaction between thought and language (Goodman 1976).

Approaches that take an *interactive* view of reading propose that both the strict bottom-up and top-down models are too naive and simplistic. Reading is seen as bidirectional in nature, involving the application of higher order mental processes and background knowledge as well as features of the text itself. Examples of such a model typically posit reading component skills that are hierarchically organized. Such components could be labeled 1) vocabulary knowledge and sight word recognition; 2) phonetic decoding skills; 3) relational knowledge and prediction from context; and 4) comprehension skills (Carr 1982). In these models, it is assumed that if sight word recognition is successful, then information can be delivered to higher-level skills that make associations between the incoming lexical items and hence help the lower level skills by narrowing the possible new pieces of information that would be acceptable to complete a coherent message. However, as Grabe (1991) notes, the term is used in different ways by different writers. Sometimes writers who use the term *interactive* mean an interaction among the different reading skills, while others refer to the term as relating to the reader interacting with the text.

Bottom-up approaches

Assumptions in traditional bottom-up approaches can pretty much be captured in Carroll's (1964: 62) definition of reading:

> We can define reading, ultimately, as the activity of reconstructing (overtly or covertly) a reasonable spoken message from a printed text, and making meaning responses to the reconstructed message that would parallel those that would be made to the spoken message.

The key features here are the PHONEME–GRAPHEME CORRESPONDENCE notions and the information- processing view of reconstructing an existing message. The process is assumed to require the processing of all graphemic information on the page. The most prototypic model of the uncompromising bottom-up approach is that proposed by Gough (1972), which he calls *one second of reading*. Gough describes how the reader passes through a reading process in which the visual system scans the series of letters one by one. Gough states, 'I see no reason, then, to reject the assumption that we do read letter by letter. In fact, the weight of the evidence persuades me that we do serially from left to right' (335).

Through this process, the reader registers the characters in milliseconds and decodes them into phonemic units. In addressing the issue of how the letters are turned into meaning, Gough continues:

> I will assume that the contents of the character register are somehow transposed into abstract phonemic representations. If, as Chomsky and Halle argue, the orthography of English directly reflects this level of representation, little processing will be required; otherwise, more complex transformations … will yield a string of systematic phonemes that can be used to search the mental lexicon.

(Gough 1972: 338)

Gough sees this process, in English at least, as proceeding serially from left to right. He sees little problem with ambiguous interpretation of lexical items such as *bass* (as fish or type of guitar), since he claims that 'we have found no evidence (as yet) that disambiguation takes place until after lexical search' (338). Word recognition takes place prior to comprehension. Once the lexical entries are associated and produce some comprehension, through the psychologically divine intervention of a mechanism Gough terms *Merlin*, then meaning goes to 'The Place Where Sentences Go When They Are Understood' (340), or PWSGWTAU. There is then a re-association of the input with phonological rules which may result in some vocal output. It is telling that reading becomes 'sentences' that go someplace when understood rather than 'propositions' or 'concepts'.

A second theory based on bottom-up processing is the initial incarnation of the framework proposed by LaBerge and Samuels (1974). Subsequent versions incorporated more interactive processes in such a way that comprehension of particular parts of text influence subsequent mental processing. However, the initial model focused on the development and application of AUTOMATICITY in reading skills applied in a linear manner. A distinction between automatic and control processing is assumed. As the processing of any macro-level reading skill becomes automatic, all of the subskills associated with that macro-level skill also become automatic and place fewer demands on working memory. As reading skills such as letter identification become automatic, they require less attention. The notion of attention is key to the model since it is assumed that we can only attend to one thing at a time, but we may be able to process many things at a time so long as no more than one requires attention. The analogy LaBerge and Samuels present for automaticity is basketball:

> In the skill of basketball, ball handling by the experienced player is regarded as automatic. But ball handling consists of subskills such as dribbling, passing, and catching, so each of these must be automatic and the transitions between them must be automatic as well. Therefore, when one describes a skill at the macro level as being automatic, it follows that the subskills at the micro level and their interrelations must also be automatic (295).

In essence, if reading is viewed as having the two levels of decoding text and comprehending text, then as decoding becomes more automatic, attention can be placed on comprehending the text. Hence, reading, in part, involves detecting graphic features, determining the letter code associated with those features, identifying a spelling pattern across all letters, and determining the visual word code. The visual word is then associated with the reader's phonological memory and then with semantic memory. This process becomes more automatic over multiple experiences. The relationship between learning to read and accomplished reading is summed up in the following statement:

> In the early trials of learning we assume that attention activation must be added to external stimulation of feature detectors to produce organization of the letters into a unit. In the later trials, we assume that features can feed into letter codes without attentional activation, in other words, that the stimulus can be processed into a letter code automatically

(LaBerge and Samuels 1974: 299)

Thus, the reader does not bypass the process of phoneme–grapheme correspondence, but rather becomes more automatic at processing, and in the process frees up cognitive resources for comprehension. Over time, the reader may become sufficiently automatic that the visual code will be able to be associated directly with word meaning. Although there is some room for feedback or SCHEMA activation, as in processing the phrase *Her hair is r__*, the LaBerge and Samuels model is clearly a linear processing explanation of reading (Samuels and Kamil 1984).

As can be seen from the discussion above, the bottom-up approaches to reading focus fairly directly on issues of rapid processing of text and word identification. Emphasis is placed on the reader's ability to recognize words in isolation by mapping the input directly on to some independent representational form in the mental lexicon. In general, this mapping is seen to be independent of context. In many cases, the reliance on context is seen as a strategy used by poor readers rather than by good readers (Nicholson 1993). The argument is that poor readers are also poor at mapping text to immediate meaning, and, thus, must rely on context as a compensatory strategy.

The linear information-processing approach of bottom-up models has a great deal of appeal to many researchers who are primarily interested in how a reader reads rather than in what the reader comprehends. However, several researchers have focused their attention on the comprehension process itself, and have developed views that have been labeled as top-down approaches to reading. While the bottom-up approaches basically follow some variant of Perfetti's (1977) view that reading comprehension is equal to language comprehension, plus decoding, plus some minor other contributing variable, top-down approaches are generally congruent with Goodman's (1968) assertion that in examining reading:

> We are looking at it as a total process. This psycholinguistic process is exceedingly complex. To understand it we must consider the language and the systems of language that make possible communication. We must consider the relationship of oral and written language. We must consider the special characteristics of written language and special uses of written language. We must consider the characteristics and abilities of the reader which are prerequisite to effective reading.

Goodman 1968: 15)

Top-down approaches

Kenneth Goodman and Frank Smith are most closely identified with early theories associated with top-down approaches to the reading process. As with bottom-up approaches, few people currently adhere to the strong form of this model. In general, however, the model begins with a view of reading as what Goodman terms the *psycholinguistic guessing game*. Readers use their knowledge of syntax and semantics to reduce their dependence on the print and phonics of the text. He specifies four processes in reading: predicting, sampling, confirming, and correcting. While bottom-up models are generally linear, Goodman's model values the cognitive economy of linguistic information over graphemic information. This model of decoding allowed either:

grapheme → meaning

or

grapheme → phoneme → meaning

Although the model shows that the reader utilizes phoneme–grapheme correspondences, it prefers the cognitive efficiency involved in a reliance on existing syntactic and semantic knowledge. The reader makes guesses about the meaning of the text and samples the print to confirm or disconfirm the guess. In this way, reading is an active process in which the reader brings to bear not only knowledge of the language, but also internal concepts of how language is processed, past experiential background, and general conceptual background. In this model, efficient reading is not the result of close perception and identification of all textual features. Rather, it results from skill in choosing the minimum cues necessary to produce correct guesses. In Goodman's (1976) words:

> Reading is a selective process. It involves partial use of available minimal language cues selected from perceptual input on the basis of the reader's expectation. As this partial information is processed, tentative decisions are made to be confirmed, rejected, or refined as reading progresses.
>
> *(Goodman 1976: 498)*

As evidence in support of this model, Goodman and others present studies of reading using *reader miscue analysis*. This method involves looking at the types of errors readers make while reading aloud. The research tends to show that reading errors are related to the syntactic and semantic contexts of any particular lexical item. So, a reader might read *hoped* for *opened*, *a* for *the*, *he* for *I*. In each instance the part of speech remains the same and represents a reasonable prediction of what the word might be. This fact is taken to indicate that guessing and sampling are taking place as text is transformed into meaning. Goodman's more holistic interpretation of the reading process is certainly consistent with his later association with the Whole-Language approach to teaching.

Smith (1971, 1994) also focuses on the top-down nature of reading. A continually moderating factor in the process is the severe limit on the amount of information the visual system can process into the reader's short-term memory, and the interaction or trade-off between the visual and non-visual processes. For Smith, it would simply take too much time for a reader to process all visual cues. In addressing the role of short-term memory and long-term memory, Smith (1971, 1994) views prediction and use of context as factors that mediate the bottlenecks of memory during reading. He places extreme importance on background knowledge (variously termed *schema* or *schemes, schemata* or *schemas*) in a person's construction of meaning during the processing of virtually any type of information, including print. He states:

> Knowledge of relevant schemes is obviously essential if we are to read any kind of text with comprehension. A child who does not have a scenario about farming is unlikely to understand a story about farming or a reference to farming in a textbook.
>
> *(Smith 1994: 15)*

Additionally, Smith supplied the notion of redundancy in language as an explanatory factor that obviates the need for the reader to attend to every letter or word in a text. As an example, he provides the following unfinished sentence: *The captain ordered the mate to drop the an-* (Smith 1994: 56).

There are four sources of information that help the reader finish the sentence: visual, orthographic (spelling), syntactic, and semantic. Whereas we would need complete visual information if the word appeared in isolation, its context helps eliminate other alternatives. Thus, we are more likely to accept *anchor* than *answer*, *anagram*, or *antibody* (57) as the most likely appropriate completion of the sentence. Additionally, the redundancy is only productive to the extent that it reflects something the reader already knows. In order to utilize the orthographic redundancy, the reader needs to know that the letter *b* is not likely to come after the *an-* in the example sentence above. Further, the reader needs to know that *anchors* are associated with *captains* in some way. According to Smith, the redundancy and application of prior knowledge in the reading process is important because of the limits to the amount of new information that a reader can process at any one time. This is in direct contrast to the view of those who accept the bottom-up approach and assume that readers just get faster at the process.

Smith sees reading as purposeful and selective in that readers attend only to what is necessary to their current purposes. As such, reading is an active process based on comprehension and is anticipatory in nature. The implications of this view are that reading instruction should take place when comprehension of a text is possible, rather than focusing on isolated phoneme–grapheme correspondence activities and drills.

Interactive approaches

Currently, most researchers and teachers have accepted some version of an interactive model of reading which acknowledges a great deal of communication between the differing bottom-up and top-down processes. These interactive approaches allow explanations for many variables in the reading process. Also, the different interactive models will tend to have biases which lean either toward the bottom-up approaches or to the top-down approaches. This in part reflects whether the interactive frameworks focus on the process of reading where the key is on the interaction of componential cognitive processes in fluent reading, or whether the interactive focus is on the product of the reader's interaction with the information in the text and the reader's background knowledge during comprehension (Grabe 1991). Further, the explanatory focus may assume that the most important features of concern are: 1) the automatic application of lower-level skills independent of comprehension (Ehri 1995; Esky and Grabe 1988; Gough 1995; Rayner and Pollatsek 1989; Stanovich and Stanovich 1995); 2) the interaction of background knowledge and text (Anderson and Pearson 1984; Carrell 1983; Hudson 1982, 1991); or 3) the role of social, contextual, and political variables affecting the reader's process of meaning making (Maybin and Moss 1993; Parry 1993; Street 1993a, b).

The first of these explanatory foci is exemplified by Rayner and Pollatsek (1989: 26) when they state that their major emphasis is on the process rather than the product of reading. They continue:

> Some cognitive psychologists who study the product of reading would also want to argue with us concerning our bias towards understanding the process of reading. To their way of thinking, what people remember from what they read may be more important than how they go about the chore of reading. However, our response to such a point is that understanding the process by which some mental structure is created almost logically entails understanding that structure. In contrast, understanding what gets stored in memory may not reveal much about the processes that created the structure.

(Rayner and Pollatsek 1989: 27)

Such an approach lends itself to what is frequently termed the *autonomous* view of reading (Street 1993a, b). In this view, it is possible to examine the reading process outside of its context through isolated reading passages, eye-movement technologies, speed of response protocols, etc. Reading is seen as a skill that can, indeed must, be understood independently from issues of general comprehension. Context can aid in the process, but has less direct influence than the cognitive processing of print.

The second orientation to reading mentioned above, that associated with the interaction of background knowledge and text, is reflected in Smith's (1994) discussion of two aspects of language. He asserts that language has a surface structure, the observable characteristics of language as it exists in print or speech, and it also has a deep structure, the meaning that is obtained from the message. The focus is on the interaction of the writer's intentions and the reader's interpretations. In this view, there is no one-to-one correspondence between the surface structure of language and meaning (Smith 1994: 27). As evidence, Smith points out that such structures as *the cat is chasing a bird* and *a bird is being chased by a cat*, and *a warm-blooded feathered vertebrate is pursued by the domesticated feline* all share very similar meanings despite having very different surface structures. Further, there are strings with the same surface structures with different meanings, such as *flying planes can be dangerous* and *visiting professors may be tedious* as well as *the chickens were too hot to eat* (27). The print is necessarily processed in fluent reading, but the print is mediated by meaning, not mediated by subvocal speech. Meaning can be brought to print directly and oral reading is an added process, not an intermediate phase in comprehension. In such views of the interactive nature of reading, priority is given to the process of sampling the text, making predictions about the intended meaning, and then evaluating the message through subsequent reading.

The third orientation to reading mentioned above assumes the necessity of addressing social context, and is associated with the New Literacy Studies (Street 1993a: 81). Such approaches reject the notion that cognition can be abstracted from social persons and cultural contexts in their focus on concepts such as literacy events, or events in which reading and/or writing play a role. This orientation, then, sees reading and writing together rather than as separate *skills*. It is not really possible to examine literacy; rather, one examines some context of a literacy event and the social, personal, and political roles of the literacy event. Furthermore, it is necessary to look at literacy practices. Literacy practices relate to social assumptions surrounding the conventions people have internalized regarding appropriate and conventional literacy behavior, whether written or spoken. Issues regarding whether a person is expected to read critically and suspiciously, the topics and genres that one selects, and other social conceptions of the role of reading and writing, are important in any examination of reading and reading processing. By locating the practice of reading in relation to reading tasks and social context, such a view avoids the traditional dichotomy between ideas of literate and illiterate. Literacy becomes a relative term associated with particular practices, and focuses on local literacies rather than 'distant literacies' (Street 2003). So, the interactive process of reading involves not only the processing of text on a page or elsewhere, and cultural background knowledge, but also the power relationships in the society which have produced concepts of the reading process.

It is with these three perspectives in mind that we now proceed to examine some of the characteristic interactive models. The focus is on interactive models, given that most current pedagogical approaches focus on some form of interactive model. The various models are presented in the chronological order of the most influential articles that describe each. This order of presentation, rather than a presentation ordered by similarity of the model concepts, is adopted primarily to indicate the diversity and contemporaneousness of thinking about reading models throughout the late 1970s and 1980s.

The Rumelhart model

Rumelhart (1977) proposes that successful reading is both a perceptual and a cognitive process beginning with a flutter of patterns on the retina and ending with a definite idea about some author's intent. A reader uses interacting sensory, semantic, and pragmatic information in a non-linear manner throughout the process of reading. In supporting this interactive view, Rumelhart points out: 1) that the perceptions of letters often depend upon the surrounding letters; 2) that perceptions of words often depend upon the syntactic environment in which we encounter the word; 3) that our perception is influenced by the semantic environment of the word; and 4) that our perception of syntax depends upon the semantic context in which the string appears. The implication, then, is that higher-level processes affect lower-level processes at times.

In his model, graphic information enters the process through a *visual information store* (VIS, in Rumelhart's terms). A cognitive *feature extraction device* selects the important features of the graphic input. A *pattern synthesizer* takes this information along with syntactic, semantic, orthographic, lexical, and pragmatic knowledge (context) in order to produce the most probable interpretation for the graphic input. The reading process is the result of the parallel application of these sensory and non-sensory sources of information. Each of these knowledge sources continually evaluates probabilities against a set of hypothesized interpretations. Through this process, a hypothesis can be accepted, rejected, or be the source of a new hypothesis until the reader comes to some decision.

Rumelhart notes that this model is complex and less clear as a model of prediction than bottom-up sequential models. However, he proposes that the knowledge sources have particular features. At the *featural knowledge level*, features are extracted from the graphic input in the basic level of processing. If hypotheses cannot be accepted, the reader can go back to get additional features for reducing uncertainty. The *letter-level knowledge* source scans the feature inputs and, as it evaluates the features, posits a letter hypothesis. This source also takes into account the relative frequencies of different letters in the language, requiring more evidence for lower-frequency letters such as *q*, in English, than for more frequent letters such as *e*. The *letter-cluster knowledge* makes hypotheses about the possible letter sequences that are likely to form units in the language. So, if, in English, a *q* is found, a *u* is postulated to be the next letter. The *lexical-level knowledge* source and the syntactic knowledge source follow the same pattern as the other sources in predicting, confirming, and generating hypotheses. Rumelhart admits that the *semantic-level knowledge source* is less easily characterized than the others. However, he concludes that it must operate essentially like the others as it evaluates lexical hypotheses for the plausibility of the hypothesized meaning given the reader's knowledge and theories of how the world operates.

The Kintsch and van Dijk models

While Rumelhart includes the lower level processing features, Kintsch and van Dijk (Kintsch 1988, 1998; Kintsch and van Dijk 1978; van Dijk and Kintsch 1983), present a model based on comprehension of text. They do not provide a model for how the lower-level processing takes place, but acknowledge that it must. In presenting a comprehension model, they see little fundamental difference between comprehension through reading and comprehension through listening. Their model is conceived at a level higher than those associated with the CHANNEL or MODALITY of input and hence, their approach differs markedly from the approaches which favor a bottom-up process approach in that it is:

> only concerned with semantic structures ... the model only says when an inference occurs and what it will be; the model does not say how [an inference] is arrived at, nor what precisely was its knowledge base.

(Kintsch and van Dijk 1978: 364)

In this explanation of the comprehension process, texts are first organized into a coherent whole, then condensed into their gist, and then these operations generate new texts and ideas. As with the Rumelhart model, readers are involved in predicting a sequence of events happening, and making inferences as to the possible, likely, or necessary facts in order to predict missing propositions that make the entire sequence of propositions coherent. In this comprehension model, complex processes operate in parallel and sequentially in ways that reduce strain on the processing system.

A key component of the model is the assumption that text is interpreted as a set of propositions that are ordered by various semantic relations among the propositions. Some of these propositions are related through explicit textual relations, while others are mediated through the reader's specific or general background knowledge regarding possible and probable relations. Comprehension of the discourse reflects attention at two levels, *microstructure* and *macrostructure*. The microstructure represents the local level of individual propositions in the text, while the macrostructure represents the global nature of the discourse as a whole. The two levels are related by a set of semantic *macrorules*. From this perspective, it is assumed that there are pragmatic rules, consistent with GRICEAN MAXIMS, that writers (or speakers) do not generally state what is assumed to be known by the reader (or listener). Hence, an explicit text provides those propositions necessary to fill in the void and provide coherence for the reader (or listener). Consequently, the text presented is what is necessary to provide interpretation conditions. Thus, the textual propositions are not only locally related, but also globally constrained to a larger discourse topic. This focus on inferences and the cyclic nature of the process is a key feature in defining this as an interactive model.

The model relies heavily on the reader's discourse structure schemas. Typical examples of these are the structure of a story, the structure of an argument, or the structure of a psychological report. These schematic structures play important roles in comprehension and production. Knowledge of these structures allows readers to determine the importance of expressions in the discourse, and thus how to evaluate the relevance of any particular proposition in the overall context. In processing the text, readers examine the propositions for coherence. If a text base is found to be coherent, it is accepted for additional processing. However, if a proposition is not consistent with other propositions already processed, new inference processes are used to fill in any gaps and make the text base coherent.

So, a model is proposed that is cyclical in its confirming of argument overlap in the propositions to be processed. The process is seen as automatic and has low resource requirements. In each iteration, certain propositions are retained and others excluded. Throughout this process, it is assumed that memory requirements will change depending upon the reader's task. Thus, the probability of recalling the propositions may vary depending upon whether the reader's task is recall, summarization, or synthesis (Mannes and Kintsch 1987). In this model, such factors as familiarity may have complex effects. Familiarity with text material may lead to the material being processed in larger chunks and retained more effectively. Lack of familiarity with the material may lead the readers to continue a closer processing of the text in order to glean new propositions with a view that finding additional information will help with organizing what is being held in the memory buffer. However, the model distances itself from a strong reliance on the reader's pre-structured schemata. Rather, although the reader relies on a knowledge net, the propositions are not full scripts, but are merely a 'skeleton script—an ordered list of episode names' (Kintsch 1998: 83–4). Additionally, the reader's goals control the use of macro-operations. Text comprehension is always controlled by specific schema applications. If a reader has specific goals, such as answering a set of pre-specified questions, the purpose may override the specific schema structure. Likewise, if a reader lacks specific goals and a text has ambiguous schema structure, different readers will instantiate different schemata in an unpredictable manner. This may result from the different interpretations of purpose across readers.

The Kintsch and van Dijk model indicates an approach that is driven by a concern with comprehension of a message. It provides insight into how different readers may develop different concepts of a message's meaning, and builds in the factor of reading purpose. Here, reading is seen within interactions among the context, the reader, and the text.

The Just and Carpenter model

Just and Carpenter (1980) proposed a model of reading which they based on evidence from eye-fixation research. They focus on what is considered to be an essential difference between listeners and readers, the fact that readers can control the rate of input. Because of this, they assert that by examining where a reader's eyes pause while reading a text it is possible to learn about the reading comprehension process. This model has been influential in its contention that reading is heavily dependent upon close text processing. Through their research utilizing eye fixations, they claim that:

almost every content word is fixated at least once. There is a common misconception that readers do not fixate every word, but only some small proportion of the text, perhaps one out of every two or three words. However, the data to be presented in this article (and most of our other data collected in reading experiments) show that during ordinary reading, almost all content words are fixated. This applies not only to scientific text but also to narratives written for adult readers.

(Just and Carpenter 1980: 329-30)

This model relies fundamentally on research (McConkie and Rayner 1975; Rayner 1978; Taylor 1962) that asserts that readers cannot determine the meaning of a word that is in peripheral vision. This view is fundamentally different from that of Smith and Goodman in that readers do not simply sample lexical items from the text in order to confirm predictions. It is a view closely allied to the bottom-up perspective of reading, although it does allow each level of processing to influence other levels. Just and Carpenter note that the gaze duration during reading varies considerably from word to word and, they claim 'we can try to account for the total duration of comprehension in terms of gaze duration on each word' (330). The assumption here is what they term the *eye-mind assumption*, that the eye remains fixated on a word as long as the word in being processed. The amount of time it takes to process a newly fixated word is reflected in the duration of an eye fixation. This follows from their *immediacy assumption*, that a reader attempts to interpret each content word as it is encountered. This immediacy assumption is the key as to why Just and Carpenter's model is considered an interactive model. In their view, interpretation takes place at all levels simultaneously, encoding, choosing a meaning for the word, determining reference, syntactic interpretation, and discourse level evaluation. None of the levels of processing is deferred.

As a consequence of the assumptions about processing, the model asserts that natural reading comprehension processes can be examined through eye-fixation durations. In this view, there is no appreciable delay between what is being fixated on and what is being processed. Research has shown that eye fixations are of short duration on FUNCTION WORDS such as articles and prepositions, but are longer on infrequent content words and at the end of sentences. Just and Carpenter interpret the length of eye fixations on content words as evidence that readers essentially process about 80 per cent of the content words in a text.

Just and Carpenter see the production systems of comprehension as involving both serial and parallel productions. Memory is seen as a process of the activation of associated concepts upon the processing of the encountered term. In addition to these parallel productions, there are slower serial productions which operate on variables as well as constants which associate an action with a class of conditions. The serial operations are seen to operate in the foreground while the parallel processes operate in the background to activate relevant semantic and episodic knowledge.

The five stages of the reading model are: 1) get next input; 2) encoding and lexical access; 3) case role assignment; 4) interclause integration; and 5) sentence wrap-up. The factors that interact in each of these stages affect the duration of the process and, consequently, the length of gaze fixation. A key feature of this model is its heavy reliance on sequential on-line processing by the reader. It further assumes that readers process a great deal of the textual material in normal reading processing. However, Just and Carpenter do note that this processing applies to readers who are given a text appropriate to their age and reading level, and that the eye fixation data assumes that the reader is not skimming or scanning in order to carry out some purpose other than what is viewed as conventional reading activities.

The Stanovich model

A key feature of interactive models is that a pattern is synthesized using information that is simultaneously applied from the reader's sources of knowledge. These sources may be orthographic knowledge, vocabulary knowledge, syntactic knowledge and background, or semantic, knowledge. Stanovich (1980) notes, however, that few researchers have examined the interactive nature of the reading process to explain individual differences in reading ability. He presents an argument for an interactive model that incorporates an assumption that a deficit in one of the component subskills of reading may cause a compensatory reliance on another skill that is present. Thus, while Just and Carpenter (1980) provide an explanation of how knowledge at one level (for example, syntactic knowledge that the next word must be a noun) can intervene to reduce the amount of processing at other levels (for example, lexical search), Stanovich attempts to show how a lack of ability in a lower level (for example, poor word recognition skills) can be compensated for by higher-level skills (for example, extra reliance on contextual factors). This approach explains that, contrary to top-down approaches, which assume that higher level processes are less involved in the performance of poor readers, given a deficit in a particular process the reader would rely on more sources of knowledge regardless of his or her reading level. Thus, given some deficit in a lower-level process, poor readers might actually rely more on higher-level contextual knowledge sources.

The Anderson and Pearson schema-theoretic view

In their discussion of first language reading, Anderson and Pearson (1984) do not present a full reading model that explains the process from the moment of eye fixation through to comprehension. Rather, they focus carefully on

the role of schemata, knowledge already stored in memory, in text comprehension. Although discussed briefly in the Kintsch and van Dijk (1978) and
Kintsch (1998) discussion, the notion of schemata will be an important one
throughout much of the rest of the issues in this book, so it will be dealt with
in some detail here. Anderson and Pearson note that the interaction of
new information with old knowledge is what we mean by *comprehension*.
Much of the focus of their discussion involves the role of schema theory
associated with Bartlett (1932) and work in Gestalt psychology. According
to this view of learning, already known general ideas subsume and anchor
new information. Bartlett studied the recall of an American Indian folktale
translated by Franz Boas, *The War of the Ghosts*. Here, readers' memories
for the story were studied over time. Bartlett does not provide detailed
information regarding the subjects in the study except to point out that there
were 20 subjects, seven women and 13 men. He notes, however, that the story
was from a 'level of culture and a social environment exceedingly different
from those of my subjects' (64). He further refers to them as 'educated and
rather sophisticated subjects' (64).

He found that in general, information from a new story that fits with the
reader's prior knowledge was recalled while other details were omitted or
rationalized with meaning not in the original. Also, he noted that salient
events for particular persons changed order depending upon the person's
interests. The stories that were recalled were consistent with previously held
concepts, or, as noted above, schemata.

In presenting their *schema-theoretic view of reading*, Anderson and Pearson
(1984) claim that an adequate account of the structure of schemata will
include: 1) information about the relationships among the components; 2) a
major role for inference; and 3) acceptance that during language comprehension, people probably rely on knowledge of particular cases as well as abstract
and general schemata. They note that each schema will be normative rather
than fully elaborated. That is, the schemata will be general in nature, not
specific to every previous experience. They argue that this is about the only
way that we can account for comprehension in exceptional cases, such as
reading about a three-legged dog. Apparently, four legs is not an inalienable
characteristic of *dogness*.

Part of the focus in the Anderson and Pearson view is on the structure of the
schemata. In their explanatory example they use the notion of a ship
christening. There are certain features that are essential and assumed. For
example, there is an assumed well-known person who breaks a bottle of
champagne across the ship's bow. Further, a schema is not simply a list of
entities associated with a particular event, such as the ship christening. Rather,
the relationships within the schema involve knowing the significance of the
parts in terms of the whole. This claim is based on research that indicates how
sentences that are integrated in some way are remembered more successfully

than sentences that are isolated. Further, there is generally room for some variation in how tightly any event matches the internalized schema. They provide the following hypothetical newspaper article as an example:

> Queen Elizabeth participated in a long-delayed ceremony in Clydebank, Scotland, yesterday. While there is still bitterness here following the protracted strike, on this occasion a crowd of shipyard workers numbering in the hundreds joined dignitaries in cheering as the HMS Pinafore slipped into the water.

(Anderson and Pearson 1984: 260)

Here, *christening* is not explicitly mentioned as a term. However, the mention that the Queen is participating in some ceremony that caused a ship to slip into the water provides strong matches to the christening schema. Further, the information extraneous to the christening about the protracted strike does not challenge the identity of the event as a ship christening.

Anderson and Pearson note that while most discussions of schema theory emphasize the use of schemata in the process of assimilating new information, they are concerned with how a schema may be modified in light of new information. For example, a ship-christening schema may change if the reader discovers that the platform is not decorated with national colors draped over the side. However, language users are flexible in what they see as necessary conditions. If some particular christening did not have bunting draped across the side, most readers would not declare that the ceremony was not a ship christening. Thus, during language comprehension people will rely both on particular cases as well as more general schema structures.

The schema-theoretic view of cognitive processing recognizes inferencing as a key process and acknowledges the role of inferences as central to the comprehension process. Anderson and Pearson identify four kinds of inferences in the reading comprehension process: 1) inferences involved in deciding what schemata among many should be called into play; 2) inferences involved in assigning roles within a schema, such as deciding which character will be in the celebrity slot at a ship christening; 3) inferences that assign default values to a schema, what is typically meant when we say that someone has made an inference; and 4) inferences that particular events rule out the possibility of a particular interpretation. Apparently, the inferences that are important for a coherent interpretation of the text will be made at the time of reading. Thus, as an author presents a new concept, the reader is involved in some level of problem solving. The more familiar the topic and the easier the inferencing process, the more a reader is involved in matching new information to old information. Thus, reading involves processes along a continuum of:

Matching ⟵⟶ Problem solving.

Schemata also have an effect upon the remembering of processed text by readers. Anderson and Pearson present results from a number of studies that demonstrate how readers remember different parts of a text depending upon the role or purpose they have been assigned to adopt. Information may be important from one perspective, that of a potential thief, but not important from another perspective, that of a florist, for example. As will be discussed later, this differential purpose in information comprehension has implications for comprehension assessment and the diagnosis of reading disorders.

The Pearson and Tierney reading/writing model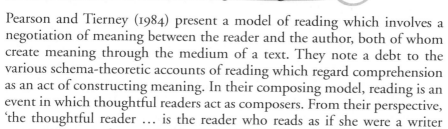

Pearson and Tierney (1984) present a model of reading which involves a negotiation of meaning between the reader and the author, both of whom create meaning through the medium of a text. They note a debt to the various schema-theoretic accounts of reading which regard comprehension as an act of constructing meaning. In their composing model, reading is an event in which thoughtful readers act as composers. From their perspective, 'the thoughtful reader … is the reader who reads as if she were a writer composing a text for yet another reader who lives within her' (144).

This view assumes that authors write with the intention that readers will create meaning, and readers will read with the expectation that authors have been considerate in providing sufficient clues about the meaning of the text to enable him or her to reconstruct in close approximation what the author initially intended. This view is derived from pragmatic theories of language which posit that every speech act, utterance, or attempt at comprehending an utterance is an action. From this perspective, context becomes very important in that knowing *why* something was said is as crucial to interpreting the message as knowing *what* was said. Failing to recognize an author's goals can interfere with comprehension of the main idea or point of view. The assumptions readers make about the author's intentions, as well as the reader's own intentions, determine which parts of any particular text are considered important. From Pearson and Tierney's perspective, reading is an act of composing rather than recitation or regurgitation, whether the language transaction is 'between a reader and a writer, a writer and his inner reader, or a reader and her inner reader' (147).

The model focuses on the *thoughtful* reader with the four interactive roles of *planner*, *composer*, *editor*, and *monitor*. As a *planner*, the reader creates goals, mobilizes existing knowledge, and decides how to align him/herself with the text. That is, readers make decisions as to the extent to which they feel they will agree with the text or will be interested in the topic of the text. This process involves something like recognizing whether one is reading Rush Limbaugh or Karl Marx and consequently establishing an attitude toward the text. As a *composer*, the reader searches for coherence, often needing to fill in gaps with inferences about the relations within the text. This is an active process in which the reader attempts to find the organizational devices that are either explicit or implied by the author. In the role of *editor*, the reader stands back and examines his or her developing interpretations. The reader questions the text for the extent to which the message appears to be sensible. Simultaneously with the above three roles, the reader acts as an executive or *monitor*. This monitor role directs the three previously mentioned roles, deciding which particular role should dominate at any particular moment in the reading process. This model assumes a great deal of collaboration between the reader and the author, collaboration with the text, as well as collaboration among the four internal reader roles.

Perfetti's model

Perfetti's Verbal Efficiency Theory (VET) (Perfetti 1985, 1988, 1991) provides an example of an interactive model that is very constrained by a bottom-up approach. In contrast to the limited interaction in the LaBerge and Samuels' model, discussed in the bottom-up approaches above, Perfetti (1991) claims that learning to read is a matter of 'incrementing a store of graphemically accessible words' (33). In his *restricted-interaction model,* interaction is restricted to letter features, letters, phonemes, and word level units. The model places restrictions on interactions:

> Its interactions are restricted to occur only within the specific data struc-
> ture of lexical formation (i.e. letters, phonemes, and words). It allows no
> influences from outside lexical data structures, no importation of know-
> ledge, expectancies, and beliefs. Skilled word recognition is context-free.
>
> *(Perfetti 1991: 34)*

Thus, in the Perfetti model, there is a very clear and restricted bottom-up view of reading. However, the model includes the two components of *local text processes* and *text-modeling processes* that provide for some interactive relationships in reading.

Local text processes encode the contextually appropriate meanings, the propositions that the text holds, and integrate the propositions across the text. First, the lexical access phase of semantic encoding results in an activation of all the possible meanings associated with a word. This is followed by associating the most appropriate semantic meaning for the proposition in the context. Second, the propositional encoding of each word as a contextu-ally appropriate semantic object allows the creation of initial propositions. As subsequent text is read, the reader assembles words into propositions, and new propositions are integrated with previous propositions held in memory. All of this occurs within a limited-capacity working memory where '[t]he trick is to quickly integrate the assembled propositions into a representation that can survive in memory' (Perfetti 1988: 111). The processes that integrate text are a continuous component of the reading process. The integrations depend partially on linguistic signals that link to memory. These signals may be word repetition, pronominal reference, and definite articles. Each proposition is displaced from working memory quickly during processing of subsequent words and their associated propositions. If they are needed in the integration of subsequent propositions, they are recalled from memory. The cognitive processes that lead to lexical access and integration of words into propositions involve such processes as feature extraction, pattern recognition, letter identification, and word meaning association.

Text modeling involves the processes that the reader uses to combine knowledge about concepts, including background knowledge, with the text propositions to create a representation of the meaning. That is, comprehension involves much more than creating a list of propositions integrated in some manner. The reader uses background schemata to fill the gaps in the propositional base. Comprehension is only achieved through the creating of inferences based on a background knowledge that makes the propositions make sense as a whole. The schemata applied include knowledge of text structure as well as situational schemata. During reading there is a continual updating of the text model by reconciling incoming text processing with background knowledge of the world.

The central tenet of VET is that the comprehension of a text is partially restricted by the efficient operation of the local processes. In this view, verbal efficiency is an interaction of product and cost. By definition, 'verbal efficiency is the quality of a verbal processing outcome relative to its cost to processing resources' (Perfetti 1988: 120). For the process to be efficient, semantic, orthographic, and phonetic components must be automatic. Short-term memory can activate only a limited amount at any given time. Cognitive processes are automated in order to reduce the amount of attention that is needed. Skilled readers will have automated letter and word identification through repeated exposures. This allows the attention-demanding activities of comprehension and application of prior knowledge, critical to reading, to be addressed. In essence, individual differences in reading proficiency are the result of how efficient the local processes are.

The McClelland, Rumelhart, et al. model

James McClelland, David Rumelhart, and several other researchers with the appellation 'The PDP (parallel distributed processing) Research Group' have developed 'an alternative framework for viewing cognitive phenomena' (Rumelhart, Smolensky, et al. 1986: 7). The PDP, or connectionist, framework argues that mental operations must operate in a parallel manner because, similar to Smith's arguments, a set of serial mental processing operations would simply take too long and would short-circuit the entire cognitive process if any particular step was faulty. The achievement of information-processing tasks requires 'the simultaneous consideration of many pieces of information or constraints' (McClelland, Rumelhart, and Hinton 1986: 3). In addition to rejecting the role of serial cognitive processing, connectionist explanations of language processing posit an intelligent system which operates without the need for learning explicit rules. Such a system recognizes that the information-processing system involves a large number of interacting units that form hypotheses based on expected probabilities, in reading for example, that any particular letter, word, sentence, or idea would occur given what has already been processed. The connection units represent a hypothesis of some sort. Each connection can be either positive or negative in the sense that hypothesized probabilities might be the result of either of two conditions: the condition that if A occurs, B generally occurs, or the condition that if A occurs, B generally does not occur.

Part of the appeal of PDP models for reading is that they help to provide a metaphor for the interactive nature of reading across the different levels of language processing. They provide for the multi-directionality of graphic, syntactic, semantic, and schematic influences. With a mutilated string such as *de_t*, we can predict certain possibilities: *b, f, n*, for example. We can pretty much rule out *d* or *q*. However, if we have information that this string exists in a passage discussing a nation's economic condition as in *the rising national de_t*, that knowledge will help to disambiguate the possible letter as *b*, and hence disambiguate the word. The models explain how the mind considers multiple options from different levels simultaneously. In many ways connectionism may be seen as a type of stimulus–response psychology in its assumptions that the mental connections that a learner builds up are not necessarily rule-governed. Associations over time build up sets of probabilities that incoming information is related or is not related. These associations are responsible for comprehension.

The Rayner and Pollatsek model

Rayner and Pollatsek (1989) present a primarily bottom-up information-processing biased model that acknowledges that top-down processes do interact with bottom-up processes. They attempt to clarify the relationship between eye movements and other processes. The Rayner and Pollatsek approach is seated much more than the other models in human physiology and the physical characteristics of human visual mechanisms. Further, they acknowledge that their model is vague in its explanation of the role played by higher-order processes.

A primary rationale for their strongly bottom-up oriented model is based in their focus on visual-acuity limitations in the reading process. Any line of text can be visually divided into foveal, parfoveal, and peripheral regions. The foveal region of fixation is narrow, the parafoveal region is somewhat wider, and the peripheral region is everything else that is in sight. Because of the anatomical structure of the retina, visual acuity is greatest in the foveal center of vision and erodes outward through the parafoveal region and the peripheral region. This is the result of the visual receptors in the retina, rods and cones. The central foveal region is primarily made up of cones and the region away from the foveal area is increasingly made up of rods. Cones are designed to process detail and are for acuity. The rods are designed to detect movement and to permit discrimination of brightness and shading. As a consequence of this physical structure, the acuity needed for reading is only present in the center of vision. Thus, in order to discriminate the details of any letter or word, the eye must move in a way to place the fovea over the part of the text to be read. This movement is seen as the key to pattern recognition, and hence to reading.

The Rayner and Pollatsek model of reading distinguishes those processes that are observable, such as eye movement and fixation time, from memory structures such as long-term memory and working memory that are not externally observable. Initial processing begins with foveal word processing and parafoveal processing. Foveal processing involves the letter and character processing within the word that is currently in fixation, while the parafoveal processing is attending to the next string of characters in order to determine where the next fixation will occur. Lexical access occurs after the eye fixation, but can be very rapid, particularly if the parafoveal preview of the word has provided sufficient information to minimize the actual lexical processing time. This model allows lexical access to proceed directly from textual pro-cessing or indirectly through application of phoneme–grapheme correspon-dence. Once lexical access of the fixated word has been completed, the eye movement continues to the next word. Since acuity is limited, the next word is normally the point of fixation, but because of parafoveal processing the first few letters have already been processed, speeding lexical recognition of the word. This is taken to explain why eye-movement research sometimes shows extremely short fixation durations as well as occasions when initial eye fixation appears to occur at the end of a word. As each word is accessed, the meaning of the fixated word is incorporated into a text representation that is being constructed in the reader's working memory. Infrequent or difficult words may require two or more fixations.

Once lexical access has been achieved, Rayner and Pollatsek acknowledge that their model moves into 'deeper and deeper water' (1989: 476). Working memory involves an inner speech mechanism that presents a literal represen-tation of what has been read. Other aspects of working memory transform the accessed lexical output to syntactic and semantic representations. The syntactic parser operates rapidly and when the semantic component finds inconsistencies, the system reverts to the eye-movement processor and the eyes regress or linger on a particular word. Likewise, as inferences are made, they are monitored and if unsuccessful, a signal of 'don't understand' (477) causes changes in eye movement and interrogation of working memory in order to devise some alternate interpretation.

As can be seen from the previous discussion, this is one of the reading models that focus on explaining observable processes rather than using observable processes to explain comprehension. It focuses on eye movements as they relate to working memory and long-term memory. Further, this is primarily a serial model of reading in its view that incoming information is converted fairly rapidly into meaning and that the active processes of the reader are employed primarily as fix-up mechanisms when some trouble occurs.

Mathewson's model of attitude influence

A final interactive model of reading addresses the role that attitude and motivation play in the reading process. Mathewson (1976, 1985, 1994) developed a model that focuses on how attitude interacts with *intention to read* and consequently how *intention to read* interacts with *reading*. Over the course of about twenty years, Mathewson (1994) refined a model which placed attitude as central but which could also explain why much research into the direct effects of attitude on comprehension failed to consistently predict reading attainment. The model posits that attitude is a tri-componential construct 'with evaluation as the cognitive component, feeling as the affective component, and action readiness as the conative component' (1133). *Conative* here refers to aspects of the individual reader's personality type, volition, preferred method of putting thought into action, temperament, etc. The three components of attitude toward reading influence the intention to read, and the intention to read affects reading behavior. However, there are other external influences on intention to read other than initial attitude. There are external effects for appropriate setting and state of mind such that an inappropriate setting would perhaps preclude reading, but it does not mean that a negative attitude toward reading has been created.

Attitude toward reading may also be modified by a change in goals by the reader. For example, if a reader is presented with a topic that is not particularly of interest to her or him, it might be assumed that the intention to read would be slight. However, if the reader knew that a comprehension examination was going to follow the reading, the goal may shift from understanding the uninteresting content to doing well in an examination. It is this moderation of goals that Mathewson proposes as one reason that attitude-questionnaire research results often do not show positive correlations between topic interest and comprehension. Attitude toward reading may be different from evaluation of content. External motivators to read during a test, for example, may override initial topic attitude. These external motivators are certainly pertinent for second and foreign language readers in terms of developing feelings of success. The 1994 model provides additionally for feedback during the reading process associated with such features as: 1) satisfaction with affect developed through reading; 2) satisfaction with ideas developed through reading; 3) feelings generated by ideas from the reading process; 4) ideas reconstructed from the information read; and 5) how the reading affects values, goals, and self concepts. All of these can have effects upon the reader's prevailing feelings about reading, action readiness for reading, and evaluation beliefs about reading. The second or foreign language reader who initially has a strong motivation to read a particular topic may become frustrated with highly complex text and develop a negative attitude, at least temporarily.

One of the important contributions of the Mathewson model is precisely that it puts issues of motivation at the forefront. It helps explain how a reader's motivation may change over time, and how important it is to address affective issues in the teaching of reading. Mathewson's suggestions for instruction include establishing classroom settings that support favorable reading intentions, minimize external incentives to justify reading, encourage students to read satisfying materials, and help students read text of suitable difficulty.

New literacy approaches

What may be seen as *new literacy* approaches have evolved over the past two decades or so and emphasize a social and anthropological approach to reading that de-emphasizes the role of the AUTONOMOUS READER. These approaches emphasize the multiple literacies embedded in social and societal contexts and criticize research on reading that focuses on reading skills in isolation. They challenge the epistemological bases of prior claims about reading in their insistence that literacy is inherently contextually based, and that cognition cannot be abstracted from social persons and the culture of the reader (Street 1993a). Further, literacy practices are seen as never being neutral, but as always being embedded in ideological contexts involving societal constructions of power and control. The implications are, as noted above, that any study of literacy events (Heath 1983), any event in which reading, writing, or a combination of the two is involved, must account for the socially and culturally situated concrete event and the associated literacy acts, (such as taking lecture notes, looking at overhead transparencies, and using the information to write a term paper in a conventional format). As Street (1993a) notes, this perspective sees the term *culture* more as a verb than as a noun (84). Cultural practices lead to expectations regarding what an appropriate reading, or literacy, act is. Characteristic of the new literacy approach is a fundamental questioning of the definition of text as a reader–text interaction and the definition of what counts as pertinent knowledge (Bloome 1993). According to Bloome, reading research has traditionally converted anthropological issues, such as cultural diversity, into such psychological factors as character recognition, background knowledge, or schemata. His general concept is that reading research has focused on the relationship between psychological factors and how those factors affect reader–text interactions. The new literacy approach, on the other hand, focuses not on reader–text interactions, but rather views reading as a social and cultural event around written language. Reading is seen as part of a social and cultural process that establishes, maintains, or changes social relationships, and it frequently emphasizes the non-school practices of literacy. Street (1999) argues for 'approaches to language and literacy that treat them as social practices and as resources rather than as a set of rules formally and narrowly defined' (1). This perspective foregrounds these social relations rather than reducing concepts of reading simply to the reader–text processes.

Bloome (1993) proposes that viewing reading as a social process requires recognizing, and examining, *author–reader interaction* as well as '*social relationships among people during a reading event*' (100–1). The first of these involves seeing that any particular author assumes a particular role (such as expert, friend, reporter, etc.), selects a particular genre, dialect, tone, and linguistic features. This author-in-the-text interacts with some reader-in-the-text who imputes social roles and may accept or reject the author's assumed roles. The social relationships during a reading event revolve around the social construction of the reading event by the reader and the writer. This construction is related to whether the person is reading in a group, reading for a discussion, reading alone in order to avoid being involved in a discussion, reading to prepare for a discussion, etc. How people go about reading will be affected both by the role that text has in their daily lives and by the status relationships implicit in any given reading act (Parry 1993). This situating of reading in a social context presents a much different view from traditional psychological approaches. There are implications about the extent to which we can generalize about reading within or across contexts. The goals of such an approach are not to generate decontextualized principles at some abstract level, but to derive theoretical insights within particular cultural events.

Street (1997) focuses on the concept of 'literacy practices' to specify the particularity of cultural practices associated with reading and/or writing in given contexts. There are multiple literacy practices and cultures in any single cultural domain. Literacy practices in this sense are not only observable behaviors around literacy, but also the meanings of the events. Thus, there may be school literacy practices as well as home literacy practices. There are multiple literacies that vary across time and space and are situated within relations of power (Street 2003). Indeed, Street poses the 'ideological', as opposed to the autonomous model, which he asserts is a synthesis of the two approaches. That is, the autonomous model separates out the technical features of literacy such as phoneme–grapheme correspondence, as though it could add the cultural components later when needed. However, the ideological model does not ignore technical skill or cognition in reading and writing, but sees them as existing within cultural wholes and power structures (Street 1993b).

Other writers who are sympathetic with the new literacy approach eschew the *objectivist* notions of there being a meaning within the text that can be determined to be right or wrong in any assessment (McCormick 1994). Rather, this view is that the readers construct the meaning as individuals within a culture, and that their interpretation is not necessarily an incorrect interpretation given their background. All reading in some sense is misreading. Given the complexity of the role of background knowledge, context, and the inherent need for reading to be selective and organizing, reading is necessarily partial (Bartholomae and Petrosky 1986). The primary issue, then, becomes not that some readers miss the mark, but rather 'whose misses matter' (6). It is this that raises questions of institutional power. Indeed, it affects whether students will even attempt to take on roles that allow them to interpret differently from their teachers or others in power. However, this view has primarily been applied to literary texts and has had limited study with text genres such as medical texts or chemistry laboratory instructions.

Summary and conclusions

As this brief overview of first language reading models points out, each of the various models attempts to capture important aspects of the reading process. Some focus primarily on the cognitive processing needed to turn images on a page into some basic meaning. Others take a broader view of just what is important about reading as an applied ability in society and the world. Some of the models assert reading to be a linear process while others view it as involving parallel processing. Some of the models, such as those of Just and Carpenter and Rayner and Pollatsek, place most emphasis on the observable psychological aspects of reading, such as eye fixation, while others, such as Rumelhart or Anderson and Pearson, focus primarily on factors that affect comprehension or miscomprehension.

As we now turn to second language reading issues, we will be well served to keep these different perspectives in mind. We will also be well served to be alert to the fundamental differences between a first language reader and a second language reader. These differences come into play when we attempt to account for such variables as age, first language literacy, reading purpose, and second language proficiency, among many other factors that are important in understanding various facets of second language reading and learning.

Discussion and study questions

1 Briefly, what are the historical developments in first language reading theory?

   A What are the primary differences between the bottom-up, top-down, and interactive approaches?

   B What contributions did Goodman and Smith make?

   C What was the contribution of the Stanovich model? What is *compensatory processing*?

   D How do the various current models incorporate orthographic rules, syntax, semantic knowledge, and context of lexical items?

   E What are the implications of Pierson and Tierney's reading/writing model?

2 There has been a change in research from product concentration to process orientation. Process orientation has implications for improving instruction in reading. What implications might this change have for instructional activities such as explicit scanning, skimming, or speed reading?

3 According to Barnett, what are the problems with model building in reading processes and instruction?

4 In the schema-theoretic model of reading, Anderson and Pearson note the following:
   • the interaction of new information with old knowledge is what we mean by comprehension
   • information from a new story that fits with the reader's prior knowledge is recalled while other details are omitted or rationalized with meaning not in the original
   • advance organizers can help comprehension
   • the author of a story suggests information to the reader and if it is a new concept then comprehension (meaning making) resembles problem solving.

   What implications does this have for determining whether a student has comprehended a passage or not?

5 Anderson and Pearson claim that an adequate account of the structure of schemata will include: 1) information about the relationships among the components; 2) a major role for inference; and 3) acceptance that during language comprehension, people probably rely on knowledge of particular cases as well as abstract and general schemata. What types of research would be needed to support these claims?

6 Look back at the different text selections in Chapter 1. Which model or combination of models just discussed focus on the processing and comprehension of the different selections?

3 SECOND AND FOREIGN LANGUAGE READING ISSUES

Introduction

As noted in Chapter 1, explanations of second or foreign language reading inevitably have to address the question: 'Is it a reading problem or a language problem?' Alderson (1984) indicates that it is necessary to address this because it is central to sorting out the causes and origins of second and foreign language reading problems. He notes that many teachers believe that the reason their students cannot read English well is because they cannot read well in their first language, thus assuming that reading is a transferable process from the first language to the second language. Others focus on the students' knowledge of the linguistic and lexical components of the target language, emphasizing the need for a second language threshold of ability. As Carson et al. (1990) point out, adult language learners have access to two primary sources while constructing a second language system. They have knowledge of their first language and they have second language input. Learners rely on both of these as they acquire literacy skills.

Views of second language reading

Hulstijn (1991) notes that it is important to address questions of whether good or poor second language readers read in the same way in their first language. He considers it to be of significance in two ways. First, our understanding of second language reading proficiency would increase if we could link it to theories that exist in first language research. Second, research that has been conducted in first languages will be important for understanding second language reading if processes in the two languages are similar. This chapter addresses the issues regarding the relationships among first language reading ability, second language proficiency, and second language reading ability. Issues of particular first/second language reading relationships such as the role of syntax, vocabulary, skills, and cognitive and metacognitive skills will be addressed in subsequent chapters.

First language readers and second language readers differ in a number of important ways. First, second language readers are likely to be already literate in their first language. Their pre-existing reading skills may influence their concepts of what reading is all about, and they may transfer their first language reading skills to the second language. This transfer of the first language skills may either assist or interfere in the second language reading. For example, while first language skills may facilitate in situations where the orthographies are similar, as with English and Spanish, the first language skills used to read such LOGOGRAPHIC languages as Chinese may be too specific to transfer to the reading of an alphabetic language. Second, reading in the first language typically begins after speaking is relatively advanced in that language, but second language learners typically do not have mastery of the spoken language prior to beginning reading instruction. The acquisition of the reading skill is likely to be very different in the absence of speaking or in the absence of a knowledge of the syntax and vocabulary of the target language. Third, there is a great cognitive difference between child first language readers and adult second language readers.

Alderson (1984) points out that traditionally, there have been two contrasting views of the second language learner, exemplified by those of Jolly (1978) and Coady (1979) versus Yorio (1971) and Clarke (1978, 1980). Both Jolly and Coady claim that success in reading a foreign language depends crucially upon one's first language reading ability rather than upon the reader's level of English. Coady states:

> We have only recently come to realize that many students have very poor reading habits to transfer from their first language, and thus, in many cases, we must teach reading skills which should have been learned in first language instruction.

(Coady 1979:12)

Yorio and Clarke, on the other hand, hold the view that reading problems of second or foreign language learners are generally the result of imperfect knowledge of the language, and they point to native language interference in the reading process. This lack of linguistic control causes what Clarke (1980) terms a 'short-circuit'. Yorio writes:

> The reader's knowledge of the foreign language is not like that of the native speaker; the guessing or predicting ability necessary to pick up the correct cues is hindered by the imperfect knowledge of the language.

(Yorio 1971: 108)

In laying out the possible relationships that might provide some explanation of second language reading performance, Alderson (1984) poses the following possible hypotheses:

1   Poor reading in a foreign language is due to poor reading ability in the first language. Poor first-language readers will read poorly in the foreign language and good first-language readers will read well in the foreign language.

2   Poor reading in a foreign language is due to inadequate knowledge of the target language.

He then notes two of the many possible modifications to these hypotheses.

1a Poor foreign language reading is due to incorrect strategies for reading that foreign language, strategies which differ from the strategies for reading the native language.

2a Poor foreign language reading is due to reading strategies in the first language not being employed in the foreign language, due to inadequate knowledge of the foreign language. Good first-language readers will read well in the foreign language once they have passed a threshold of foreign language ability.

(Alderson 1984: 4)

In support for hypothesis 1 he notes that bilinguals generally read well in both languages, indicating some transferability of the initial reading ability. Additionally, there is some evidence that the transferability may be in either direction. However, there are studies that indicate that bilinguals do not appear to transfer, or that they transfer inappropriate, first language reading strategies. Alderson uses this as partial support for his hypothesis 1a, though we would want to modify the second clause to include strategies that are appropriate for reading the native language. Some bilinguals do not read well, due to differing strategies being appropriate for different languages, such as English and Farsi, or English and German. To the extent that structures, MORPHOLOGY, and orthography are different in the two languages, such as the use of case markers and the capitalization of nouns in German, components not generally available in English, then the strategies will necessarily be different and transfer might be counterproductive. Indeed, low second language proficiency readers may overly rely on first language reading strategies. Akamatsu (1999) found support for the differential availability of first language reading strategies between languages that are alphabetic (Farsi) and those that are not (Chinese and Japanese). Learners from non-alphabetic languages had more difficulty processing upper and lower orthographic case alternations (for example, the reading of the phrase 'cAsE aLtErNaTiOn') than did those readers from alphabetic first languages. Such findings lend support to Cummins' (1981) assertion that 'concepts developed in L1 can easily transfer to L2 given adequate exposure to L2' (21–2).

Alderson indicates two potential sources of evidence for hypothesis 2. First, Alderson, Bastien, and Madrazo (1977) present results from a study examining the relationship between reading in Spanish and reading in English for students at a university in Mexico. The results indicated that there was a higher correlation between English proficiency and English reading comprehension scores than there was between Spanish reading and English reading. Second, Uljin and Kempen (1976) found that structures in Dutch and French that were very different from a contrastive-analysis point of view did not interrupt comprehension. In this case, the readers' conceptual knowledge and strategy use compensated for low-level structural differences. Thus, background knowledge, including strategy knowledge, rather than knowledge of the second language structure, affected comprehension. As support for hypothesis 2a, Alderson presents Clarke's (1978) research which indicates that there may not be any direct transfer of ability or strategies from language to language. Instead, there is a threshold of second language competence that must be reached before successful second language reading is possible. This explanation is consistent with Cooper's (1984) findings that unpracticed readers differed from practiced readers primarily in their inability to use the linguistic cues in the larger context to determine meaning, as well as in weaknesses in vocabulary knowledge and understanding of affixation. He concluded that the higher the reader advances in grammar and discourse, the better he or she will be.

However, there has been some support for a hybrid variety of hypotheses 1 and 2 which states that there is no absolute language threshold below which there is no comprehension whatsoever. Goodman and Goodman (1978) looked at reading miscue analysis of second language groups (Navajo, Hawai'ian Samoan, Arab, and Texas Spanish) as well as second dialect groups (Downeast Maine, Appalachian White, Mississippi Rural Black, and Hawai'ian Pidgin). All of the students were in second, fourth, and sixth grades and were considered average readers by their teachers. The interviews about their reading that followed an oral reading of a text were in the students' first language. After looking at the miscues across the languages and dialects, Goodman and Goodman concluded:

> there is a single reading process which underlies reading, no matter what the language background or relative proficiency of the reader. Demonstrated differences, then, are not in the process but in how well it is controlled. Any effects of lack of complete receptive and productive control will either (a) be noticeable but superficial in which case the

process can still be relatively efficient and effective or (b) be somewhat dis-
ruptive to comprehension or (c) limit the ability of the readers to express
what they have understood.' (3-1)

The second language groups showed less ability to preserve meaning than to
preserve syntax in the oral reading. There was first language phonological
interference and a number of miscues were generated by: 1) unfamiliar or
unusual lexical items; 2) sentences loosely supported in the paragraph
context; and 3) sentences with weak syntactic structure, such as lists of
nouns. The second dialect students showed fewer semantically unacceptable
miscues than the second language groups, indicating that vocabulary was an
important factor in the generation of miscues. Goodman and Goodman's
conclusions were:

> Among our second language readers we can see the effects of varying
> stages in control of English on our subjects' reading. But we can also see
> that subjects need not be totally proficient in both productive and recep-
> tive English to learn to read English and to get considerable meaning from
> their reading. The language limitations interact with cultural and experi-
> ential factors and all may affect reading. One cannot read an unknown
> language. But as the language becomes known, speaking or writing, read-
> ing or listening involve the graphophonic, syntactic, semantic systems,
> the strategies of sampling, predicting, confirming, correcting, the sensory
> to perceptual to syntactic, to semantic cycles. These are at work even as
> language control develops.

(Goodman and Goodman 1978: 3–22)

From this perspective, then, the first language reading processes are applied,
though some of them may not be fully applied until language ability has
improved. Goodman and Goodman do not see a particular threshold for the
variety of reading processes that are needed to process some level of syntax
and semantics. However, all of the languages they examined had alphabetic
orthography.

A further complication in answering the question of first and second language
relationships arises with respect to the kinds of literacy acts that are in
question. Learners in higher education environments engage in distinct genre
types and tasks that may very well not be present in the first language learner's
repertoire of reading. For example, the reader may be reading in order to write
a literature review, prepare a presentation, or to understand what took place
in a meeting by reading the minutes. Contextualized reading may involve
unfamiliar genres or discourse types that are new to all readers, whether they
are first language or second language readers. As the notion of reading and
literacy are broadened, answering questions about the particular relationships
between first and second languages becomes even more complex.

We will now review the most prominent studies addressing the relationships introduced above between first language and second language components. However, care should be taken to not over-interpret the strength of the results and their implications. Much of the early research on the relationship between first language and second language reading ability is purely correlational. This raises two potential problems in generalizing the findings. First, many of the studies of bilinguals do not use BALANCED BILINGUALS. This lack of uniformity across studies often creates conflicting results and conclusions. Further, many of the studies were hampered by a restriction in range of the ability levels in the first language and second language subjects by virtue of using intact classes or homogeneous learners. This restriction makes correlational interpretation difficult. Second, there are questions regarding the sources of variability in the first language reading ability. Here the issue is why some subjects are identified as not being good readers in their first language. That is, is the variability due to socioeconomic status, cultural values toward reading, psychomotor difficulties, etc.? It is the case that some of the studies use adults and some use school-age subjects in the process of measuring first language reading ability. The notion of a good reader is more difficult to pin down when we are dealing with adults than with children across grade levels.

Three additional problems with many of the studies stem not from problems with using correlational approaches, but with restrictions in the way the studies were conducted. First, much of the early research into the first language and second language reading ability research was typically carried out using cloze tests and short modified passages. It takes a leap of faith to equate these forms of instrumentation with reading ability in general. It can certainly be argued that we have moved beyond the need to base so much research on short, modified passages and cloze paragraphs. Second, several studies often take a rather limited definition of the term *reading*. Some studies focus on narrow processing while others include more global literacy activities. Third, a limitation for many of the studies rests with the ways in which the researchers operationalized such characteristics as 'high-ability learners' and 'low-ability learners'. Usually, the definition is entirely relative to the particular sample of learners that were available to the research project. These learner characteristics differ across the studies, such that subjects that are defined in one study as 'high-ability' might not be considered as such in another study. Finally, there is an unfortunate variability in the quality of the research designs, sample sizes, and reporting of statistical data across the studies. Given these questions with the research studies, it should not be surprising that there are frequently conflicting findings about the nature of the relationship between first language and second language reading ability.

Research into first language and second language relationships

Studies tend to find a strong relationship between second language linguistic ability and second language reading ability as well as a moderate relationship between first language reading ability and second language reading ability, depending upon second language ability level. Several studies have examined the relationships and are summarized in the next section of this chapter.

In a correlational study looking at the relationship among first language reading ability, second language proficiency, and second language reading ability, Perkins, Brutten, and Pohlmann (1989) placed 158 Japanese students into one of three levels based on their paper-and-pencil TOEFL test scores. The groupings were: level 1, n=32, TOEFL=270–374; level 2, n=106, TOEFL=375–429; level 3, n=20, TOEFL=430–469. In addition to the TOEFL, the students were given random parallel reading comprehension tests, one in Japanese and one in English. They found an overall positive relationship between first language reading and second language reading as well as a relationship between second language proficiency, as measured by the TOEFL score, and second language reading. Further, they found that there were relatively weak relationships between first language reading and second language reading at level 1 and level 2, with correlations at .19 and .24 respectively. However, at level 3 the correlation reached .64. Thus, the higher the learner's second language ability, the stronger the relationship is between first language and second language reading. These findings provide support for the argument that there is some general threshold at which the first language reader begins to be able to transfer first language reading skills and strategies.

In a subsequent study, Carson et al. (1990) further examined the literacy relationships between first language and second language. They looked at data for 48 Chinese and 57 Japanese learners studying in four universities in the United States. Using a cloze test and stand-alone essays they examined the relationship between first language reading and first language writing, second language reading and second language writing, first language reading and second language reading, as well as first language writing and second language writing. They found moderate, but significant, correlations between the first language reading and second language reading scores. The results are presented in Table 3.1 below.

These results tend to indicate a moderate relationship between first language reading and second language reading. They lend mixed support for the reading/writing model of Pearson and Tierney (1984) mentioned in Chapter 2, except for the first language reading/writing relationships for Japanese and the second language reading/writing relationship for Chinese. The findings

Comparison	Chinese (n=48)	Japanese (n=57)
L1 reading × L2 reading	r=.366**	r=.509**
L1 writing × L2 writing	r=−.019	r=.230*
L1 reading × L1 writing	r=.271*	r=.493**
L2 reading × L2 writing	r=.494**	r=.271*
*p<.05 **p<.01		

Table 3.1: Correlations of language by skill (Carson et al. 1990)

suggest that some transfer of reading ability is possible, possibly supporting Alderson's hypothesis 2a, but that this transfer may differ depending upon first language background. However, caution must be exercised in interpretations from this study. First, the subjects here have a relatively narrow distribution of second language ability. With additional subjects of lower and higher language ability, the correlations are likely to increase, as seen in the Perkins et al. (1989) study. A second potential problem is with the appropriacy of using the cloze procedure with Chinese and Japanese text, languages in which there may be problems identifying word and sentence boundaries. At any rate, the study does lend some support for the idea that first language reading ability may transfer to second language reading, particularly for the Japanese. This appears to be intuitively reasonable given that the Japanese language does contain some phonemic and syllabic features in common with English.

Carrell (1991a) attempts to answer some of the issues raised by Alderson in terms of second language ability. In her study, she examines the metaphoric equation:

L2 Reading = L1 Reading + L2 Language Proficiency.

She notes that:

> other groups of researchers have argued that reading ability in a second language appears to be largely a function of proficiency in that language, or that at least some minimal threshold of proficiency needs to be attained in that language before good readers' first language reading strategies can be transferred ...

(Carrell 1991a: 159)

She compared the performance of adult Spanish speakers learning English and adult English speakers learning Spanish on tests of each language. Her results indicate significant effects for both first language reading ability and second language proficiency on second language reading performance. However, there is no clear relationship regarding which is most important. For example, for the Spanish first language speakers, first language reading ability had the greatest predictive power while for the English first language speakers, the second language proficiency was the greatest predictor. These last results may be due the fact that the English language speakers overall had a lower proficiency in the second language than did the Spanish first language speakers. Yamashita (2002) also looked at the 'L2 Reading = L1 Reading + L2 Language Proficiency' equation with Japanese university EFL students. She found that both first and second languages were important, but that second language ability was most important. This appears to be due in large part to the students in her experiment not having reached the threshold level in the second language for the first language literacy skills to transfer.

These findings are consistent with the Perkins et al. (1989) results which show a stronger relationship between first language and second reading for the higher-level learners. The results seem to indicate that once the readers become more advanced, first language reading ability becomes increasingly important. So, while both variables appear to affect second language reading, the second language threshold may be on a sliding scale, and we are far from having determined what that threshold may be and whether it is different for reading activities other than those that have been used in studies up to now.

As with the Carson et al. (1990) study, there are several limitations in generalizing too far from Carrell's study. First, the reliabilities of her test instruments were very low at .60 for the English texts and .68 for the Spanish texts. Second, the equation for first language reading and second language proficiency only accounted for about 40 per cent of the variance on the second language reading test in total. Presumably part of that low value is due to poor reliabilities in the study. However, there is still a great deal of variability in reading ability left to explain in order to determine precisely what the primary source of second language reading is.

Bossers (1991) examined the relation between first language reading, second language reading, and second language ability as well as attempting to determine whether one could in fact demonstrate the existence of some language threshold. In this study, 50 native speakers of Turkish enrolled in Dutch as a second language courses or in other tertiary-education contexts were assessed in terms of their first language (Turkish) reading ability, their Dutch language ability, and their Dutch reading ability. Using regression analysis, Bossers shows that both second language ability and first language reading play a substantial role in second language reading, more so than in Carrell's (1991a) study, accounting together for approximately 72 per cent of the variability in second language reading scores. However, although both variables were significant, second language ability accounted for nearly four times more than first language reading ability. Thus, both variables do appear to play a role in explaining a second language learner's reading ability, with second language ability playing a greater role in this particular study. In a follow-up analysis, Bossers examined the issue of whether there is an identifiable second language threshold ability level that mediates the relative relationship between first language reading ability and second language reading ability. The subjects of the study were broken into two groups. The subjects with the lowest second language reading ability, the lowest 70 per cent of the scorers, were examined using regression analysis and it was found that second language ability was the only significant variable. On the other hand, for the top 30 per cent of the second language readers, only first language reading ability was a significant predictor. This finding would appear to indicate that there may indeed be a threshold level before which learners are limited in their ability to transfer their first language reading abilities to the second language reading context.

While Bossers' findings are important, there are still several questions that need to be addressed. The primary issue is that dividing a group of learners into the lower 70 per cent and the top 30 per cent still does not give a very clear picture of what the threshold ability level looks like. We have only a description relative to the particular subjects in the study. Further, it is not clear why 70 per cent and 30 per cent were selected as the criteria. In selecting these criteria, there remained only 15 subjects in the top group. It may very well be that the limited sample size caused it to appear that second language knowledge was not a significant predictor at the advanced level. Nevertheless, the study lends additional support to the views that both first language reading ability and second language ability play an important role in second language reading ability. We still have to determine what the threshold levels are. Are they 30 per cent, 40 per cent, 50 per cent, etc.? Additionally, the Bossers study omits descriptive statistics about the test results as well as information regarding the reliability of the instruments used. This information would be very helpful in interpreting the implications for the research.

Lee and Schallert (1997) examine Alderson's hypothesis 2a, namely that there will be little or no effective transfer of first language reading strategies until the learner has reached a threshold level of second language ability, but that first language reading strategies will play a larger and larger role as the learner's second language ability increases. In their study, they gave a test of second language proficiency, a test of second language reading ability, and a test of first language reading ability to 809 Korean students in grades 9 and 10 in Korea. For analysis, they divided the students first into ten groups of equal size, and then into five groups, each group representing 20 per cent of the second language proficiency scale of obtained scores. Analysis found that first language reading ability and second language proficiency accounted for 62 per cent of the variability in second language reading, with second language proficiency contributing more than first language reading ability.

These results support Carrell's (1991a) finding that while both contribute, first language reading ability contributed less to second language reading ability than did second language proficiency. Further, their results indicate that for the top 60 per cent of the groups, there was a strong relationship between increases in first language reading score and second language reading score, whereas there was little such relationship at the lower proficiency levels. This would again indicate that there is a language threshold at which a learner's first language reading skills begin to contribute to second language reading ability. However, it was still the case that there was a modest relationship between first language reading and second language reading, although a strong form of the threshold hypothesis such as that held by Clarke (1980) and Yorio (1971) would predict no relationship.

The Lee and Schallert study used a common test to determine second language proficiency rather than simply using language course membership. In this way they bypassed some of the problems that exist in other studies which have based ability on class membership. However, as with most other studies, problems remain in generalizing from the results of the study. First, the regression analysis indicates that second language proficiency contributes more than first language reading ability. This has been found in the majority of studies in this area. However, it is not clear whether these findings are due to the fact that this relationship is the true relationship, or is due to a restricted range in the first language reading ability. In this study, the means on the 20-item first language reading test were as follows in Table 3.2:

These results indicate relatively low means at 35.5 per cent to 55.5 per cent with narrow standard deviations. The regression results indicate first language reading contributed less than second language ability in part because there was little variability and because the reliability on the first language reading test was a low .68. Thus, much of the variability that did exist may not have been systematic variability.

A second issue with generalizing from the Lee and Schallert results relates to their definition of second language proficiency. Here second language proficiency is 'knowledge of vocabulary and of grammatical structures' (1997: 717). Their operationalization of this was a test with 40 grammaticality

	Middle School				High School			
	Males (n=203)		Females (n=183)		Males (n=235)		Females (n=188)	
	x	sd	x	sd	x	sd	x	sd
L1 reading	8.0	3.5	7.1	3.4	10.9	3.3	11.1	2.8

Table 3.2: Means and standard deviations on L1 reading test (Lee and Schallert 1997)

judgments and 40 vocabulary items. This definition does not include many aspects of language proficiency, such as knowledge of register, comprehension, or textual knowledge. Without the inclusion of these broader aspects of proficiency, the results of the study may actually be underestimating the effects of second language proficiency on second language reading performance.

A final issue regarding the Lee and Schallert study has to do with generalizing about what the threshold level might actually be. The instrument for assessing second language reading was made up of two passages from the Metropolitan Achievement Test (1964–71), Form F (Elementary) (720). The first language reading test was made up of passages that were at the grade-level of the students in the study. Given that all of the reading passages were simplified to some extent, there is no way to determine how relatively high or relatively low the second language linguistic threshold may or may not be. This will have implications for how much weight is actually given to the importance of the threshold on second language reading ability. For this study, it was relatively low, at about 40 per cent of the scale band. If the students had been reading unsimplified material, the results would have undoubtedly been somewhat different.

Fecteau (1999) examined the relationship between first language and second language reading of literature for more advanced-level foreign language learners. Subjects were studying in a university-level French literature course. They read excerpts of two stories, one in the original French and one an English translation. After reading, the learners recalled everything they could from the segment that they had read, and took a short multiple-choice test over the passage. A subset of the subjects had recent second language ability test scores. Fecteau found that first language recall scores predicted second language recall scores, and first language multiple-choice scores predicted second language multiple-choice scores. However, for the subset with second language ability scores, it was not the case that second language ability predicted second language recall or second language multiple-choice scores. She found that the subjects with the highest-ability scores did not always recall the most and those with the lowest-ability scores did not always recall the least. Apparently recall is more complex than the language-ability test format could describe. Thus, it appears that we have some insight into what the threshold might look like for reading literature. Fecteau's subjects had on average had 6.8 semesters of language study. They were apparently able to transfer their first language literature reading skills to reading second language literature. However, Fecteau notes that the findings that second language ability did not predict second language recall and multiple-choice scores should be viewed as tentative since the study was carried out on only 24 subjects.

A further concern in how first language and second language abilities relate to one another rests with how the factors are language processing specific and how they might differ over various tasks that the reader encounters. Donin and Silva (1993) attempt to differentiate aspects of second language reading comprehension specific to reading in the second language from those factors that are generally relevant to understanding text in any language. In their study they examined the propositional recall and reading time for English-dominant Canadian bilinguals as they read English or French nursing materials. The nurses either read an English text and reported in English, read a French text and reported in English, or read a French text and reported in French. The study found that reading time was slower while reading the French texts, indicating, not surprisingly, that there are differences in the input processing between first language and second language text reading. This is consistent with the view that the readers are employing high-level conceptual processing to compensate for limitations created by a lack of automaticity on the semantic and syntactic level. However, the study also indicated that for these intermediate-level speakers of French, the amount of propositional text recalled from the French texts was almost as high as that recalled from the English texts when the subjects recalled the text in English rather than in French. This indicates that much of the literature that finds a 'short-circuit' may have confounded comprehension and production, depending upon the type of assessment measures that were used. However, much more research needs to be conducted in this area, especially given that the Donin and Silva study employed a very small sample size, 18 in one segment of the study and nine in a second segment. Further complicating the reaching of a simple answer on the basis of this study is the fact that it focused on occupation-specific texts and the results may have limited generalizability to other reading contexts.

An additional factor in determining which of Alderson's hypotheses most closely explains the second language reader's situation is how performance on different tasks might affect the reading process. Taillefer (1996) examined the relationship between first language reading and second language reading, along with the notion of a second language proficiency threshold, across two different tasks. The first task was a scanning activity in which French university students in social science searched for key words and numbers in English texts of two and five pages in length. The second task involved the same students reading a two-page text, then answering agree-disagree and multiple-choice questions. The study found both first language reading ability and second language proficiency to be significant predictors of foreign language reading, but to differing degrees, depending upon the particular task. For the scanning task, first language reading ability was the only significant predictor of performance, and that significance held only for the more proficient second language students. For the task that required the students to read and answer the questions, second language proficiency was the only significant predictor of performance, and that was true only for those students more proficient in the second language. Thus, there appears to be a differential importance of the role first language reading ability and second language proficiency play, depending upon the particular reading task. More demanding reading tasks may call on greater need for second language proficiency. Further, the study suggests that the use of first language reading ability aids the second language reader only after the reader has a threshold of second language ability. Unfortunately, the Taillefer study can only be suggestive because of limitations with the study. First, there is a question of how reading was operationalized in the scanning activity. It would not be surprising that second language proficiency, as measured by TOEFL and a cloze passage, would be of little importance in an activity that only involved scanning for key words and numbers. Scanning in actual practice is goal-oriented and is generally more complex than this. Second, just as Carrell (1991a) found that first language reading ability was more effective only for the second language students, as opposed to the foreign language students in her study, the Taillefer results may not be generalizable to second language readers. Third, and perhaps of more importance, the study did not report the TOEFL results, either for the entire cohort or the high and low level examinees. Consequently, it is neither possible to estimate just how able the students in the study were, nor what level of ability the potential threshold might be.

Finally, in looking at the relationships between first and second language reading, there can also be a variation on the way in which Alderson's hypothesis 1a is cast. New reading strategies may be applied which differ from those of the native language, but, rather than detracting from reading in the second language, actually assist. Second language readers have access to two languages. Mental translation may be employed in coping with the second language reading. Kern (1994) notes that counter to some notions that translation is to be avoided at all times, it may not only be used as a 'crutch'. It may be a developmental tool in the process of learning to comprehend the new language and assist by helping to reduce the cognitive load involved in mental processing. Kern sees mental translation as processing the second language into the first language while interacting with the second language. He examined 51 students at an American university in their third semester of French. They were divided into three French proficiency groups on the basis of their scores on the ETS French Reading Comprehension Test (ETS 1980). Students were interviewed in a think-aloud type procedure. They read a text one sentence at a time at the beginning and again at the end of the semester. Instances of translation were identified as to whether they indicated comprehension or not. Students in the lower ability group reported more instances of translation than those in the higher groups, and the results indicate a tendency for less translation to occur over the course of instruction. Also, the proportion of translation associated with comprehension was greater in the higher-ability groups, indicating that the differing ability groups may have been using translation qualitatively differently. Overall, the study indicated that mental translation may facilitate generation and conservation of meaning by reducing cognitive load, but translation diminishes as learners become more proficient.

Summary and conclusions

Throughout the studies of the relationship between first language reading ability, second language proficiency, and second language reading performance, there has been a general trend that indicates that there are interrelationships between all three. Further, there has tended to be a finding that second language proficiency plays a greater role than does first language reading ability. Yet there are also results that indicate this last finding may depend upon the reader's level of proficiency and upon what particular reading task is involved. The role of the reading task and text type have yet to be thoroughly researched in second language studies. More research is needed in the area, research which attempts to include subjects who represent variability in both first language reading ability and second language proficiency, and which uses a range of authentic materials and tasks that can inform us regarding the nature and uniformity of the threshold across different types of reading. Basically, the field is in no position to describe the nature of the language ability threshold and how it interacts with different tasks and readers at the current time.

However, the findings that second language proficiency is of most importance at lower levels of second language proficiency presents consistencies here with what Perfetti (1985, 1988, 1991) termed the Verbal Efficiency Model in that the lower-level language learner has automated very few of the local text processes. As a result, most of the reader's effort and attention are devoted to the processes of lexical access and elementary propositional encoding. Basically, those activities swarm the reader's working memory and drain all of its capacity. Such features as syntactic function words, morphology, and vocabulary have not been automated sufficiently to release attention to the text work of encoding propositions within and across sentences, inferencing requiring memory searches, plus interpretive and critical comprehension of text. The extent to which attention is allocated systematically to these local text processes will, in part, be due to similarities between the first language and second language in terms of orthographic systems, language family memberships, cognate size, and other features that distinguish the languages.

Although there is a frequently demonstrated relationship between second language ability, first language reading ability, and second language reading ability, the interactions are many, depending upon second language proficiency level and whether the learners are in foreign or second language contexts. Further, in the equations that look at the different relationships, the researchers obtain different amounts of the second language reading ability that is explained by the two predictors: Carrell (1991a) found the two variables explained 40 per cent of the second language reading ability; Bossers found 72 per cent; and Lee and Schallert (1997) found 62 per cent. Several questions arise from these findings. First, what factors can explain the remaining 30 per cent to 70 per cent of second language reading performance? Second, how are the results affected by the relatively narrow range of texts and text types that have been used in the research? Third, what precisely is the threshold level and how much does it vary across tasks and text types? Finally, what types of remediation can affect the relationships among the variables? Many of these questions will be addressed, though most likely not completely answered in the rest of this text.

We still cannot satisfactorily answer Alderson's (1984) hypotheses in a definitive manner two decades after they were posed. However, an implication for reading instruction is that the processing load of second language reading at early levels of proficiency must be addressed in some way. The studies are fairly consistent in showing that learners with very little exposure to the second language have difficulty in reading. Thus second language reading instruction must find ways to avoid continually frustrating the reader. This can be accomplished through the use of modified texts to fit readers' ability levels (Day and Bamford 1998), or it may be through identifying tasks whose difficulty matches the reader's ability. Both of these approaches have positive and negative aspects. It is too early to answer the question of exactly how to accomplish this. However, this issue will be addressed through the remainder of this book. Also, we will see that the two factors of the second language threshold and reading ability itself both interact with the topics in the rest of the text. The language threshold will be of concern as we look at second language processing of different text structures and genres of text, and second language reading ability will be important as we examine metacognitive strategies in reading.

Discussion and study questions

1   Bossers (1991) and Carrell (1991a) attempted to examine the issues raised by Alderson. The research attempted to examine the relation between first language reading, second language reading, and second language ability as well as to determine whether one could in fact demonstrate the existence of some language threshold. How did their findings differ?

2 Lee and Schallert (1997) examine Alderson's Hypothesis 2a, namely that there will be little or no effective transfer of first language reading strategies until the learner has reached a threshold level of second language ability, but that first language reading strategies will play a larger and larger role as the learner's second language ability increases.

A What findings did they obtain in the relationships of the variables and top group versus the bottom group?

B What does this indicate in terms of a threshold effect?

C How might the relative restricted range of first language reading scores affect the results of this study?

D Lee and Schallert defined second language proficiency as 'knowledge of vocabulary and of grammatical structures' (717). How might this affect the generalizability of the study?

3 Throughout the studies of the relationship between first language reading ability, second language proficiency, and second language reading performance, there has been a general trend that indicates that there are interrelationships between all three. Which has tended to play the largest role in second language reading? Why? What additional types of research are needed in this area?

4 The studies use various approaches to measure second language reading ability. Make a list of the different approaches. What additional tasks do you think would be useful in addressing the issue of second language reading ability?

5 Which of the views of second language reading do you tend to support? That of Jolly and Coady that focuses on lack of transfer? That of Clarke and Yorio that focuses on a 'short-circuit' due to language deficit? What about Goodman and Goodman who view reading as a single underlying process regardless of language and ability? What conclusions do you make regarding Alderson's hypotheses?

4 READING SKILLS

Introduction

A fundamental concern in second language reading involves the identification and nature of *reading skills* and whether those skills that exist are situated within an ordered hierarchy. The reading and literacy literature is replete with references to *reading skills*, *higher-level skills*, and *lower-level skills*. However, the precise meanings of the terms are not always transparent.

Much of the basic work in the literature about reading skills comes out of research and concerns in first language reading that was first carried out in the 1970s and 1980s. Some of that research addresses the processes of children learning to read, turning written language into oral language, and the stages that they go through in order to become mature readers (Clymer 1968; Gibson and Levin 1975; Goodman 1968; Gordon, 1982; Just and Carpenter 1987; Lunzer, Waite, and Dolan 1979; Perfetti 1991; Rayner and Pollatsek 1989; Strain 1976). Because so much of the initial literature into skills has focused on the first language education of children learning to read, it is important to examine the implications for second and foreign language reading rather closely. As previously noted, unilaterally adopting concepts and terminology from the first language literature must be done with caution, if at all. Nevertheless, they are an important starting point and source of common vocabulary. This chapter examines issues in reading skills and the next chapter will be somewhat of an extension devoted specifically to issues of reading strategy acquisition, instruction, and use. As will become clear, this division is not always clearly a dichotomy as it is not always easy to distinguish skills from strategies.

Reading skills in the first language

It is difficult to clearly discuss the concerns around reading skills without addressing the overlap of several terms and concepts. There is a need to recognize how the term *skill* is used in multiple ways. The terms *skills*, *subskills*, *processing strategies*, *ability*, and Stanovich's (1980) term, *knowledge sources*, are terms used variably in the applied linguistics and language teaching literature. The distinctions in usage can depend upon whether the term is used to refer to a language component or to an individual reader's ability to perform. Richards, Platt, and Weber (1985) define language skills as being:

> the mode or manner in which language is used. Listening, speaking, reading, and writing are generally called the four language skills … Often skills are divided into subskills, such as discriminating sounds in connected speech, or understanding relations within a sentence.

(Richards et al. 1985: 160)

Harris and Hodges define skill as 'an acquired ability to perform well; proficiency' (1981: 298). Thus, the term can be used to denote a reading behavior such as making appropriate phoneme–grapheme correspondence, or it can be used to indicate a relative level of reading ability as in the concept of a skilful reader. This ambiguity in the use of the term *skills* can be seen in the following excerpt from Proctor and Dutta (1995):

> First, skill is acquired through practice or training. A defining characteristic of the skills discussed in this book is that they are not innate but must be learned. Second, skilled behavior is goal directed. Skill develops in response to some demand imposed by the task environment on the organism, although some learning may occur that is incidental to that demand. Third, skill is said to have been acquired when the reading behavior is highly integrated and well organized. Through experience, the components of behavior are structured into coherent patterns. Finally, cognitive demands are reduced as skill is acquired, freeing limited mental resources for other activities. From these characteristics, we derive our definition of skill: Skill is goal-directed, well organized behavior that is acquired through practice and performed with economy of effort.

> As stated earlier in the chapter, most skills involve the entire information-processing system. However, at a gross level, skills can be divided into those with primarily perceptual, motor, or cognitive components.

(Proctor and Dutta 1995: 18)

In this example, skill is used both as a skill level ('well organized behavior that is acquired through practice and performed with economy of effort') as well as separate types of behavior ('skills can be divided into those with primarily perceptual, motor, or cognitive components'). In the present discussion, the term will be used to indicate different reading processing activities rather than as relative ability level.

Additionally, in much of the literature there is a mixing of the terms *reading skill* and *reading process*. In part, much of this last conflation depends upon whether the author is primarily concerned with pedagogy or with psychology. Finally, at times the discussion focuses either on reading skills or comprehension skills, and in some discussions comprehension skills are seen as being entailed in reading skills while at other times they are seen as distinctly different cognitive processes.

Throughout the next few sections of this chapter about whether skills are separable and hierarchically ordered, we will find studies that view reading skills as decontextualized abilities existing outside of any particular literacy context. It is proposed here that this assumption is one of the reasons we find conflicting results from various studies. For example, if it is proposed that *inferring unknown vocabulary from context* is a skill of some particular difficulty or facility, then there is no acknowledgement that some texts are co-operative for inferring unknown vocabulary while other texts are not, nor is it acknowledged that some lexical items may be easier to infer than others. The relative salience of skills as they are operationalized in empirical studies will affect whether they are seen as separable skills or not, and this relative salience will be due to the context of the literacy act in which the reader is engaged.

As we examine the differing views of reading skills, we can see how underlying assumptions about language and research affect the different reading worlds that are being presented. Which of these worlds we favor will affect what we do in the reading classroom and the shape of the language teaching materials we design. It will affect whether a class adopts a skills-centered syllabus or focuses more closely on task- and performance-based contextual activities. It will affect how the reading activity is discussed and the extent to which we focus on the relationship between first and second language behaviors. Consequently, it is important to take a close look at how reading skills have been identified and described in the reading literature.

Separability of skills

Generally, reading skills are represented in categories representing: 1) word attack skills; 2) comprehension skills; 3) fluency skills; and 4) critical reading skills. Word attack skills (sometimes called DECODING SKILLS) represent the skills necessary to convert orthographic symbols into language. This set of skills requires that the reader recognize that the script represents units of language, such as phonemes, syllables, and words. Some of the subskills of this skill type would be recognizing syllable patterns, converting strings to sound on occasions, recognizing upper- and lower-case letters and recognizing word boundaries. Comprehension skills represent the ability to use context and knowledge to derive meaning from what is read. Examples of comprehension skills would be grammatical competence and knowledge of morphology, syntax, mechanics, using context to gain meaning, using schemata as aids, using METACOGNITIVE knowledge, recognizing text structure, and predicting what will come next in a text. Fluency skills are directed at allowing the reader to see larger sentences and phrases as wholes, a process which assists in reading more quickly. Fluency skills would involve such abilities as sight word recognition and recognizing high-frequency letter clusters, rapid reading, and possessing an extensive vocabulary. Finally, critical reading skills provide the reader with the skills to analyze, synthesize, and evaluate what is read. This process involves such activities as seeing the cause-and-effect or comparison relationships in the text, or adopting a critical stance toward the text. There is a great deal of variety in the specific skills that are identified by various teachers and researchers as well as a lack of precision in the language used to describe the skills.

In an examination of how reading skills have been viewed in pedagogical circles, Rosenshine (1980) examined the comprehension skills identified from five authoritative educational sources. The first was from Science Research Associates (Shub et al. 1973). The second source was from the skills tested on the 1973 National Assessment of Educational Progress. The third was from the scope and sequence chart for Scott Foresman's reading series (Aaron et al. 1976). The fourth was from textbooks by Harris and Smith (1976). The final source was from the reading program developed by the Wisconsin Research and Development Center (Otto and Askov 1974). In their examination, they found that there were common general reading skill categories specified in all five sources and that they fell into three different types of skills, all of which appear to be associated with comprehension skills. The first type of skill could be termed *locating details*. This is the simplest of the skills and involves recognition, paraphrase and/or matching. The second type of skill group is labeled *simple inferential skills* and is made up of such skills as understanding words in context, recognizing the sequence of events, and recognizing cause and effect relationships. The third group was labeled *complex inferential skills* and relates to working with longer texts than in the second skill type. This group might comprise such activities as recognizing the main idea, drawing conclusions, and predicting outcomes. Although Rosenshine found that there were many skills in common among the five sources, he also noted that all but Harris and Smith had unique skills that did not fit within the three types of common skills. In some cases this had to do with how specific the authors were in defining a particular skill. Rosenshine notes that some teachers and researchers might believe that rather than a skill called *recognizing the main idea*, it might be more justifiable to split the skill into *recognizing the main idea* in different text types such as a narrative or exposition. In general, Rosenshine finds some consensus that reading involves at least the following seven subskills across the three general reading skill categories:

– recognizing sequence
– recognizing words in context

– identifying the main idea
– decoding detail
– drawing inferences
– recognizing cause and effect
– comparing and contrasting.

However, he also notes that many sources break these down further into subskills. Such subskills might reflect the recognition of different clues in reading, such as recognizing synonym or antonym clues, summary clues, or clues provided by tone, setting, and mode, etc. In some cases lists such as these led to over 30 different skills and subskills. In addition, discussions of reading skills frequently discuss *lower-level skills* and *higher-level skills*. The lower-level skills tend to be related to word-attack skills, while the higher-level skills tend to be linked to reading comprehension skills.

This notion of lower-level skills being linked to word-attack skills may in part be a historical product of the way reading has been taught to children in first language contexts, most of whom already have a relatively well-developed oral first language but have had little experience matching the sounds and words of the language to a print representation. This concept reflects the twin processes in reading of automatic text recognition versus recoding known oral language through text. Just and Carpenter (1987) take a reading fluency and compre-hension development focus, and note that there are two routes in text decoding, 'direct visual recognition' and 'speech recoding' (327). They report that fluent readers rely primarily on direct visual recognition while children and early readers make greater use of speech recoding. In early first language reading, the accuracy and speed of word-decoding skill is a strong predictor of comprehension, a stronger predictor than listening comprehension ability. However, in later school grades, listening comprehension becomes a better predictor of reading comprehension than word-decoding skill (Just and Carpenter 1987: 328). Thus, as decoding skill improves, differences in reading ability are controlled more by a general comprehension factor. Stanovich (1986) posits that any causal relationship between phonological sensitivity and word recognition is developmentally constrained. That is, the relationship is confined to the very early stages of reading acquisition (Stanovich 2000). Likewise, Doctor and Coltheart (1980) found a shift from phonological to visual encoding as age increased when the readers were attending to meaning rather than attending to remembering the text. This indicates that as readers mature they have less dependence on phonological encoding and develop more reliance on the visual code. The research findings indicate that children initially convert print into sound to help in comprehension, but as they develop increased reading skill they rely more heavily on visual processing in comprehension.

This last factor regarding type of processing in comprehension reveals another source of confusion in the literature about the nature of reading skills. It is important to be explicit about what constitutes reading and the concomitant implications for reading skills. Clymer (1968) points out that some authors define reading as responding orally to printed symbols while others view reading as the change that takes place in one's knowledge as a result of having interacted with a text. Those who take the first view restrict their view of reading to those instances in which the outcome of reading could only take place in the narrow context of the reading activity, not in any other form of communication. This, then, restricts the focus of reading skills to word perception. Bruck and Waters (1990) state, for example, '[a]lthough reading may critically rely on the ability to recognize a word, once it has been recognized the reader must employ general language comprehension mechanisms to understand the decoded items.' (189). In this instance, reading is identified as visual decoding while reading comprehension is just a special case of a general comprehension ability. In one approach, the skill of interest is *visual word decoding* while in the other the skill of interest is *comprehension of written text* or the subskills that make it possible.

For example, Gordon (1982) indicates that 'there are three distinct sets of competencies that a student must develop in order to become an effective reader: reading skills development, reading comprehension, and reading research and study skills' (41). He goes on to present the type of breakdown for a reading program that spans first language K-8th grade in Table 4.1 opposite.

This three-part breakdown conceptually corresponds to what might be termed lower-level skills (decoding), higher-level skills (comprehension), and strategies (METACOGNITION). It is interesting to note that in this categorization 'reading' skills are separate from 'comprehension' skills. The reading skills are heavily focused on letter–sound correspondence. It is clear that this collection of skills is pitched at a much earlier level of student than those that Rosenshine described above.

The component skills approach to reading is one of the approaches that views skills as reflections of cognitive processes. The approach attempts to view reading as 'the product of a complex but decomposable information-process-ing system' (Carr et al. 1990: 5). Proponents see this 'decomposable' system as consisting of a specific number of mental operations, or component skills, that are distinct from one another and empirically separable. Although the skills are separable, they work in concert with one another and may exert more or less influence depending upon the reading task and reader require-ments. Levy and Hinchley (1990) contend that there is likely to be no single organization of the multiple-component skills that characterizes a good reader or a poor reader. Rather, good readers may organize their skills differ-ently depending upon whether they are dealing with a speeded task, a com-prehension reading task, or a memory-based task. Thus, skill may incorporate

---

Reading skills development

Names of letters	Vowel diagraphs	Root words
Introduce words	Silent letters	Prefix and suffix
Consonants	Plurals	Synonyms
Vowels	Compound words	Antonyms
Sight words	Context clues	Homonyms
Blends	Contractions	Multiple meaning
Word division	Rhyming words	Pronunciation key
Consonant diagraphs	Hard and soft 'c' and 'g'	Word definitions

---

Reading comprehension development

Categorizing	Summarize	Figurative language
Sequencing	Predict outcomes	Literary forms
Follow directions	Recognize emotions	Evaluate characters
Read for facts	Make inferences	Evaluate settings
Retell story	Reliability of source	Factual conclusions
Main idea	Compare and contrast	Fact, fiction, and opinion
Key words	Make judgments	

Reading research and study skills

Alphabetize	Classify books	Atlases, maps, graphs
Table of contents	Information from	Cross-referencing
Dictionary skills	various sources	Use of index
Encyclopedia	Use of glossary	

Table 4.1: Gordon's (1982) three sets of competencies

organizational flexibility in reading as opposed to some fixed model in which the different component skills consistently operate in the same fashion in relation to one another. This provides some acknowledgment that literacy acts present the reader with different goals and purposes. Such a view also generates additional named reading skills, such as *organizational flexibility*.

Brown and Haynes (1985) note that for component skills 'there are no firmly established set of required subskills for reading' (22). However, they indicate that research from a number of lines of evidence identifies six skills that can be viewed usefully:

1 systematicity of variations in patterning of letters in the perception of graphic features
2 application of orthographic rules in phoneme–grapheme correspondence
3 vocabulary knowledge
4 use of semantic and syntactic context
5 ability to hold information in short-term memory
6 co-ordination of word knowledge and textual information to elaborate comprehension.

In any examination of these skills, Brown and Haynes (1985) note that there is also a need for some other general measure of reading comprehension in addition to tests measuring each of these skills in order to examine the correlational structure of the differing component skills as variables. Carr et al. (1990) indicate that a focus on direct teaching of the skills associated with the various component skills using activities such as direct instruction and practice of identifying gist, using context to determine word meanings, and extensive instruction in phonics, can improve reading ability in first language children.

Thus, there are differing definitions of reading skills and differing assumptions about at what level of description they are separable. The extent to which skills are discretely defined comes in part from whether one is taking a developmental view or a more general cognitive-processing view.

Hierarchy of skills

In many models of skills, over time the focus of attention may change from lower-level skills to higher-level skills as reading ability is acquired, requiring less attention and becoming more automatic (Brown and Haynes, 1985; LaBerge and Samuels 1974; Logan 1979). That is, the lower level skills involving visual perception and phonic analysis become automatic with practice and require less conscious monitoring. This releases attention capacity to deal with comprehension aspects of reading.

It is apparent from the discussion on reading skills that many educators and researchers have identified reading skills at different levels of detail. This is one of the central issues in determining whether there are separable skills. The levels of skill descriptions presented in Table 4.2 are taken from Lunzer et al.(1979).

Most of us would agree that the Level 1 skill of 'decoding print' is a skill different from the Level 1 description 'making sense'. However, there may be quite a bit of overlap in all of the Level 3 descriptions regardless of designations such as decoding print, making sense, or questioning. This concern with how fine to draw a particular skill goes to the heart of whether there appear to be distinct and separable skills. As the skill becomes narrower in scope, the more difficult it is to find distinct examples of reading acts that are not comprised of more than one skill. Further, as the reading act is made up of more than one skill, it becomes more and more difficult to measure the skill without it being overpowered by the existence of overlapping skills. This factor in turn makes it difficult to determine whether the skills are truly separate. As we begin to look at the different approaches to determining whether reading skills represent a hierarchy of skills, this problem with identifying specific skills will become more apparent.

Level 1	Level 2	Level 3
Decoding print	Identifying letters, words, phrases	Scanning, fixating, anticipating, categorizing, testing, matching, verifying
Making sense	Assigning meaning to phrases and sentences	Anticipating syntactic and semantic categories, matching, verifying
Questioning	Noting discrepancies between different statements or between what is read and what is known	Retrieving material from long-term memory, comparing, inferring

Table 4.2: The process of reading: three levels of description (Adapted from Lunzer et al. (1979))

In terms of any implicational hierarchy order of comprehension skills, Clymer (1968) presented a taxonomy, developed by Barrett (N.D) in an unpublished paper. The taxonomy is divided into five ordered skill levels: (a) literal comprehension; (b) reorganization; (c) inferential comprehension; (d) evaluation; and (e) appreciation. According to Clymer, these categories are ordered to move from easy to difficult in terms of the demands of each category. The Barrett taxonomy is shown in Table 4.3. It is interesting to note that, in this taxonomy of reading skill, the lowest level of reading skills discussed earlier, such as Gordon's (1982) names of letters, silent letters, etc., or word-attack skills in general are not listed. The reader is assumed to be beyond that initial stage of text processing.

Barrett's taxonomy was clearly influenced by Bloom's more general processing taxonomy (Bloom 1956), which attempted to define levels of cognitive and affective processing that represent different levels of educational objectives in areas other than reading comprehension. As with Barrett's taxonomy, Bloom's taxonomy assumes that the lower-numbered levels are more basic than those with higher numbers. Although intuitively somewhat reasonable, the presentation of such orderly categories may indicate more precision in categories than may psychologically exist. It is not at all clear that in Barrett's taxonomy *Inferring character traits (3.6)* is more basic or essential than *Judgments of fact or opinion (4.2)*. There is certainly more overlap in the categories, and tasks devised to reflect each category, than the list suggests. Additionally, the taxonomy does not reflect in any reasoned way that background knowledge will have a significant effect upon the difficulty of any given category or how context in general will modify the proposed difficulty or ease.

There have been a number of studies to determine whether there is empirical support for the distinctiveness of reading skills, and for whether there is any

1.0 Literal Comprehension
    1.1 Recognition
        1.1.1 Recognition of Details
        1.1.2 Recognition of Main Ideas
        1.1.3 Recognition of a Sequence
        1.1.4 Recognition of Comparison
        1.1.5 Recognition of Cause and Effect Relationships
        1.1.6 Recognition of Character Traits
    1.2 Recall
        1.2.1 Recall of Details
        1.2.2 Recall of Main Ideas
        1.2.3 Recall of a Sequence
        1.2.4 Recall of Comparison
        1.2.5 Recall of Cause and Effect Relationships
        1.2.6 Recall of Character Traits

2.0 Reorganization
    2.1 Classifying
    2.2 Outlining
    2.3 Summarizing
    2.4 Synthesizing

3.0 Inferential Comprehension
    3.1 Inferring Supporting Details
    3.2 Inferring Main Ideas
    3.3 Inferring Sequence
    3.4 Inferring Comparisons
    3.5 Inferring Cause and Effect Relationships
    3.6 Inferring Character Traits
    3.7 Predicting Outcomes
    3.8 Interpreting Figurative Language

4.0 Evaluation
    4.1 Judgments of Reality or Fantasy
    4.2 Judgments of Fact or Opinion
    4.3 Judgments of Adequacy and Validity
    4.4 Judgments of Appropriateness
    4.5 Judgments of Worth, Desirability and Acceptability

5.0 Appreciation
    5.1 Emotional Response to the Content
    5.2 Identification with Characters or Incidents
    5.3 Reactions to the Author's Use of Language
    5.4 Imagery

Table 4.3: Outline of the Barrett taxonomy of cognitive and affective dimensions of reading comprehension

1 Recalling word meanings*
2 Drawing inferences about the meaning of a word from context
3 Finding answers to questions answered explicitly or merely in paraphrase*
4 Weaving together ideas from content
5 Drawing inferences from the content*
6 Recognizing a writer's purpose, attitude, tone, and mood*
7 Identifying a writer's technique
8 Following the structure of a passage*.

*=identified as unique in Davis (1968)

Table 4.4: The eight reading comprehension skills addressed by Davis (1968, 1972)

hierarchical ordering of those skills identified as distinct. One of the first language researchers most identified with the proposition that there are separable processes or skills involved in reading comprehension is F. B. Davis (1944, 1968, 1972). Davis originally posited nine operational skills of comprehension among mature readers. Thus, he was not addressing the early prerequisite skills of letter identification or phoneme–grapheme correspondence. In his 1968 study, he reduced the hypothesized skills to be examined to eight. These are listed in Table 4.4. Of these eight, Davis found five variables to be unique contributors to comprehension through multiple regression. These were 1, 5, 3, 6, and 8, indicated with an asterisk (*).

He noted that:

> comprehension in reading among mature readers is not a unitary mental skill. It is apparently a composite of at least five or six underlying mental skills. Whether there is a hierarchy of these skills by which one or more must be available to the reader before he can call on others is not shown by the data.

(Davis 1968: 655)

Through subsequent factor analysis, Davis (1972) determined that he could specify four unique factors or skills. These four skills were:

1 knowledge of word meanings
2 drawing inferences from the content
3 finding answers to questions answered explicitly or in paraphrase in the passage and weaving together ideas in the content
4 drawing inferences about the meaning of a word from context.

Davis (1972) notes that while there are four unique skills in reading comprehension, his findings do not show evidence that the skills 'can be arranged in a clear-cut order of cumulative agglomeration of simple skills in more complex

skills.' (672). Thus, while he does claim to identify distinct reading comprehension skills, he does not see that they represent a hierarchically ordered set
of skills. It is not clear what interpretation to make of the fact that the skills are
different in his 1968 study from those in his 1972 study. For example, drawing
inferences about the meaning of a word from context was not unique in the
first study but was unique in the second. This most likely is a function of the
two different statistical types of analysis used in the two different analyses.

Two subsequent studies re-examined Davis' original data using different
statistical procedures. Spearritt (1972) concluded that the statistical
approach taken by Davis in his factor-analytic study did not employ the
most comprehensive procedures, and he reanalyzed Davis' data using a
different statistical approach. The four skills he identified were:

1 Recalling word meanings
2 Drawing inferences from the content
3 Recognizing a writer's purpose, attitude, tone, and mood
4 Following the structure of a passage.

He notes however, that vocabulary is the best differentiated of the four identified skills. The other three skills were highly intercorrelated and the tests
measuring them may actually measure one basic ability termed 'reasoning in
reading'. However, this may be a product of the tests rather than bringing the
skills themselves in question.

Lunzer et al. (1979) set out to examine the status of eight item types representing comprehension skills. Their eight types are represented in Table 4.5.

They developed items for each type of skill across four different passages.
Each test consisted of an extended passage, followed by approximately 30
questions. The tests were administered to 257 pupils in their last year in one
of four British primary schools. Reliabilities for each test were reasonably
acceptable, ranging from .83 to .85. Their factor analysis produced six factors
for each of the four tests. However, the item types on the different tests were

---

1 Word meaning
2 Words in context
3 Literal comprehension
4 Drawing inferences from single strings
5 Drawing inferences from multiple strings
6 Interpretation of metaphor
7 Finding salient or main ideas
8 Forming judgments.

Table 4.5: Comprehension skill item types (Lunzer et al. 1979)

associated with different factors and were inconsistent with one another. Thus, the structure of the items is apparently test specific. When they put all the items of each type into the analysis, regardless of passage, they obtained a single factor that accounted for 71 per cent of the total variance. They concluded that the individual differences in reading comprehension across readers is not the result of a multiplicity of specialized aptitudes, and they certainly did not find support for any hierarchy of difficulty in the skills they examined. In short, an apparent unitary construct of reading emerged from their study.

There have been numerous other attempts in the first language literature to identify skills and their ordering, primarily using factor-analytic techniques to identify reading skills and any possible hierarchy of those skills. Lennon (1962) examined 12 such studies. He generalized across the studies and identified four basic reading skills: a) general verbal factor; b) comprehension of explicit information; c) comprehension of implicit information; and d) appreciation. However, in fact, half of the studies identified only a single factor, and the other studies varied in the number and type of skills that were identified. In part, the discrepancies that have been found, and which cloud the issue of whether there are distinct reading skills, are often methodological in nature. First, many different existing tests ranging from comprehension to reading speed to letter recognition have been used in the different tests, and little attention is given to the reliabilities of the tests, Thorndike (1973) being the exception.

Additionally, in terms of question difficulty on a reading test, the particular text may be the largest source of difficulty for the reader, not the item type. A scientific text may require a very difficult literal-interpretation item while an item on a less difficult text may ask for an easy inference. While there may be some general order for item type within passages, any taxonomy will have to contain the caveat 'all other things being equal …' However, it is a reality of literacy acts that 'all other things being equal' rarely if ever occurs. For one thing, background knowledge will differ and this will affect the difficulty of answering a word-in-context type item. Likewise, in addition to the text being the source of difficulty, the particular task that is required of the reader will affect difficulty. Whether an examinee is asked to select a multiple-choice item or to write out the answer will affect the relative difficulty.

Further, the interpretation of factors in factor analysis is as much an art as it is a science. Perhaps a different approach is needed, one that does not equate correlation of skills with absorption of skill. That is, from the factor-analytic approach, when test items identified with different skills correlate highly, it is assumed that they are no longer separate skills. The view of the componential model offers some alternate approaches to interpreting highly correlated skills. In this view, the correlations are reflections of the different strength of relationships, and simply because two skills, or subskills, such as phonological awareness and word recognition, are highly correlated, does not mean that they are part of the same skill. To some extent, this approach requires that research adopt an *a priori* confirmatory type approach to future research. Through such approaches as structural equation modeling, rather than exploratory factor analysis, skills and their separability can perhaps be more adequately and reliably identified.

However, that doesn't help us much right now. Whether at the present time we accept that there are separable skills or not will be due in large part to our particular academic orientation. There are researchers who attempt to take a skill and decompose it into its smallest intuitively meaningful parts ('There are several distinct skills in reading.'). There are other researchers who are looking to combine whatever information is available in order to come up with the most parsimonious and least complex explanation ('There is only one reading factor.'). Consequently, we should expect much disagreement about whether there are skills. However, there appears to be scant evidence that those skills that have been identified are hierarchically ordered in any way other than the basic letter-decoding skills are essential for application of any of the other reading skills. Rather, we should conceptualize reading as a multifaceted information-processing activity requiring any number of subcomponents. Any one of these subcomponents can lead to reading differences across individuals. It is clear that ease and facility of orthographic and phonological processing, as well as word-recognition ease, are important contributors to efficient reading.

On skills and their hierarchical nature in the second language literature

There have been several attempts to develop skill lists and hierarchies in the second language reading literature. Much of the interest in this work is designed to recognize that second language learners are generally older when they begin to read the second language than the normal age of beginning reading instruction in the first language, are already literate in their first language, and have more specific needs than early first language learners. The research into skills in second language has taken one of two primary orientations. The first examines the role of the traditionally termed lower-level word processing skills while the second examines the role of comprehension skills in second language reading. The research into lower-level processing skills is reflected in studies by Brown and Haynes (1985) and several studies by Koda (1987, 1992, 1997, 2005). The research into the separability and ordering of second language reading comprehension skills is reflected in work by Munby (1978), research on the guidelines of the American Council on the Teaching of Foreign Languages (ACTFL) (Higgs 1984), and work by Alderson and Lukmani (1989), Alderson (1990), Hudson (1993), and the Common European Framework (North 2000).

Lower-level processing in second language

Brown and Haynes (1985) examined differences in visual and orthographic coding skills of Japanese, Arabic, and Spanish speaking learners of English. The selection of these language groups was motivated by the different script types represented by the three languages. Spanish largely uses the same alphabet as English. Arabic has a different script, but one that is alphabetic in principle, while Japanese uses a system that is a combination of phonological, syllabic, and logographic symbols. The research was designed to examine differential visual and orthographic processing skills due to the differing nature of the first language writing systems.

To the surprise of Brown and Haynes (1985) in a task requiring the matching of orthographic strips as same or different, although the Spanish readers were faster and made fewer errors than the Arabic readers, the Japanese were the fastest and most accurate at this orthographic recognition task even with words up to ten letters. The Japanese were also fastest in matching same and different numeric strings, while the Spanish and Arabic speakers were basically equal. However, on a read-aloud task, the Japanese speakers were slower and less accurate than the other two groups. Further, the Japanese showed a greater sensitivity to whether the words were familiar or unfamiliar, indicating that they relied more on sight word knowledge than phoneme–grapheme clues. The Japanese readers appeared to have more difficulty in connecting visual symbols to spoken units. Brown and Haynes speculate that these results may be due to both the literacy and educational background of the learners. First, the Japanese appeared to process the letter combinations visually rather than phonologically, as they would in their first language. Spanish and Arabic speakers, on the other hand, were accustomed to alphabetic writing systems that have a generally clear and consistent sign–sound correspondence. Second, the Japanese educational system has generally tended to value reading over speaking in second language instruction.

The study appears to indicate that first language skills are applied to second language contexts, at least for skills associated with orthographic processing and letter recognition. However, there are problems with basing too much on the study. The study does not report data about the different language groups in terms of their proficiency levels. Nor does it report descriptive or inferential statistics in adequate detail. However, it does provide initial support indicating different word-attack skills among the languages and indicates how those skills may be transferred from the first language to the second language context.

Koda (1987, 1990) provides additional support for the finding that Japanese readers transfer the visual-processing skills from their first language to the second language when reading English, though this process appears to be a tendency rather than an either/or dichotomy. She investigated the relationship between orthography and cognition in reading a second language. She notes that script systems can be logographic, in which each symbol represents an entire syllable, or orthographic, in which each symbol represents a single phoneme. The different representations of the role of print in the different writing systems, as well as processes of perception and cognition, would be expected to differ for users of each orthographic system. Koda (1987) summarizes past research showing that orthographies that are sound based involve more phonological coding than those that are meaning based. However, some research has also found a phonological trace in logographic language processing, indicating the need for readers to supply phonological information to retrieved logographic meaning. Koda posits that it is 'reasonable to conjecture that phonological recoding of lexical items is vital in reading sentences and texts, whether written in sound-based script or meaning-based script' (133).

Koda's (1987) study investigated the phonological inaccessibility assumed for logographic readers reading a sound-based second language. Twenty-six Japanese students were divided into two groups. One group was presented with pronounceable names (for example, *doffit*) associated with pictures of fish. The second group was presented with the same pictures but associated with unpronounceable names (for example, *dfofti*). After learning the names, subjects read a passage describing the fish, using either the pronounceable or unpronounceable forms the subjects had learned. Koda found that, in contrast to English-speaking readers, the Japanese readers in her study read the unpronounceable passage in a significantly shorter amount of time than the pronounceable passage. The results suggest that the Japanese transferred their second language reading skill to the second language reading in that phonological recoding is not a common strategy among Japanese readers reading Japanese.

In two subsequent studies, Koda (1989, 1990) investigated first language orthographic influence on processing involved in second language reading with readers from language backgrounds with contrasting orthographies (Arabic, Japanese, Spanish, and English). Two passages were employed. The first passage described the characteristics of five fictitious fish, and the second described the characteristics of five imaginary cocktails. In the experimental condition, Sanskrit symbols were used in place of the names of the fish and cocktails. In the control condition, pronounceable English nonsense words were substituted for the Sanskrit symbols. Half of each experimental and control group read one of the passages while the other half read the second passage. After reading the passages, the subjects were given a recall test in which they were asked to match the names of the fish/cocktails to their characteristic descriptions in the passage. The results showed that subjects spent considerably more time on the Sanskrit passages than on the English nonsense versions across the groups. This indicated that phonological inaccessibility significantly impeded reading regardless of language background. However, it was found that reading speed was significantly slower in the readers with the alphabetic phonological languages (Arabic, English, and Spanish) than the morphographic readers (Japanese). The results appear to indicate that the different phonological coding strategies are used among subjects with contrasting orthographic systems, and that some phonological processing skill transfers from first language to second language. That is, the Japanese readers transferred their reading skill character recognition and the alphabetic readers transferred their phonologically related skills.

Haynes and Carr (1990) again investigated lower-level first language reading skills on second language reading. They examined skilled readers whose first language was Chinese while reading English as a second language. In Chinese, characters map primarily on to meaningful syllabic units of speech while English maps primarily on to phonemic units. Haynes and Carr note that readers of English often show evidence of phonological recoding during the reading process but that Chinese characters do not appear to elicit much evidence of this when the sentences are simple and consequently do not place high memory demands on comprehension. The study involved a two-stage component skills approach. The subjects were 28 university freshmen (low group), 32 seniors (high group) in a university in Taiwan, and 15 American undergraduate volunteers from a general psychology class at a large mid-western university. The first stage of the study compared visual-processing efficiency of English alphabetic stimuli by first language Chinese readers at the two levels of English proficiency (low and high) with performance of native readers of English. The subjects were engaged in matching same or different pairs of orthographic strings that were: 1) orthographically irregular strings; 2) orthographically regular non-words; and 3) real English words. The subjects were also asked to match strings of digits in order to determine whether the processing of matching was language specific or a more general process. The second stage of the research involved comparing individual differences at the visual-orthographic level to reading outcomes such as: 1) comprehension; 2) speed of reading; and 3) ability to learn new lexical items from context. The study also included measures of vocabulary knowledge, English grammar, English listening comprehension, and Chinese reading comprehension. Relevant findings from the study were:

1 The comparison of words, pseudo-words, and letter strings was used to indicate whether the presence of orthographic structure improved the level of recognition. The finding was that the English readers benefited from the existence of the orthographic cues to a significantly greater extent than did the Chinese readers in terms of speed and accuracy.

2 The more advanced Chinese learners of English did not differ from the lower-level Chinese learners in terms of speed of reading or reading comprehension. However, the advanced-level learners were significantly better in terms of the vocabulary-learning measures. Haynes and Carr take this as an indication that the longer exposure to English orthography provided an advantage for this aspect of reading comprehension.

3 Correlations between all the measures indicate a relative lack of relationship between the measures of comprehension and those of reading speed. Further, Chinese reading comprehension scores by the Chinese native speakers correlated with English reading comprehension scores but not with measures of English reading speed. However, the measure of orthographic same-different recognition was related to reading comprehension. In general, the findings indicate that speed and comprehension are different and that the factors that constrain speed and those that constrain accuracy are different.

4 Despite the dissociation of reading comprehension and reading speed in general, both these factors were associated with new word learning. For Haynes and Carr, this indicates that both speed and accuracy may be factors in lexical acquisition. This is consistent with the limited-capacity models of interactive reading which see accuracy and speed as factors in integration of word clues.

The results generally indicate that the low-level skills of orthographic processing are both different in kind from comprehension skills and that the particular type of orthographic-processing practices in general first language literacy acts are transferred to some extent into second language orthographic processing.

Koda (1992) also examined the relationship between lower-level processing skills and second language reading comprehension. Her focus was on the processes involved in extracting visual information from print, such as word or letter identification. She examined the concept that deficits in lower-level processing skills put a strain on short-term memory and hence hinder text integration. This limited-capacity model, similar to that discussed in Haynes and Carr (1990), posits that when a reader is preoccupied with lower-level processing, less cognitive capacity is available for the higher-level text-processing skills. Koda notes that research 'suggests that the reading process is heavily dependent upon visual information contained in the text, and that successful performance is determined largely by efficiency in sampling visual information details' (503). She predicts, then, that because of differences between Japanese and English script, second language learners of Japanese will suffer in reading comprehension to the extent that they have problems processing Japanese script.

Fifty-eight American college students enrolled in first-year Japanese took a battery of tests. For reading comprehension, they took a cloze test, a paragraph comprehension test, and a sentence comprehension test. Verbal processing was measured using two types of speed recognition tasks: word recognition in both Kanji and Hiragana, as well as letter recogniton in Hiragana text. Koda predicted that test performance on the comprehension measures would largely be determined by word recognition of both Kanji and Hiragana. The second prediction was that, because grammatical morphemes such as case markings and verb tense are written in Hiragana, letter-identification ability would predict cloze test performance. Since the sentence-level comprehension test did not require INTERSENTENTIAL PROCESSING, it was predicted that readers would have more capacity available for processing and thus verbal processing would not affect the sentence comprehension performance as much as it would the cloze and paragraph comprehension tests.

The results of the study indicated that the three verbal processing tests correlated highly with the text comprehension scores, but less well with the sentence comprehension measures. Results indicated that at early stages of ability, Kanji recognition was the single significant predictor of comprehension while as ability increased, Hiragana word recognitions entered as a significant factor. The reason for this, Koda speculates, is that because Kanji are linked directly to a word meaning while Hirigana are linked to sounds that are added together to create a word, it may be easier to make a symbol-to-word connection than symbol-to-sound connections. Thus, initial retrieval of Kanji may be more salient when full control over the sound system has not yet been formed. The analysis further found that letter identification was the only significant predictor for the cloze tests, as predicted. Finally, none of the verbal processing measures significantly predicted the sentence comprehension test scores, lending support to the limited-capacity argument about early reading processing.

However, the multiple-regression approach taken here requires large samples, larger than those used in this study. Again, descriptive statistics and reliabilities are not reported so it is difficult to extrapolate from the study to other contexts. Without descriptive statistics it is not possible for us to see just how low or high in ability the subjects were. Further clouding the implications of the study is the fact that a lot of the interpretation rests on which particular Kanji and Hiragana were selected for the test instruments.

In a review of the literature on first language orthographic processing, Koda (1997) again explores the effect of orthographic processing on word identification. She again argues for the importance of visual-information control in the text as a key factor in reading. Here she attempts to clarify the nature of orthographic knowledge and its function in second language contexts, noting that current vocabulary studies show reading proficiency to be correlated with the ability to infer meaning of unknown words from context (Chern 1993). Failure to use context may be due to word misidentification. She notes that many identification errors result from insufficient information being derived during orthographic processing. First language research has indicated that poor readers are inefficient in their lexical retrieval from print (Perfetti 1991; Stanovich 1991). Thus, reading is dependent to a large degree on visual information. She further reiterates from her previous studies that linguistic features essential to sentence comprehension and production vary from language to language. In many instances, cross-linguistic variations in processing are consistent with what would be predicted based on the morphosyntactic features of the particular first language.

For Koda, the fact that Japanese employs three major orthographic systems (logographic, syllabary, and alphabetic) is an essential factor to take into account when examining second language reading processes by Japanese learners learning English or English first language speakers learning Japanese. Again, she argues that, since lower-level processing plays a crucial role in reading comprehension, since different processing is required in the processing of different languages, and since previous research has indicated that some first language processing is transferred to second language, then orthographic knowledge plays a more central role in second language reading than many have previously assumed. In essence, then, Koda sees these low-level skills as part of a hierarchical ordering of reading comprehension skills. They are necessary but not sufficient skills in successful reading.

The research by Brown and Haynes (1985), Koda (1987, 1989, 1990, 1992, 1997), and Haynes and Carr (1990) consistently indicate that lower-level processing in second language is affected by visual and orthographic coding. Further, this coding in many cases is affected by the orthographic conventions of the learners' first language. Efficient visual processing is essential for lexical access, and consequently is essential for comprehension. As long as the learner is at a low level of processing ability, comprehension will be impeded.

Higher-level skills in second language

For potentially higher-order skills, Munby (1978) presents a taxonomy across the second language skills of listening, speaking, reading, and writing within a communicative framework. Some example skills that are most identified with reading are presented in Table 4.7. The numbers to the left of each skill represent the original designation of skills 1–54 provided by Munby (1978).

Munby (1978) developed his taxonomy of skills in order to provide teachers and materials writers with a basis from which to select skills appropriate for students with particular goals and needs. It is not clear the extent to which the skills in the taxonomy are viewed in a strict hierarchy of difficulty. Munby states, in relation to skills in groups 20–3 that, 'the ability to perform skills 20, 21, 22.1, and 23.1 appears to involve operating at a lower (or grosser)

17. Recognizing the script of a language
    17.1 discriminating the graphemes
    17.2 following grapheme sequences (spelling system)
    17.3 understanding punctuation

19. Deducing the meanings and use of unfamiliar lexical items, through
    19.1 understanding word formation:
        19.1.1 stems/roots
        19.1.2 affixation
        19.1.3 derivation
        19.1.4 compounding
    19.2 contextual clues

20. Understanding explicitly stated information

22. Understanding information in the text, not explicitly stated, through
    22.1 making inferences
    22.2 understanding figurative language

32. Understanding relations between parts of a text through grammatical cohesion devices of
    32.1 reference (anaphoric and cataphoric)
    32.2 comparison
    32.3 substitution
    32.4 ellipsis
    32.5 time and place relaters
    32.6 logical connecters

39. Distinguishing the main idea from supporting details, by differentiating
    39.1 primary from secondary significance
    39.2 the whole from its parts
    39.3 a process from its stages
    39.4 category from exponent
    39.5 statement from example
    39.6 fact from opinion
    39.7 a proposition from an argument

44. Basic reference skills: understanding and use of
    44.1 graphic presentation, viz. Headings, sub-headings, numbering, indentation, bold print, footnotes
    44.2 table of contents and index
    44.3 cross-referencing
    44.4 card catalogue
    44.5 phonetic transcription/ diacritics

continued

45. Skimming to obtain
45.1 the gist of the text
45.2 a general impression of the text

54. Relaying information
54.1 directly (commentary/description concurrent with action)
54.2 indirectly (reporting)

Table 4.7: The taxonomy of reading skills (Adapted from Munby (1978))

level of delicacy than that for related skills such as those at 32.' (119). More generally, the taxonomy goes from skill 17.1, 'discriminating sounds in isolate word forms', to 54, 'relaying information'. However, skill 39, 'distinguishing the main idea from supporting details', does not appear in any logical way to be a less demanding endeavor than skill 44, 'basic reference skills: understanding, and use of' and 44.2, 'table of contents and index'. Still, the taxonomy does present skill 54, 'relaying information', in a way that is consistent with a reading-to-write or literacy-act basis. With more specificity of the tasks that indicate actual literacy acts, this provides a form of contextualization of the reading skill.

It is important to note that Munby developed his taxonomy outside of an empirical framework, much like the Barrett and Bloom taxonomies discussed earlier. He first identified a set of communicative needs. He then reflected on what skills would be necessary for the realization of different communicative activities and extrapolated those skills to relationships within the taxonomy. Thus, the relative order and separability of the skills presented are not based on any of the statistical procedures discussed in the preceding section.

Mecartty (1998) investigated whether performance on reading skills was uniform across learners and reading texts, and whether the skills formed a hierarchy for non-native readers of Spanish. In this study, 38 fourth-semester students of Spanish and 30 in the fifth semester of study in a Midwestern US university were chosen to contrast the skills in two ability levels. The subjects read two text selections, each four pages long. The skills isolated were: 1) locating details—recognition and paraphrase (skill-1); 2) simple inferential skills—understanding words in context and recognizing cause/effect (skill-2); 3) complex inferential skills—recognizing main ideas and drawing conclusions (skill-3). The three-way repeated measures Analysis of Variance (ANOVA) indicated a three-way interaction among level, passage, and skill. There was also a main effect for skill and interactions between skill and level and skill and passage. Post hoc tests showed no significant difference between skill-1 and skill-2, but skill-3 was significantly different from skill-1 and skill-2. However, of primary importance in the study is the indication that the variables attributed to passage and skill are constantly in interaction with one another. Thus, while skill-1 and skill-2 do not appear to be different (to the extent that they have similar means), skill-3 is different from them, and there is an overriding indication that they operate in consort throughout the reading process. Mecartty indicates that the findings show a hierarchy to the extent that skill-3 was more difficult than the other skills regardless of the combination of passage or level. However, what is not clear from studies such as this is how homogeneous the test items are as representative samples of a skill. The study included only two items per passage of each skill type. In essence, a study is needed that generates a large number of all three skill types and then examines the extent to which there is overlap of the skill distribution, not just the mean of each skill group. The degree of overlap across skill designations is a central concern in deciding the extent to which we feel comfortable asserting any hierarchical nature of skills. This is particularly relevant for the Mecartty study given that the paper does not report descriptive statistics or reliability estimates for the test.

Alderson and Lukmani (1989) investigated whether there existed 'identifiable separate levels of comprehension' (260) in the context of an English examination for students needing to show evidence of their English reading ability. They examined the issue from two directions. First, nine teachers at the Institute for English Language Education at the University of Lancaster were given the task of examining a test and determining what each item was testing, and then to specify whether they felt the item was measuring lower-, middle-, or higher-level abilities. They were then given an envelope with a list of reading skills and asked to indicate which of those skills were tested on the examination they reviewed. The results indicated very little agreement among the teachers on the levels being tested by the different items. Additionally, the judges were unable to consistently specify which reading skill the particular items represented. In fact, their determinations were often as divergent as one judge's indicating that an item was measuring 'explicitly stated information, gist', with other judges indicating that the item measured 'knowledge of literary style; distinguish related items' or 'understand coherence; pick out main ideas'. Alderson and Lukmani found overall that 'for something less than half of the items involved, it is possible to say that some identification of level seems to be possible judgmentally' (265).

In order to examine the issue further, Alderson and Lukmani carried out an empirical phase of the study involving an examination of the performance of 100 students at Bombay University, India, on the examination under investigation. The analysis involved the 14 items that had achieved agreement by the judges in the previous stage of the study. According to the *a priori* classification, this 14-item test contained five lower-level items, four mid-level items, and five higher-level items. The results showed a slight tendency for the higher-level items to be more difficult. However, they found this to be only a slight tendency. For example, they found the percentage of correct scores for lower-level questions to range from 42 per cent to 89 per cent, while the middle-level skills ranged from 52 per cent to 73 per cent and the higher-level skills ranged from 42 per cent to 64 per cent. One of the lower-level items and one of the higher-level items tied as the most difficult items. Apparently, item difficulty does not closely align with proposed level of comprehension.

Their conclusions from the two phases of the study are that there are no clearly defined isolated skills or definite implicationally ordered levels of skill hierarchy such that an examinee must answer test items for the lower-level skills in order to answer items assessing the putative upper-level skills. Indeed, they found that the higher-order skill items had a much lower item discrimination than the lower-order skill items, indicating that many of the lower-level students were answering higher-level skill items with more ability than would be expected in a hierarchy. It very well may be that these higher-level skill items are indeed measuring cognitive abilities rather than reading specific abilities. In that case, there is no reason to believe, as Alderson and Lukmani point out, that lower reading ability will necessarily interfere consistently with the application of cognitive ability.

In an extension of the Alderson and Lukmani (1989) study, Alderson (1990) focused on two different tests, tests for which there is more published data available. The tests are the Test of English for Educational Purposes (TEEP) and the English Language Testing Service (ELTS) test. Both tests were based on Munby's taxonomy, and assume that Munby's taxonomy is ordered such that lower-level skills are a prerequisite for the higher-level skills. First, Alderson selected 18 experienced teachers of ESL to complete three tasks based on the TEEP: 1) rate each skill ostensibly tested on the TEEP as to whether each was a higher- or lower-level skill; 2) inspect the TEEP reading test and match each item to the skills ostensibly tested; and 3) judge whether each test item is testing a higher- or lower-level skill.

The judges showed substantial disagreement as to which skills were higher- or lower-order skills. Only 'understanding explicitly stated ideas' received unanimity in the judgments. Nine of the 14 skills had disagreements among the judges of 30 per cent or more. In their evaluation of which reading skill each item was testing, the judges showed similar disagreement. On one item, although the judges differed from one another markedly, they also all selected skills different from that designated by the test designer. The two items with the most consistency of judgment had discrepancies of 24 per cent and 41 per cent respectively. Finally, when the judges matched each item with whether it was a higher- or lower-level item, there was disagreement approaching chaos, and some of the judges changed their rating of whether a particular skill was lower or higher based on the item content. Thus, the study reinforces the findings from the Alderson and Lukmani (1989) study using a different test with different judges.

In the empirical phase of his study, Alderson examined the test results from previously administered tests. For the TEEP, he found that the items that were targeted as higher-order items by the test writer had a mean facility of .65 whereas the items that were supposed to be lower-level items had a mean item facility of .53. That is, the proposed lower-level items were more difficult for the examinees than the supposedly higher-level items. A further analysis focuses upon those items in which there was relative agreement among the judges who rated the items previously. In this instance, as well, there is little relationship between ranked difficulty and examinee performance. In order to address this in more detail with a larger sample of items, Alderson took the results from seven different TEEP tests. Again, there were no systematic results supporting assigned level of reading difficulty and performance across the seven tests. Finally, in order to further test the findings, Alderson examined results on seven forms of the ELTS test, a different type of test from those used in the study just discussed and in the Alderson and Lukmani (1989) study. Again, the results showed no systematicity in the relationship between reading skill designation as represented by test items and score. For three tests, the higher-level skills were more difficult; in three tests there was no difference between the higher- and lower-level skills, and in one test the higher-level skill items were easier than the lower-level skill items.

In 1993 I investigated the role of reading skills and skill levels using item-response theory to help identify and delimit the role that particular skills play. In this examination, I hypothesized that:

1   A skill or subskill will have a narrow bandwidth of difficulty.
2   Skills or subskills may be at different levels depending on whether their general dispersion is at a more difficult or less difficult location on the difficulty continuum.
3   A skill or subskill will have very discriminating items, that is, high slope values.

(Hudson 1993: 66)

Subjects for the study were Spanish-speaking chemical engineering students studying English for specific purposes at a university in Mexico. Each of three forms of a reading test comprising a grammar test, a test of reading comprehension, and a multiple-choice cloze test measuring general reading ability was administered to approximately 200 students. Items on the test were categorized according to the task or item type they represented. The reading skills associated with items for each subtest were characterized as indicated in Table 4.8.

Three judges rated the items according to the category they represented. Items were placed in the category identified by at least two of the three judges. The results show that of all the skills, only specific direct information

---

Subtest and reading skill
Reading comprehension subtest
1 Specific direct information: a fact contained in the passage that can be answered by a single term or number
2 Specific restatement: a phrase or clause taken directly from the text
3 Gist: a question that can be answered by comprehending a section of the text and selecting the appropriate answer that is a paraphrase of the text
4 Graph/chart: a question that directed the students to a chart, illustration, or graph to answer the question

---

Grammar subtest
1 Simple verb tense: tenses including simple present, copula, and simple past
2 Connectors: logical connectors such as *because, thus, therefore*, and *consequently*
3 Passive voice
4 Modal verbs
5 Perfective tenses
6 Relative pronouns: pronouns in relative clauses, including reduced relative forms
7 Progressive: present or past

Multiple-choice cloze
1 Reading comprehension/grammar: understanding prepositional information at an interclausal level, but item emphasizes syntax over vocabulary
2 Reading comprehension/vocabulary: the processing is long-range (i.e., interclausal), but a lexical choice is required to solve it
3 Grammar/reading comprehension: the source of item difficulty involves relatively short-range grammatical constraints—usually a few words on either side of the blank or within a single grammatical phrase or clause
4 Vocabulary/reading comprehension: the primary aspect of this category is vocabulary, although it also invokes reading comprehension in that the reader must understand the information presented within clause boundaries.

Table 4.8: Reading skill by test type (Adapted from Hudson (1993))

appears to have a consistent order in relation to the others. Its mean score indicated that it was an easier task type than the others. Likewise, specific restatement items had a high discrimination and a relatively identifiable bandwidth for difficulty. However, each of the skills generally represented a wide band of difficulties, indicating a violation of the initial hypothesis described above. That is, the items associated with the different skills did not tend to have homogeneous difficulty values.

The results from the study indicate that the current analogy of reading as an interaction of top-down and bottom-up processes and skills is a restricting metaphor. The processes and skills are definitely interactive. However, the interaction appears to be other than top-down interacting with bottom-up, at least for readers at all but the lowest ability. Rather, it is important to emphasize the overlapping parallel interactions between language skills, interactions that are independent of skill levels designated as higher or lower, top-down or bottom-up. It is likely that there is more variation within skill levels than between levels of reading skills. Consequently, we need to re-examine models using levels and discrete categories. Most likely, the skills and processes that are the basis for reading are much more numerous and complex than existing taxonomies can accommodate. Different skills, knowledge, and vocabulary are differentially related depending upon the context, purpose, text, length, time, etc. associated with individual readers.

Summary and conclusions

In general, both the first language and second language literature related to reading skills argue against the existence of strictly hierarchically ordered reading skills. Further, there appear to be broad categories of skills, such as word-attack skills, comprehension skills, fluency skills, and critical reading skills rather than a detailed list of numerous discrete reading skills. The application of identified skills, further, appears to be mediated by such factors as text, purpose, and content. While the detailed lists of skills may be helpful in curriculum development and scope and sequence charts associated with textbooks and series, the actual operationalization of simple unitary skills is problematic. Reading acts and literacy events are sufficiently complex that they involve multiple skills and skills that are not unitary in their structure.

Discussion and study questions

1 From the review of the literature, how many reading skills do you identify as important? What are they? Is it a problem that skills appear to overlap?
2 To what extent do you think reading comprehension is a reading skill as opposed to a general language ability? How will your answer to this question affect the kinds of activities you would include in a reading course or program?
3 Alderson found difficulty in determining skills or levels of difficulty associated with skills. What does this imply for learning to read and for testing reading? In his study, he indicated that in pedagogical circles, skills may be higher in a hierarchy of values attached to the skills rather than actually implicationally ordered. Do you consider this correct, and if so, how is it important?

4 Hudson asserts three hypotheses regarding skills. What are they? To what extent do you believe that these are correct hypotheses? Were they shown to exist in the present study?

5 What factors can affect the stability of reading skills and their difficulty? In looking across the various studies, what is your view of the stability, and our ability to identify, reading skills?

6 Look at one of the extended lists of reading skills such as that by Barrett or Munby. Select one of the skills and try to write a test item that would allow you to test the skill. What are some of the problems you have with generating more than one item for the skill that would measure roughly the same ability?

5 STRATEGIES AND METACOGNITIVE SKILLS

Introduction

While the last chapter focused on the reading skills utilized by readers, this chapter addresses the role of reading strategies and metacognitive skills. The relevant areas of concern in the first language literature are first examined, and then the findings and implications from a second language perspective area addressed.

It would be useful at this time to clearly define the characteristics that distinguish skills, strategies, and metacognitive skills. However, previous literature does not help in this regard. As noted in the last chapter, some literature restricts reading skills to visual and auditory processes of decoding, and attributes the rest of the text-mediated meaning-making endeavor to cognitive or comprehension skills. Other researchers restrict reading skills to automatic processes and contrast those to the view that strategies are conscious and deliberate repair strategies. This question of whether or not to restrict strategies to 'consciousness' is a central issue in considerations of strategy importance. Wellman (1988) states that:

> the term strategy more narrowly denotes some routine or procedure *deliberately* employed to achieve some end ... In my usage, therefore, strategies include only deliberate or intentional attempts to help oneself, for example, to help oneself remember ... To be a strategy, the means must be employed deliberately, with some awareness, in order to produce or influence the goal.

(Wellman 1988: 5; emphasis in original)

However, Richards, Platt, and Weber (1985) define strategy as:

> procedures used in learning, thinking, etc. which serve as a way of reaching a goal. In language learning, learning strategies ... and communication strategies ... are those conscious or unconscious processes which language learners make use of in learning and using a language.

(Richards et al. 1985: 274)

In these two perspectives, there is a dissonance regarding intentionality in strategy application. One reason for the difference in viewpoints may arise from how one views the consequences of a reading skill/strategy such as scanning being automatic in some cases and intentional in others. How are we to conceptualize this apparent contradiction? This is addressed by Paris, Wasik, and Turner (1996) when they state that:

> *Skills* refer to information-processing techniques that are automatic, whether at the level of recognizing phoneme–grapheme correspondence or summarizing a story. Skills are applied to text unconsciously for many reasons including expertise, repeated practice, compliance with directions, luck, and naïve use. In contrast, strategies are actions selected deliberately to achieve particular goals. An emerging skill can become a strategy when it is used intentionally. Likewise, a strategy can 'go underground' … and become a skill. Indeed, strategies are more efficient and developmentally advanced when they become generated and applied automatically as skills.
>
> *(Paris et al. 1996: 610–11)*

Such a description allows the distinction of skill versus strategy to be a cognitively derived distinction rather than one that is behaviorally based.

Another metaphor for the relationship between metacognition and skills has been developed by Crowley, Shrager, and Siegler (1997) in their discussion of the relationship between metacognitive and associative accounts for strategy discovery and use. In their account, metacognitive mechanisms provide the assets required to explain the explicit part of cognition. These mechanisms are adaptable and responsive to the particular goals of problem solving. Associative operations, on the other hand, attend to explanations of that part of cognition that is implicit, non-conscious, fast, and sensitive to the problem-solving environment. In other words, metacognitive mechanisms assume that strategies are invented and selected by explicit reflection on the nature of the task demands, knowledge of strategies available, and prior history of addressing similar tasks. Associative operations, then, assume that strategy selection is determined by:

> a set of learned correlations among tasks, actions, and outcomes. Usually, the correlational knowledge is implicit rather than explicit … If the chosen actions lead to success, the links between them and the task will be strengthened, making it more likely that they will be chosen in the future.
>
> *(Crowley et al. 1997: 463–4)*

Associative mechanisms thus operate in an automatic manner, being applied unconsciously. However, metacognitive mechanisms can override the associative mechanisms if it is consciously acknowledged that a new, and perhaps broader, strategy is needed to solve a new and unique, even if only slightly different, task. In Paris et al.'s (1996) terms, then, the associative mechanisms represent the strategies that have gone 'underground'.

Additionally, some of the literature that focuses on cognitive and metacognitive strategies integrates reading strategies and the processing control of metacognitive acts (Baker and Brown 1984). This is in part due to how metacognitive skills are essential in the marshaling of appropriate strategies. Without developed metacognitive strategies, inappropriate and unproductive reading strategies might be applied. Other researchers, such as Oxford (1990), view strategies as the steps taken by students to enhance their own learning in general, with metacognitive strategies being one of several categories of learning strategies available to the learner. Such proposed divisions result primarily as a result of a focus on a broad range of strategies, some directly language-based and some being affectively grounded and related to emotions and motivation. Phakiti (2003) notes that 'unless *the role of concurrent consciousness or intention* is considered, reading skills and reading strategies cannot be distinguished' (24). It should be kept in mind that not all strategies are metacognitive, and not all metacognitive skills are strategies. Because of the multiple uses of the terms, the following discussion will first attempt to disambiguate the terms as clearly as possible.

Strategies and metacognition in first language research

Basic reading comprehension strategies

From the last chapter, common concepts of reading skills (as opposed to comprehension skills) usually focus on word identification or other such low-level processes. On the other hand, conceptions of reading strategies generally focus on creating and maintaining meaning. A reading strategy can be described as any interactive process that has the goal of obtaining meaning from connected text, and reading skills operate within the context of such reading strategies. The strategies of predicting, confirming, monitoring, reflecting, and evaluating are consciously brought to bear. Strategies operate to lessen demands on working memory by facilitating comprehension processing.

Paris et al. (1996) present text-processing strategies promoting comprehension that are applied prior to, during, and after reading. Pre-reading strategies are summarized in Table 5.1. Pre-reading strategies involve several of the traditional academic study skills foci. For example, there is a recognition of the importance of establishing a positive physical environment when possible,

Pre-reading strategies	While-reading strategies	Post-reading strategies
1 Establishing a good physical environment	1 Checking comprehension throughout the reading activity	1 Appreciation of text and writer
2 Setting reading purpose	2 Identifying the main idea	2 Revisit pre-reading expectations
3 Accessing prior knowledge	3 Making inferences	3 Review notes, glosses, text markings
4 Asking questions based on the title	4 Recognizing patterns in the text structure	4 Reflect on text understanding
5 Semantic mapping	5 Looking for discourse markers	5 Consolidate and integrate information
6 Skimming for general idea	6 Monitoring vocabulary knowledge	6 Review of information
7 Previewing the text: examining headings, pictures, title, etc.	7 Predicting the main idea of each paragraph	7 Elaborate and evaluate
8 Reviewing instructions	8 Glossing	8 Determine what additional information is needed
9 Identifying text structure and genre	9 Comparing what is read with what is known	9 Apply new information to the task at hand
10 Determining what is known about the topic	10 Evaluating value of what is being learned	10 Relate the text to own experience
11 Predicting what might be read	11 Rereading text or skipping ahead	11 Critique the text

Table 5.1 Comprehension strategies (Paris et al. 1996)

and setting such reading purposes as: 1) gaining information; 2) performing a task; 3) experiencing and enjoying literature; or 4) forming opinions. Similarly, the strategies of accessing prior knowledge through skimming and previewing of the text involve becoming physically familiar with the text, its title, headings, pictures, etc., along with reading and reviewing any associated instructions that are provided in educational contexts. The reader aligns him/herself with the text, text type, and genre. Here the reader decides what is currently known about the topic, what he or she wants to gain from reading the text, and how success will be determined. Based on all of this information, predictions are made about possible information and content topics that may be encountered while reading.

While reading, the reader uses many recursive on-line strategies in constructing meaning (Paris et al. 1996). The strategies are iterative in that the current meaning that the reader has can change throughout the cyclic applications of the skills of the reading process. These iterative strategies are identified in the second column of Table 5.1, but their order is not intended to imply any linear, sequential, or hierarchical order of importance.

In successful reading, comprehension is checked throughout the reading activity. The realization of this strategy involves the reader as an active agent in the comprehension process. The reader also identifies the main idea. Identification of main idea is a complex strategy requiring the reader to comprehend what has been read, evaluate the importance of the information covered, and synthesize the information into a concise concept (Paris et al. 1996). This main idea (concept) is continually revised and, depending upon the text, may eventually split into multiple main or important ideas that the reader evaluates as significant. Identifying the main idea of a text is dependent upon text factors in addition to overall reading skill development. Readers are better able to identify clearly stated main ideas than implicit main ideas, and are better able to identify the main idea when it is presented early in a paragraph than when it appears later in the text (Bauman 1984, 1986). However, 'main idea' may be defined by the reader as something other than what the author views as the main idea. The reader is reading for a purpose, and that may involve finding only a subset of the author's main ideas, or indeed, something that the author may have seen as of relatively minor importance.

Appropriate inference generation is a strategy that points out the frequent difficulty of separating skills and strategies. Frequently, inference making is an automatic process. However, second language research points out that beginning and poor readers often have difficulty answering inferential comprehension questions (Hansen and Pearson 1983). That research has also indicated that poor and early readers can be taught to apply an inferential comprehension strategy to their reading. While reading, the reader is able to recognize patterns in the text. The reader attends to whether different sections of the text follow a regular organizational pattern, or whether the text follows a particular familiar and conventional organization such as comparison/contrast or cause/effect. Related to text-pattern recognition is the strategy of looking for discourse markers throughout the text. These can help the reader orient her/himself to the argument structure and intertextual relationships. This includes looking for discourse markers such as: enumerators (*in the first place, second*), chronological markers (*at first, later, then*), contrast indicators (*however, on the other hand*), or summarizers (*thus, in conclusion, finally*). Particularly in second language contexts, the reader will need to monitor vocabulary and address any problems associated with unfamiliar lexis. In this, the reader may use background knowledge to make sense of text, place the new word into a group with other similar known words to determine meaning, guess the general meaning of a word by using context clues, associate a word with a known word in order to determine meaning, link the vocabulary with a cognate in the first language, or resort to dictionary use. Readers also continually employ a strategy of comparing what they know with information within the text they are reading. This serves both to confirm comprehension and to alert the reader to any mis-match between the incoming information and relevant known information. The new information may be compatible with given information or provide an expansion and elaboration of current knowledge. Likewise, the new information may lead to a clarification of prior existing incorrect knowledge. The reader engages in evaluating whether the new information is to be accepted or not, and evaluates the value of what is being read in the text. This evaluation is directly tied to the purpose that the reader has already established for reading. Aligning reading practices with purpose allows the reader to determine which portions of text will be attended to and which portions of the text are not currently of value in achieving the reader's current goal. While reading, the reader may decide to reread particular passages for clarification or may skip ahead to determine where the text is going. This strategy of stepping outside the generally linear processing of text reflects the flexibility needed in mature reading. Research has indicated that less skilled readers frequently read in a linear fashion without rereading problematic sections of the text (Garner and Reis 1981).

Post-reading strategies tend to be task, purpose, and affect determined. The reader is simply attempting to finish an assignment and he or she may simply put the reading aside and go on to the next activity. However, readers may also be motivated to learn content from the text and to complete a particular assignment or project. Examples of post-reading strategies were presented in the third column of Table 5.1.

In pleasure reading, the post-reading task may simply be appreciation of the text, message, and writer. However, in instructional or applied contexts the strategies may be more directed. A reflection on text understanding will allow the reader to determine whether he or she understands the text well enough, or whether parts should be read again. The decisional criteria will be based upon what task is at hand. Readers will need to consolidate and integrate the information from the text. They will also need to review the information that was presented in the text. The form that these two strategies take will be determined by the nature of the task that is to be accomplished. For example, if the reader has a goal of synthesizing information from the particular text with information from another text, the consolidation and integration will be done with the content and structure of the second text in mind. Likewise, what information is selected for review will depend upon the purpose of the synthesis. The reader will elaborate the information from the text with known information, and will evaluate the sufficiency of the text. This, in turn, will allow him or her to determine what additional information is needed. Finally, the reader will apply the new information from the text to the task at hand. After reading a portion of text from a manual, he or she may now be able to assemble a piece of equipment, cook from a recipe, answer test questions, etc. The application of post-reading skills such as these functions to fulfill the task that prompted the reading to take place initially.

The examples in Table 5.1 are far from constituting a comprehensive representation of the many strategies that have been proposed. As with skills, each of the strategies can be divided and subdivided. In their examination of studies using verbal protocols to study skilled reading, Pressley and Afflerbach (1995) identified well over one hundred different strategies across the studies. In their summary of skilled readers they conclude:

> The conscious processing that goes on during skilled reading can be enor-mously complex … Still, there is a striking orderliness to the processing that occurs. That is, it is possible to summarize all the thinking that goes on into a number of categories that are familiar to cognitive psychologists and reading response researchers. Thus, skilled readers know and use many dif-ferent procedures (strategies) in coming to terms with text: They proceed generally from front to back of documents when reading. Good readers are selectively attentive. They sometimes make notes. They predict, para-phrase, and back up when confused. They try to make inferences to fill in the gaps in text and in their understanding of what they have read. Good readers intentionally attempt to integrate across the text. They do not settle for literal meanings but rather interpret what they have read, sometimes constructing images, other times identifying categories of information in text, and on still other occasions engaging in arguments with themselves about what a reading might mean. After making their way through text, they have a variety of ways of firming up their understanding and memory of the messages in the text, from explicitly attempting to summarize to self-questioning about the text to rereading and reflecting. The many procedures [*viz.* strategies] used by skilled readers are appropriately and opportunistically coordinated, with the reader using the processes needed to meet current reading goals, confronting the demands of reading at the moment, and preparing for demands that are likely in the future (for example, the need to recall text content for a test).

(Pressley and Afflerbach 1995: 79–80)

This summary statement of good reader strategies indicates the complexity of the task facing the skilled reader, as well as the many potential pitfalls facing the less skilled reader. Just how this process is carried out, how the strategies are orchestrated, is the focus of the next section on metacognitive skills.

Metacognition and automaticity in application of reading strategies

The development of metacognition as an important focus of education generally, and language education in particular, is partially a result of educators describing and promoting strategic learning. Metacognitive skills play a strategic role in such problem-solving cognitive activities as reading comprehension, writing, language acquisition, and logical reasoning. (Flavell, Miller, and Miller 2002). Metacognition refers to knowledge of or regulation of cognitive endeavors. As such, it is basically cognition about cognition. It involves knowledge about one's cognitive system and conscious attempts in regulating cognition. Metacognition is distinct from cognition in that cognitive skills help one to perform a task, whereas metacognitive skills help one understand and regulate the performance on the task (Schraw 1998).

Some researchers argue that metacognitive knowledge precedes metacognitive control. In this view, learners must first become aware of structures of text, as well as knowledge of the task, possible strategies, and their own characteristics as learners, before they can strategically and efficiently control the processing of those text factors (Armbruster, Echols, and Brown 1983). Such a view of metacognitive control indicates that knowledge of cognition includes three components: declarative knowledge, procedural knowledge, and conditional knowledge. (Baker 1989; Paris, Lipson, and Wixon 1983; Schraw and Moshman 1995; Schraw 1998). The first includes knowledge about ourselves and our learning, about what factors affect us, and about the structure of tasks and activities. Procedural knowledge includes knowledge about strategies such as guessing words in context, SUMMARIZING, or looking for the main idea in a text. Conditional knowledge refers to the knowledge we have about why and how to use different strategies.

As Flavell et al. (2002) state, people have 'knowledge and beliefs not only about politics, football, electronics, needlepoint, or some other domain, but also the human mind and its doings' (164). Metacognition in reading represents the planning, monitoring, and evaluating of the reading process, where planning involves identifying a purpose for reading and selecting particular actions to achieve the reader's goals, monitoring involves regulating and redirecting the reader's efforts during the course of reading to accomplish that goal, and evaluation involves the reader appraising her or his cognitive ability to carry out the task. Metacognition, then, acts as a type of executive control over the application of the particular reading strategies that will be employed. It involves both what is known about cognition and how that cognition is managed. There are a number of metacognitive skills, as indicated in Table 5.2.

Flavell (1982) and Flavell et al. (2002) subdivide metacognitive knowledge into knowledge about *persons*, *tasks*, and *strategies*. This three-way distinction

Understanding the conditions under which one learns best
Analyzing the problem at hand
Allocating attention
Identifying which important aspects of a message apply to the task at hand
Separating important information from less important information
Understanding explicit and implicit task demands
Determining what performance components are important for the
    particular task
Determining how to strategically proceed
Monitoring to track attention and comprehension
Internal checking to determine success of achieving goals
Revising, modifying, or terminating activities strategically
Determining what internal and external feedback to explore
Initiating and maintaining repair.

Table 5.2: Example metacognitive skills

focuses on the objects of the metacognitive knowledge base, and links knowledge of the world to domains of metacognitive processing.

Knowledge of *persons* includes any knowledge a person has about how people operate cognitively. It is the awareness a reader has of his or her own characteristics (background knowledge, interest, skills, self-efficacy, and deficits) and of how these affect language processing and learning. This knowledge is translated into changes in reading behavior that reflect regulation of reading. Research suggests that successful students tend to relate information in texts to previous knowledge, where less successful students show little tendency to use their knowledge to clarify the text at hand. Flavell et al. (2002) indicate that person knowledge includes the three categories of: 1) cognitive differences within people; 2) cognitive differences between people; and 3) universal properties of human cognition. The first type involves the person's knowledge that, for example, he or she is better at math than at geography. The second category involves such comparisons as the knowledge or belief that the reader is more empathetic than other people. The third category includes the general awareness that people can understand, fail to understand, or misunderstand a message.

Knowledge of *tasks* involves two subcategories: 1) understanding the nature of the information that is encountered; and 2) comprehending the inherent demands of the task. The first of these subcategories relates to how familiar one is with the information encountered as well as how well organized and complete the information is. For example, an ordered list of information is easier to process than a randomly presented list of information with no headings or organizational structure. The second subcategory involves the differential difficulty of different tasks. For example, it is easier to read and comprehend two passages than it is to write a synthesis of the very same information. Likewise, it is generally easier to answer a multiple-choice exam question than to recall the exact wording of some sample of text.

The third category of metacognitive knowledge and control indicated by Flavell et al. (2002) involves knowing *strategies* for monitoring an individual's cognitive progress and how to remedy comprehension failures. The reader must apply strategies to self-regulate his or her reading process. In applying metacognitive strategies the reader relies on what has been learned in the past about achieving cognitive goals. For example, when a reader recognizes that comprehension is suffering because of inattention, he or she can apply the strategy of recognizing the need to pay attention and not 'wool-gather'. Additionally, the successful reader has learned to spend more energy reviewing more difficult material than easier or more familiar material (Flavell et al. 2002). These strategies are not just for repair, they are also for self-regulation. For example, when a reader pauses while reading an article or other text and then scans forward, counting the number of pages left to read, in order to decide whether to continue reading or to find a convenient stopping point that will allow proceeding to another task because of time constraints, the self-regulation is not for repair. Rather, it is a strategy to stop at a text juncture that will enhance storage and retrieval when the reader subsequently resumes the reading task. Knowledge of strategies would also involve such activities as looking for text structure within the passage.

These metacognitive strategies reflect 'knowledge or cognitive activity that takes as its object, or regulates, any aspect of any cognitive enterprise' (Flavell et al. 2002: 164). The type of executive control in metacognition reflects some of the 'fuzziness' that was pointed out in defining the differences between a skill and strategy as being predicated on conscious awareness. For example, most readers of English have the metacognitive knowledge that letters on a page are supposed to represent words that are strung together to convey a meaning. However, that knowledge is generally not consciously needed because reading letters has become automatized. Thus, the letters in sentence 1 below would be read quickly without conscious thought.

1   Saturday is generally a good day for shopping.

2   *SATURDAY IS GENERALLY A GOOD DAY FOR SHOPPING.*

However, sentence 2 might be more problematic to some readers because of font unfamiliarity. The reader would recognize the elements as words made up of letters, and his or her metacognitive skills would marshal letter recognition strategies to read the sentence. Readers might try to determine which letters can be recognized and predict the remaining letters in a cloze type completion process. Other readers might attempt to pronounce the segments in the hope of creating some recognizable match that fits with known vocabulary.

This adaptation reflects the interaction noted by Crowley et al. (1997) between metacognitive knowledge and associative mechanisms that was discussed previously. They note that since metacognitive knowledge is potentially verbalizable, it can be accessed and modified through reflection. It can be discussed and considered out of a particular context. Associative mechanisms are realized in a network of connections and strengths, and operate without the requirement of consciousness in an automatic way that allows a freeing-up of processing resources. Brown (1987) explains that an activity such as looking for the main idea in reading comprehension can be seen as a cognitive strategy when it serves the goal of reading comprehension, or as metacognitive when it is used to self-evaluate comprehension.

Similarly, Anderson's (1975, 1990) approach of co-ordinating metacognitive and associative knowledge is designed to explain how skills are automatized. Strategies are initially explicit plans which need conscious metacognitive control to achieve the desired goals. After there is sufficient practice with the strategies, the strategies are translated into a procedural representation that is not dependent on conscious control through metacognitive monitoring. In fact, this new representation may, to use a computer analogy, overwrite the original metacognitive representation. An example of such a process that has become so automatic that a verbal representation would be difficult is how adults tie their shoes (Crowley et al. 1997). They perform this action automatically, but would have to reinvent the strategy in order to teach someone else how to do it or if they were presented with huge, thick, and cumbersome shoestrings. The procedural knowledge is no longer readily available.

Brown (1982) makes a distinction between knowledge about cognition, and regulation of cognition. The first, 'knowledge about cognition' can be stable, though fallible or late in developing. It remains relatively consistent within individuals. 'Regulation of cognition', however, can generally be relatively unstable, resistant to articulation, and age independent. It can change rapidly from situation to situation. This distinction suggests that self-regulation is most likely to be more context than age dependent. A reader may show effective self-regulation in one context but not another. Further, in some situations a child may show self-regulation where an adult does not. Regulation may also be affected by such factors as anxiety, fear, self-concept, or interest. That it is resistant to articulation indicates the general inaccessibility of regulatory processes to awareness.

This relationship between knowledge of cognition and regulation of cognition again parallels some of the concerns regarding the relationship between metacognition and associative mechanisms (Crowley et al. 1997). There is a recognition that problem-solving strategy use is sometimes explicit and effortful, and sometimes implicit. Crowley et al. posit that the relationship between metacognitive knowledge and associative knowledge is a 'competitive negotiation'. In their view:

> (t)he metacognitive and associative systems maintain separate representa-
> tions and decision-making processes. Metacognitive knowledge is explic-
> it and potentially verbalizable and may be expressed as production rules,
> plans, or heuristics. Associative knowledge is implicit and non-
> verbalizable and might be best expressed as statistical associations among
> units of action and problem solving contexts.

> *(Crowley et al. 1997: 480)*

At each stage of problem solving, the two systems compete to identify a solution. The results of this competition rest upon how much of the domain-
specific knowledge the associative system includes and the extent to which
the metacognitive system perceives a need to intervene by altering the
problem-solving goals. They contend that this type of competition can
account for changes in strategy use over time.

Metacognition and reading

Research indicates that readers use many different strategies, but that
distinctions exist between good/experienced readers and poor/younger
readers. Good/experienced readers tend to use the most effective strategy
that leads to complete processing of the text. Lovett and Flavell (1990)
showed that awareness of strategies is in part a function of age and experience.
Their study examined how three groups of readers, first graders, third graders,
and undergraduates, approached the tasks of memorizing a list of words,
matching words to a picture, and both memorizing and matching words.
The results indicated that the more experienced readers understood the
concept that a rehearsal strategy would help list memorization, and word
definitions would help comprehension of new words. The less experienced
readers did not recognize memorization and comprehension as distinct
operations requiring different strategies.

Additionally, research has indicated that poor/younger readers demonstrate
deficits in: 1) identifying the purpose of reading; 2) flexibility of strategy
application; 3) coping with failures of comprehension; 4) identifying
important information; 5) recognizing textual organization; 6) identifying
and fixing syntactic or semantic anomalies that are encountered; 7) effectively monitoring comprehension; 8) application of their repertoire of strategies;
9) relating new information to known information; 10) level of metacognitive
awareness; and 11) number and effectiveness of strategies used. (August,
Flavell, and Clift 1984; Baker 1989; Brown 1982; Garner 1990a; Flavell
et al. 2002; Ryan 1981). Additionally, research indicates that the general
effectiveness of comprehension-monitoring behavior explains a significant
amount of variability in reading comprehension (Zinar 2000). Thus, there

is strong evidence that metacognitive ability affects the success of reading comprehension in first language readers.

Differences noticed during comprehension monitoring can be due to comprehension problems, uncooperative text, or unfamiliar vocabulary, among other things. This mismatch creates a dissonance realized as an unease or feeling of confusion and triggers some form of repair. Readers then begin to exert their control in order to make a coherent text representation. Successful readers possess the necessary linguistic knowledge, background knowledge, and strategies, and their metacognitive knowledge selects the strategy or strategies that will repair the dissonance. If the repair allows the reader to fix the text or internal representation such that the two instantiations are congruent, the reader typically attributes the problem to the text. If the two cannot be reconciled, the reader generally (rightly or wrongly) attributes the problem to his or her own comprehension abilities. After the reader resolves the comprehension problem, he or she continues to evaluate subsequent text information determining whether the developing text representations continue to remain congruent (Hacker 1998). However, there remain instances of comprehension failure that are not repaired through this metacognitive process. Hacker (1998) has indicated several sources of comprehension failures that result from failures of monitoring or controlling comprehension. These are indicated in Table 5.3.

1   Readers lack linguistic or topic knowledge necessary to monitor or control sources of dissonance.
2   Readers possess necessary linguistic or topic knowledge but lack monitoring or control strategies.
3   Readers possess strategies but lack metacognitive understanding about where and when to apply them.
4   Comprehension and/or control are too demanding of the reader's resources, thereby hindering his or her ability to control reading.
5   The standard or standards of evaluation used by the readers are inappropriate for the levels of text representation that need to be monitored.
6   Sources of dissonance are resolved by the incorrect inferences readers make during the comprehension process.
7   Comprehension and/or monitoring are too demanding of the reader's resources thereby hindering his or her ability to monitor reading.
8   Although not specifically noted in the model, but implicit in all controlled cognitive processes, readers lack motivation to monitor or control their reading.

Table 5.3: Reading failures due to metacognitive comprehension monitoring or control (Adapted from Hacker (1998))

These failures at comprehension are reflections of inappropriate monitoring and control of the reading comprehension process, or of linguistic or topic knowledge deficiencies.

Strategies and metacognition in second language reading

As noted above, learners utilize an array of strategies to assist them with the acquisition, storage, and retrieval of information. There has been quite a bit of research on the relationship between strategic reading and successful or unsuccessful second language readers, much of it paralleling the first language research findings, though the studies have typically been carried out with older learners than in the first language literature. Not surprisingly, as we examine the use of reading strategies by second language learners, we are again faced with questions regarding whether any infelicities in use are the result of reading problems or result from language deficits. Additionally, although there is some indication that strategy use is affected by instruction, we cannot always be clear whether strategy use is a reflection of good reading, the cause of good reading, or some of both.

In an early second language reading study, Hosenfeld (1977) employed think-aloud protocols to identify the relationships between different reading strategies and successful or unsuccessful second language reading. She asked 40 students, half identified as proficient and half identified as non-proficient, to think aloud as they read. Hosenfeld found a relationship between certain types of reading strategies and successful or unsuccessful foreign or second language reading. Her successful reader: a) kept the meaning of the passage in mind during reading; b) read (translated) in 'broad phrases'; c) skipped words viewed as unimportant to total phrase meaning; and d) had a positive self-concept as a reader. By contrast her unsuccessful reader: a) forgot the meaning of sentences as soon as they decoded them; b) read in short phrases; c) seldom skipped words as unimportant, viewing words as 'equal' in terms of their contribution to total meaning; and d) had a negative self concept as a reader. In general, there was a failure to successfully apply several of the strategies identified in Table 5.1 by Paris et al. (1996).

Readers approach a text with a history of how they have dealt with text in the past. They have an internal default that sets how they initially attempt to comprehend. Devine (1984) investigated the theoretical orientation and reading performance of a small number of students who were at a beginning/low level of English ability in a community-based ESL program in Michigan. Her research examined two primary hypotheses: 1) readers have an internal model of reading that can be articulated; and 2) the internal model will affect reading performance. Three sets of data were collected from each subject: an oral reading interview, a sample of oral reading, and a retelling of the oral reading.

Transcripts of reading interviews provided information indicating the units the subjects focused on or thought were important for effective reading. Information from the transcripts allowed the subjects to be classified as sound-, word-, or meaning-oriented readers. Thus, the transcripts indicated that the readers possessed internalized models of the reading process that they could articulate reasonably well.

A miscue analysis was carried out on the transcripts of the subjects' oral reading, and a comparison of the types of miscues produced indicated that they were consistent with the articulated reading type. The sound-oriented subjects had high average scores for graphic and phonemic similarity to the text words and a high percentage of non-words, indicating a central concern with reproducing the sounds/letters of the text rather than with preserving meaning. The word- and meaning-oriented subjects appeared to focus less on the words and letters of the words in the text than did those with a sound orientation. The meaning-centered subjects produced miscues which were semantically acceptable more frequently than was the case with the other two orientations. Statistical analysis indicated a significant difference for the readers in the use of the graphic, phonemic, syntactic, and semantic cueing systems. Thus, the subjects' internalized model of reading influenced the type of print information they attended to during oral reading. Evaluations of the retellings of their oral reading selections indicated that the meaning-centered readers demonstrated good to excellent comprehension while the sound-centered readers were judged to have either poor or very poor comprehension of the text meaning. However, the results were not categorical with the word-centered group. Some were judged poor or very poor and some were judged very good or fair. This last result indicated that while the theoretical orientation that a reader possesses affects comprehension at the extremes, the middle orientation has sufficient variability to indicate the need to use caution in attaching attributes to transitional statuses. Some of the word-centered readers were still near the sound-centered phase of development and some had moved closer to the meaning-centered readers.

A basic issue in second language research regarding reading strategies relates back to the *first language* ⟷ *second language* relationships discussed in Chapter 3. Are first language strategies transferred to the second language or are different strategies generated anew in processing the new language? Knight, Padron, and Waxman (1985) looked at whether there were differences in either the type or frequency of strategies reported by younger English–Spanish bilingual and English monolingual students. Their research was designed to examine whether there are observable differences in the cognitive strategies of bilingual and monolingual readers. Taped structured 30-minute interviews were carried out with 23 Spanish-speaking ESL students and 15 English monolingual students in the third and fifth grades. The students read a passage about 120 words in length matched to their reading ability level

1 Rereading
2 Selectively reading
3 Imaging (i.e., having a picture in mind)
4 Adjusting speed
5 Assimilating with personal experiences
6 Concentrating (i.e. thinking about the story and keeping it in mind)
7 Assimilating with passage events (thinking about some event that happened earlier in the story) or thinking about previous events
8 Noting/searching for salient details (i.e. remembering specific details, important details, or details that were different)
9 Summarizing
10 Predicting outcomes (i.e. trying to guess what will happen next in the story)
11 Self-generated questions (i.e. a questioning comment about the story)
12 Student perceptions of teacher expectations (i.e. reading in anticipation of questions the teacher might ask)
13 Rehearsal.

Table 5.4: The reading strategies identified by readers (Knight et al. 1985)

as determined by a standardized graded word-list test. Each student read the passage, stopping regularly at pre-determined intervals to describe the strategies they were using. The thirteen reading strategies identified across the subjects are presented in Table 5.4 above.

English monolinguals most often cited the strategy of concentrating, while they cited the strategy of anticipating the teacher's expectations least. In contrast, the bilingual students cited this last strategy the most. The categories of imaging, noting details, and predicting outcomes were not cited by any bilingual student during the interviews. The use of three strategies, concentrating, noting details, and self-generation of questions was reported significantly more often by monolinguals than bilingual students. Generally, monolingual subjects used about twice as many strategies as bilingual students. Knight et al. indicate that this is a cause for concern since the use of varied reading strategies has been tied to enhanced reading comprehension. They suggest that this discrepancy may result because the bilingual students may not have had enough time to develop these strategies in their first language and may have been assigned English texts too early, leading them to overly concentrate on decoding. Unfortunately, although they had a measure of overall ability, Knight et al. did not report whether parallel findings would have obtained if the students had been examined by proficiency level as well as the monolingual-bilingual dichotomy. It is not clear whether the differences in strategy use are the result of language proficiency, languages known, or lack of training in the particular strategies.

In an additional study comparing the strategies employed by first language and second language readers, Block (1986) used a think-aloud procedure to examine the strategies used by non-proficient readers, three native and six non-native English speakers enrolled in freshman remedial reading courses in the US. Each student was given two self-contained reading selections rated at approximately the ninth-grade readability level by the Fry readability formula. After the think-aloud session, the students were asked to retell the story as closely as possible, and were asked to answer a multiple-choice test with 20 questions. Block found that the following features differentiated successful from less successful readers: 1) integration; 2) recognition of aspects of text structure; 3) use of general knowledge, personal experiences, and associations; and 4) response in extensive versus reflexive modes. In the reflexive mode, readers related affectively and personally directed attention away from the text and toward themselves, and focused on their own thoughts and feelings rather than on information in the text. In addition, they tended to respond in the first or second person during the think-aloud period. In the extensive mode, the readers' focus was on understanding the ideas of the author, and they did not relate the text to themselves affectively or personally. These readers tended to respond in the third person.

There did not appear to be a systematic non-native pattern of strategy use different from a native speaker pattern for the readers in the remedial courses. Rather, in each language group, one of the readers integrated infor-mation more consistently than the others, recognized text structure more frequently, and referred to personal experiences less frequently than the others. The other readers in each group tended to make associations in a reflexive manner, failing to integrate information from the text effectively, and seeming unaware of text structure. Among the non-proficient readers Block investigated, one group, which she labeled 'integrators', integrated the information read, were generally aware of text structure, responded in an extensive mode by dealing with the message conveyed by the author, and monitored their understanding consistently and effectively. In comparison to the poor readers, better readers were more able to monitor their comprehension than poor readers; they were more aware of the strategies they used, and they used strategies more flexibly. Specifically, better readers adjusted their strategies to the type of text they were reading and to their purpose. They also made more progress in developing their reading skills and demonstrated greater success after one semester in college. Members of the other group, labeled 'non-integrators', on the other hand, failed to integrate, did not recognize text structure, and were more reflexive in that they relied much more on personal experiences. They also made less progress in their reading skill development over the semester.

The study points to several issues about strategy use by the two groups of readers. Readers differ in their overall approach to the text rather than any language-specific set of strategies. Such findings are similar to those in a later study by Sheorey and Mokhtari (2001) which indicated that both high-ability native speakers of English and ESL students showed higher reported usage of cognitive and metacognitive strategies than did the lower-ability readers of each group. The results of Block's study indicate that students used strategies but language background did not seem to account for the different patterns. That is, ESL readers did not use strategies or patterns of strategies that were different in kind from those of native speakers of English. It should be kept in mind, however, that none of the subjects in Block's study were accomplished readers.

Sarig (1987) examined the processes characterizing the performance of main idea analysis and overall message synthesis tasks in Hebrew as a first language and English as a foreign language through think-aloud protocols of ten Israeli high school seniors. Several pairs of texts equated on their readability were created in each language to be somewhat challenging based on the assessment of the subjects' reading ability. The tasks involved in the study were: 1) main idea analysis (for example, identification of main propositions and elimination of peripheral and background information); and 2) synthesis of the overall message (for example, identification of paradoxes, comparison of opposing views, and the identification of such components as counter statements, contradictions, and settling statements). The basic unit of analysis

1   Technical-aid moves: skimming, scanning, skipping text, marking and writing key elements in the text, textual marking for different purposes, margin summary, using a glossary, etc.

2   Clarification and simplification moves: syntactic simplification, decoding meanings of word and groups of words through synonyms, circumlocutions, propositional simplification, rhetorical function identification, and various forms of paraphrase

3   Coherence-detecting moves: identification of text structure, identification of people in the text and views or actions attributed to them, identification of key textual information, use of text structure for prediction about text development, overt cohesive cue use, relying on summarizing units identified in the text, identification of text focus, and other discourse coherence identification moves

4   Monitoring moves: conscious changes in planning and conducting the task, conscious decisions to delay a text section until later, deserting a hopeless text section, flexibility of reading rate, mistake correction, ongoing self-evaluation, self-directed dialogue, repeated skimming or scanning, etc.

Table 5.5: The reading moves provided by Sarig's (1988) subjects during think-aloud

in the study was the reading move (each separate action the reader took, such as highlighting a word in the text, syntactic simplification paraphrases, and the identification of incompatible information). The think-aloud protocols and observations yielded the four types of reading moves shown in Table 5.5.

The results of the study show that the different move types function across task performance in almost identical ways in both languages. Coherence-detecting moves accounted for approximately a third of all moves in both languages. An examination of whether the moves promoted or deterred comprehension of the text indicates that technical aid moves actually interfered with comprehension more than they aided it. Clarification and simplification, on the other hand, promoted comprehension much more than they deterred it. The data were classified according the stages of the problem-solving process: proposition identification stage, main idea detection stage, and synthesis of the overall message stage. Correlations for the occurrences of reading move type in first language and second language are high with one exception. The correlation for first language and second language comprehension-promoting moves during the proposition identification stage was low at $r = .54$. While there might be some language specific issues with this process, the other move types have correlations between first language and second language of $r = .74$ to $r = .84$.

Another interesting finding in Sarig's study is an examination of the extent to which the reading moves were unique to the particular learners and the number of strategies used by each reader. The results indicated that there was a great deal of variability among the readers in terms of which reading moves they used. That is, each reader appeared to use similar moves in reading the two languages, but they tended to use different moves from one another in solving the reading problems they encountered. The results also show very little difference between the readers in terms of the number of moves they used. This finding, that the variety of the reading move repertoire used by all of the readers does not distinguish between high and low task scorers, appears to challenge other findings that have indicated that low-ability readers were less strategic than high-ability readers in the number of strategies they use. Upton (1997), for example, found that lower-proficient second language readers used fewer strategies in general, relied more on local text-based strategies, and demonstrated a pattern of using their first language as a strategic tool much more than higher proficient readers. However, the findings by Sarig may reflect a lack of true reading variability among the ten readers in the study. Still, the findings that readers tend to use the same or similar strategies across languages, and that the strategies vary from person to person, lend support to the view that readers transfer some aspects of reading from first language to second language.

Relative strategy use by bilinguals in their first language and second language is an important concern in the teaching and assessment of second language

reading. Calero-Breckheimer and Goetz (1993) studied 26 bi-literate third-
and fourth-grade students whose first language was Spanish as they read in
English and Spanish. Like Sarig, the study addressed the question of how
strategy use differed in the two languages. The bilingual program in which
the students participated provided instruction in the student's first language
while offering structured and sequenced instruction for mastery of English
language skills. Thus, the students had initially developed basic literacy skills
in Spanish. Spanish and English versions of two stories at the second- and
third-grade difficulty level were used in the study. Each story was presented
one line at a time via a computer that recorded the reading time for each line,
and the time for rereading of any previously encountered text. After the story
was read, each student was asked what kind of strategies had been used, completed a strategy checklist, retold the gist of what happened in the story, and
answered a multiple-choice test. The results show the students reporting
about the same number of strategies regardless of language. Likewise, the
students tended to use the same number and type of strategies when reading
in English and Spanish, with a correlation of $r = .89$. There was no significant
difference between languages on the multiple-choice comprehension measure
or on the gist recall measure. The study indicates that reading skills initially
developed in the first language can be transferred to the second language relatively quickly, at least with this age group. It serves to underscore the concern
presented by Knight et al. (1985) that the participants in their study may have
been transitioned into English too early.

The first language literature described previously in this chapter indicated
that less able readers used fewer reading strategies and employed more inappropriate strategies. As with this literature, most studies in second language
indicate that lower-proficiency readers tend not to recognize the need to
employ reading strategies to resolve problems they encounter with text
(Padron and Waxman 1988; Zhang 2001). Padron and Waxman designed a
study to examine the reading strategies of young ESL readers. Their study was
populated with 82 third-, fourth-, and fifth-grade Hispanic ESL students.
The students were administered a 14-item Likert-type reading strategy questionnaire in order for them to identify the strategies they felt that they used.
A standardized reading comprehension test was also taken by the students
twice over a four-month period in order to examine the relationship between
the self-reported reading strategies and reading comprehension gain. Seven
of the strategies were found to be positively related to students' reading and
seven strategies were found to be negatively related to their achievement.
These relationships are shown in Table 5.6.

The results indicated that the most cited reading strategies were: 1) asking
questions about the parts of the story that were not understood; 2) checking
through the story to see if everything is remembered; 3) imaging or picturing
the story; and 4) looking up words in the dictionary. On the other hand, the

Positive

1 Summarizing in writing
2 Underlining important parts of the story to see if everything is remembered
3 Self-generated questions
4 Checking through the story to see if everything is remembered
5 Asking questions about parts of the story not understood
6 Taking notes
7 Imaging or picturing the story mentally

Negative

1 Thinking about something else while reading
2 Writing down every word
3 Skipping the parts not understood
4 Reading as fast as possible
5 Saying every word over and over
6 Looking up words in the dictionary
7 Saying the main idea over and over

Table 5.6: Positive and negative strategies related to reading achievement (Adapted from Padron and Waxman 1988)

least cited reading strategies were; 1) reading as fast as possible; 2) thinking about something else while reading; 3) writing down every word; and 4) skipping parts not understood. The results of the questionnaire were compared to results on the reading task. The findings are congruent with previous metacognitive research conducted with monolinguals which found that lower-achieving students use less sophisticated and at times inappropriate reading strategies during reading (Brown, Armbruster, and Baker 1986). A multiple regression analysis found that in addition to the pretest, two of the strategies listed were significant predictors of reading posttest results. Both thinking about something else while reading and saying the main idea over and over were negative predictors, meaning that the higher the frequency of using these that the students reported, the lower their reading scores were. The results indicate that there is a relationship between second language reading proficiency and the types of reading strategies that are used, though whether or not they are causal is not clear. That is, thinking about something else while reading or saying the main idea over and over may result from being a poor reader, not be the cause of poor reading.

Further studies support the finding that there is a relationship between the type of strategies used and second language reading proficiency. However, as seen above, not all reported strategies are related to success in second language reading. Carrell (1989) undertook a study into the metacognitive awareness of second language readers about reading strategies in both their first and second language, and examined the relationship between their metacognitive awareness and comprehension in both first and second language reading. Two groups of subjects of varying proficiency levels were involved in the study. The first group included 45 native speakers of Spanish at intermediate to advanced levels of English enrolled at an ESL intensive program at a US university and the second group consisted of 75 native speakers of English studying intermediate to advanced levels of Spanish. However, in general, the English first language group was at a lower level of second language proficiency in Spanish than the Spanish first language group was in English. A metacognitive questionnaire was developed to elicit relevant demographic information and to tap the subjects' metacognitive awareness and judgments about silent reading in their first and second language. The questionnaire included sections on: 1) confidence in reading the language; 2) how they institute and carry out repairs when something goes wrong as they read; 3) perceptions of effective/efficient strategies; and 4) things that make reading the language difficult for them. Subjects were also tested in both their first and second languages on reading two texts in each language, answering comprehension questions pertaining to the text, and responding to the metacognitive questionnaire.

The findings of Carrell's (1989) study indicated that no questionnaire items associated with confidence or repair strategies were significantly related to reading performance for either group of subjects. For first language reading, local reading strategies such as focusing on grammatical structures, sound–letter, word–meaning, and text details tended to be negatively correlated with reading performance. For second language reading, the Spanish first language and English first language groups differed somewhat. With the Spanish first language group reading English, the more they agreed that they could distinguish main ideas from supporting details, the better they performed. For the English first language group reading Spanish, the more they felt that they could question the significance or truthfulness of the author, the better they performed. For both groups, not surprisingly, the more they disagreed with the statement that they 'gave up when they did not understand', the better they performed in reading the second language. In general, the better readers in both groups did not focus on local or bottom-up processing while the lower-level students did focus more on bottom-up processing.

Three qualitative studies, Block (1992), Jiménez, García, and Pearson (1996), and Kern (1997) present additional insight into the relationship between strategy use and reading ability. Block collected think-aloud protocols from 25 subjects. These subjects were placed into one of four groups: 16 proficient readers of English (eight monolingual first language English readers, and eight non-native speakers of English), and nine non-proficient readers (six were non-native speakers of English and three were monolingual first language

English readers). She focused on two strategies that emerged from analysis of the think-alouds: search for a pronominal referent, and dealing with an unknown vocabulary item. Block found that the monitoring process appeared to be comprised of three components: evaluation of comprehension, action, and checking the success of the action. Her findings were that control of the various stages seemed to depend more on reading ability than on whether the reader was a first or second language reader. She found that the proficient native readers used the process the most completely and efficiently, with the proficient ESL readers being just as efficient and almost as complete. The less proficient native English speakers and the less proficient ESL readers were neither as adept at recognizing that a problem existed nor in identifying the source of a problem. The less proficient ESL readers appeared to be more aware of their failures to comprehend than the less proficient native speakers, but both lacked the resources to remedy the problem. Even when the less proficient readers expressed recognition of a problem, they did not appear to know what to do, supporting the contention by Baker (1985) that evaluation and regulation of comprehension are separate processes.

Jiménez et al. (1996) examined the strategies of bilingual Latina/o children who were both successful and less successful readers of English. Both prompted and unprompted think-aloud protocol, interview, prior knowledge, and passage recall protocol data were collected. The data indicated 22 different strategies that fell into one of three strategy categories: 1) text-initiated strategies (for example, using text structure, focusing on vocabulary); 2) interactive strategies (for example, inferencing, questioning); and 3) reader-initiated strategies (for example, using prior knowledge, monitoring). There were three strategies that were unique to the successful readers: 1) they consciously transferred information across languages; 2) they translated from one language to another; and 3) they openly used cognate vocabulary as they read. The less successful readers employed fewer strategies and were often ineffective in resolving comprehension difficulties in either Spanish or English. Further, the successful readers were more determined to understand what they read, while even when the less successful readers identified problems, they often did not resolve them. The less successful readers tended to adopt a single interpretation of a text or text segment and resist changing even in the face of contradictory information. Finally, the less successful readers did not appear to know how to use their knowledge of Spanish to enhance their comprehension of English text.

Kern (1997) reported on a case study of two English first language university students reading in French as a second language, one a 'good reader of French as second language,' and one who was less able. Kern demonstrated, consistent with Anderson (1991), that no strategy is an inherently 'good' or 'bad' strategy. Similar strategies were employed by both 'good' readers and 'bad' readers. For example, using prior knowledge may sometimes be an effective strategy for one reader in one reading situation, but not for another reader or in another reading situation. As Anderson noted, successful second language reading comprehension is

> not simply a matter of knowing what strategy to use, but the reader must also know how to use it successfully and know how to orchestrate its use with other strategies. It is not sufficient to know about strategies, but a reader must also be able to apply them strategically.

> *(Anderson 1991)*

Likewise, Kern concluded that there are good and bad uses of the same strategy, and that the difference between a 'good' use and a 'bad' use of the same strategy rests with the context in which they are used, how the strategies are used, and how they interact with other strategies. In other words, Kern says, the difference is with how the strategies are 'operationalized.'

While strategies are related to success by good and poor readers, the role they play throughout the language development process is not always evident. Schoonen, Hulstijn, and Bossers (1998) carried out an important study on the role metacognitive and language-specific knowledge play on reading comprehension in both first language and second language. They first point out that one of the problems with previous studies that have examined the relationship between first language reading ability and second language reading ability was a frequently rather simplistic operationalization of first language reading. It was frequently viewed as 'general reading skills' without any acknowledgement that first language reading is also dependent upon first language-specific knowledge, vocabulary knowledge in particular. They, thus, see a need to view the first language variable as language-specific knowledge as well as more general reading skills. The study used a first language vocabulary measure to tap the language-specific knowledge and a metacognitive knowledge test to tap more general, transferable reading ability. They assumed that since the metacognitive knowledge test measured general reading ability, it could be used to assess second language general reading ability as well. In a sense, then, this puts first language and second language reading ability on a common scale that could identify which metacognitive components in first language did or did not transfer to the second language. They subdivided metacognitive knowledge into the four subcomponents in Table 5.7.

The study aimed to determine at which grade and academic level a reading strategies instructional program could appropriately be implemented. It explored how the relation between first language and second language reading proficiency is mediated by more language-specific knowledge (as shown by the vocabulary measures) and by the more general reading skills (as shown by the four components of metacognitive knowledge indicated above).

1   Self knowledge: perceptions or understandings of oneself as a learner or thinker

2   Task knowledge: understanding of the cognitive demands of a task

3   Strategic knowledge: knowledge of processes that are effortful, planned, and consciously invoked to facilitate the acquisition and utilization of knowledge. This includes both cognitive strategies, those that contribute directly to the solution of a problem, and metacognitive strategies, those that evaluate and monitor how well the selected cognitive strategy works.

4   Plans and goals: knowledge of the goals that may be established and the general plans that may be invoked.

Table 5.7: Subcomponents of metacognitive knowledge identified by Schoonen et al. (1998)

Specifically, they wanted to examine these relationships in grades 6, 8, and 10 for first language and in grades 8 and 10 for second language. The subjects were the 486 (out of 685) Dutch students who had complete data on all tests and questionnaires in first language and 274 of the subjects who completed the second language reading and vocabulary tasks. Since grade 6 is the first year of EFL instruction it was deemed that this group would not be useful for analysis.

Each of the four components of metacognitive knowledge was measured with items directed at specific aspects of the component. Reading comprehension in Dutch and English was measured using a standardized national test. Vocabulary was measured in first language with multiple-choice items and in second language with a translation test from English to Dutch. The results for the first language data indicated that almost two-thirds of the variability in reading comprehension related to vocabulary and metacognitive knowledge: 64 per cent for grade 6, 62 per cent for grade 8, and 65 per cent at grade 10. Further, the data indicate that at grade 6 metacognitive aspects play hardly any role at all, while at grades 8 and 10 the contribution is substantial. The findings in relation to second language for the grade 8 and 10 students show that second language vocabulary is the best predictor of second language reading comprehension in both grades, but that at grade 10 the relative importance of vocabulary seems to decrease and the importance of metacognitive knowledge increases. Additionally, metacognitive knowledge is a significant predictor on its own. The findings are interesting in showing how for lesser ability readers, vocabulary plays a much greater role than do metacognitive skills. However, the reverse is found to be true as the students mature and begin to handle more demanding and difficult material. At the higher levels, reading becomes a more complex overall skill requiring comprehension monitoring and knowledge of such factors as text structure, and this appears to happen in both first language and second language.

A pertinent point on much of the research in this section was made by Singhal (2001). While many of the studies have examined strategy use by different types of readers (successful versus less successful, good versus poor, and so forth), such artificial dichotomies can be limiting. Such broad categories may also overlook subtle and important differences and similarities between learners and their strategy use. Frequently, the designations of successful/non-successful, high/low, good/poor, etc. are normative decisions based on rank order on a test or other scale. Those subjects in each category who are near the cut-off point may not be very different from one another.

Second language strategy and metacognitive training

There have been a number of intervention studies in second language reading strategy research which have included varying amounts of overt metacognitive training. These studies provide insight into the conditions under which such training and instruction might be successful (O'Malley and Chamot 1990).

Some studies into the role of strategy training have focused on training of text-structure feature recognition and understanding. Explicit instruction in text structure was provided in Carrell (1985) in order to determine whether such instruction would facilitate reading comprehension. The subjects were 25 high-intermediate proficiency ESL students in an intensive English program. The subjects received text-structure training for five successive one-hour sessions during a one-week period. The training sessions covered four text structures: 1) collection of descriptions; 2) causation; 3) problem/solution; and 4) comparison. The training sessions began with simple short and easy text passages and built during the week to longer and subtler passages. Each session contained explicit reviews of the training objectives and the main points of the previous session. Subjects were given study packets explaining the benefits of the strategy, and checklists for the monitoring and regulating of their own learning. A control group of subjects received the same reading materials, but performed various linguistic operations with the text. Both groups were administered a pre-test and a post-test, with a delayed post-test given only to the treatment group three weeks after the first post-test. The tests covered only the discourse types of comparison and collection of descriptions. The results indicated that the treatment group showed a significant gain in their recognition and use of the text structure while the control group did not. The delayed post-test showed that the gain persisted after three weeks. More importantly, the treatment group recalled a significantly larger number of idea units from the test passages than the control group, indicating an effect on reading comprehension of the text-structure training. As with the text-structure recognition test and the delayed post-test, the reading comprehension gain persisted after three weeks. Finally, analysis of the subjects' recall protocols indicated that the treatment group's advantage over the control group after training was maintained across high-, mid-, and low-level idea units. This study, then, indicates that training in text structure can benefit at least relatively high-level second language readers' reading comprehension.

Hamp-Lyons (1985) examined a 'text-strategic' training approach, which involved training on an extensive list of text characteristics in a small-scale classroom-based study. The study is informative about strategy training in part because teachers in a naturalistic language program setting instituted it. Based on a pre-test, the 24 subjects of heterogeneous Asian languages (Malaysian n=13, Korean n=3, Chinese n=3, Japanese n=2, and Vietnamese n=1) with TOEFL scores of 500–50 were placed into one of three classes in the regular program. All subjects used the regularly assigned textbook. Two groups received a 'traditional' instructional program while the other received the text-strategic training. Rather than focusing on literal, inferential, and critical comprehension questions of the traditional instruction, the text-strategic approach de-emphasized the comprehension questions associated with reading passages and focused on discourse features such as the structure of the text, cohesion and coherence, anaphoric reference, and logical connectors. After 16 weeks of instruction, the subjects received a post-test. The strategic approach had a significantly higher gain score than the groups that received the traditional training, as well as a significantly higher post-test score. The study points out that teachers working within regular language courses can have an effect using strategic training in the second language classroom.

Barnett (1988) investigated the relationships among reading strategies and perceived strategy use on reading comprehension in a two-part study, the first looking at strategy use, and the second looking at the effect of a teaching intervention designed to help students develop more effective reading strategies before, during, and after reading. The subjects were 272 college-level students in fourth-semester French classes. Fifteen of the course sections were taught with a standard four skills approach, and four of the classes were taught with a strategy-training orientation that focused on skimming, scanning, guessing, and predicting. During the tenth week of the semester, the students: 1) read an unfamiliar French passage and wrote a recall protocol in English; 2) answered six questions related to amount of background knowledge they had about the story context; 3) indicated strategy use by reading portions of a new unfamiliar text and at intervals selecting the most likely text that would logically follow; and 4) answered a questionnaire in English about the types of reading strategies they thought they used. The results indicated that comprehension increased with use of the strategy of reading through context, and with increasing self-perception of effective strategy use. Additionally, the treatment group had significantly higher scores for strategy use, as measured by their predictions of what would come next in the text. However, the groups did not differ in terms of perceived strategy use. More importantly, the two groups did not significantly differ in terms of their comprehension scores. This last finding presents another case in which the quality and intensity of the strategy instruction may be of importance.

Just as research has shown that strategy use differs with reading ability, researchers involved in training have been interested in whether success of instruction differs depending on ability level. Kern (1989) focused on the effects of strategy instruction on the reading comprehension and inferential ability of intermediate-level French students. The study was interested not only in whether direct strategy instruction was effective, but also whether it was differentially effective depending upon second language reading ability. Fifty-three third-semester French students were placed into one of two treatment groups: 1) the experimental group that received explicit instruction in reading-strategy use in addition to normal course content; and 2) a control group that received the normal course content without the strategy training. For the treatment group, the reading-strategy instruction was integrated into the normal course curriculum. The treatment centered around: 1) word analysis (cognates, prefixes, etc.); 2) sentence analysis (questioning strategies, attention to cohesive devices); 3) discourse analysis (diagramming, cloze, inferring word meaning from context, hypothesis formation about prediction, main idea identification); and 4) reading for specific purposes (solve a particular problem, identify author's attitude, find the primary problem being presented). Each subject was given a pre-test and a reading task think-aloud interview about his or her reading strategies. Two measures were obtained from the reading task interview on both the pre-test and post-test: a comprehension measure and a word inference measure. Subjects were categorized as low-, mid-, or high-ability level based on their pre-test scores. At the end of one semester of instruction, subjects were given the post-test reading task interview. For the comprehension measure, the strategy-training group obtained a statistically higher gain than the control group. It was also found that there was a statistically significant difference in comprehension gain between the strategy-training group and the control group subjects within the low-ability level. However, this was not found for the middle- or high-ability levels, although the middle-level training group gain score was almost three times that of middle-ability control subjects. The lower-ability groups were assisted to a high degree by the strategy training, whereas the middle- and upper-level groups benefited approximately to the same degree as one another. For the inference measure, the strategy-training group showed a significantly higher gain than the control group, but there were no differential effects based on level of ability. Thus, the study does indicate that strategy instruction affects comprehension, but the degree to which it is differential depending upon reading ability level is still not clearly answered. Also, since the subjects were all in the third semester of French, it is not clear just how much actual difference in ability there was between the low group and the high group.

Auerbach and Paxton (1997) present a qualitative study describing a reading program that brought many of the reading research tools such as think-aloud protocols into the classroom in order to lead the students to examine their own first language and second language reading strategies and to involve them directly in strategy discovery. The students were enrolled in a pre-freshman intensive language program, and were given individual assessments at the beginning and end of the course through think-aloud protocols. The course was designed to enable the students to become researchers of their own reading in order to promote their metacognitive skills and reading strategies over one semester with four hours of instruction per week. The 20 students in the study kept journals and strategy logs, took tests and quizzes, wrote papers about themselves as readers and the changes they underwent, and participated in interviews. At the beginning of the course, the students' initial strategies, conceptions, reading contexts, feelings about reading, and reading histories were examined. The findings from the initial data indicated that the students saw second language proficiency as the biggest problem facing them in second language reading, and by and large they disliked reading English deeply. Materials based on the students' reactions to a questionnaire concerning their ideas of what reading involved, their general second language reading problems, and their strategies were presented and discussed very early in the course in order to invite them to begin thinking about formal models in terms of their own processes. They examined what other readers in the class did strategically in both first language and second language reading, and began to decide what led to more successful reading. All of the initial readings were narratives about reading and learning to read. The middle part of the course was divided into three sections that focused on the reading phases of pre-reading, during-reading, and post-reading strategies such as those in Table 5.1. At each step students brainstormed the strategies they used. This activity showed students the diversity of strategies and approaches that are used by different readers. Then a strategy was modeled by the teacher and the students kept strategy logs about each strategy they were presented. Excerpts from the logs were used as handouts for class discussion. Student comments in their strategy logs indicated that throughout the course of the instruction, they became increasingly comfortable, skilled, and critical in their evaluation of the strategies, and increasingly able to evaluate not only which strategies worked for them, but also developed growing conditional knowledge regarding when and why to use the particular strategy. About halfway through the course the students began pleasure reading in addition to academic reading. According to Auerbach and Paxton, the end of semester interviews and the final think-aloud indicated several changes in the students' reading strategies:

1   They had increased the number of strategies they had to draw from and improved in their confidence, and indicated that they had changed in how they felt about reading English.

2 They sampled from various parts of the text in order to take control of it, something not evident in the initial evaluations.

3 Their use of strategies appeared more natural and not forced as they each learned which strategies worked best for themselves.

4 They had the vocabulary to articulate the detailed strategies that they were using while reading.

5 Most were no longer text-bound at the level of words.

6 They prioritized higher-level meaning-centered strategies, and recognized that there was no single strategy or set of strategies that worked.

7 Most had improved their comprehension.

8 They talked about how they brought their own prior knowledge and thinking to the text.

9 They realized it was not just a lack of second language proficiency that impeded reading.

Thus, the approach of involving the students in their own learning in an internal way can change the way students read and feel about their reading. This research shows one approach to developing metacognition in concert with strategies.

In another qualitative study of how instruction affects strategy use and perception, Jiménez (1997) presented a case study of five bilingual Latino students with low literacy levels in English, students who were reading up to four grade levels below their current seventh-grade placement. The focus of the training program was an assumption that a reading program that emphasizes comprehension and the use of strategic reading processes can improve word recognition and reading fluency. The program included the components of: 1) culturally relevant and familiar text; 2) a focus on comprehension, stressing important reading strategies; and 3) provision of opportunities to build reading fluency. Data were collected from think-aloud protocols in which the student was presented with a text, asked to read each line of the text silently, and then asked to explain in as much detail as possible what he or she been thinking during the reading. Instruction involved eight lessons over a two-week period. Reading texts were three children's books and a language experience text dealing in some way with the Mexican staple food, corn. The language experience text was created from the oral texts of the students as they discussed two ears of corn, packages of tortillas, and a sack of corn flour. This was designed to show the students the value of using prior knowledge while reading. The strategies that were taught included: 1) resolving the meanings of unknown vocabulary; 2) how to integrate prior knowledge; and 3) how to formulate questions. Strategies were modeled for the students and they were encouraged to implement the strategy presented each day. On subsequent days strategies were reviewed and demonstrated again. At their initial interviews, the students appeared to understand that learning to read requires effort and that knowing how to read is a desirable goal, but their comments also appeared to indicate that they saw reading as a somewhat mysterious process. By the end of instruction the students provided evidence of taking a more active role in their reading. They actively asked questions and connected textual information with their prior knowledge. The students also appeared to have made connections of a metacognitive nature in that they verbalized the awareness that reading requires thinking and on occasion explicitly labeled their strategy use, such as questioning, which was then implemented. Several of them also developed explicit strategies for addressing unknown vocabulary. The study provides insight into how reading can be made a little less mysterious and how selection of appropriate texts is an important tool in strategy training.

However, not all aspects of strategy instruction have led to successful instruction. Janzen (2003) examined the effect of strategic reading instruction with third-grade Navajo students. One group of students received strategic reading instruction over the course of a school year while a comparison group in the same school received more traditional instruction. In the strategic instruction classroom, the students averaged about one and a half hours of reading work per week. At the beginning and end of the year students were given a standardized test measuring general reading proficiency and a questionnaire about their conscious knowledge about reading strategies, and at the end of the school year they were given a think-aloud protocol. The strategic reading instruction followed a four-part division: discussion, modeling, student reading, and review. The strategies that were covered included predicting, previewing, asking questions, identifying a purpose for reading, and thinking about what the reader knows before reading. At the end of the training, there was no significant difference between the two groups on the standardized test of reading proficiency. On the post-questionnaires, the students in the strategic instruction group provided more responses than they did at the beginning of the training, and provided a greater variety of responses than the control group. The think-aloud protocols also showed that the intervention students showed fewer instances of negative reading behaviors. Overall, the intervention students demonstrated a wider variety of behaviors than the control group, and more behaviors relating to the overall story rather than decoding single word behaviors. Thus, the study shows that although the intervention group did demonstrate more facility and knowledge of reading strategies than the control group, they did not improve significantly on their reading proficiency.

The various second language studies tend to show significant positive effects found for strategy training when compared with control groups or traditional approaches to instruction. As with the first language training studies, there is evidence from these second language training studies that reading-strategy training shows significant positive results. However, such training varies in effectiveness depending upon second language ability and the depth of the training.

Implications for instruction

An important goal of reading instruction should be to help learners become strategic readers (Baker 2002; Palincsar 1986). The research just examined offers several implications for effective strategy training. While the particular form of the strategies taught will need to develop from the learner's own particular context, Brown and Palincsar (1989) and Palincsar and Brown (1984) have presented the six strategies that have been found consistently to affect comprehension. These are: 1) clarifying the purpose of reading in order to determine the appropriate strategy to use; 2) activating relevant background knowledge and linking it to the text; 3) allocating attention to important pieces of information in the text; 4) evaluating content for internal consistency and compatibility with prior knowledge; 5) self-monitoring and self-regulation of comprehension; and 6) drawing and testing inferences regarding the text message. These six strategy families can form the basis for selection of strategies in instruction.

A number of educators have discussed characteristics of instruction designed to encourage learners to become more strategic (Baker 1994; Gourgey 1998; Janzen and Stoller 1998; Rhoder 2002; Rosenshine and Meister 1994). First, instruction is most effective when the instructor: 1) carefully explains the nature and purpose of the strategy; 2) models its use through reading and thinking aloud; 3) provides ample practice and feedback for the students; 4) reminds students of the benefits of strategy use, and encourages the independent transfer of these skills to new learning situations; and 5) provides a content base so that strategy learning is embedded in authentic purposes.

Additionally, instructional time for direct-strategy instruction and modeling must be made available for strategy instruction to be effective. Implicit instruction does not appear to be very effective, particularly for those students who are having problems. The strategies that are taught must be determined through task analyses of strategies needed. The strategies should be difficult for the students to apply, but not so difficult that they become frustrated. If the activity is too easy, the readers can forget the need to be strategic in their reading. It is important to consider how particular strategies are applied and the contexts in which they are needed. Strategies need to be taught over a sufficient duration for the training to be effective and should be presented over a number of contexts with a variety of texts. In this sense, the learners will need to be able to use the strategy automatically before they can monitor its success and helpfulness.

A number of educators recommend using think-aloud procedures to assist with COMPREHENSION STRATEGIES. Often, the approaches follow the Duffy and Roehler (1989) approach that begins with the teacher as model and gradually turns responsibility over to the students. Wilhelm (2001) provides eight steps in using think-aloud techniques to teach general-process strategies. These are presented in Table 5.8.

Step	Activity	Comments
1	Choose a short section of text.	Should be interesting and challenging to students
2	Decide on a few strategies to highlight.	Explain the think-aloud process to students and what strategies they will be trying. Also, explain how these strategies will be helpful.
3	State the purposes.	Enjoy a good story? Write a summary? Study for a test?
4	Read the text aloud to the students and think-aloud as it is read.	Read slowly and stop often to report, target the strategies that are the focus, perhaps stop and predict aloud.
5	Have students underline the words and phrases that appear in the strategy.	What words helped to make an inference and make predictions?
6	List the cues and strategies used.	Students make a list of signals that prompt strategy use. Discuss which cues helped and which did not.
7	Ask students to identify other situations in which they might use the strategies.	This is aimed at transfer contexts.
8	Reinforce the think-aloud with follow-up lessons and phases.	Teacher does / student watches Teacher does / students help Teacher does / students do Students do / teacher helps Students do / teacher watches and assesses

Table 5.8: Steps in using think-aloud approaches to teach strategies (Adapted from Wilhelm (2001))

These general steps lead the students through the process of identifying strategies associated with particular reading purposes. Gradually, the responsibility for strategy development is turned over to the students and the teacher becomes an assistant.

Summary and conclusions

The discussion above has indicated the difficulties with distinguishing between reading skills and strategies solely by seeing skills as subconscious and strategies as conscious activities. The same activity can represent skill application in some contexts and strategic moves at other times. In discussing reading strategies, we need to recognize that they represent not only repair actions, but also a repertoire that is of importance in strategy marshaling, monitoring, and regulation throughout the reading process, particularly in that strategies are applied in connection with the reader's primary purpose for reading, the literacy act in which the reader is engaged. Further, the literature reviewed has shown that there are not sets of strategies that are uniquely used by proficient readers and sets of strategies that are uniquely used by poor readers. The same skills are often employed by both good and poor readers, but they are employed with differing levels of success. The types of strategies that a reader applies are often somewhat idiosyncratic in that the particular strategies that are used differ across individuals. However, in general the more successful readers appear to use more strategies than less successful readers. Apparently, metacognitive strategies play an increasing role in identifying good readers from poor readers as the reader progresses (Shoonen et al. 1998). The research also appears to indicate that direct training of strategies and metacognitive skills is both possible and productive. However, such training needs to be modeled and demonstrated, not presented as lists of strategies practiced on texts that are of little interest or for purposes that are not embedded in the reader's own life.

Subsequent chapters in this text address specific areas of second language reading that affect comprehension success. These areas include both content and formal schema, vocabulary, and reading-writing relationships. As those areas are addressed, specific forms of strategic instruction will be presented.

Discussion and study questions

1 The discussion of research has presented a number of different reader strategies. What are these strategies? How can they be categorized in a way that is meaningful? Make a list of the strategies mentioned and categorize them.

2 What are some of the assumptions in the research related to meta-cognition and the instruction of metacognition? Which do you agree with and which do you not agree with?

3 What relationships have been found between metacognitive-strategy use by native speakers and non-native speakers? Have the metacognitive strategies discussed been successful in aiding comprehension? How does language proficiency affect the results?

4 Auerbach and Paxton present a description of a reading program that focused on learners who were actively involved in their own strategy use expansion. In what types of programs would this approach likely work? In what types of programs would this approach perhaps not work well?

5 Examine several reading textbooks for how they address (or fail to address) the issues raised in the readings and discussions of strategies and metacognitive skills in reading. To what extent does the text address:

A Problem-solving techniques such as: guessing word meanings from context and evaluating those guesses, recognizing cognates and word families, skimming, scanning, reading for meaning, predicting, activating general knowledge, making inferences, following references, and separating main ideas from supporting details?

B Pedagogical approaches for developing successful strategies involve pre-reading activities such as: brainstorming for appropriate background knowledge, imagining text content from a title or illustrations, activities while reading like discussing word formation and word meanings in context, and post-reading global comprehension activities requiring students to summarize or get the gist?

C Metacognition: understanding the implicit and explicit task demands, or purpose, identifying the important aspects of a message, focusing attention on the major content rather than trivia, monitoring ongoing activities to determine whether comprehension is occurring, engaging in self-questioning to determine whether goals are being achieved, and taking corrective action when failures in comprehension are detected?

6 CONTENT SCHEMA AND BACKGROUND KNOWLEDGE

Introduction

The literature on reading notes two different types of SCHEMA, or background knowledge, that the reader brings to bear on a text. The first class of prior knowledge has to do with content schema relevant to the content area and cultural knowledge. An example of this is the 'ship christening' schema that was presented in Chapter 2 in the discussion of Anderson and Pearson's (1984) schema-theoretic model of reading. The second type of schema is formal schema. This represents the background knowledge the reader has regarding how syntax is used to structure text, cohesive relations, and the rhetorical organization of different text types. This chapter will focus on concerns of content schema, or background knowledge, while the next chapter will focus on formal schema issues.

Before proceeding, a note about terminology in *schema* theory needs to be made. The term *schema* is sometimes used as a singular term with *schemata* as the plural noun form. However, the literature also often uses the term *schema* in a generic or non-count sense as in terms such as 'schema theoretic' or 'types of schema'. Further, a schema may be very well developed and robust, as in all of the things that we would accept might take place in church. It may not be the case that an individual has one schema for the sermon, another for Sunday school, and yet another for communion. In one of the earliest uses of the term, Kant (1963, Smith translation) writes:

> Indeed, it is schemata, not images of objects, which underlie our pure sensible concepts. No image could ever be adequate to the concept of a triangle in general. It would never attain that universality of the concept which renders it valid of all triangles, whether right-angled, obtuse-angled, or acute-angled; it would always be limited to a part only of this sphere. The schema of the triangle can exist nowhere but in thought. . . . This schematism of our understanding, in its application to appearances and their mere form, is an art concealed in the depths of the human soul, whose real modes of activity nature is hardly likely ever to allow us to discover, and to have open to our gaze. This much only we can assert: the image is a

product of the empirical faculty of reproductive imagination; the schema of sensible concepts, such as figures in space, is a product and, as it were, a monogram, of pure a priori imagination, through which, and in accordance with which, images themselves first become possible. These images can be connected with the concept only by means of the schema to which they belong. In themselves, they are never completely congruent with the concept. On the other hand, the schema of a pure concept of understanding can never be brought into any image whatsoever.

(Kant 1963: 182–3)

The term is used in its generic form here, meaning all possible triangles and 'images connected with a concept by means of the schema to which they belong'. This usage will continue here, incorporating the plural, *schemata* when distinctly referencing multiple instances.

Introduction to content and cultural schema

As noted the discussion in Chapter 2 of Anderson and Pearson's (1984) schema-theoretic view of reading, an area of major importance in the reading process relates to how background knowledge/schemata and cultural under-standing affect text comprehension. As Freire and Macedo (1987) state:

Reading does not consist merely of decoding the written word of language; rather it is preceded by and intertwined with knowledge of the world. Language and reality are dynamically interconnected. The understanding attained by critical reading of a text implies perceiving the relationship between text and content.

(Anderson and Pearson 1984)

Background knowledge plays a role in terms of facts known and assumptions held about the world, what have been termed scripts, plans, or goals (Shank and Ableson 1977). Here we refer to the nature of a reader's default concepts about events and settings. Prior knowledge may have a facilitating effect because a reader who already has an elaborate schema can more easily fit incoming textual information into that schema. Background knowledge can also be related to values and judgments that are made about an event by a reader, values that are due to social experience and cultural mores. Both of these aspects of background knowledge will affect the extent to which a second language reader constructs a meaning that is in any way consistent with the meaning a first language reader is likely to construct, as well as whether two first language or two second language readers construct the same meaning. As Malik (1990) states, echoing Goodman (1984), 'Because comprehension results from reader–text transaction, what the reader knows, who the reader is, what values guide the reader, and what purposes or interests the reader has will play a vital role in the reading process' (207).

However, the reader's background knowledge does not simply represent the contents of a repository filled with random relevant and irrelevant ideas. The background knowledge also reflects expectations of importance, relevance, and structure. Sometimes these expectations reflect biases, and these colored expectations can become goals and self-fulfilling prophecies in the comprehension process. When considering the role of background knowledge, we should not view schema as controlling immutable structures. If this were so, we would be hard-pressed to explain how learning and conceptual change take place. Rather, the knowledge structures are part of more complex coding that involves propositional representations, bottom-up word-meaning generation, and mental imaging. There is an interaction among all of these coding sources (Nassaji 2002; Sadoski 1999). The application of mental representations involves processes of constraint satisfaction through which the reader determines the extent to which the emerging message is consistent, or satisfying.

Prior knowledge and first language reading

This chapter examines the effects that background knowledge has been shown through research to have on text comprehension and recall. A fairly rich tradition of studies in this area exists, and indicates how background knowledge can affect comprehension, even among children, who might be expected to have less well developed and internalized background schemata than adults. Dochy (1994) summarizes results which indicate that 30 per cent to 60 per cent of reading test variability can be explained by prior knowledge. For example, Lipson (1983) studied the effect of background knowledge on the reading performance of children in the fourth through sixth grades who were of differing religious backgrounds. The subjects were from two subcultures within a larger society, Catholic and Jewish. Half of the subjects (n=16) were Catholics attending a private Catholic school and half (n=16) were Jewish attending a Hebrew day school. Each of the subjects read three passages: a culturally neutral passage entitled *The Ama*, a passage entitled *First Communion*, and a passage entitled *Bar Mitzvah*. After reading each passage, the subjects wrote a free recall of everything they remembered about the passage and answered ten recall questions. Lipson found a significant effect for group by passage in terms of reading time, with each group taking less time to read the culturally familiar passage. The analysis further found that the groups recalled more explicit and implicit propositional information from the familiar passages than from the less familiar passage. A similar pattern was found for the recall questions. The results support the concepts that background knowledge may assist in comprehension of a text. However, it is also important to note that the subjects tended to make more errors in their interpretations of the unfamiliar text, distortions such as thinking that the Torah was something to be worn or that the communion wafer was left behind by Jesus. Thus, schemata that mismatch the context of the target text can create distortions and intrusions that are perhaps as detrimental to comprehension as a complete absence of prior knowledge.

It appears from the research that prior knowledge of a topic increases the amount of information that is recalled from a text on that topic. Reynolds et al. (1982) also report on the effects of personal knowledge and cultural background on text interpretation. In their study, African-American and white eighth graders read a letter about an incident at school that could be interpreted as either a school cafeteria fight or as an instance of 'sounding.' 'Sounding' is a type of ritual insult found primarily in the African-American community. The object of sounding is to establish status in the peer group by demonstrating skill at insulting the opponent's family members and making derogatory allusions regarding the personal attributes and behaviors of those relatives. The students in the study read a short letter allegedly written by a boy to a friend who had moved away. The letter described a school day, highlighting an episode in the school cafeteria. Again, the episode could be interpreted as a fight in the cafeteria or as an instance of sounding. The results suggest that cultural schemata influence reading comprehension. African-American subjects tended to indicate that the text was about a sounding scenario, while the white students interpreted the text as being about an actual fight. Reynolds et al. hypothesize that culture influences knowledge and that knowledge affects reading comprehension.

Further, a great deal of first language research has demonstrated that prior knowledge significantly affects memory performance over and above aptitude (Marr and Gormley 1982; Schneider, Körkel, and Weinert 1989). Given that background knowledge can affect recall of information from a text, a question arises as to the relationship between background knowledge and reading ability in text comprehension. Recht and Leslie (1988) examined whether prior knowledge or reading expertise had the greater effect on recall. They note that research has indicated that good readers have better recall than do poor readers (Ryan 1981), and that good and poor readers have been found to have similar short-term recall when text topic is familiar (Taylor 1979). Recht and Leslie divided 64 seventh- and eighth-grade students into four categories of reading ability and knowledge about the sport of baseball: 1) high-ability/high-knowledge; 2) high-ability/low-knowledge; 3) low-ability/ high-knowledge; and 4) low-ability/low-knowledge. The subjects read a passage describing a half inning of a baseball game. A replica of a baseball field was presented along with wooden figures of baseball players. The subjects moved the players to re-enact the reading passage and also provided a verbal account of the action. Subsequently, they were asked to recall the passage and sort randomly selected sentences from the passage into their importance for the narrative. The analysis showed that the memory recalls of the high-knowledge readers were significantly better than the recalls of the low-knowledge readers, regardless of reading ability, both quantitatively and qualitatively on the re-enactment activity, the verbal retelling, and the recall summarization. Further, subjects with low knowledge but high reading ability did not score better than the low-knowledge/low-ability subjects. Thus, high knowledge of a topic appears to provide a support that takes a load off short-term memory and allows for compensation for lower general reading ability.

Although background knowledge has been shown to assist compensation by challenged readers, it is important to take into account Lipson's (1983) finding that background knowledge can also distort and intrude on the reading process. That is, the reader's reliance on background knowledge can be disadvantageous at times. Two studies (Reutzel and Hollingsworth 1991; Reynolds et al. 1982) provide evidence that while a text may be read with some fidelity in the short term, its long-term reconstruction may reflect previously held opinions.

Background knowledge can affect both short-term and long-term interpretations of text information. As discussed above with the sounding study, Reynolds et al. (1982) note that readers create meaning from a text by processing the words and sentences against the backdrop of their own personal world knowledge and opinions. Any reader's personal knowledge is conditioned, in part, by such variables as age, ethnicity, gender, race, religion, nationality, occupation, political affiliations, and other salient cultural features. In support of this view, they reference a long research tradition that has examined the effects of beliefs on how texts are processed and what is remembered from them. Read and Rosson (1982) examined prior views on the value and hazards of the nuclear power industry. They developed a questionnaire that identified people who either strongly supported or strongly rejected nuclear power. Participants read a passage about a fire at a nuclear power station. A multiple-choice test was administered after the reading but showed little influence of beliefs on immediate comprehension of the text. Both groups' answers reflected fidelity with information in the text. However, when the test was administered a week or two later, the participants distorted the content in ways that tended to coincide with their prior held views about the safety and desirability of nuclear power. Participants who had been in favor of nuclear power rejected anti-nuclear statements which were not supported by information in the passage while tending to accept pro-nuclear statements that were spurious. Those opposed to nuclear power demonstrated the opposite pattern. Thus, there is a tendency for readers over time to fit the information from a text to their own conceptions of what is correct.

Reutzel and Hollingsworth (1991) obtained similar results in their study of the effect of attitude on reading and remembering of text. In their study, 58 sixth-grade students were randomly assigned to one of three groups. Each of these groups was then taught lessons about the fictitious country of Titubia. One group was taught about the paradise of Titubia, one group was taught of the miserable and tragic Titubia, while the third group was taught a straightforward neutral set of lessons about Titubia. The purpose of these sets of instructions was to create attitudes in order to compensate for previous findings that once prior knowledge is controlled, there are no significant effects associated with topic-related attitude. After the instruction, students were presented with stories about Titubia that were either positive or negative, and were then given a recall test and a multiple-choice probed recall test. The findings showed no significant differences on either test for the groups' immediate performance on the two passages. However, when the students were administered the same instruments three weeks later, the favorable attitude group recalled significantly more idea units on the positive passage than did the negative attitude group, and the negative attitude group recalled significantly more idea units on the negative passage than did the positive attitude group. Parallel results were obtained for erroneous idea-unit intrusions and scores on a multiple-choice delayed test. Thus, the results lend support to the schema-theoretic view about the effects that attitudes can have in the reading comprehension process. Topic-related attitudes influence the long-term reconstruction of memories of a text, but are frequently not strong enough to change immediate recall of the text. Findings such as these also lend support to the constructivist views of reading that comprehension is not necessarily something that happens after reading a text and is fixed. Rather, comprehension can take place over a long period of time, even after the text has been absent for a considerable duration.

So, prior knowledge and attitudes can color the long-term memory of a text's meaning. However, research has also indicated that in some cases prior knowledge based on experience and affiliation can also affect the immediate interpretation of text. Spilich et al. (1979) had previously examined the effects of schemata for listening comprehension, a process often seen to be very close to reading comprehension. In their study, again using baseball as in the Recht and Leslie (1988) study, subjects with high knowledge of baseball and subjects with low knowledge of baseball listened to a contrived account of a half inning in a baseball game. Spilich et al. held the assumption that processing of textual information consists of a matching procedure which matches the input information with the individual's current schemata. Thus, it was hypothesized that the high baseball knowledge subjects should be able to process the information more readily than the low baseball knowledge subjects. Their results showed that the high-knowledge subjects recalled significantly more propositions from the input than did the low-knowledge subjects. The high-knowledge subjects' recall was superior with respect to the names of the teams playing, the inning that was presented, the batting averages of the players, and the record of the pitcher. The high-knowledge subjects tended to integrate sequences of the goal-related actions in the game better, recall information in the appropriate order better, and provide a more coherent recall than the low-knowledge subjects. These findings lend further support to the view that schemata affect the comprehension of text.

Anderson et al. (1977) conducted an experiment that involved female music majors and male physical education majors. The participants read an ambiguous text that could be given an interpretation of either a prison break or a wrestling match. They also read the text discussed in Chapter 1 that could be interpreted in terms of an evening of card playing or an evening of music playing by a quartet of amateur classical musicians. The scores on a disambiguating paper and pencil test, and theme-revealing disambiguations and intrusions in free recall, showed striking relationships to the subjects' background. Physical education majors tended to give a wrestling interpretation to the wrestling/prison break passage and a card-playing interpretation to the music/card passage. The female music education majors showed the reverse interpretations. Unfortunately, it is not clear whether gender or major caused the particular pattern of interpretations.

Explicit biases can affect immediate interpretations of a text when textual content does not explicitly constrain interpretation. Gaskins (1996) asked 72 eighth-grade students in three different groups to read a fictitious passage about a particularly violent basketball game between Boston and Philadelphia. The game ended in a fight between players on both teams. According to the text, both teams committed the same number of fouls and physical plays, and responsibility for the altercation could be attributed to either team. One of the groups of readers was composed of avid Boston fans while another group was composed of very strong Philadelphia fans. A third group in the study read a passage that was identical to the first passage except that the game involved two teams that the readers were uninvolved with. Immediately after reading the passage, the students were asked to recall the events of the passage and answer three questions. The students 'were asked if they thought one team fouled more or played rougher than the other, which team they thought was responsible for the fight, and if they thought the referees called the game evenly or favored one team over the other' (391). On the three questions, there was a significant difference in the way the groups answered. The Boston fans said the fight and physical contact were the responsibility of Philadelphia, while the Philadelphia fans blamed the fight and roughness on Boston. Neither group claimed that the referees were biased against their team. The third group, the uninvolved group, tended to indicate that the responsibility for the fight and physical roughness was equally shared by both teams. Thus, as with Read and Rosson's (1982) nuclear power passage results, a reader's attitudes and affiliations affected the interpretation of the text.

In contrast, background knowledge can also affect the extent to which new information that may be at odds with existing knowledge is learned from text. Lipson (1982) examined the ability of children to learn new information depending upon the extent to which they had prior knowledge of the topic that was read. Here, 28 third-grade students were given a pre-test on knowledge of topics about which they would subsequently read. They were asked to identify any questions about which they did not have information. On the subsequent tests, the students correctly answered information that they had correctly answered on pre-test, a not surprising result. However, it was also the case that they were more likely to correctly answer questions that they had indicated a lack of knowledge about on the pre-test than to correctly answer items that they had answered incorrectly on the pre-test. Thus, they appeared to be able to use information from text better when they had no prior knowledge than when they had held a contrary view. Lipson notes that the subjects were remarkably impervious to changes in their schemata regarding familiar topics. One of the subjects stated the following on a recall about the reading topic of *insects*: 'Insects have/the spider has eight legs. Insects usually have six legs. A spider is an insect.' (258).

On the pre-test the subject had indicated that a spider was an insect. He was willing to accept that spiders had eight legs, yet he was unwilling to change his opinion that a spider was an insect, even though the text explicitly stated that insects have six legs. His response was made consistent with his prior knowledge rather than accommodating the new contradictory information from the text. Here we have not an absence of background knowledge, but a qualitative mismatch between a schema that is held and the incoming information from the text. In such instances, the reader may build inappropriate meanings based on inappropriate and incorrect inferences, making it more advantageous to acquire completely new information rather than to correct old information that is inaccurate.

This effect of background knowledge has implications for how and whether readers learn new information from texts. Alverman, Smith, and Readence (1985) looked at the effects of background knowledge that is incompatible with information presented in a reading passage. Here they presented subjects with two texts, one of which had information that was counter-intuitive to the readers' existing knowledge structures. The subjects were presented with a passage on snakes and a passage on sunlight. The 'snake' passage contained information that was compatible with prior knowledge while the 'sunlight' passage contained several points that were incompatible with the knowledge that the students already possessed. In the study, half of the group members were provided with an opportunity prior to reading to activate their background knowledge by writing everything they knew about the topic. This was termed the 'activator' group. The second group, the 'non-activator' group, wrote about a topic unrelated to the topics in the text. The results indicated that the information in the 'sunlight' text had very little influence on changing the incompatible views that the subjects held prior to reading the passage. In recall protocols, the subjects continued to provide information incompatible with the text they had just read, and on multiple-choice tests they selected options that were incompatible with the information presented in the text. The scores for both the 'activator' group and the 'non-activator' group were higher on the 'compatible' passage than on the 'incompatible' passage. There was no overall main effect for group membership, meaning that 'activators' and 'non-activators' performed very much alike Interestingly, however, there was a compatible/incompatible text-by-group interaction. The 'non-activator' group produced fewer incompatible recall ideas than did the 'activator' group. The difference is slight, but it could indicate that the activation exercise actually entrenched the incompatible concepts held by the readers. These findings should serve as a caution to teachers who use schema-activation activities prior to reading. It does not indicate that such activities should be avoided; rather it makes clear the possibility that the activities may not serve the learners well at times. There may be a GARDEN PATH EFFECT which leads the reader-to-be astray.

Fincher-Kiefer (1992) examined the proposal that readers with domain knowledge generate anticipatory, knowledge-based inferences as they construct a mental representation of a domain related text. The study involved providing subjects who possessed differing degrees of baseball knowledge with a text describing a baseball game. The study was concerned with two types of inferences: those inferences used to maintain referential coherence within the text and inferences involved in prediction of a highly likely action or event. The first type of inference is locally text based while the second contributes to the mental representation of the text. A local inference would be of the type 'Chase swings and hits a high drive to left-center field. We have a tie game!' (15). In this case the inference that Chase hit a home run is required for the second sentence to fit with the first. A global inference is of the type 'Martin is up. There are runners on first and second with no one out. The Shark's third basemen, Jensen, is playing very deep' (15). Here, Fincher-Kiefer claims that the global inference is that Martin would bunt in that it represents a consequence of the information in the sentences. The subjects in the study were university students in the US who took a baseball knowledge test and were rated as having low knowledge, intermediate knowledge, and high knowledge about baseball. Reading ability scores showed no differences by group membership. Pairs of sentences based on a radio account of a baseball game were selected that prompted either local inferences or global inferences. Fincher-Kiefer examined the reading time of processing the different inference types. The results indicated that the reading times on the global inference statements for the intermediate- and advanced-knowledge subjects were significantly faster than the reading times for the low-knowledge subjects. Further, for both the high-knowledge and intermediate-knowledge groups, the reading times for the statements of the global inferences were significantly faster than the reading times for the local inferences. The low-knowledge group showed no significant difference between the reading times for the local and global inferences. The study supports the view that the goals of low-knowledge and high-knowledge readers may be different while processing a text. The high-knowledge reader focuses more on domain-related text to construct a representation of the text. A low-knowledge reader, on the other hand, focuses much more closely on local coherence issues in order to construct a representation.

Low-knowledge and high-knowledge readers may utilize different methods in identifying the main idea of a passage. Afflerbach (1990) addresses the influence that prior knowledge has on strategies that are used by experts reading both in their own field of study and in an unfamiliar field. Basically, he was examining how topic familiarity or lack of familiarity affected the strategies utilized to find the main idea of a text. The study involved verbal protocols from four anthropology and four chemistry doctoral students reading materials from both fields of study. Afflerbach looked at strategies for presenting the main idea of a reading text:

1 Draft-and-revision strategy: The reader does not find his or her construct-ed main idea to be satisfactory, and revises it as if it were a first draft.
2 Topic/comment strategy: After reading the text, the reader is only able to state the topic of the passage. He or she merely comments upon the topic.
3 Automatic construction: The reader automatically identifies the main idea, bypassing working memory, without using any repair strategies.
4 Initial hypothesis testing: The reader constructs a reasonably accurate initial hypothesis based on the title and initial paragraphs, and then mon-itors while reading to determine the adequacy of that initial hypothesis.
5 Listing strategy: The reader searches the text for important related words, concepts, or ideas that may be used to construct the main idea of the passage.

As might be expected, Afflerbach found that the draft-and-revision strategy was used more when the reader encountered unfamiliar text content, and the automatic-construction strategy was used more often with familiar text content. Similarly, the initial-hypothesis strategy was used significantly more often with familiar text content than with unfamiliar text content, but the listing strategy was used more often in the reading of unfamiliar topic domain texts. However, there was no significant difference in use of the topic/comment strategy for either familiar or unfamiliar text content. Afflerbach concludes that when the text content is unfamiliar, the reader has to reconstruct relevant background knowledge to produce a schema that accommodates the unfamil-iar information. A deficiency of prior knowledge contributes to the reader's dependency on comprehension strategies before the main idea is constructed.

Content schema across cultures and languages

The role of background knowledge in second language reading has been an issue of concern for some time. Given the fairly well established research findings that prior knowledge can affect the recall and comprehension of readers within a particular culture, it should be expected that there would be cross-cultural and cross-linguistic effects as well. Such effects may result from readers attempting to fit their default schematic concepts on to the incoming information or from low text-processing ability forcing a reliance on prior knowledge for compensation in the comprehension process. The cross-cultural effects may manifest themselves through comprehension of text in ways very different from any reasonable first language interpretation, unusual content preferences, increased reading rates for second language text, and non-conventional interpretations of what parts of a text are important. The second language research on the topic of content schema or background knowledge has looked at several variables and their interactions. Much of the research examines issues of cultural background on text interpretations or attitude toward the reading text. Other research addresses the relative effects of background knowledge, text complexity, text type, or some combination of these three variables. These effects and interactions are discussed in the remainder of this chapter.

Cultural background

Some of the more obvious cross-cultural effects on reading are due to different social conventions between the first language culture and the second language culture. Professor John Povey of UCLA in the late 1970s used to relate such a development in his course on teaching literature to EFL/ESL students. He recalled teaching an English literature class in West Africa using a story by John Updike entitled *A and P*. In the story, Updike develops the character of Sammy, the 19-year-old narrator of the story who is maturing from adolescence into adulthood. The story takes place in the summertime of 1960. Sammy works at a local A and P grocery store not far from Boston near the beach, and the story chronicles his last day working there. Three girls come into the A and P wearing their bathing suits as they shop. Sammy presents himself as an airy nonchalant distant teenager, superior to the older people who frequent the store, showing disdain and distance from what he sees as conventional lives. As he watches the three girls walk barefoot through the store in their bathing suits he imputes an intellectual vacuousness to them, much as he does to others who come into the store or who work mindlessly as employees. However, when his boss humiliates the three girls, Sammy attempts to stand up for them. He winds up quitting his job, thus pitting himself against his parents and striking out on his own. John Povey related how his West African students could not get past the three girls in the bathing suits. The class turned into a discussion of their lifestyle, professions, motivations, morality, etc. In essence, the story became a story about the three girls, not about Sammy and his emotional development as an adolescent. Sammy, in essence, became a relatively minor character in the students' minds, and they could not be convinced otherwise. In this example, cross-cultural differences affect not only comprehension, but radically alter what is considered primary in the reading passage.

However, cultural interpretations can also result from conflicting internalized scripts for the prototypical structure of cultural events. Steffensen, Joag-Dev, and Anderson (1979) examined the influence on reading comprehension of differences in cross-cultural knowledge and beliefs. They employed two cultural groups of subjects, Indians from India and Americans. Each group read two passages, one about a typical Indian wedding and one about a typical American wedding. The results showed that the subjects read the passage reflecting their own culture faster than the passage about the other culture, recalled a larger amount of information from the familiar passages than from the others, made more culturally appropriate elaborations of their native culture passage than the less familiar culture passage, and made more culturally-based distortions of information in the passage not reflective of their culture. The subjects distorted and elaborated information in the text based on their values, perceptions, and expectations. In short, it was apparent that cultural knowledge affected what was attended to as important in the reading passage.

Pritchard (1990) found similar results regarding how cultural schemata appear to influence readers' level of comprehension for other conventional cultural events. In his study, proficient 11th grade readers from the US and the Pacific island nation of Palau read culturally familiar and unfamiliar passages in their native language. The two passages were in the form of a letter from a woman to her sister detailing the events at a typical funeral in one of the two cultures. While funerals are common to both cultures, they vary in the events associated with them. The example Pritchard gives is that in Palauan funerals the family members are much more personally involved than in the US, in that they typically transport the body, dig the grave, and conduct the services personally. Further, funerals are more social in nature and may involve singing and dancing. Three religious representatives of each culture read the letters and made suggestions for changes in order to ensure that they were accurate representations. The subjects read the passages in a think-aloud condition, answered an attitude questionnaire, and then wrote a recall protocol in which they attempted to recall everything they could from the familiar and unfamiliar texts. The recall protocols were analyzed for the number of idea units recalled, number of distortions, and number of elaborations. The subjects recalled significantly more idea units from the cultural-ly familiar passage than from the unfamiliar passage. Further, there were significantly more distortions in the recall of the culturally unfamiliar passage than in the familiar passage, and more elaborations appeared in the culturally familiar passage than in the unfamiliar passage. These findings appear to support the findings by Steffenson et al. (1979) that background knowledge can influence comprehension of texts that include partially ritualized cultural events.

In a study examining the effects of schema and beliefs on second language reading comprehension and attitude toward text, Abu-Rabia (1996) looked at both Israeli Arabs reading texts based on traditional Arab stories and traditional Jewish stories and at Jewish Israelis reading texts with Western content. The subjects were also given an attitude questionnaire designed to determine whether the learner had an instrumental or an integrative orientation toward the target language. The subjects were 80 Jewish and 70 Arab 14–15-year-old students at two intermediate schools in Israel. The Israeli Jewish students studied English for four hours each week and the Israeli Arab students studied Hebrew for five hours a week as part of their regular school schedule. The culturally familiar texts were translated into the reader's second language while the culturally unfamiliar texts were translated into the reader's first language. Each reading passage was followed by a ten-item multiple-choice comprehension test. Arab students' comprehension scores were significantly higher on the tests associated with the Arab stories than on those associated with Jewish stories, regardless of whether the text was presented in Arabic or Hebrew. The Israeli Hebrew readers also showed a significantly higher comprehension for the texts based on culturally familiar content than on the culturally less familiar texts based on Western content. As with the Arab readers, the finding showed a higher effect for content than for the language in which the information was presented. Thus, the results of both the Israeli Arab and Israeli Jewish contexts support the role of schema theory as with the previously examined studies. Unfortunately, however, the Abu-Rabia study did not present the actual texts used in the study. Because of this, it is not possible to determine the extent to which the texts were culturally embedded and how familiar the topics were to the subjects. However, the results are consistent with findings by Nelson (1987) who found that Egyptian adult readers recalled significantly more material from texts focused on their own culture and preferred reading that material to material with an American context.

Carrell (1988) also notes that while having the appropriate background knowledge is a necessary condition for comprehension, it is not a sufficient condition. That is, the schema must be activated in the reading process. A failure to activate the appropriate schema may be due to the reader not recognizing the context. Such a failure to recognize the context may have several causes: the reader may be strongly expecting some other topic or point of view; the reader may be distracted; or, as Carrell and Wallace (1983) point out, there may not be sufficient textual cues to signal the content. In their study, they investigated the individual and interactive effects of context and familiarity on the comprehension of second language readers. In this study, they developed texts which were opaque, i.e., which contained sentences such as 'The task is extremely simple. It is not even necessary to do each one separately—they can all be done at more or less the same time ...' (308). This passage was designed to be about brushing teeth. Further, the texts were on topics that were very familiar to all students (brushing teeth), moderately familiar (setting a mouse trap), or unfamiliar to most students (sonar). Participants in the study were presented with the texts either with a picture and title, or without a picture or title. The results indicated that the contextualization aided the native speakers but did not help the non-native speakers, even for advanced-level ESL students. The second language readers remained text-bound and did not use the context to activate their schema as an aid to comprehension.

Yet prior knowledge is not always a facilitating factor in second language reading. Hammadou (1991) examined the effects of prior knowledge on the recall of text by foreign language students studying French and Italian in an American university. The students were in levels 101 and 104 of the language courses fulfilling the university language requirement. The students were given three newspaper articles to read. They then recalled what they had read after each passage. When they had finished the recall of the three texts, they were given a list of the topics that they had just read about and asked to rank order these according to their familiarity with the topic. The recall protocols were scored according to the percentage of possible propositions contained in each. The results showed no significant difference between comprehension of familiar and unfamiliar topics across all readers. The results also showed no significant differences between the familiar and unfamiliar recall for the more proficient readers and the less proficient readers. The study further failed to find a significant relationship between background knowledge and number of inferences in the recall protocols. In this instance, then, it appears that background knowledge may have played no significant role in second language reading comprehension. However, this lack of a demonstrated effect may in fact be due to problems internal to the particular study, problems that Hammadou readily acknowledges. First, it may be the case that the 104 level students are still novice readers of the languages. Thus, the absence of an effect for proficiency may be due to the fact that there actually were not two significantly different levels of ability. Secondly, the subjects were asked to rank order the three topics of the readings according to their familiarity. Rank ordering can mask the actual differences in degree of familiarity. In fact, the method of rating their knowledge on a three-point scale of familiarity may not actually elicit information about the amount of background knowledge the reader has. Further, the subjects rank ordered the topics after they had read the passages. Thus, they may have been ranking the perceived difficulty level of the texts. In any case, the study does not find support for schema as an aid to second language reading comprehension, regardless of proficiency level. Additional research is needed to examine the validity of this approach to tapping background knowledge.

Chen and Donin (1997) obtained results that contradicted those of Hammadou (1991) with more advanced second language readers. Their study involved 36 native Mandarin-speaking students in Montreal. Each read biology texts via computer in English and Chinese that were matched in terms of number of propositions, propositional types, text structure, number of technical terms in biology, and syntactic complexity. It was assumed that the biology majors would be high background knowledge and the engineering majors would be low background knowledge for biology. Time of reading was considered an indication of lower-level lexical and syntactic processing while amount of free recall was taken to be a measure of semantic higher-level processing.

The results of Chen and Donin's study indicated that when reading in English, the high background knowledge readers read faster than the low background knowledge readers, but this was not the case when reading Chinese. Additionally, the high background knowledge readers recalled more propositions from the texts across languages, and English language proficiency between the subjects did not make a difference. That is, high-knowledge readers had an advantage regardless of whether they were in a high English ability group or not. This conflicts somewhat with the Hammadou finding that familiarity did not enhance scores. This result may have obtained because of differences in the two studies regarding the language threshold of the participants mentioned in Chapter 3. The Chinese readers in the Chen and Donin study were more advanced in their second language, English, than Hammadou's subjects were in theirs, French and Italian. The Chinese readers were students in courses that were largely English medium, so they were well beyond the 101 and 104 college level students in Hammadou's study. For the Chinese participants, background knowledge was the primary factor, not relative language ability.

Thus, cumulatively, these studies indicate that cultural interpretations can affect text comprehension. Culturally familiar topics are recalled in more detail and tend to have fewer false intrusions and misinterpretations than less familiar topics. In addition, the effect for background knowledge appears to be influenced by the relative second language ability level of the readers. However, the literature is not consistent as to whether it also takes less time to read familiar texts. This is likely to be a factor that is related to text charac-teristics, task, as well as topic familiarity. The findings of studies on know-ledge and inferencing lend support to the view that background knowledge plays a role in the types of learning that take place during reading. Further, these studies tend to support the notion that background knowledge facilitates the reading process, to the extent that speed of processing is a reflection of reading ease.

Cultural background and text complexity

In addition to the role of background knowledge, second language researchers have been interested in the extent to which background knowledge interacts with text difficulty. Johnson (1981) looked at the effects of both language complexity and cultural background on reading comprehension of conventional folk tales. In her study, a sample of 46 Iranian intermediate- to advanced-level ESL students and 19 American subjects were presented with two stories, one that was based on Mullah Nasr-el-Din from Iranian folklore and the other based on the American folk tale of Buffalo Bill. Each story had a linguistically adapted (simplified) version and an unadapted version. The subjects from each cultural group were randomly assigned to two groups. One group read the unadapted texts and the other read the adapted texts. After reading, the subjects were asked to recall the story in writing as well as to take a multiple-choice test on explicit and implicit information from the text. The results showed that the level of syntactic and semantic complexity had less of an effect than the cultural origin of the story. The ESL subjects recalled more propositions from the Iranian-based story than from the American-based story with no effect due to language complexity (i.e. adapted versus unadapted). Both the Iranian and American subjects recalled more propositions from the culturally familiar story. It appears that when the Iranian subjects confronted a culturally unfamiliar component in the story, they were unable to utilize even simplified language to disambiguate the text. However, the study does not present external information regarding the language level of the subjects in order to determine whether the adapted text was much easier than the unadapted text, or whether the adapted text was at the students' level of language ability. Nevertheless, the finding that content familiarity can overcome linguistic complexity has implications for how classroom materials are selected and presented. Clearly, linguistic simplification alone is not the complete solution for students reading at levels near the language threshold level.

Clearly, teasing out the relationships between text characteristics and background knowledge or topic familiarity is not easy. Barry and Lazarte (1998) examined the role of background knowledge, text complexity and reading topic on subjects' recall of text and the types of inferences that the subjects made. In their study, students in their junior and senior years of high school studying third-and fourth-year Spanish were presented with texts of different levels of syntactic complexity, defined as the number of embedded clauses in the sentences of the text. Further, they had a high-knowledge group which had studied a lesson on the Incas of Peru, and a low-knowledge group which had little or no knowledge about the Incas. Subjects were presented with three reading passages about Incan history and life. The results indicated that the high-knowledge readers constructed a richer and more accurate representation of the texts than did the low-knowledge readers. They showed that high-knowledge readers in second language elaborate the more complex text with knowledge-based inferences, thus resorting to a more top-down process when increased syntactic complexity requires more attentional resources. Low-knowledge readers, on the other hand, relied considerably more on bottom-up strategies that were primarily propositional representations of the text. The study found that for the total number of inferences in the recall protocols there was both a significant effect for background knowledge and for syntactic complexity, but that the effect for background knowledge was greater. Further, they found there was an effect for background knowledge, but not for syntactic complexity, in terms of the proportion of incorrect inferences made by the readers.

Carrell (1983) examined the interaction of variables on two levels of ESL readers and one group of native English speakers. She examined how readers were affected by three variables in the selected texts: contextualization versus non-contextualization; text transparency versus non-transparency; and familiar topic versus novel topic. The two texts selected were adaptations from Bransford and Johnson's (1973) Washing Clothes text (discussed in Chapter 1) and another or their texts generally referred to as the Balloon Serenade text, texts that are ambiguous as to the topic of the passage. The subjects read the two passages which were in one of four conditions: 1) a non-concrete text which was contextualized with pictures and title; 2) a concrete text which was contextualized with pictures and title; 3) a non-concrete text which was not contextualized with pictures and title; and 4) a concrete text which was not contextualized with pictures and title. After reading the text, subjects recalled as much as they could remember from the passage in English. Carrell found that while native speakers utilized context (presence of title and picture), text transparency (presence or absence of concrete lexical items), and familiarity in a top-down processing mode to make predictions about what a text will be about, the non-native speakers of English did not process text in the same way. Neither the advanced nor high-intermediate ESL readers in her study appeared to utilize context or textual clues. In effect, they were not efficient top-down processors. Further, only the most advanced ESL readers were affected by familiarity. Thus, the non-native readers failed to use background information until they were relatively advanced readers because, according to Carrell, they were essentially linguistically bound.

However, subsequent studies have had findings contrasting with those of Carrell (1983). Lee (1986) replicated the Carrell study with the exception that during the recall of the texts the subjects used their first language to produce the recall, rather than their second language as in the Carrell study. His subjects were enrolled in third-year Spanish classes at the University of Illinois (Urbana/Champaign). He found that all three components of background knowledge (context, familiarity, and transparency) played some role in comprehension and recall of the Spanish texts. Additionally, he found an interaction effect among the three variables. The results of the study show that context was significant only in the familiar/transparent passage. Additionally, recall of the novel topic was enhanced only when no title or picture preceded the passage. Thus, he found that the use of pictures was differentially effective. This should not be surprising in that it stands to reason that not all pictures are of equal quality or relevance to a particular passage. Finally, his research points out that by allowing the subjects to respond through their first language, different results as to the role of background knowledge may be found. Lee's findings differed from those of Carrell in several ways. First, he did not find a familiarity effect. Further, he found a two-way interaction between context and familiarity, as well as a general three-way interaction. Thus, Lee's study does not support Carrell's finding that non-native readers do not show an effect of background knowledge on reading, comprehending, or recalling the target language passages.

In another study using the passages employed by Carrell (1983) and Lee (1986), Roller and Matambo (1992) found that second language readers did use background knowledge while reading. This study involved Zimbabwean students who were very proficient second language speakers of English. Here, the subjects' native language was Shona, a Bantu language. They were in their 13th year of schooling. However, English was the language of instruction, and except for their African language courses, all schooling was in English. Eighty students were randomly assigned to one of the four following experimental conditions: 1) English with no picture; 2) English with a picture; 3) Shona with no picture; and 4) Shona with a picture. All of the subjects read both the familiar passage (Washing Clothes) and the unfamiliar passage (Balloon Serenade). They found significant main effects for language, and for familiarity. The students performed better in English, their second language, than in Shona. They also performed better on the unfamiliar Balloon Serenade passage than they did on the familiar Washing Clothes passage, supporting Carrell's finding. There was no main effect for context. Their findings of an interaction of context by familiarity are similar to Lee's findings. Subjects who saw the picture recalled more on the Washing Clothes passage than those who saw no picture, but the subjects who saw no picture performed better on the Balloon Serenade passage than did those who saw a picture.

There are a few issues that should be taken into account when interpreting the studies just mentioned which used the Washing Clothes and the Balloon

Serenade passage and their associated pictures. It is not at all clear that washing clothes is in fact a more familiar topic than a serenade, given the effect of modern media. Far more movies and television programs have shown a serenade than someone washing clothes as a salient event. In fact, given that all three studies using this passage failed to show that it was more familiar, there is fairly strong evidence that washing clothes was not necessarily familiar to all of the subjects in the various studies. Second, the passages were intentionally written to be ambiguous. In many instances pictures associated with the passages may not disambiguate the text at all for many readers. However, there does appear to be some indication that background knowledge plays a role in text processing. It is not clear whether the interactions of context by familiarity are due to interference of the pictures or whether it is simply the case that unfamiliar topics are best comprehended when energy is placed on reading the text rather than attaching meaning to a graphic associated with the text. This is an area that still requires more research with non-contrived passages.

Cultural background and text genre characteristics

Text complexity has also been viewed in terms of genre rather than merely in terms of syntactic complexity or specific cultural differences. Although the next chapter explicitly examines in detail the role of formal schema knowledge by readers, there are additional questions about the relationships that exist between content schema and formal schema as reflected by text structure. Malik (1990) expressed concern that so much of the literature on the role of schema in second language reading has been conducted using narrative stories rather than expository text of the type readers encounter in different content fields. He compared Iranian ESL university students in the US on their comprehension of a culturally familiar passage about Iranian myths and a culturally unfamiliar passage about Japanese myths. Both passages came from the *Encyclopaedia Britannica*. Each subject read one text and then the second text after a one-week interval. The subjects were told prior to reading that they would be asked to recall as much of the material as possible. Idea units from the texts were identified and weighted as important or not important. The results show that the reading comprehension was significantly higher for the culturally familiar text than for the culturally unfamiliar text. There was no significant difference between the subjects' reading speed on the two passages, unlike the results in Steffensen et al. (1979). Further, the subjects were less able to distinguish important information from less important information in the culturally unfamiliar text than in the culturally familiar passage. Malik concludes that the use of schemata most likely played a role in the superior comprehension of the familiar topic. Further, he concludes that a schema enables a reader to distinguish important information from less important information. However, there are some caveats in interpreting Malik's findings. First, he inappropriately uses multiple t-tests without any adjustments in the significance level. Thus, his finding of significant differences may reflect chance differences. Second, it would have been useful to see whether Japanese reading the two texts reacted in the same way that the Iranian subjects did with reference to familiar and unfamiliar myths. Finally, it is not clear that the myths were uniformly familiar to everyone from each culture.

Carrell (1987) investigated the simultaneous effects of both culture-specific content schema and formal schema with ESL students. One group of students had a Muslim background and the second group had a Catholic background and were primarily Spanish speakers from Central and South America. The reading passages were based on two fictionalized characters, one from each culture, 'Ali Affani', and 'St. Catherine'. Each text contained an episode about the early life of the character and the later part of the character's life, and concluded with the character's death. Two rhetorical versions of each text were constructed: 1) straight chronological order (familiar form); and 2) an interleaved order in which the early part of the character's life was presented second (unfamiliar form). After reading each text, the students answered multiple-choice questions and wrote a recall of the text without referring back to the text. The results of the study indicated that content of the text was a stronger predictor of performance than was the familiar or unfamiliar organization of the text. Thus, reading familiar content was relatively easy even when that content was in an unfamiliar format. Subjects familiar with the content of the texts tended to recall more propositions representing main topics and main idea units. However, the rhetorical form did have some impact on the recall protocols in that the passages read in the interleaved format tended to have recall protocols that merged the two episodes without a clear delineation that one part of the text was about the character's early life and the other about the character's later life. However, in general, the research indicates that topic familiarity is of more importance than familiarity with text structure, at least for such short texts with single central characters as the focus.

Many of the studies discussed thus far point out an additional research problem which also contributes to the conflicting research results in many other studies as well. This issue involves the inherent problem with operationalizing the construct of *background knowledge*. Some researchers use self-report strategies whereby the subjects of the study rank order their familiarity with a list of topics. This frequently becomes problematic to the extent that the subjects of the study actually know how much they know about a topic. For example, Hammadou (1991) asked her subjects to assign a number from 1 to 3 to each set of topics, either sports, cinema, and biography, or AIDS, the stealth bomber and Sudan. Recall that in this study, there was no significant effect for background knowledge, a result that may be in part due to the fact that the subjects had to decide whether they knew what the stealth bomber was in general, or whether they needed to know about how it operated from a technical perspective. Other researchers have used multiple-choice tests about a particular topic, vocabulary tests in a topic area, recall protocols, structured questioning, and completion. Valencia et al. (1991) found that different types of measures that assess background knowledge had inconsistencies in their correlations and that different measures elicited different amounts of information. They thus recommend multiple forms of assessment. With both the self-report and the approaches that sample content more broadly, a common concern is just how narrowly to define the background knowledge area so that it is indeed a definable area, not just a topic of common knowledge, yet is not so narrow as to be accessible only to experts in that particular field.

Summary and conclusions

There is a great deal of evidence that indicates a relationship between content schema and reading comprehension. Familiarity with the topic of a text is essential for readers in either first language or second language to understand, or even approximate, a writer's message. However, the exact nature of the interaction is not clear. As noted in Chapter 3, there are issues regarding a linguistic threshold and the ability to activate background knowledge in order to facilitate comprehension. An additional issue that clouds implications from the research is that many variables have not been controlled in the research. Subjects of many different ages, backgrounds, levels of ability, first languages, as well as those who are ESL versus those who are EFL versus those taking modern language classes such as university Spanish or French classes, have all been included in the research. The inter-actions of those variables are still not clear. However, considerations of background knowledge cannot be ignored when attempting to understand second language reading comprehension. Further, this is more than an issue of how much prior knowledge the reader has. It also concerns the quality of knowledge, of how that knowledge is organized and the depth and flexibility of the knowledge by the reader.

Carrell (1988) looks at much of the earlier research into the effects of back-ground knowledge on second language reading. She notes that there are many conflicting research findings on second language readers' use of schema. Some studies (Carrell 1983; Carrell and Wallace 1983) show that second lan-guage readers may not effectively utilize knowledge-based processes. They may not utilize contextual information they are supplied with to facilitate comprehension. These readers appear to engage almost exclusively in text-based processing rather than applying background knowledge in the comprehension process. However, other studies of second language reading have found that readers often rely too heavily on top-down background knowledge processes that cause interference. Thus, some readers are reluctant risk takers, sticking closely to the printed word, while others are much more impetuous in their knowledge-based processing. Carrell notes that one reason for over-reliance on the text is an absence of the appropriate knowledge structures for top-down processing. Such an absence of the appropriate content schemata may lead some readers to rely totally on the text-based processes while others may rely on the closest schema they have and will attempt to reconcile new information with that schema.

Discussion and study questions

1 Several of the studies discussed report on the effects of personal knowledge and cultural background for children and adults reading texts. What concepts are developed regarding the following with respect to second language reading, second language reading instruction, and second language reading materials selection:
   A age, sex, race, religion, nationality, occupation?
   B children and adults having differing amounts of background knowledge?
   C the existence of cultural universals?
   D any potential interactions between linguistic complexity of the text, linguistic proficiency of the reader, and the reader's background knowledge?
   E systematicity of transfer of first language reading ability to second language reading?
2 A concern raised by Reynolds et al. (1982) is that the existence of cultural schema could have effects on whether tests or materials introduce bias against minority groups. Given that many studies of the effect of cultural schema are based on different cultures, perhaps in different places, involving subjects who are reading passages based on different cultural assumptions, do you see any complications in interpreting their study as relating to second language readers? That is, given that the passages were directed toward a minority culture within a larger educational environment, are there any caveats we might want to make for contexts in which the minority culture has access to the majority culture via television and other media, while the majority culture has much less access to the minority culture?
3 Roller and Matambo (1992) found that learners used background knowledge. They also found that their readers performed better in second language than in first language. How can you explain the findings?

4 Gaskins' (1996) study looks at how emotional involvement (as opposed
   simply to background knowledge) can affect interpretation of connected
   text. The study confirms that the more emotionally involved a reader is,
   the more difficult it is for that person to critically analyze the text. Data
   from his Table 1 (395) are presented below. At least two issues seem to arise
   from this study: 1) How do we interpret the results in Table 1 regarding the
   number of 'equal' responses; and 2) How do we translate such findings
   based on reading about a basketball game to reading of academic text if we
   are concerned about successful reading of academic text?

Group	Philadelphia/ Rapid City	Boston/ Topeka	Equal
Question 1 – Responsibility for the rough play			
Avid 76ers fans	1	13	10
Avid Celtics fans	9	3	10
Control group	4	7	13
Question 2 – Responsibility for the fight			
Avid 76ers fans	4	12	8
Avid Celtics fans	12	3	9
Control group	6	7	11
Question 3 – Favoritism by the referees toward one team			
Avid 76ers fans	0	5	19
Avid Celtics fans	5	0	19
Control group	4	5	15

*Table 1: A summary of the responses to the interview questions (From
Gaskins 1996)*

5 Carrell (1988) assumes that ESL readers will sometimes over-rely on
   text-based processes, and try to construct the meaning totally from the
   text. There is a basic belief here that trying to construct the meaning totally
   from the textual input is virtually impossible, because no text contains all
   the information necessary for comprehension. Do you agree with this
   assumption that no text contains sufficient information necessary for its
   comprehension? Why or why not? How can different types of texts vary
   in this?

6 Many of the studies note that readers will sometimes over-rely on top-
   down processing. That is, if no relevant schema is available, readers will
   substitute the closest schema they possess and try to relate the incoming
   textual information to that schema, resulting in schema interference.
   Where do 'appropriate schemata' come from? In other words, how do
   'relevant schemata' initially get activated?

7 Do readers and writers share equally in the responsibility to ensure that relevant schemata get activated?

8 Several of the studies also indicate that previously held opinions affect interpretation and memory. What is the relationship between opinions and schemata?

9 How is the relationship between cultural identity and the individual often oversimplified? How can the expectations of task demand differ across cultures and individuals within that culture?

10 Can you think of instances in which conflicting internalized scripts for cultural events affected your own or others' comprehension of an event or story?

11 How would you measure 'background knowledge' of a particular topic? Pick a topic and explain how you would measure this.

7 FORMAL SCHEMA AND SECOND LANGUAGE READING

Introduction

In the introduction to Chapter 6, it was noted that both content and formal schemata may affect how a second language reader comprehends a text. That chapter also discussed the role that content background schemata may play in reading comprehension by second language readers. The present chapter will examine how formal schemata may interact with a reader's comprehension processes. The surface-level manifestations in a text present phenomena that can assist second language reading. That is, there are internal structures to a text that may aid (or perhaps hinder) the reader's success. Further, these structures are situated in social life. Formal schemata represent the reader's knowledge relative to the language, conventions, and rhetorical structures of different types of text. Each of these aspects of formal schemata, as with content schemata, plays a role in how a reader establishes the coherence of a particular text. Further, as with content schemata, formal schematic knowledge need not be conscious knowledge. As it addresses formal schemata and the second language reading process, this chapter examines the roles of ORTHOGRAPHY, syntax, cohesion, and TEXT STRUCTURE. The related, but distinct, issues of contrastive rhetoric and genre in different discourse communities will be addressed in Chapter 8.

Orthographic and phonemic knowledge

As discussed earlier, learners learning a second language are often already literate in their first language. To the extent that this is true, they will have existing knowledge that the graphic features they encounter on a page or screen are to be translated into language with a meaning. Also, as noted in Chapter 4, readers are sensitive to the rules of their script or writing system whether that system is LOGOGRAPHIC (Chinese characters, Japanese Kanji, Korean Hanzza), syllabic (Japanese Kana, Korean Hangul), or alphabetic (Arabic, English, Hebrew, Spanish), with each corresponding symbol representing a word, morpheme, syllable, or phonological segment.

Logographs (logo = word, graph = written sign) primarily represent the meaning of words or morphemes, only secondarily representing the sounds of the words. Phonetic scripts, on the other hand, have the sounds and sound sequences of morphemes and words as a basis. However, the logogram versus phonogram distinction is not in fact a complete dichotomy of orthographic principles. Both Chinese and Japanese have cases in which characters are primarily phonetic representations of syllables or parts of syllables with little regard to any symbol–meaning correspondence (DeFrancis 1989; Unger and DeFrancis 1995). Indeed, some scholars prefer the term sinographic to logographic (Birch 2002; Henderson 1982) because Chinese characters are not completely logographic in nature, given the presence of written RADICALS in approximately 80 per cent of the characters.

The extent to which learners' first language orthographic features are similar to those of the second language will affect the ease with which they make the transition into fluent second language reading. For example, although readers come from a language that uses the same alphabetic script as that of the target language, the languages will differ in terms of the distribution of letters, general length of the written words, amount and types of diacritical marks, allowable consonant clusters, and frequency of upper and lower case, etc. (Ferreiro 2002). Further, even if the alphabetic system is somewhat different from the target language script (for example from Spanish to English or Greek to English), learning will be easier than if the learner is from a non-alphabetic script (for example from Chinese to English) or is moving from an alphabetic script to a logographic orthography (for example from Spanish to Chinese). For example, this sentence **gradually becomes** MORE *complex* TO process as **THE orthography** CHANGES from the FAMILIAR.

Given the differing orthographic units, cognitive processes in reading may be seen to vary both in how the phonological code operates, and in contrasting strategies that may be used to access the phonological codes (Koda 1995). However, research has indicated that readers of logographic orthographies also use phonological encoding to access short-term memory in the reading process (Koda 1995). Strategies in phonemically represented languages vary according to the extent to which there is a clear consistent one-to-one correspondence of letter to sound. For instance, Spanish and Serbo-Croatian have much closer correspondences between letter and sound strings in each language than do English and French. With logographically represented languages, the phonological information is not clearly represented graphically, though Chinese characters do contain some phonological information through radicals associated with single characters, as just noted. Sounds are arbitrarily assigned to the graphic representation and are not directly derivable (Koda 1995). Thus, dialects of Chinese employ the same characters for words that have unintelligible pronunciations to speakers of different dialects. As a result, decoding of such characters involves memory-search strategies as well as a certain amount of arbitrary sound assignment to unfamiliar symbols.

Just as second language learners apply their existing first language content schemata to the reading process, it appears that they may apply their first language orthographic processing strategies when reading in a second language as well. Mori (1998) examined how readers from morphographic (Chinese and Korean) and phonographic language backgrounds (English) processed novel Japanese pseudo-characters that were either phonologically opaque or phonologically accessible. The pseudo-characters contained differing combinations of outer and inner radicals associated with the pronunciation of the character. The subjects had completed approximately 100 hours of Japanese study at the college level. Subjects were shown the characters and then engaged in a memory task for the new characters. The results indicated that subjects from the morphographic language backgrounds processed the phonologically inaccessible and accessible symbols equally well while the subjects from the phonological orthography background performed better on the phonologically accessible pseudo-characters than on the phonologically inaccessible pseudo-characters. Thus, the two groups applied orthographic processing strategies that were consonant with those from their own first language. Their knowledge of how script is processed in their first language was applied to the unique characters in the target language. Native Chinese and English speakers learning to read Japanese attend to visual and phonological information differently. Chikamatsu (1996) showed that Chinese readers learning Japanese relied more on visual information in Japanese kana than did English readers, while the English readers attended to the phonological information in the Japanese kana more than the Chinese readers did. Word recognition differs between languages depending upon the language and characteristics of the writing system, and the ability to deal with the differences in the writing systems depends to a large extent upon reading proficiency in each of the languages (Chitiri et al. 1992).

Akamatsu (2003) examined the interaction of first language orthographic processing in second language reading of connected text. She was concerned that much of the research into second language orthographic processing has been done utilizing pseudo-words or non-words processed as single words without contextual clues. The study used case manipulation of letters in longer text. For example, one of her texts begins 'ThErE iS nO aBsOlUtE lImIt To ThE eXiStEnCe Of AnY tReE' (230). The subjects were native speakers of Farsi (alphabetic), Chinese (logographic), or Japanese (logographic and syllabic). The three groups did not differ significantly in their English reading ability based on TOEFL and Gray Oral Reading Test results. Each subject read case-alternating texts and normal texts at easy, moderate, and difficult text levels and answered comprehension questions. Reading times were recorded. As might be predicted, the results showed that the passages printed in normal case were read significantly more quickly and accurately than those in alternated case, and easy passages were read faster than moderate passages which were read faster than the difficult passages. The Chinese and Japanese first language subjects read significantly more slowly than the Farsi readers, but there was no difference in comprehension scores. Thus, first language orthographic processing may affect word recognition efficiency, but does not necessarily negatively affect comprehension.

Differences in knowledge of how orthographic systems operate can affect the success of reading in a new language. The formal schematic knowledge by native readers of English that phonetic orthographies can contain grammatical elements such as tense markers (-ed) and part of speech indicators (-tion) is useful strategic information, while native readers of Chinese will not necessarily have that knowledge because Chinese writing does not represent syntactic features in this way. Likewise, the formal knowledge that an alphabetic system containing combinations of 26 letters can represent all words of the language is important in how one goes about processing the text. Finally, native readers of such consonantal languages as Arabic and Hebrew which do not necessarily explicitly mark all vowels will have knowledge about processing texts in those languages that native readers of English, which explicitly provides most vowels in each word, will not. Thus, the formal knowledge a reader possesses about how script operates can affect reading success in a new second language reading context.

Syntax and language structure

As noted in Chapter 3, accounts of a learner's second language reading proficiency will need to include an examination of the learner's general syntactic, morphological, and lexical knowledge. These interact with one another and with the characteristics of the text and tasks the reader confronts. The role that syntactic knowledge plays in second language reading comprehension would on the face of it appear to be pervasive. It appears self-evident that a second language reader's command of grammar is essential to comprehension of the text meaning. Indeed, many of the traditional readability-based approaches to text modification are based almost entirely on syntactic simplification of texts. However, the strength of the role that syntax plays is quickly attenuated by the recognition that there must be some minimum linguistic threshold, as mentioned previously, for the reader to be able to process text, and the role of direct syntactic control may diminish as the reader passes this threshold.

The level of control will need to be both in terms of recognizing the salient features and being able to process the syntactic system with some efficiency.

For example, look at the following sentence (Langacker 1972: 157):

pama-lu tyulpin wanta-re-lna
pama   = man
lu   = ergative case marking
tyulpin = tree
wanta   = fall
ri   = causative affix
lna   = future marker

Regardless of how accomplished a reader the learner is in his or her first language, little comprehension of this sentence will happen unless the learner understands the syntactic and morphological features of Tyapukay, a language of Australia. The learner will not understand that the sentence means 'The man will fell the tree'. The fact that future aspect is indicated by an affix rather than a particle and that the causative marker is also an affix are essential pieces of formal schemata that are necessary for comprehension of the sentence.

One reason that syntactic formal schemata are of interest to second language researchers is reflected in accounts of how this knowledge affects the ease or difficulty of texts that the second language readers may encounter. In short, the issues involve questions about how to create textual input that is more comprehensible to the language learner. The research presents no clear-cut unambiguous account of this relationship. Barnett (1986) addressed several issues concerning syntax and vocabulary in reading through investigations of the relative importance of lexical/semantic and syntactic knowledge in reading comprehension. She points out that past research into these relationships has produced conflicting findings, noting that some research indicates that readers have a much easier time reading a syntactically simplified text than they do with topically and structurally similar unsimplified texts. On one hand, simplification can make a text more comprehensible for a reader (Aronson-Berman 1978), while other studies have shown that syntax is not a large issue in comprehension, particularly for readers who are the intended audience of a text. Charrow (1988), for example, contrasted two types of altered technical texts in first language reading. One type of alteration involved the syntactic simplification of the text while the other involved revision to increase the clarity, cohesion, and text structure (see the next sections in this chapter for more on this topic). The version modified for clarification, cohesion, and text structure produced greater gains in comprehension than did modification along syntactic lines. Ulijn and Strother (1990) similarly found no differences in comprehension of English for science and technology texts whether the texts were simplified or not. However, Barry and Lazarte (1995) found that the effect of a second language reader's familiarity with content could be cancelled out by text containing complex embedded clauses in Spanish. Other research indicates that readers engaged with a technical text have more difficulty with content words than with syntactic function words (Ulijn 1980). Additionally, Hatch, Polin, and Part (1974) indicated that although first language readers attend to content words more than to syntactic function words while reading, ESL readers focus on both function and content words because the syntax is unfamiliar to them.

Several additional studies have looked at the role of text simplification in reading comprehension. Blau (1982) examined the effect that manipulation of sentence structure had on readers' comprehension of text. In her study, she developed three versions each of 18 short passages. Version 1 was comprised of short simple sentences; version 2 was made up of complex sentences with clues to underlying relationships; and version 3 consisted of complex sentences without the clues to underlying relationships. Vocabulary and content were held constant across the three versions. Each paragraph was followed by two or three multiple-choice comprehension questions. The passages and associated questions were given to college and eighth-grade students in Puerto Rico. For both groups, the more complex version 2 was comprehended better than the supposedly easier version 1. Her results indicate that short relatively simplified syntax does not result in text that is more comprehensible. So, simplification of syntax itself is insufficient in making complex text easier to comprehend.

In two related studies, Strother and Ulijn (1987) and Ulijn and Strother (1990), the role of syntactic simplification was examined for readers whose native languages were English, Dutch, Chinese, Spanish, and Arabic, as well as a small number of other languages, while they were reading English for science and technology texts. A text related to computer mass storage was simplified to avoid nominalizations, passives, and participial constructions, thus producing a text more suitable as a 'common language' version. The text was given to computer science majors and humanities majors, followed by ten true/false questions. The study also looked at the length of time it took each subject to read the passage. It was found that there were no significant differences between the groups reading the authentic or the simplified text either in terms of comprehension or reading time. Nor were there differences between the computer science majors and the humanities majors. Thus, they found no results indicating the effectiveness of syntactic adaptation in order to make texts easier for comprehension. In this study, then, the role of syntax in comprehension is not simply one of apparent linguistic complexity.

Leow (1993) examined the effects of lexical and syntactic simplification, type of linguistic item (present perfect versus present subjunctive), and amount of language exposure, as measured by number of semesters in a Spanish as a foreign language course. Although the study was primarily focused on how these variables affected intake, it is revealing about how formal syntactic knowledge affects reading. The results indicated that simplification did not assist students who had not been exposed to the target forms. Rather, subjects who had been exposed to the present perfect and the present subjunctive recognized more of the target forms than those who had not been exposed to the forms. Thus, not surprisingly, overt knowledge of the syntactic forms facilitates their recognition in connected text.

However, there have been studies indicating that syntactic modification of texts may have a facilitative role for some learners. Yano, Long, and Ross (1994) studied the effects of simplified, elaborated, and unmodified text on reading comprehension. They found that both simplified and elaborated text versions increased comprehension of short texts over unmodified versions of the same texts. Likewise, Oh (2001) found that simplified and elaborated text generally increased comprehension over unmodified text. However, she found that this improvement was only the case for her higher-level English ability subjects. Neither simplification nor elaboration significantly improved comprehension for her lower-level language ability subjects. Elaboration and simplification improved comprehension about the same amount, though neither was statistically significantly higher than the unmodified versions of the text for these learners. These findings are interesting in that they appear to indicate that very low-level learners may take advantage of the redundancy of content material in reading difficult texts to a greater extent than they take advantage of syntax that is simplified, and considered linguistically easier. Further, the findings by both studies, that elaboration of text can improve comprehension about as well as simplification, create questions as to how much of the reading problem is actually due to syntactic complexity, given that the elaborated texts were much longer and complex than the simplified passages. However, it is also the case that the studies do not indicate whether the two types of modification improve overall reading ability over time as opposed to simply making a particular text more accessible.

The relative contribution of lexical and syntactic knowledge is also an issue that is of frequent concern. There has been some anxiety that reading instruction over the past decades has led to an abandonment of attention to syntax in favor of a focus on vocabulary. In order to clarify the relationships, Barnett's (1986) study examined the hypothesis that 'the ability of English-speaking readers to comprehend a French text depends more on lexical/semantic analysis than on syntactic analysis' (344). She administered multiple-choice cloze tests based on two French reading passages to fourth-semester students of French during their third week of class. The correct choice for half of the items depended upon knowledge of syntax while the other half required knowledge of vocabulary. After completing the cloze passages, the students were provided with a longer version of the original text and were asked to recall as much of the passages as they could. The number of propositions recalled was used as the measure of comprehension. Using the results on the cloze tests, the students were classified into groups having high, medium, or low knowledge of vocabulary and syntax. The results of the study indicated a possible interaction between syntax and vocabulary on recall. However, the students with low syntactic knowledge were not aided regardless of their vocabulary score. Likewise, high syntax scores did not aid students with low vocabulary knowledge. At the upper levels of both syntactic and lexical knowledge there was an interaction such that high syntax could aid medium vocabulary and vice versa. Barnett's conclusions are that vocabulary not be stressed to the exclusion of syntax since syntax appears to play a significant role in comprehension.

Thus, there appears to be a level in both syntactic and lexical knowledge that is minimally needed for comprehension of a second language text, taking us back to the threshold issues raised in Chapter 3 and elsewhere. Unfortunately, the Barnett study does not reveal information regarding the qualitative nature of the threshold itself. First, as with many other studies reviewed so far, her groups were determined by dividing the students into three approximately numerically equal groups. This practice obscures any actual differences that might exist as meaningful *levels* of competence. For the syntax cloze items, the range of scores in each level was: low = 10–17; medium = 18–24; high = 21–24. For the vocabulary items, the ranges of scores were: low = 10–15; medium = 16–18; high = 19–24. Given the narrow ranges in scores for the medium and high groups, the students may not actually have represented different groups in terms of language ability. However, the standard deviations and general descriptive statistics are not reported, so it is not possible to determine what the distribution of scores is actually like. Any aberrant score by a student in any one of the groupings could radically affect the results.

Although there appears to be a limited systematic relationship between syntactic complexity and the comprehensibility of a text, there certainly is some relationship between knowledge of grammar and reading ability. Alderson (1993) reports on a project that compared results from a grammar test with those from reading tests covering such areas as 'science and technology', 'life science', 'arts and social sciences', and 'general non-academic reading'. He reports relatively high correlations (.58 to .80) between the grammar test and the different reading tests. Additionally, in a factor analysis, the reading and grammar tests formed one factor while tests of writing formed a second factor. Thus, there is clearly some relationship between grammatical knowledge and reading ability. Formal knowledge of syntactic features plays a role in text comprehension, but it again appears that it is at the lowest levels of syntactic knowledge that it plays the largest role. That is, once the second language reader has reached some as yet undefined threshold of grammar ability, its impact is reduced in terms of text comprehension.

Cohesion

Cohesive relations are defined as those linguistic features which link one sentence to another without reference to a higher level of analysis (Irwin 1986). Knowledge of how cohesion is realized within a text is essential to interpreting the relationships between textual propositions. As Grabe and Kaplan (1996) note, '[c]ohesion is the means available in the surface forms of the text to signal relationships that exist between sentences or clausal units in the text' (55). Cohesion is achieved through the overt linguistic marking devices (present, absent, implied, or elided) that provide connectedness between sentences, clauses, etc. Cohesion is different from coherence. Coherence involves the connections between the discourse propositions and the context in which they are embedded, while cohesion involves the connections within the textual discourse itself (Campbell 1995). As such, cohesion may aid in establishing coherence. Coherence relies on cohesion, text organization, situational consistency, congruence with the reader's background knowledge, etc., and occurs when the interpretation of some textual element in the discourse is dependent on that of another linguistic element. Connectives such as *although, thus, because, however, consequently*, and *therefore* provide the reader with the relationships between the ideas represented in sentences or clauses. Similarly, referential markers such as *he, this, their*, etc. provide cohesive elements in connecting referents across sentences, clauses, and paragraphs. Moe and Irwin (1986) contend that cohesive relations that tie sentences together help the reader establish a coherent representation of the message. The cohesive devices provide a reader with knowledge about the relationships that are seen to exist between one element of information presented by the author to 'knowledge which is presupposed, either within the text (anaphoric or cataphoric reference, substitution, ellipsis, conjunction) or outside the text (exophoric reference)' (Frederiksen 1977: 314).

Many linguists have provided descriptions of various types and roles of cohesion in text. Grimes (1975) discusses cohesion as 'the way information in speech relates to information that is already available' (272). For him, text information is linguistically blocked into units based on the amount of information that the author believes is new information to the reader. Making this connection, under what Haviland and Clark (1974) call the 'given-new contract' between the author and the reader, establishes textual cohesion. Under this contract, the writer is required to be relevant, to co-operate, and to consider what the reader knows or does not know. Cohesive elements are used to relate the known information to the new information.

Van Dijk (1977) offers a broader view of 'coherence'. He defines coherence intuitively as 'a semantic property of discourses, based on the interpretation of each individual sentence relative to the interpretations of other sentences' (93). Many components of language simultaneously contribute to a text's cohesion. These include components as varied as connectives, implications, verb frames, property relations, condition–consequence relations, general–particular relations, and other semantic relations linking clauses or sentences, which are all viewed as contributing to the coherence of a text. Frequently, coherence relations are implicit rather than explicit because making every coherence relation explicit through cohesive markers would produce a text that is unnatural in being overly complete (Irwin 1986). Van Dijk provides the 'topic' and 'comment' notions parallel to the 'given' and 'new' distinctions of Haviland and Clark discussed above. In this framework, the text can be seen in units of proffered topics which are then expanded upon with comments that supply new information from the author's perspective.

The reader, in either first language or second language, must be aware of the way cohesive ties are structured in order to construct meaning. Halliday and Hasan (1976) have perhaps been most closely identified with the concept of textual cohesion. They define cohesive ties as instances in which words are linked by one of five types of cohesive relationships. These relationships include: 1) referential (pronouns); 2) substitution of one word with another; 3) ellipsis; 4) conjunction, additive, adversative, causal, and temporal; and 5) lexical cohesion, including reiterations and collocation. These are the formal mechanisms which authors use to tie textual material together. Referential relations include cohesion of the type provided by pronouns as in 'Mary drove to the market. She bought some milk'. Substitution relations result when one word or phrase is exchanged for another as in 'Bob likes dogs. Everybody he knows does.' Ellipsis involves the omission of a repeated linguistic element such as 'Would you like to go to the store?' followed by 'I already have'. Conjunction involves the suppliance of a linking relationship between clauses such as 'He planted the seeds before the season was over'. Lexical cohesion involves reiteration or the use of collocations. Examples of reiteration in lexical cohesion would be of the type 'Henry bought himself a new Jaguar. He practically lives in the car'. As examples of collocational cohesion, Halliday and Hasan (1976) present a passage on Yosemite by John Muir in which the following collocational chains occurred: 'mountaineering, Yosemite, summit peaks, climb, ridge; hours, whole day, sundown, sunset, all day, minute; wallowing, sinking, buried, imbedded; ride, riding, ride, travel, travel, travel, flight, motion, flight' (287). The basic argument for the relationship between cohesion and coherence, then, is that generally the greater the number of cohesive markers that are in a text, the greater the coherence, and, further, that the greater the continuity of the marked relationships, the greater the coherence (Hasan 1984).

Some first language research has demonstrated relationships between certain cohesive relations and processing difficulty (Irwin 1986). In terms of co-reference, when one lexical unit refers to another such as Halliday and Hasan's reference, ellipsis, substitution, and some lexical relations, Kintsch et al.

(1975) found that the number of word concepts in a passage was related to reading time and recall of propositions. Apparently, reference assists comprehension and the inclusion of reference markers helps predict reading time and comprehension. For semantic relatedness, Carpenter and Just (1977) found that reading time diminished if the target sentence contained a noun that was entailed by the verb in the sentence preceding it. Entailment is something like 'Many of the students were unable to answer your question' entails 'Only a few of the students grasped your question'. It basically refers to the relations of lexical items with high semantic content versus items such as 'go'. Another example would be 'The dog wagged its _____.' Here there is a strong default for 'tail'.

With connective concepts, van Dijk (1977) and Halliday and Hasan (1976) claim that conjunctions and connectors help comprehension and reading speed, specifically for younger and lower-ability readers. Marshall and Glock (1978) found that explicit conditional relationships, with some subjects, were recalled better than implicit conditional relationships. This assistance of explicit connective concepts has implications for the traditional practice of simplifying text through shortening sentence length. Finally, Graesser (1978) proposes the 'relational density hypothesis' in which it is asserted that the probability of recall of any proposition in a text is a function of the number of other propositions to which the proposition is related. Thus, readers remember highly cohesive text better than less cohesive text. However, it should be kept in mind that no matter how many cohesive elements there are, the underlying semantic relations must make sense in order for us to identify the cohesive markers.

Several studies in first language reading have demonstrated that readers have better comprehension of texts with more cohesion (Beck et al. 1984). Additionally, texts that have been modified to produce clearer cohesive relationships between propositions are comprehended more thoroughly, and create greater awareness of the role played by central events in the causal sequence (Beck et al. 1991). In a review of the relationship between content schemata and formal text-structure schemata, Roller (1990) proposed that the influence of cohesion, as reflected in text structure, interacted with the reader's background knowledge of the text content. The basic argument was that text structure would be most important in comprehension when the reader has moderate familiarity with the content, but decrease in importance as the reader has more familiarity with the content. McKeown et al. (1992) examined Roller's hypothesis of the interaction of text structure and cohesion. Fifth-grade students who were soon to read about the American Revolution in their regular social studies class were provided with background knowledge that contextualized the historical period in terms of cultural and geographical characteristics. Following this instruction, the students read four segments of text materials that were either the original school text or a version of that text revised to incorporate more cohesive relationships among the propositions within the text. The results indicated that the more cohesive text segments were read better than the original text across each of the segments. However, there was a cohesion by text segment interaction, indicating that the advantage for the revised texts was not equal across all four of the text segments. Thus, there were times when ease or difficulty of the segment content still overrode the effect of more versus less cohesive text.

A slightly different take on this interaction of cohesion and difficulty was found by Linderholm et al. (2000) regarding comprehension by college-level readers reading texts at different levels of difficulty. In this study, Linderholm et al. took two texts at different levels of difficulty based on the number of causal connections, referential connections, and explicitly stated goals. The cohesion in the two passages was revised to restore temporal order, repair coherence breaks, and increase explicitness of relationships. They found that both lower- and higher-ability readers benefited from the increased cohesiveness for the initially difficult passage, but not for the initially easier text. In this instance, the easier text apparently already had cohesive ties that were sufficiently explicit given that the basic propositional relationships were not conceptually difficult. It was the more difficult text that became more comprehensible in the text revised to improve coherence. Thus, while increased textual cohesiveness and content background knowledge play a role in comprehension and text memory, such factors as text difficulty and perhaps text length will still feature heavily in the reading process. The reader's knowledge and use of formal schema features interact with other text features.

The role that knowledge of cohesion plays in second language text processing is not clear. Degand and Sanders (2002) found that the presence of causal markers benefited both first language and second language readers of French and Dutch. However, as with much of what has been discussed so far, the second language threshold level is not clear in terms of its effect both on text processing and the reader's reliance upon cohesive markers. Horiba (1993, 1996) focused on the role that level of language ability plays in comprehending causal relationships and reporting of text propositions. These studies note that coherence-based inferences, such as identification of causal and anaphoric relations, are essential in building a coherent text representation. However, in second language reading, the smooth application of text comprehension processes are likely to be disrupted as a result of the reader's inadequate control of the language and limitations of information-processing capacity. Horiba (1996) asserts that since some processes may be prerequisite to other processes, a disrupted process at one level is likely to influence subsequent processes at higher levels. In order to examine the second language reading process of higher- and lower-level interactions, Horiba (1996) conducted a study with four groups: English first language learners of

Japanese as a second language, one high-ability group and one intermediate-ability group, a group of Japanese native speakers, and an English native-speaking first language group. Three types of data were collected: sentence reading times; written free recall of propositions from the story; and verbal think-aloud reports from half of the subjects. After the first recall of the text, the reader read the story again and repeated writing the free recall. The findings indicated that the high-coherence texts were more memorable than the low-coherence texts for the first language readers, but this distinction was not true for the second language readers, except for the advanced second language group on the second reading recall of the text propositions. The data suggest that language competence affects comprehension and recall, and only those learners with high language proficiency were sensitive to the degree of causal coherence, recalling more information from the high-coherence texts than from the low-coherence texts. There is, thus, a confirmation that level of language will affect how well a reader can utilize cohesive devices in a text. Chung (2000) also found that lower-ability second language readers were more sensitive to cohesive devices than more advanced readers.

Some care should be taken in interpreting the causal role of cohesive ties and comprehension. The specification of cohesive ties will not in itself ensure successful text processing by readers. Naturally, processing cohesive ties is most easily accomplished in relatively non-complex descriptions. Al-Jarf (2001) examined the difficulties with cohesive ties encountered by 59 relatively advanced Arabic first language learners of English. The subjects in the study received direct instruction in Halliday and Hasan's (1976) five types of cohesion, and were then tested on the cohesive ties of reference, substitution, conjunction, and ellipsis. Subjects were asked to read a text and write the referent for each anaphor and identify each cohesive tie. The subjects had most problems with processing substitution ('thing' for previously mentioned 'toy') than for any other type of cohesive marker. Ellipsis and reference were the next two most difficult, while conjunction processing proved relatively unproblematic. There were low correlations among the different categories of cohesive relations. The pattern of errors revealed that the strategy used in the errors tended to relate an anaphor with the closest noun that was familiar to the reader. Thus, cohesive relations will be most accurately processed in texts with the fewest participants, not necessarily in the text with the most clearly presented cohesive relationships.

Carrell (1982) offers some cautions about over-interpretation of the role cohesion plays in text coherence. Her arguments are in response to Halliday and Hasan's (1976) claim that '[c]ohesion does not concern what a text means; it concerns how the text is constructed as a semantic edifice' (26). She provides an argument that contrary to the notion that text is coherent because it has cohesive markers, in point of fact text has cohesive markers because the text propositions are coherent. That is, the cohesive markers are a logical consequence of coherence rather than the cause. She bases this argument on the schema-theoretic view that text comprehension is the matching of incoming information with known information, citing research by Tierney and Mosenthal (1980, 1981) which finds no correlation between a text's rated coherence and the quantity of cohesive markers. Further, Freebody and Anderson (1981) found that vocabulary difficulty had dramatic effects on comprehension, but that the number of cohesion markers did not affect comprehension. Finally, the adequacy of the Halliday and Hasan model of cohesion has been challenged because it was initially based primarily on British fiction, particularly Lewis Carroll's *Alice in Wonderland* (Johns 1980). However, much expository text, such as business correspondence and technical writing, uses graphic material and tables, which require different types of cohesive devices to maintain coherence (Campbell 1995).

Additionally, Myers (1991) has noted that cohesive relations differ depending upon type of audience expected by the author. More on this will be discussed later in the discussion of genre analysis and discourse community, but often a great deal of knowledge is required in order to recognize cohesion in text, particularly highly specialized and scientific or technical text. Myers shows that scientific texts and popular texts on a similar topic employ cohesive elements differently. Popular texts on scientific topics, such as those one might find in a newspaper, employ narrative cohesive elements like those discussed in Halliday and Hasan (1976), while more academic scientific texts assume specialized knowledge on the part of the reader. Myers argues that readers of scientific articles 'must have a knowledge of lexical relations to see the implicit cohesion, while readers of popularizations must see the cohesive relations to infer lexical relations' (5). He asserts that a reader's perception of cohesion depends upon a knowledge of what the text is doing. That is, scientific texts need to be understood within the larger processes of scientific argument in scientific communities, while popularizations of science employ different cohesive elements and construct a different narrative of science. Thus, cohesion is a product, in part, of the interaction between an author and the readership.

All of this discussion by Carrell and Myers is not to dismiss the role that cohesion may play in text comprehension. It merely serves as a caveat to the notion that cohesion itself is the cause of coherence within a text. A second language reader's formal knowledge of how cohesive markers operate will affect the ease with which the text is processed and consequently will affect the reader's level of text comprehension. Additionally, knowledge of the system through which cohesion is established can assist second language readers when they confront trouble in text comprehension. The reader can explicitly examine troublesome text to reestablish the cohesive thread within the text.

Text structure

The previous section has indicated some of the effects of cohesion on coherence and comprehension. This section examines research that addresses the role that text structure plays in reading. The term text structure refers to how the ideas in a text are structured to convey a message to a reader (Carrell 1992). Clearly, some of the ideas presented in a text are central to the message and others are less central. Hence, text structure designates how concepts are related as well as which concepts are subordinated to others (Meyer 1999). Research over the past three decades has shown that knowledge of text structure interacts with comprehension. This research has generally focused on the two areas of narratives and expository prose, approaching the internal structure of each genre in different ways.

Narrative

A great deal of the research on text structure has examined the narrative.

Graesser, Golding, and Long (1996) note that narrative discourse has a special status in research and theories of discourse, language use, and literacy in general. People acquire a knowledge of story structure prior to school while the structure of expository text requires explicit instruction and training. Further, narratives are read more quickly than expository text, and scores on recall and comprehension tests are generally higher for NARRATIVE TEXTS than for expository texts. The conceptual basis for narratives lies in sequences of experiences and events that are based in a culture. This grounding provides a source of background knowledge for use in constructing meaning (Graesser et al. 1996). Narratives represent experiences based on events that are organized in knowledge structures that can be predicted by the reader. Several narrative prose studies have looked at schematic textual superstructures (Rumelhart 1975; van Dijk and Kintsch 1983). This research has shown that narratives have a rather hierarchical structure that can be used by readers to aid comprehension. According to Mulcahy and Samuels (1987), these narrative text structures help 'identify, define, and explore the goals of a protagonist and reveal the problem-solving strategies of story characters as they attempt to reach a goal' (248).

Several 'story grammars' have been proposed to account for the internal structure that ties the individual sentences within a narrative together (Mandler 1984; Mandler and Johnson 1977; Rumelhart 1975; Thorndyke 1977; van Dijk and Kintsch 1983). A story grammar is designed to present the hierarchical relationships among story components such as setting and episode, hierarchical relationships that are represented by the story schema. A reader familiar with the narrative schema will look for these components in processing the text and they will guide the reader. The story grammar attempts to describe what elements of a narrative will be most salient to readers, and, by implication, what will be most and least comprehensible.

Story grammars have a number of commonalities in their features (Graesser et al. 1996). Among these common features is that each has a set of rewrite rules that express component regularities. As an example, the following rules have been adapted from Mandler (1987) and Graesser et al. (1996).

1 Story → Setting + Episode(s)
2 Setting → description of the characters, time, location
3 Episode → Beginning + Development + Ending
4 Beginning → an event that initiates the Complex Reaction
5 Development → Complex Reaction + Goal Path
6 Complex Reaction → Simple Reaction + Goal
7 Simple Reaction → an emotional or cognitive response
8 Goal → a state that a character wants to achieve
9 Goal Path → Attempt + Outcome
10 Attempt → an intentional action or plan of a character
11 Outcome → a consequence of the Attempt, specifying whether or not the goal is achieved
12 Ending → a reaction.

Additionally, Beginning, Outcome, and Ending can serve as nodes that supply opportunities for additional episodes. Each episode contains such components as the initiating event, the protagonist's internal response, some attempt to reach a goal, a consequence of that attempt, and a reaction following from the protagonist's attempts to reach the goal (Mulcahy and Samuels 1987). The first rewrite rule above posits the primary constituents of a story as a setting plus one or more episodes. The second rewrite rule provides the substance of a setting. The third rule indicates that the constituents of an episode are Beginning, Development, and Ending. The remaining rules represent the types of information that can be assigned to the nodes when the text is interpreted. Graesser et al. (1996) show example text statements that may be attached to the different node categories:

Setting: Once upon a time there was a lovely princess who lived in a castle near a forest.
Beginning: One day the princess was walking in the woods and she encountered a large ugly dragon.
Simple reaction: The princess was startled and frightened.
Goal: The princess wanted to escape from the dragon.
Attempt: When she started to run away…
Outcome: The dragon breathed fire in her path.
!
!
Ending: The princess was happy to be home again.

(*Graesser et al. 1996: 180*)

Thus, a story grammar assigns a hierarchical constituent structure when it is applied to a particular story. Each phrase, clause, and statement in a text is assigned to a particular node. Superordinate information in the hierarchy is more important than any subordinate information. It would, thus, be expected that episode 1 would be more salient than episode 2 and episode 3. Further, it would be expected that episode 4 is less salient than episode 3. A test of the story grammar is whether readers reproduce a representation of these relationships in recall protocols. Together, according to Mandler (1984, 1987), these constituents represent a prototypic story schema that readers internalize. Studies have shown that subjects restructure stories to fit this canonical structure. Even when presented stories with interwoven episodes, subjects provide a story with distinct episodic structure when retelling the story (Mandler 1978; Mandler and DeForest 1979).

Mandler (1987) presented subjects with 12 different stories organized in three different ways. The first four stories consisted of a setting and two episodes temporally organized in such a way that one episode ended and another unrelated episode began. The second four stories consisted of a setting and two episodes, but the second episode was contingent upon the outcome of the first episode. The last four stories, with the most complex organization, consisted of a setting and two episodes with the second episode embedded in the first episode. For the first two structures, subjects overwhelmingly organized the sentences of the story into the canonical story structure. There was less agreement on the third type of organization. In general, the data from the study indicate a hierarchical structure in the relationship between episodes as well as between setting and episode.

There are indications that although the underlying hierarchical narrative story structure is recognized by most first language readers from about the third grade on, schematic knowledge of narrative structure is reflective of overall reading ability. Fitzgerald (1984) systematically presented 166 fourth- and sixth- graders with components of a narrative with different parts of the Mandler and Johnson (1977) story grammar visibly missing. The narratives could be missing the story grammar component of Setting, Beginning, Reaction, Attempt, or Outcome. As they read, the readers were asked to predict orally what should or could come in the incomplete section of the story. For the most part, there was a strong tendency for the readers to predict the correct category for the deleted text. This indicates that the readers maintained a general sense of the narrative structure. Further, there was a tendency for the better readers to expect the appropriate categories more often than the poorer readers, and to predict more accurately. Two subsequent studies (Hinchley and Levy 1988; Rahman and Bisanz 1986) confirmed the findings that although all of the readers were sensitive to some degree to the canonical story schema, better readers were more able to use the structure and more capable of dealing with non-standard narrative presentations. Finally,

Wilkinson, Elkins, and Bain (1995) found that lower-ability readers evidenced reduced sensitivity to story structure and generally recalled less information from story grammar categories.

A primary criticism of story grammars is that they apply most reliably only to straightforward simple and relatively short stories (Graesser et al. 1996). When a story has shifting points of view or is complex in terms of the relationships between episodes, story grammar becomes less useful in explaining the hierarchy of the story. Thus, with stories that have unpredictable consequences that alter the plot, story grammars fail to capture the relationships between constituents. Likewise, story grammars are structural in nature and do not explain the background knowledge needed to comprehend a story or reflect a representation of story motives such as revenge or desire. These deficiencies limit the explanatory value of story grammars.

Several other approaches to the explanation of how narrative texts are comprehended have been developed. There are *causal network* approaches (Trabasso and van den Broek 1985; van den Broek 1988), *conceptual graph structure* approaches (Graesser 1981; Graesser and Clark 1985), *script and plan* approaches (Shank and Abelson 1977), *story point* approaches (Wilensky 1982), *plot point* approaches (Lehnert 1981), *setting-episodes* approaches (Stein and Glenn 1979), and *thematic affect* approaches (Dyer 1983) to name some. Each approach attempts to explain the ways that narratives are comprehended and stored. Each assumes that there is some essential set of structural and conceptual components that define a narrative and are used in its comprehension. Knowledge of the prototypic narrative structure assists the reader in comprehending and remembering elements of the story they have read.

Expository text

While narrative has a structure that is temporal and causal, the connections in EXPOSITORY texts tend to depend upon logical relations. Several different taxonomies of expository text types have been proposed. Meyer (1975) proposes *antecedent/consequent, comparison* or *contrast, collection, description,* and *response.* Van Dijk and Kintsch (1983) propose text structures such as *argument, definition, classification, illustration,* and *procedural descriptions.* Calfee and Curley (1984) present a taxonomy of exposition with levels of type specification: 1) *Description* (definition, division and classification, comparison and contrast); 2) *Illustration* (analogy, example); 3) *Sequence* (process, cause and effect); 4) *Argument and Persuasion* (deductive reasoning, inductive reasoning, persuasion); and 5) *Functional* (introduction, transition, conclusion). The complexity of categorizing expository text into clear and exclusive classes points out how the category divisions tend to be abstract example structures describing subcomponents within an overall text. The overall text is composed of different organizational units that are marshaled by the writer to accomplish the overall goal of presenting explanatory information in an organizational manner with which the reader is familiar.

Research into expository text has indicated for some time that there is a relationship, or relationships, between text structure and text processing. The two most commonly used text analysis systems, Meyer (1975, 1985) and Kintsch and van Dijk (1978), van Dijk and Kintsch (1983), have slight differences in how they view the text. The Kintsch and van Dijk approach employs the notion of *propositions* as the basic unit of meaning while Meyer's system uses the *idea unit* (Weaver and Kintsch 1996). Propositions are viewed as the smallest unit of text that can logically be proven false. Propositions consist of predicates and arguments, where predicates are typically the relationships between objects while arguments are the objects and concepts identified in the text (Kintsch, 1998; Kintsch and van Dijk 1978; van Dijk and Kintsch 1983). However, an idea unit expresses one action or event, and can generally be related to a single verb clause. Meyer (1985) notes that 'unlike propositional analysis, our units do not give separate status to modifiers, conjunctions, connectives and the like' (71). It is not necessary to go into detail here about the differences between the two systems in order to discuss the relative importance of the text grammars in reading research. Meyer (1985) provides a detailed comparison and concludes that the Kintsch and van Dijk system is more efficient for scoring immediate-recall protocols while the Meyer approach is more advantageous in situations where less textually explicit accuracy is important, such as in delayed-recall contexts. However, although the sample size was very small in her study, Meyer (1985: 52) found a correlation of .96 between the two systems on recall scores. In short, both systems provide hierarchical descriptions of the ordering of the text propositions/idea units and base their predictions of how salient various parts of a text will be on the text organization.

Kintsch (1998) sees propositional representations as being underlying representations related to underlying meaning more closely than sentences in a text. This is because, in his view, sentences are mapped on to the syntax of a language whereas propositions represent the most salient semantic relations. In short, he argues that propositions are the mental semantic processing units.

Further, Meyer (1975, 1985) and van Dijk and Kintsch (1983) emphasize that there are microprocesses and macroprocesses involved in text comprehension. These processes reflect the differential manner in which the reader processes micropropositions and macropropositions. Interest in micropropositions is generally concerned with the interrelationships among the propositions and how each new proposition relates to what has already been presented (Meyer and Rice 1984). As such, it focuses on the coherence issues discussed previously. Macroprocesses are related to global comprehension of the text while microprocesses have to do with close comprehension of the text that proceeds phrase by phrase, clause by clause, and sentence by sentence in a very bottom-up fashion. The two levels may not be directly related.

In looking at how text structure affects comprehension, Kintsch and Yarbrough (1982) presented subjects with essays that were either in 'good' or 'bad' rhetorical form. The texts that were in good form closely followed a familiar text structure containing explicit organizing cues, cohesive ties, as to the text structure. In the ill-formed texts, the cues were missing and the ordering of the text violated the typical text order. The content of the passages remained the same regardless of how well formed the passages were. The subjects were given global comprehension measures as well as cloze passages relating to the content of the texts. The researchers found that the subjects performed better on the well-formed texts than on the ill-formed texts when assessed through the comprehension measures. However, the subjects performed no differently on the two forms of the texts when assessed with the cloze passages. They interpret this to indicate that text structure is important for macroprocesses of global comprehension, but it may be less important for the microprocessing of text elicited by the cloze procedure.

It is assumed that a reader's formal knowledge about canonical text structures can be useful for the organizational schemata that the structures offer (Kintsch 1982). Knowledge about prototypical text type will play an important role in the reader's employment of comprehension strategies. Kintsch (1982) argues that there may be some text-type specific comprehension strategies such that when a reader encounters a text that is identified as a specific type (for example, 'argument'), a set of comprehension strategies will be employed to deal with that text type. For example, if a reader is reading a 'definition', he or she will expect a particular form with perhaps one or more genus propositions, each with several differentiating notions, which will eventually answer the question 'What is it?'. However, the reader must be aware that the text is a definition if he or she is to utilize the definition strategies.

Following up on the research just discussed, Van Dijk and Kintsch (1983) contend that discourse strategies associated with rhetorical forms, text structures such as *argument, definition, classification, illustration*, and *procedural descriptions*, are used by experienced readers to organize the text they are reading (254). Thus, texts that are clearly organized according to a familiar structure should be easier to comprehend than texts that have no clear structure. A complication for the reader will be that it is rarely the case that a text is of a single structure. An expository text might contain a brief history of the development of a product that the reader has purchased, instructions to perform some act, a warning about dangers involved, a short narrative describing what happened when someone performed the act incorrectly, and a description of the tools that will be needed. The experienced reader will have the formal schemata that include the recognition that text structures may change. The recognition of these structures is carried out in an ongoing manner in that the original Kintsch and van Dijk model (1978) recognizes that the reader does not construct a textbase only after having completed the entire paragraph, chapter, book, etc. Rather, the textbase is constructed in real time and affected by the reader's limited short-term memory capacity.

Meyer (1975, 1977) examined how certain expository text types affect memory as they interact with content schemata and processing strategies. Meyer and Freedle (1984) argue that the higher a text is on a scale of internal organization, the more facilitative it is for comprehension. They argue that the order from least to most organized expository text types are: *description, collection, causation, comparison*, and *problem/solution*. The five basic groups of textual structure differ in terms of the type and number of organizational components. Meyer and Freedle (1984) argue that the *description* relationship is the least organized while the *problem/solution* structure is the most organized. They argue that *problem/solution* has all of the organizational components of the *causation* relationships with the addition of overlapping propositions in both the problem segment and the solution segment.

In order to test their hypothesis, they conducted two studies on English first language graduate students listening to English passages. In the first study, they took content related to the topic of dehydration and put the information in four versions of a listening passage, with each version representing a *causal, problem/solution, comparison*, or *collection of descriptions* organization. (They essentially collapsed the description and collection structures into one category.) In the second study, they examined the relative effects that the two organizations of *comparison* or *collection of descriptions* structure would have on recall of a listening passage. The results from the first study showed a significant advantage in proposition recall for *causation* and *comparison* structures over the *collection of descriptions* structure. It is not clear why the *problem/solution* structure was not significantly higher than *collection of descriptions* on number of recalls. In the second study, two groups of subjects listened to a passage about killer whales. Those subjects who listened to the *comparison* passage recalled a significantly higher number of text propositions than did those who listened to the *collection of descriptions* texts. Thus, both studies showed that discourse structure can affect comprehension and memory. An obvious issue here is to what extent this finding can be generalized to reading contexts, particularly second language reading contexts.

However, text structure does not act in isolation in the reading process. Berkmire (1985) examined the interrelationships among text structure, background knowledge, and purpose of reading, in effect looking at the interaction of content and formal schemata. Berkmire had physics and engineering college majors and music majors read three texts. One text was on the topic of a new laser annealing technique (laser text), a second text was about the history of musical notation (notation text), and a third passage was about parakeets as pets (parakeet text). The parakeet text was used as a control text, while the laser text was familiar to the physics majors and the notation text was familiar to the music majors. The subjects were either instructed to read for the main idea, or were given three questions to answer after reading. The reading passages were presented on a computer terminal one sentence at a time, and reading rate was monitored. After reading the text twice, the subjects were presented with six sentences measuring high-level, intermediate-level, or low-level content structure, and were asked to identify which sentences had appeared in the text they had just read.

The results of the study showed that while reading the laser text, the physics majors read high content structure sentences at a faster rate than the intermediate or low content structure sentences. The music majors were slower overall with this text and did not read information high in the content structure at a rate that was different from the rate they read the low-level content structures. While reading the musical notation text, the two groups reversed these outcomes. The music group read the high content sentences faster than the intermediate or low content structure sentences, while the physics majors were slower overall and their reading rate did not distinguish between the high content structure and the low content structure. With the parakeet text, both majors read high content structure faster than intermediate or low content structure sentences, and each major read at approximately the same rate. The results show that sentences containing information located high in the content structure were read faster than sentences containing information lower in the content structure by those subjects whose background knowledge was related to the text topic. However, when the subjects did not have specialized knowledge of the topic, the text structure was either less helpful or not helpful at all. When reading the control parakeet text, both groups read the high content sentences faster than the lower-level content sentences. This suggests that as an expository text becomes more specialized, the role of text structure may diminish with decreasing familiarity with the specialized topic. It further indicates that as information in a text 'fits' with existing knowledge it is easy to comprehend and is therefore processed more quickly. In the texts used in this study, the intermediate and low content structure sentences contained new information that required additional processing time.

The studies discussed here appear to show that, at least for first language readers, text structure can affect reading comprehension in several ways. First, the particular rhetorical structure may elicit particular strategies associated with that structure, as posited by van Dijk and Kintsch (1983). Second, the particular rhetorical structures vary in their ease of processing. Third, superordinate propositions that are higher in the text structure are recalled better than subordinate propositions lower in the text-structure representation. Groups of propositional units that are related to one another in the hierarchical structure are recalled more readily and more often than propositions that are weakly related to other propositions.

Text structure and second language reading

The previous discussion has examined research into the role of text structure in first language reading. However, it is important to examine how the issues play out in second language reading. A primary question revolves around: 1) the knowledge of text-structure strategies by second language readers; 2) the relationship of first language text structures to second language text-structure processing; and 3) the effectiveness of text-structure instruction on second language reading comprehension. These areas of interest are not completely independent in that they overlap and interact with one another.

Narrative text structure

Several studies have looked at how narrative texts are processed by second language readers. Carrell (1984a) examined whether a simple story schema influences ESL subjects as they read stories in English. Her subjects were each presented with three stories. The stories either followed a two-episode standard sequential order, or the same story with content from the two episodes interleaved in a non-conventional text pattern, analogous to the Mandler (1984, 1987) studies. Twenty-four hours after reading the stories, the subjects were asked to recall the stories as well as possible in writing. Carrell found that the subjects who read the standard-order texts recalled more story nodes than did the readers of the interleaved non-conventionally ordered stories. Further, there was a significant difference in the number of story nodes per episode that were recalled between the two groups. Those who read the standard-order stories recalled more than did the readers of the interleaved stories. Additionally, many of the readers of the interleaved stories produced recalls rearranged into the standard order with the episodes ordered in the conventional sequential organization. Thus, the formal story schema tended to operate during the retrieval of the story information, a finding indicating that readers do rely on text-structure strategies for comprehension and retrieval of story information. This sensitivity to violations of narrative text structure by second language readers parallels the interference that first language readers had with the expository text-structure violations in Kintsch and Yarbrough (1982).

The role that second language proficiency plays is a major concern in terms of how it interacts with text-structure knowledge and use. Walters and Wolf (1986) examined language proficiency, text content and text structure with two groups of non-native English readers, all native speakers of Hebrew at Tel Aviv University. They examined these variables to determine whether the story grammar structural categories of *setting, initiating event, internal response/goal, attempt, consequence,* and *ending* would hold across language ability. They were particularly interested in whether the second language readers would corroborate findings from other story grammar studies of first language which indicated better recall of *settings, initiating events,* and *consequences* (Stein and Glenn 1979). Further, they wanted to determine whether this order was violated in different stories. Two groups of non-native English subjects participated in the study. The first group, designated EFL, consisted of 20 intermediate EFL students who had not completed the university's English requirements. The second group, designated Fluent, had completed all English requirements as well as advanced study in English. Subjects were presented with four short texts between 86 and 104 words in length. Three versions of each passage were developed: the original story with normal ordering of events; a partially mixed order which had the consequence moved from fifth position to third position; and a fully randomized-order version in which the statements were never in their canonical order. Subjects were randomly assigned to one of the versions of each story and asked to read the story for recall. The results of the study indicated that there was considerable variation across stories in the amount of recall for the different story grammar categories, but that there was much more regularity in the Fluent group's recall than in the recall by the EFL group. As was to be expected, the results showed that the recall order was more typical for the standard-order and partially mixed versions of the texts than with the fully mixed order. Further, the Fluent group had higher recall overall than did the EFL group. It thus appears that language proficiency does play a role in the processing of narratives. However, it is not clear whether this has to do with the initial reading of the text and recognizing it as a story, particularly with the fully mixed-order text, or with the structuring of the recall during its production. With the original standard-order text the language proficiency effect is less strong on the recall of the categories. For the partially mixed order, however, language proficiency played a greater role in differences of recall. This may indicate that unconventional text order qualitatively affects the lower-proficiency readers to a greater extent than it does the more able second language readers.

Other studies have attempted to determine the extent to which knowledge of text structure, particularly narrative structure, affects comprehension in languages other than English as measured by recall. Horiba, van den Broek, and Fletcher (1993) examined how recall of a narrative reflected attention to surface-level meaning-preserving features as opposed to top-down text-structure preserving features. The study involved 47 Japanese 12th-grade students in Japan, and a control group of 72 American undergraduate students in the US. The students received four stories, two of which were fillers and not of interest in the recall component of the study. After reading all four stories, they were asked to write in their native language everything that they remembered about the texts. The recalls were then translated back into English and matched against the idea units in the original story. The recalls were scored for the extent to which they matched verbatim or in a close paraphrase to the original text, termed *meaning preserving*, or the extent to which they also preserved the structure of the original text even though some misunderstanding of the language may have occurred, termed *structure preserving*. The results showed, not surprisingly, that the first language group had significantly higher recall in both categories than the second language group. Further, the results showed that second language readers had significantly higher recall of the structure-preserving features, thus showing that these readers did use their knowledge of text structure in their recall of the story. However, although the first language group showed sensitivity to the hierarchical level of the information according to the Johnson and Mandler (1980) approach to episode relationships, the second language group did not. This indicates more of a reliance on locally situated texts, such as lower-level causal relations, than on more global thematic organization of the entire text. This finding parallels the implications from Horiba (1993) previously discussed in the discussion of text cohesion in second language reading, lending support to the idea that the second language reader uses top-down knowledge about how a text is structured.

Most of the studies on the relationship of narrative structure and second language comprehension have been conducted with stories that have had fairly simple one- or two-episode structures. Riley (1993) examined the effects of story structure on a longer 850-word folk tale in French containing eight episodes. She had three levels of English first language speakers studying French read one of three versions of the story. The levels were Level One (end of first year French), Level Two (end of second year French), and Level Three (students who had completed courses beyond the fourth semester of French). The story was analyzed based on the story grammar of Johnson and Mandler (1980) and manipulated to form three versions: 1) an 'ideal' story structure; 2) a flashback; and 3) a story grammar violation structure with interleaved episodes. (420). Thus, the reorganization of the second version created a story that began with a flashback, where no actual violation of the story structure existed. The third story organization involved the reorganization of episodes, much as with Walters and Wolf (1986), moving episodes out of chronological sequence and breaking up episodes. The subjects in the three ability levels were randomly assigned to one version of the text. They read the story and then retold the story in English. The protocols were scored for the number of nodes accurately recalled. The results showed that Level Three students scored significantly higher than the other two groups and that Level Two students scored significantly higher than Level One. They further show that the canonical organized unmodified text produced significantly more recalled nodes than either of the other two text organizations. There were no significant differences between story organization 2 and organization 3. Only the highest-level students recalled both the original version and the flashback organization significantly better than the story grammar violation. The interaction of story organization and language level, thus, indicates differences between the three groups of subjects. Text structure had the biggest effect on the middle-level readers where the canonical structure was significantly more memorable than the other two organizations. Level One and Level Three, however, showed the least effect for text structure. Level One was at a very low-ability level and consequently the text, regardless of text structure, was just too difficult. Text structure did not assist the subjects very much. However, for Level Three readers no significant differences existed between the original structure and the flashback structure, but differences were significant between the story grammar violating text and the other two. Thus, the higher-level readers could recognize the flashback version as a legitimate story organization, but were less able to piece together the text when the structure represented a violation.

Riley also examined the extent to which recall of the categories of *setting*, *beginning*, *reaction*, *attempt*, *outcome*, and *ending* were related to language level and story organization and found significant effects for both story organization and language level, indicating that these affected the types of nodes that were recalled. Further, there was a significant interaction of category by language level and story organization by language level. This indicated that the specific nature of the category differences varied depending upon level and organization. Level Two and Level Three had nearly parallel patterns of recall across the organizations, while Level One learners showed little differentiation in story organization 3, the randomized version. On organization 1, Level Two and Level Three subjects recalled *settings* and *beginning* best, followed by *attempt*. Level One, on the other hand, recalled *setting* and *reactions* better than the other categories. This would seem to show that the lowest level of students is more affected by low-level events. In general, *settings* and *beginnings* were recalled better than the other nodes, while *reactions* and *endings* were the least well recalled, perhaps because of the relative low saliency given their positions.

Expository text structure

Carrell (1984b) examined how use of text structure applied to expository text. Her research was designed to determine whether there were any differences among non-native readers of English in their interaction with English expository text representing different rhetorical structures. She divided subjects into four language groups (Spanish, Arabic, Oriental, and Other). Four passages relating to the topic of loss of body water by athletes were developed into the rhetorical structures of *collection of descriptions, causation, problem/solution,* and *comparison.* She collected immediate- and delayed-recall data as well as answers to probe questions on the idea units that were common to all four passages. Her results on the recall data show a significant difference between immediate and delayed recall, language group, and discourse type. The results show a much better recall of the tightly organized structures than for the *collection of descriptions* passages, a finding consistent with the Meyer and Freedle (1984) findings for native English speakers. For all but the Arabic group, the more tightly organized structures were recalled significantly better than the *collection of descriptions.* The results from the recall protocol organization show that those who recognized the discourse structure and used that structure in their recall recalled more information from the original text. This is consistent with the findings of Meyer and her colleagues (Meyer, Brandt, and Bluth 1980; Meyer and Freedle 1984). However, unlike Meyer's work where approximately 50 per cent of the subjects recognized and used the structure in their recall, only about 26 per cent of the non-native English speakers used the original structure as they recalled the text. It is difficult to interpret this finding directly, primarily because there are no external measures to describe the proficiency level of these particular experimental subjects. Consequently, it is not known whether this low implementation of the input structural organization was due to the language proficiency level being insufficient for the readers to recognize the input structure or because the non-native English speakers were employing qualitatively different strategies due to their own first language background. Bendetto (1986) found that readers who failed to attend to top level text structure in their first language also failed to do so in their second language, even when they were advanced second language users (for example tenth-grade ability). More on this will be discussed later in the next chapter when we look at findings from studies in contrastive rhetoric.

Tian (1990) replicated Carrell's (1984b) study in Singapore with subjects whose home language was Chinese, Malay, or Tamil. The results are similar to those of Carrell in that the *comparison* text type was recalled better than the *collection of descriptions* text type. However, there was little difference between *collection of descriptions, causation,* and *problem/solution* text structures. The findings that texts with the *comparison* text structure were recalled better than those with the *collection of descriptions,* and that there was no superiority for *problem/solution,* were also consistent with Meyer and Freedle (1984), though Meyer and Freedle did find the *causation* structure to be superior to *collection of descriptions.* The findings by Tian may be closer to Meyer and Freedle because the English language ability of the subjects from Singapore was perhaps closer to those in Meyer and Freedle's study than that for the subjects in Carrell's study. Additionally, Tian found no effect for language across the text types. The absence of an effect for language is most likely due to the fact that all of the subjects had English-medium instruction and primarily used their first language orally at home.

Instruction in text structure

A natural question that emerges from this research in first and second language reading and text-structure relationships is whether it would be effective to teach these structures explicitly in reading instruction. The previous review has indicated that there is evidence for an effect of text structure on both first language and second language reading comprehension in both narrative and expository texts, though much of this effect is inferred from the relative performance between processing a well-formed text and an ill-formed text. Several studies at different levels of instruction have indicated that first language instruction in text structure can be effective in teaching discourse organization.

Singer and Donlan (1982) provide evidence that explicitly teaching 11th-grade students the structure as well as strategies for applying the structure schema aided comprehension. In their study, they taught students both schema knowledge of narrative structure for assimilating content and a self-generation of content-specific questions for engaging the text. Two groups of 15 students were assigned to one of two groups. The first group received instruction in how to ask schema-general questions about a story. These were questions concerning the main character, the story goal, the conflicts that occurred, the outcome of the story, and the story theme. This first group of students read half of a story and then generated questions that they wanted answered. In the second group, the students answered questions supplied by a teacher. Students were then given criterion-referenced tests about the story. The group that received instruction on structure schema and self-generated questioning over time showed a significant advantage over the traditionally instructed group who worked with supplied comprehension questions.

Taylor and Beach (1984) looked at the effects of text structure instruction on expository text with first language seventh-grade students. Three groups of students were formed. One group received instruction over seven weeks in text-structure organization, the second group received conventional reading instruction in which they generated questions about the text, and the third group acted as a control group. The first group received instruction and practice regarding how to produce and study a hierarchical summary. Subjects were briefed on the material, read the assigned pages, and then worked on summaries. The summarization practice involved working on a skeleton outline from which they generated a main idea statement for each section and a key idea statement for the whole text. The second group of subjects read a passage and generated a set of approximately 15 practice questions on the main ideas. They then discussed the questions as a group and finally told a partner everything they could remember. The control group completed all pre- and post-tests, but was not given any special instruction that was not part of their regular class. For the pre- and post-tests, the subjects read one of two social science texts and then recalled the text, answered questions, wrote an opinion/example essay, and rated their familiarity of the topic. The first post-test passage was about the US two hundred years ago and today, and was rated as relatively unfamiliar by the groups. The second passage was about the energy crisis, and was rated as relatively familiar by the groups. The results showed that the experimental subjects on the first post-test passage had significantly higher recall scores than the conventional group and the control group. On the second passage both the experimental group and the conventional group had higher recall than the control group, but not different from one another. Further, the experimental group and conventional group both had higher short-answer question scores than the control group, but did not differ from one another. The experimental group had higher scores on ratings of overall quality of their writing, but not significantly higher than the conventional group. Thus, the results indicate that after receiving reading instruction focusing on text structure, the subjects in the experimental group had higher recall scores on the first passage, a passage that all three groups rated as relatively unfamiliar. On the second passage, a passage that was rated as relatively familiar by all groups, the experimental and conventional groups had higher recall scores than the control group. This finding suggests that developing hierarchical summaries may be more helpful in preparation for reading an unfamiliar passage, while for familiar topics generating questions may be just as helpful.

An important concern in the extent to which processing of text structure can be taught is whether there are particular approaches that are better than others, or whether the consciousness-raising activity itself is sufficient. To a large degree, a major consideration for interpreting the research rests with the amount and saliency of the types of instruction that have been presented to the subjects of the different studies. Slater, Graves, and Piché (1985) looked at the effect of four different types of instructional directions on recall and comprehension of high-, middle-, and low-ability ninth-grade students who were randomly assigned to one of the types of instruction. Basically in this approach, treatment was equated with the form of instructions that the subjects received as they carried out a task. The four different types of instruction varied in the extent to which guidance was provided for attending to text structure. The first two types of instruction were termed the structural organizer with outline grid (SOG) and the structural organizer alone (SOA). The SOG involved directions that: 1) described the benefits of using top-level structure as an aid for remembering information from a text; 2) defined the top-level structure of the target passage; 3) provided a sample passage top-level organization; and 4) included an outline grid of the top-level organization of the target passage for the subjects to fill in as they read. For the recall protocol, the subjects were instructed to write using the organization of the target passage. The SOA was identical to the SOG except that no outline grid was provided. The third condition, note taking (NOTE), involved directions that instructed the subjects to read the target passage carefully and take detailed notes while reading. A brief note instructed them to write down everything they could remember for the recall test. The final condition, control (CON), involved instructions identical to the third condition except that the subjects were not instructed to take notes. The results indicated that the subjects in the SOG condition recalled the largest number of idea units (propositions) of all four conditions. Further, the NOTE condition was more effective than the SOA and the CON, but the SOA was not more effective than the CON. Further, high-ability subjects scored significantly higher than the middle- and low-ability students, and the middle-ability subjects scored higher than the low-ability subjects, but there was no interaction of treatment by ability level. Here, the results indicate that the treatments that involved the most direct and productive involvement on the part of the learner, as well as providing the most guidance, were the most effective. However, given that the study provides only a one-shot exposure to the treatment and then analysis of the results from that treatment incident, it is not clear that the results indicate any type of generalizable learning by each subject, or are just a result of the particular type of instructions that the subjects get with each passage. In short, it is not clear whether this is an effective instructional technique or is simply an immediate governor on the subjects' performance.

Over a six-week instructional intervention, Berkowitz (1986) compared two experimental methods that focused on the textual organization of ideas with two study methods that did not focus on text organization. Three of the study methods are instructional methods while the fourth served as a control condition. In the map-construction (M-C) procedure, after reading the text students wrote the title of the article in the center of a sheet of paper. They then skimmed the text to determine the main ideas and these topics were written as headings around the title in a clockwise direction. The article was then skimmed again and important details were written under each of the main ideas that had been identified. Finally, boxes were drawn around each of the main idea categories and connected to the title box. Students then studied these completed maps focusing on the content and organization. The map-study (M-S) procedure provided the students with prepared maps of the texts after they read the passage. These were discussed in terms of the content and organization and the students were told to study them as with the M-C group. The question-answering (Q-A) procedure presented the students with 20 probe questions after they read the passages, and students went back to the text to check their answers to each question before actually writing an answer. Finally, the rereading (RR) procedure acted as a control condition in which the students reread the passage carefully and reflected on what they had read in a silent review/study procedure. Students then read three new passages and were tested for free recall and on short-answer tests.

The treatment lasted for approximately six instructional sessions. The results showed that the M-C group performed better than the other groups on the tests of the passages, but only significantly on one of the passages read, a passage rated by experts as best suited for mapping. In further analysis, Berkowitz looked at the results for those students who were determined to have actually mastered the study procedure taught to the M-C and Q-A groups. The comparisons for those students who mastered each of the instructional techniques showed that the M-C group scored significantly better than the Q-A group on tests of recall. Thus, when the degree of expertise at learning the study technique is taken into account, there is evidence that map-construction is an effective technique across all of the passages. However, the caveat for both the M-C and Q-A procedures is that about 25 per cent of each group was unable to learn the technique. It is not clear whether those students did not learn the procedure because of insufficient exposure to the treatment, or because the instructional methods themselves were not robust enough to be successful, or because the treatment was difficult to learn.

As part of a larger study, Meyer and Poon (2001) looked at expository prose structure training for both older adults (M $\approx$ 69 years) and younger adults (M $\approx$ 21 years). The structure training explicitly taught learners to identify and use signaling devices such as headings, preview and summary statements, and pointer words, in the text as an aid to encoding and organizing their recall. Subjects in the study were placed in a structure-strategy training group (S-S), an interest-list group (I-L), or a no-contact control group (NC). In the S-S group, nine hours of training involved direct instruction, modeling, and practice alone and in pairs. Participants learned to identify and use basic top-level structures to organize their ideas, and learned to recognize the structures in everyday reading materials. They were taught to use these structures as a framework for acquiring new information. Feedback was given individually to participants as they wrote or told partners the structure of texts that were read. In the I-L group the subjects were taught to evaluate systematically their interest in the text and use that information to monitor and increase their motivation to read by thinking of others who might find the article interesting. The N-C group received no training prior to reading a selection of texts. On total recall measures, the S-S group for both older and younger adults recalled significantly more idea units, and showed significantly greater gain from pre-test to post-test in idea units, than the I-L or N-C groups, while the last two groups did not significantly differ from one another. Additionally, participants from the S-S group recalled more main ideas and produced text summaries of better quality than either of the other two groups, and produced texts that used the organization of the original text better to structure their recall. Further, the S-S group training transferred to new tasks involving the processing of information presented via a video tape and reading of multiple texts that were more complex and longer than those used in the training and initial testing. In summary, Meyer and Poon found that structure training can be successful with both young and older adults and that the resulting increase in content schema assisted in their reading.

In general, first language studies of training appear to support the effectiveness of direct text-structure instruction. Teaching students to be aware that a text does have a reasonably predictable structure and to use it has been demonstrated to have a positive effect on comprehension. However, the studies just mentioned may actually have primarily taught the readers to be active readers. That is, the control groups typically had not had their attention called to good reading procedures while the experimental groups were provided with some instruction that focused the learners on the process.

Carrell (1985) noted that little empirical research had been reported as to whether teaching text structure facilitated second language reading comprehension, and she attempted to determine whether it was possible to facilitate ESL reading comprehension through training students in text structure. Her study included 25 university students from heterogeneous language backgrounds. Over five consecutive class periods the students in the experimental condition received explicit training in four of Meyer's expository structures: *comparison, problem/solution, causation,* and *collection of descriptions.* The control group received training in linguistic operations such as grammar, discourse connectors, cohesion, and vocabulary with the same texts, but no training in top-level text structure. The pre- and post-test procedures consisted of the students reading two passages, one *comparison* and the other *collection of descriptions,* writing an immediate recall, and identifying the overall organization of the text in an open-ended question. A delayed post-test was administered to the experimental group three weeks after the first post-test. The recall protocols were scored for the presence of each idea unit in the original text, and were analyzed to determine whether or not the recall used the text structure of the original text. Each idea unit in the original texts was coded according to Meyer (1975) as being an Introduction, Top-, High-, or Low-Level idea unit. The results indicated that the text-structure training enabled the experimental group to recognize and use the discourse types. After training, the experimental group showed significant gain from the pre-test in the subjects who recognized and used the target text structure while the control group did not show such gain. Additionally, the delayed post-test showed that the subjects retained this gain three weeks after training. Further, the experimental group recalled significantly more of the High-, Mid- and Low-level idea units than did the control group. Thus, Carrell's work indicates that direct instruction of text structure can facilitate the reading recall of second language readers, just as it was shown to facilitate comprehension by first language readers of English.

Various text adjuncts have been examined for their effectiveness in teaching text structure to second language readers. Lee and Riley (1990) presented 120 third-semester French language students with one of two reading passages, one a *collection of descriptions* organization and the other a *problem/solution* organization. The subjects were assigned to one of three conditions: 1) no framework at all prior to reading the passage; 2) a minimal framework in which the subjects were told the type of passage organization (for example a *collection of descriptions* or *problem/solution*); or 3) an expanded framework in which the subjects were given a more extensive presentation that provided context for a *collection of descriptions* or *problem/solution*. The results show that the subjects in the third group recalled a significantly greater number of idea units on the *collection of descriptions* passage than the other two groups, and these last two groups did not differ from one another. There were no significant differences for the number of idea units recalled by the group with the *problem/solution* passage. However, when only the top-level idea units were examined, the expanded framework group produced significantly more for the *problem/solution* passage, but not for the *collection of descriptions* passage. The conflicting results again indicate how the effectiveness of instruction is a complex association of interacting variables. In many ways, it is surprising that any significant results were found given the paucity of the instruction that was provided.

Raymond (1993) examined whether French as a second language reading could be facilitated by instruction in organizational patterns of discourse. Based on the work of Meyer (1975), Raymond selected the following top-level text organizational structures for inclusion in her training: *collection, description, causation, problem/solution,* and *comparison*. Part of the training involved teaching signal words identified with the structures. Examples of the signal words are:

Collection: (grouping) and, in addition, also, include, moreover, first, second, at the same moment; (sequence) before, after, later, finally, last, etc.

Description: for example, which was one, this particular, for instance, specifically, such as, attributes of, namely, properties of, characteristics are, etc.

Causation: as a result, because, since, for the purpose of, caused, led to, consequent, thus, in order to, this is why, if/then, the reason, so, therefore, etc.

Problem-solution: (problem) problem, question, perplexity, puzzle, query, need, to prevent the trouble, (solution) solution, answer, response, etc.

Comparison: not everyone, but, in contrast, all but, instead, act like, however, in comparison, on the one hand, on the other hand, whereas, unlike, etc.

The study is based on Carrell (1985) except that the training was in French, and all 43 subjects were native English speakers at a high-intermediate level of ability. The students were placed into either a control or treatment group. The subjects wrote their recall protocols in English. This study points to some of the problems that can emerge in strategy-training research that have to do with: 1) existing skills prior to training; and 2) the need for training that is intensive and engaging. The pre-test and post-test involved reading a passage, assessing the passage on a Likert scale measuring perceptions of text difficulty, memorability, etc., and then recalling the text in writing. The strategy training involved one hour for each of the target structures. Subjects were taught what the strategy was, why it should be learned, how to use it, and when to use it. The dependent measures that were used to test the effectiveness of the treatment were the number of idea units recalled, reading time, and reader assessment of the text. Raymond (1993) recognized the fact that subjects differed in their prior knowledge of the use of the structures before the study began. Thus, the pre-test recall score was used as a covariate to adjust the post-test means and allow those adjusted means to be compared. No significant differences for group were found between the strategy group and the control group. Likewise, the strategy group did not read significantly faster than the control group after treatment. Much of the outcome may have been due to the briefness and, almost necessarily, lack of depth in the actual treatment. This plus the fact that the readers most likely had strategies in their first language that could transfer to second language even without training makes the likelihood of finding a real effect for the training less.

There is some indication that text-structure instruction can be effective with young EFL learners as well as with older learners. Amer (1992) looked at the effect of story grammar on EFL Arabic-speaking sixth-grade students' comprehension of a narrative text. The students were divided into experimental and control groups. In the experimental group, the teacher asked guiding questions for each episode and questions that developed the story as a whole. Instruction lasted across seven class periods. The students were initially presented with a story to introduce them to the idea of a story grammar with setting, characters, problem, action, resolution, and theme. The teacher asked questions which elicited the elements of the story, and wrote the story elements on the board in both English and Arabic. This was done to familiarize the students with the notion of a story grammar. After this initial contact with the concept of story grammar, the main story consisting of ten episodes was introduced. Students went through the story episode by episode over subsequent class periods. The students in the control group went over the same story in a traditional manner with some silent reading and some comprehension questions. At the end of the instructional sequence, both groups of children were given a 20-item multiple-choice test to measure their comprehension of the text. They also completed a story frame, which is similar to a cloze passage except that whole phrases are deleted and a *wh*-word such as *who* or *what* is put at the beginning of the blank to guide the examinee as to what is missing. The results showed that there were significant differences between the experimental group and the control group on both measures, with the experimental group scoring highest on both. The results indicate that young EFL students can be taught to be aware of text structure, and use it, through direct instruction.

Summary and conclusions

Formal schema knowledge plays a fundamental role in first language and second language reading performance. Default concepts of how script functions, how syntax operates, what creates a cohesive text, and how text is structured exert a strong influence on how any reader attempts to process text. The second language reader needs to master these aspects of text processing at some yet to be determined threshold. However, it is clear that the more mastery the reader has, the better he or she will be.

Further, it appears that there is support for the view that both first language and second language students can be taught formal schematic concepts of text structure and can use that knowledge in recall and comprehension of the text. What has been less well studied is the intensity and duration of training that is necessary in order for students to transfer this knowledge to the processing of texts that are novel and that reflect the nature of authentic texts made up of several different substructures. The next chapter will examine two areas related to formal schema: contrastive rhetoric and genre. These areas involve the reader in an interaction with text in more social contexts than this chapter has done.

Discussion and study questions

1 How might reading an English text with its alphabetic orthography be experienced differently for readers with other first language scripts? Korean readers? Chinese readers? Arabic readers?

2 What are the issues around linguistic simplification of reading texts for learners who are at lower language ability levels? When do you think it is appropriate to simplify texts for these readers? Under what conditions would you decide to avoid text simplification? Why?

3 What are the advantages and disadvantages of examining text structure by having students construct formal outlines of texts representing different rhetorical structures?

4 What approaches to the teaching of text structure do you support? To what extent would you focus on text structure signaling devices?

5 Find a sample narrative and expository text. In groups, discuss who might read the text. Why might they read the texts? How would you apply the discussion of formal schema to assist in teaching the texts in a lesson?

8 GENRE AND CONTRASTIVE RHETORIC

Introduction

Two additional aspects of formal schema related to cohesion, coherence, and text structure are the concepts of genre and rhetorical structure, particularly as rhetorical structures differ from one language to another. In looking at genre and rhetorical structures and their effects on reading, not only do we ask whether the different genres have a cognitive and social reality, but we are also asking whether they cross languages and cultures universally or are culture-bound. This chapter will examine issues involved with genres and rhetorical organization within and across languages and cultures. When second language readers attempt to learn from written text, they are often operating under the combined obstacles of limited language control, limited content knowledge, and limited knowledge of the genre.

The discussion that follows will first present issues surrounding the nature of genre and genres in part to raise to the fore many of the discussion concerns that have framed current considerations of genre studies. This discussion also presents arguments about whether genres actually exist in any stable form. This treatment is necessary in order to explicate what contrastive rhetoric can reveal about reading and, to some extent, writing. Chapter 10 will directly address the reading-writing connection, but some of the issues raised there become evident in the discussion of genre and contrastive rhetoric. There is a growing consensus that, as Swales (2004) notes, genres may not be best seen as single, separable, 'communicative resources but as forming complex networks of various kinds in which switching mode from speech to writing (and vice versa) can—and often does—play a natural and significant part' (2). Similarly, genres often involve switching from reading to writing (and vice versa).

Genre

Swales (1990) states that 'GENRE is quite easily used to refer to a distinctive category of discourse of any type, spoken or written, with or without literary aspirations' (33). The term enters English from the French word for 'class' or 'type', and is the basis for the term *generic*, which today has come to be associated with such concepts as *generic drugs* and *non-branded generic grocery store products*. We have already addressed some genre-relevant concerns above in the discussion of such text structures as *comparison/ contrast, cause-and-effect*, etc. However, in that discussion the attention was on the structural qualities. Traditional rhetoric identifies exposition, argument, description, and narration as four distinct types of discourse that are frequently termed genres (Fairclough 1995). However, Chandler (1997) notes that it is misleading to refer to these as genres because written texts may use any number of combinations of these and other forms at the same time. Rather, it may be more productive to refer to them as modes. In the present context attention will focus on the context of the message that takes on a particular rhetorical structure or structures, on how writers and readers see the function of the text, and on how that genre is congruent with a reader's knowledge base. Bazerman (1997) sees the issue with genres as follows:

> Genres are not just forms. Genres are forms of life, ways of being. They are frames for social action. They are environments for learning. They are locations within which meaning is constructed. Genres shape the thoughts we form and the communications by which we interact. Genres are the familiar places we go to create intelligible communicative action with each other and the guideposts we use to explore the familiar.

> *(Bazerman 1997: 19)*

The term genre has recently come to be used as a characterization of almost any pattern or event, such as the *genre of the music video*, the *genre of the Presidential Press Conference*, and others (Swales 1990: 33). However, it will be used much more narrowly here and used only to refer to types or categories of written text representing *ideal types* that are recognizable in their use. The notion of *ideal types* recognizes that there are many variations in the types of genre we encounter while reading. Take for example the genre of the recipe. Some recipes are fairly terse, others provide very detailed directions, some have a bit of prose at the beginning of the recipe telling of its origins and varieties, others even tell where to obtain hard-to-find authentic spices. Still, we would recognize each of these as a recipe.

Further, it is important to distinguish genre from register (Bhatia 1993), a distinction most prominently raised by systemic linguists. Much research in the past on genre has failed to make this distinction. For example, in discussions of scientific writing, researchers are prone to define a research article style as an exemplar of the academic genre of scientific writing. However, that is a focus on register and style rather than on genre. Register constrains the linguistic features of a text while genre, reflecting the purpose of the discourse interaction, constrains the overall discourse structure (Swales 1990) as well as the level of formality or degree of technical specificity in an instance of discourse (Celce-Murcia and Olshtain 2000). Genres such as the research or business report or recipes are finite structured texts, while registers such as the language of scientific or newspaper reporting or registers such as *academese* and *bureaucratese* represent more generalizable stylistic options (Swales 1990). More discussion of this topic will follow below.

It should not be surprising that there are contentious arguments and conflicting assumptions among theorists and researchers regarding the nature and role of genres. Even the very use of the term genre is not neutral. Three general approaches to genre study have been at play since the early 1980s (Hyon 1996). These are the Sydney School approach, identified closely with the Systemic Functional Linguistics of M.A.K. Halliday, the New Rhetoric approach, which generally attempts to link studies of specific genres with their social and historical contexts (Freedman and Medway 1994), and the English for Specific Purposes approach, with a frequent focus on the practical pedagogical application of studies on particular genres in specific domains of expertise. The three approaches differ in how closely they align their studies with linguistic conventions and constructivist interpretations. However, in general they all concur that genres must be examined as representations of actions beyond a primary concern with text structure alone. For more extensive discussions of the three approaches, see Hyon (1996), Hyland (2002), or Johns (2002).

Johns (2002) presents a succinct overview of the intellectual tensions existing between differing theoretical camps in their conceptualization and use of the term genre. The first major distinction relates to whether one takes a primarily structural linguistic descriptive orientation of genre or one that foregrounds rhetorical context and grounds considerations of genre in the context of the purposes and values of members of a particular discourse community. A second tension that Johns presents relates to the relative stability and tangibility of a genre or the totally contextualized ephemeral and evanescent evolving quality of a genre. That is, can stable and clear genres be defined in such a way that a syllabus or curriculum could be designed around them? How much overlap of structure is allowed for two genres to persist as distinct genres? A third tension involves whether teachers and researchers accept the inherent power relationships that exist within genres, but view them as conventional communicative artifacts within a community, or whether they encourage students to take a critical position and resist a culture's domination of accepted text form (Benesch 2001). Finally, there are basic practical issues of how narrowly a particular genre is to be drawn. Is a genre seen on a macro level, such as narrative, or is it to be defined on the micro level of a letter to a friend describing tending a vegetable garden? Are genres the same as the traditional concepts of text types as discussed in the last chapter? Throughout the following discussion, these tensions and questions will provide a background chorus for the discussion.

Swales (1990: 45–55) provides the following observations about genres. Genres are classes of communicative events, and what turns a collection of communicative events into a genre is the presence of shared communicative purposes. Hence, it was noted that recipes can vary in level of explicitness and detail, but still share a communicative function. Swales' emphasis on shared purpose rather than simply on similarities of form recognizes that texts that have the same form may actually represent separate genres. For example, a parody can have the same form as another text but have far different purposes. Such similarities of form and language are the basis for publications such as the *Journal of Irreproducible Results* (Scherr 1986), which parodies scientific genres and registers. Likewise, a joke and a story may have the same internal structure but they represent different genres. Swales also notes that exemplars or instances of genres will vary in their PROTOTYPICAL-ITY. Thus, it will be easy to uncompromisingly identify some instances of a particular genre, but be more difficult as the text is less representative of the prototype genre. To follow the above example, we will frequently be able to clearly distinguish between a joke and a story. However, irony may be introduced into a story that in effect turns it into a joke, in terms of its purpose, but that irony may be lost on some people so that the story remains a simple narrative. Likewise, a set of chemistry lab instructions may share similarities with a recipe, but will most likely have a somewhat different register.

Paltridge (1997) discusses the relationships of genre to prototypicality. He explores:

> the question of what it is that leads users of a language to recognize particular activities as examples of particular communicative events as instances of particular genres, and what it is that leads a discourse community (Swales, 1990) to lend particular terms, or labels, to these particular events.
>
> *(Paltridge 1997: 47)*

He notes that the concept of prototypicality, though usually discussed in lexical and semantic terms, is important for discussion of genre. Central to his discussion is the frame semantics developed by Fillmore (1976), which attempts to include consideration of the cognitive and interactional frames against which language users interpret their environment and understand the messages of others. These frames are very similar to background schemata in that people have idealizations of concepts such as colors, situational scripts such as going to a café, semantic relations such as cause-and-effect, or forms of writing. These frames are units of conventional knowledge against which expectations are organized.

It is the differences between genres that are of importance in determining the effect that different genres may have on a particular reader (or writer).

Genres differ in their rhetorical complexity (Swales 1990). Thus, recipes are typically less complex than an article abstract. They also differ in terms of the extent to which they are planned ahead of the communicative event. For example, a note from a teacher requesting a meeting is likely to be planned less extensively than a research paper. Genres will differ in terms of length and formality. The recipe is shorter and less formal than the research article. Genres can also differ depending upon the extent to which they represent a universal or culturally specific tendency (Swales 1990). A legal text coming from an Anglo-American tradition proscribing particular acts may be very different from that text derived from an Islamic tradition.

Bhatia (1993) notes that it is almost impossible to explicate clearly defined criteria which make a satisfactory distinction between genres and sub-genres. For example, while it seems fairly clear that a survey article, a review article, and a state-of-the-art article can be seen as sub-genres of some genre designated as research articles, are articles from the *New York Times* and articles from the *National Enquirer* or the *Weekly World News* sub-genres of something known as newspaper articles, or are the latter so different in purpose that the articles become two separate genres? It becomes easier to distinguish the identity of genres as the discourse community becomes more and more homogeneous in its goals and formalisms.

Some genre knowledge is general, in the sense that most literate people share a representation for how a simple cause-and-effect relationship is conveyed. However, other genre knowledge is situated within specific fields, inextricably related to a writer's procedural and social knowledge (Berkenkotter and Huckin 1995). Genre knowledge is linked to accepted practice in specific areas such as how a biologist knows how to report lab results or how a statistician knows how to present data findings. The writers' knowledge of genre allows them to create an appropriate rhetorical context in which to present their ideas. This situated knowledge is acquired gradually throughout the course of the specialist's apprenticeship (Berkenkotter and Huckin 1995). Thus, we see much more clearly defined genres at the graduate level of university education than we do at the early undergraduate levels. Specializations create more distinctly restricted generic forms. But specializations alone do not create distinct genres. Functions also generate genres. PowerPoint presentations are a prime example of a genre growing out of the presentation function, and having privileged or non-privileged status in different fields and specializations.

As indicated above, genre involves much more than mere structural categories. Although genres may be characterized by regularities of structure, much current discussion of genres focuses on a different type of regularity. Genres are seen as typical ways of engaging rhetorically with situations that recur. The regularities observed in structure across occurrences of genres are seen as being due to similarities in how the genre task is socially addressed (Freedman and Medway 1994). Integral to the notion of genre is the task that the writer has engaged in and how the readers are intended to interpret the text. In addition to having prototypic schematic structures, genres represent goal-directed communicative products such as lab reports, working papers, indexes, computer search screens, reviews, letters of recommendation, progress reports, eulogies, sermons, grant proposals, and journal articles. They represent the gamut from grand literature to the mundane. The particular structure selected is a function of the communicative goal. As such, genres are both psychological and social. They represent the cognitive processing of internal schemata and structure as well as the appropriate application of socially prescribed genre categories for others who are familiar with the categories.

Paltridge (1996) comments on the relationship between genres and text types by showing how the two are related in a set of texts previously reported by Hammond et al. (1992). Table 8.1 summarizes Paltridge's findings. As Paltridge notes, it is important to see that more than one genre may share the same text type (for example Advertisement and Police report), and more than one text type can be used with the same genre (for example Formal letter).

Genre	Text Type
Recipe	Procedure
Personal letter	Anecdote
Advertisement	Description
Police report	Description
Student essay	Exposition
Formal letter	Exposition
Formal letter	Problem–Solution

Table 8.1: Examples of genres and text types (from Paltridge (1996), based on Hammond et al. (1992))

Examples of how different genres can develop different structures can be seen in the emergence of different genre structures in texts reflecting what Kachru (1997) identifies as World Englishes. For example, adaptations of two newspaper obituaries are presented below. The first is slightly adapted from a newspaper in the United States, and is fairly representative of US newspaper obituaries. There is discussion of what the person did as an occupation, what services will be held, and the person's immediate family. The second obituary, also slightly adapted, is from a newspaper published near Goa, India. It situates the person in terms of the family network. Both of the texts represent the same genre in terms of what is supposed to be accomplished within the community and what is to be included in the announcement, but they focus on different facets of the person.

Obituary 1

Mr Dean Wallace, 78, of Honolulu, formerly of Fayetville, Ark., died July 10, 2004. Born in Izard County, Ark. A former state public works administrator. Survived by daughters Elizabeth and Marcia: son, Walter; four grandchildren. Celebration of life 7 p.m. Wednesday at Punahou School, Thurston Chapel; private scattering of ashes at sea. Aloha attire. Arrangements by Valley Isle Mortuary.

Obituary 2

JUANITA MARIA FONSECA, Novangoli-Varca: Wife of late Eustaquio; mother/mother-in-law of Filomena (PWD)/Dulcina (Margao Municpal-ity), Norberta/Onesia, (D'Costa Nursery, Aquem) Deanna & Ruando Fonseca/Emelia, Elma/late Benedicto Pinto; grandmother of Antonetta, Ancel, Janice, Olivia Lourdes, Priyo, Melisa, Angelo, Varun, Joao, Delaila, and Mariano.

Another example of how different communities develop different structures for the same genres can be seen in personal advertisements in newspapers. For example, the first advertisement below is adapted from a newspaper in the United States, while the second is adapted from a newspaper in India.

Advertisement 1

SWM, 50 yrs, Academic, Athletic, Renaissance-type. Interested in lady who enjoys the outdoors, fine dining, romance, humor, etc. Non-smoker. Age no barrier. Call XXX-XXXX after 5 pm.

Advertisement 2

ALLIANCE INVITED FROM AN INTELLIGENT, BEAUTIFUL SMART HOMELY PUNJABI GRADUATE GIRL CURRENTLY LEARNING WEBCASTING AND INTERNET PROGRAMMING

ASP, JAVA AND E-COMMERCE 23/182 EMPLOYED AS A SECRETARY FOR THREE YEARS WILLING TO LIVE AND SETTLE IN UAE OR ABROAD LOOKING FOR INTELLIGENT HANDSOME FAIR HARD WORKING PROFESSIONALS NRI'S PREFERRED. EDUCATED AT LEAST UP TO GRADUATE LEVEL, CASTE, RELIGION NO BAR. BOY IS MAIN CONSIDERATON FOREIGNERS CAN ALSO APPLY IN FULL CONFIDENCE GIRLS' FATHER HAVING IMPORT EXPORT BUSINESS IN ENGLAND. e-mailxxxxx923.hotmail.com.

Both of the texts are of the personal ad genre, but are structured differently in terms of what information is included. Additionally, because the Internet is much more flexible and comprehensive, personal ads have virtually disap-peared in many mainstream newspapers (Kemper 2004). Here we see how genres can change over time, and how they are not strictly identified with their structural properties.

Discourse communities exert a great deal of control over the genres adopted to represent their knowledge and purposes. Valle (1997) examined the rhetorical, pragmatic, and textual features of life science texts from the *Philosophical Transactions of the Royal Society of London* from 1711 until 1870. She notes that across that period of time, there was a narrowing of the range of topics, from almost random reports of odd phenomena and events to systematic articles dealing with human and animal anatomy and/or physiology, or with fossil structure. Further, the structure of the texts in the journal became more formal, being primarily descriptive and empirical. The texts began to reference a literature and point out gaps in knowledge. In this sense, they begin to indicate an explicit structure with a clear introductory section presenting the statement of purpose. Here, the initial genre for scientific exchange has become molded and constrained by the discourse community of British biological scientists.

There have been a number of studies examining the different explicit structures of genres and texts such as the introductions, methods, results, and discussion. The goal has been to understand how authors strategically go about the business of presenting knowledge. One useful approach has been the rhetorical move analysis approach pioneered by Swales (1981, 1990). Hopkins and Dudley-Evans (1988) call for an analytic framework that addresses how features relate to:

1 The content of the text creator's message
2 The internal logical organization of what is presented, and the author's explicit and implicit patterning
3 The ways in which the author takes account of the audience.

Move analysis attempts to do this by indicating the functional role played by each move. It should be noted that the moves are not interpreted solely as text-structure representations. They also exist because they are related to the contextualized tasks that the author is attempting. Accomplished readers recognize these moves as parts of conventional texts. Move analysis research has been conducted to look at different sections of research articles and at how these moves differ across different content areas.

Swales' (1981) initial attempt identified four moves that authors used in the introduction section of research articles. However, because there were difficulties in separating Move 1 and Move 2, he revised his initial system (1990) into what he termed the Create a Research Space (CARS) three-move model, incorporating what had previously been Move 2 as Step 3 in Move 1 below:

Move 1 Establishing a territory
Step 1   claiming centrality, and/or
Step 2   making topic generalization(s), and/or
Step 3   reviewing items of previous research

Move 2 Establishing a niche
Step IA   counter-claiming, or
Step IB   indicating a gap, or
Step IC   question-raising, or
Step ID   continuing a tradition

Move 3 Occupying the niche
Step IA   outlining purposes, or
Step IB   announcing present research
Step 2   announcing principal findings
Step 3   indicating research article structure

In discussing the function of these moves, Swales addresses the issue of how they reflect the goals of a functional framework such as that identified by Hopkins and Dudley-Evans (1988) above. He notes that research article introductions need to re-establish in the eyes of the intended audience the significance and importance of the field of research itself and to situate the current research in terms of its significance. Further, there is a need to indicate how the particular research has wider implications in terms of its findings. The particular moves identified in the research article introduction are intended to accomplish these types of bonding with the community.

Other work on research article introductions has tended to support the general move model by Swales with some amendments for particular text types. Crookes (1986) found general support across articles in the hard sciences and biomedical sciences for the moves presented by Swales, but found that social science articles tended to differ. Social science introductions tended to be about 1.8 times the length of the other science articles and have a cyclical pattern in their development. For example, there were many instances of steps that involved a sequence such as Move 1 Step 3 → Move 2 → Move 1 Step 3 → Move 2, and so on in a recursive pattern. Brett (1994) also found introductions in sociology research articles much longer than those in other sciences. Anthony (1999) found that Swales' general framework was supported in his own analysis of introductions in software engineering research articles, but found that variations in step occurrence among different disciplines may be fairly large. For example, fewer than half of Anthony's introductions contained Steps 1-1, 2-1D, and 3-1A. He also found extensive cycling of moves in the software introductions. For example, the following appeared in one of the introductions:

A software requirements specification should be .... (Move 1)

Unfortunately, requirements specifications are often
incomplete .... (Move 2)

We know that many serious conceptual errors are .... (Move 1)

Therefore, it is important to ....   (Move 2)

Previously, we defined formal criteria for ....   (Move 1)

(Anthony 1999: 42)

Further, Anthony found that for the software engineering introductions, there was an obligatory 'evaluation of research' step that is different from the 'reviewing items of previous research' step. Both the Crookes and Anthony studies point out the need to examine how generically the CARS model is applied in different disciplines. These differences help explain why readers often have difficulty when reading information from different disciplines. It is not simply the unfamiliarity with the content material. It is also in part the way the material is presented, though it can be argued that the two are often inextricable.

A number of other researchers have examined different parts of research articles in different disciplines. Salager-Meyer (1990) found that article abstracts varied a great deal from the summary order of the research article they describe, and Hyland (2000) notes that the variations in that structure relate to how the author intends to promote his or her paper. That is, while many of the abstracts in his corpus did not include a method section or explicit introduction, almost all of them included a product statement that foregrounded the primary argument or the findings.

Several researchers have analyzed the discussion sections of different types of research articles. Hopkins and Dudley-Evans (1988) found the structure of discussion sections to be quite different from the introductions that Swales (1981) had proposed. They found a cyclical patterning for the discussion section. First, of the 11 moves they identified, they found only one obligatory move in the discussion sections of articles, statement of result, which occurred at the initial move in each cycle. Further, they found that the particular moves selected differed depending upon whether the dissertation reported satisfactory or unsatisfactory results. Dudley-Evans (1994) notes that the biology discussion section often reverses the order of moves in the introduction to the extent that the statement of the aim is presented initially rather as a final move as in introductions. He finds an overarching framework to the discussion section: Introduction, Evaluation, and Conclusion. Holmes (1997) found political science and sociology discussion sections to be very similar to those found in the natural sciences, although they appear distinct enough to be considered sub-genres. History discussion sections, however, appear to be very distinct, and involve a move, outlining parallel or subsequent developments, found in almost none of the other examined texts. Thus, although research indicates that there are broad similarities in the rhetorical structures of research article discussion sections across many disciplines, there are disciplines such as history with much different structures that the reader must be made aware of.

Brett (1994) examined the results section of sociology research articles. He found 13 moves that fell into one of three categories: metatextual categories, presentation categories, and comment categories. The metatextual categories define parts of the text that refer to data, figures, or text organization. Presentation categories are those that report present conditions, or highlight the results in an objective and impersonal manner. Comment categories are those in which the author comments upon or gives an opinion about results already presented. The results showed a cyclical pattern such as that found by Hopkins and Dudley-Evans (1988), and the statement of finding was the only obligatory move in each cycle. The typical cycle was pointer → statement of finding → substantiation of finding. However, Williams (1999) found that the research section of medical texts not only presented cyclical structures, but also presented strictly linear presentations to a much higher degree than Brett found in the sociology texts. Thus, while there are similarities within the writing patterns across academic research articles, there is some disciplinary variation in genre structure.

In order to explicate the role of genre patterns in reading comprehension, it will be useful briefly to discuss what Swales (1990) labels a *discourse community*, or what Smith (1988) terms a *literacy club*. The key contribution of the concept of a discourse community is the recognition that discourse operates within social and academic communities that have particular expectations about how communication through discourse is presented. In terms of genre and its use, Swales (1990) points out that 'knowledge of the conventions of a genre and their rationale is likely to be greater in those who routinely or professionally operate within that genre rather than those who become involved in it only occasionally' (54). The discourse community stipulates the acceptable forms of text structure allowed for transmitting information, and its members are aware of these acceptable forms and conventions. Swales (1990) offers six requirements for a discourse community. A discourse community:

1 has a broadly agreed set of common public goals
2 has mechanisms of intercommunication among its members
3 uses its participatory mechanisms primarily to provide information and feedback
4 utilizes and hence possesses one or more genres in the communicative furtherance of its aims
5 has acquired some specific lexis
6 has a threshold level of members with a suitable degree of relevant content and discoursal expertise.

As an example of a discourse community, Swales (1990) mentions a hobby group called the Hong Kong Study Circle (HKSC). This group has as its goals the fostering of interest and knowledge about the stamps of Hong Kong. The group has a diverse membership from around the world: some academics, some from the military, some blue collar, both male and female. The members of the group apparently have little in common other than an interest in stamps from Hong Kong. Communication among the members of the group principally takes place through a bi-monthly journal. Swales indicates how the conventions regarding submissions to the journal have developed into a specific set of genre-related methods for describing aspects of Hong Kong stamps. He provides an example from an auction catalog as follows:

> 1176 1899 Combination PPC to Europe franked CIP 4 C canc
> large CANTON dollar chop, pair HK 2C carmine added &
> Hong Kong index B cds. Arr cds. (1) (Photo) HK $1500

> *(Swales 1990: 28)*

Clearly, people who are not part of this discourse community will be at a disadvantage when trying to comprehend this text. The HKSC meets all six of the requirements that Swales identified as necessary to define a discourse community. Consequently, its members have some formal schema about the expected forms of interaction and conventions.

Obviously, people can belong to many different discourse communities and literacy clubs. Some of these can be central to a person's occupation, such as academic institutions and specialized associations, while others are of a peripheral nature, such as bird-watching clubs. It is through some form of apprenticeship that one becomes a full member of the discourse community and is steeped in the conventions and genres that are utilized. It would take one some time to understand the example just given, and to learn that PPC means picture post card, CIP means Chinese Imperial Post, and so on. However, over time the conventions are learned and accepted as appropriate, relevant, and correct. In order to maintain coherence, discourse communities employ what Clark (1998) terms *communal lexicons*, lexicons associated with communities of expertise. Additionally, discourse communities may have unique genres. For example, take the example of the research article abstract. It is a very peculiar genre limited to certain types of publications. Magazines do not usually have formal abstracts before each article, nor do automotive manuals tend to have abstracts. As readers experience the texts of their discourse community in more depth, they are able to classify texts into genre categories, and are able to identify the different texts shared by community designated names (Johns 1997). Johns provides several examples of what parts of genre are shared by the discourse community. These are:

1 genre names
2 communicative purposes
3 knowledge of roles
4 knowledge of context

5 knowledge of text conventions
6 text content
7 register—lexical and grammatical feature categories
8 awareness of intertextuality—how texts relate to prior texts.

Obviously, these shared types of knowledge are learned incrementally as the reader gains experience with the particular expectations of the discourse community. The more contact the reader has, the deeper the connections and understanding of the constellation of genres expected from the community membership. Hyland (2002), however, notes that not everyone is equally sanguine with the notion of discourse community and the power any discourse community exercises over writers and readers. Criticisms of the role that any discourse community may exert focus around concerns that discourse communities are ill defined, abstract, empirically elusive, and, if existent, imply static and deterministic forces that are inconsistent with how texts develop. Rafoth (1990) states that by focusing attention on conventions of language use, the notion of discourse community 'often obscures the variety, conflict, and anti-conventionalism that exists in most actual discourse communities, and thus impedes critical examination of the inherent trade-offs an individual faces in belonging to some communities and not others' (140). However, the concept appears useful in its descriptive and explanatory power, given that communities do exhibit regularities in the characteristics of text that they normatively produce. Further, recognizing the convention-bound nature of text can raise recognition of the implications of any static and deterministic inertia in the texts that readers encounter.

Contrastive rhetoric

For second language reading, a natural area of concern is the extent to which genres and associated text structure are language or culture specific and might consequently create interference in the comprehension of a text by readers from other cultures and languages. Further, it is of interest to understand whether and to what degree similar discourse communities, such as biologists and jurists, differ in different linguistic and cultural environments. The developing field of *contrastive rhetoric* has been involved in these issues for some time. Although it was primarily developed as a tool to explain characteristics of second language composition products, it has been useful in understanding potential second language reading problems as well. Contrastive rhetoric emphasized that language is a cultural phenomenon. Consequently, different cultures develop different rhetorical argument patterns. Those different rhetorical patterns, according to contrastive rhetoric advocates, may interfere in second language writing and reading.

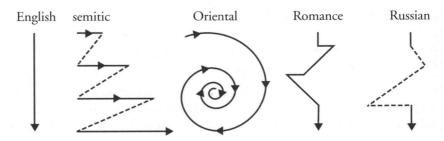

Figure 8.1: Kaplan's (1966) diagram of cross-cultural differences in paragraph organization

Robert Kaplan (1966) first articulated the concern in a seminal and somewhat controversial article in *Language Learning*. In Kaplan's view, logic and rhetoric are interrelated and culture specific, as are language and thought. According to this view, cultures developed unique rhetorical structures over time and these structures interfered with the second language writing of their members. As support for this, Kaplan provided the diagrams in Figure 8.1.

In these contrasts, Kaplan represents English rhetorical structure to be linear because an English text begins with a topic sentence, followed by supporting information. In contrast, 'Oriental' languages are indirect in their approach while Romance and Russian writing incorporate digressions and extraneous material. This incarnation of Kaplan's views on language and rhetoric is obviously much too simplistic to explain the complete rhetoric of any language or group of languages. Further, such a conceptualization was motivated by an analysis of how writers of each language group produced example texts in English, rather than a close analysis of the actual instances of rhetorical structures in the languages mentioned. The structure of a second language learner's English composition is not necessarily reflective of the first language rhetorical structures. Finally, it is not the case that a single rhetorical organization can be said to be representative of all composition in any particular language or culture.

Kaplan has subsequently recognized some of the shortcomings of the particular model presented in the 1966 'doodles' article (Kaplan 2000). In fact, Kaplan (1987) states that in his opinion 'all of the various rhetorical modes ... are possible in any language ... The issue is that each language has certain clear preferences' (10). He notes that speakers of each language consider their own language to be linear and English to represent some other rhetorical model (Kaplan 2000). Contrastive rhetoric has evolved to a position that acknowledges that the rhetoric of no language or culture can be reduced to a diagrammatic representation designated as circular or zigzag, but there is evidence that languages frequently have preferred generic or stylistic compositional forms that vary across languages (Scollon 1997). However, the original Kaplan article does reflect a sense that differing rhetorical patterns do foreground and background differing relationships. Further, his work presented an early rejection of linguistics bound by sentence-level analysis, calling instead for a linguistics based on the paragraph or beyond.

That there is something to the notion that texts in different languages utilize different organizational patterns can be seen in the opening sentence of an abstract to an article in the journal *Text* from 2001. The abstract begins, 'In this article I will suggest that Japanese texts are logically organized' (Nanri 2001: 373). That such a statement would appear in an important refereed publication indicates that there is some disagreement on the nature of Japanese text organization. Indeed, Nanri reviews a literature, albeit not empirically based, that argues a claim that Japanese writers 'just create texts without having clear goals in mind' (373). Certainly, different languages and cultures employ different logics and different patterns of writer/reader roles and responsibilities. However, there is some socially agreed-upon organizational perspective for how language artifacts are to be presented, or no transactions could be completed. Discovering how these patterns differ from culture to culture and language to language is the primary function of contrastive rhetoric.

There has been extensive work looking at the relationship between the rhetorical structures of different languages. For example, some Japanese, Korean, and Chinese compositions are characterized by four-unit rhetorical patterns that are inductively organized. In Japanese it is known as the *ki-shoo-ten-ketsu* pattern. In Korean it is known as the *ki-sung-chon-kyul* pattern. In Chinese it is termed the *qi-cheng-zhuan-he* style. Many researchers in the field of contrastive rhetoric argue that these structures lead to writing that promotes what appears to be an indirect style to Western readers (Cai 1999; Hinds 1983a, b; Tsao 1983).

In discussing the *ki-shoo-ten-ketsu*, etc. rhetorical organization, Hinds presents the following description:

ki   First, begin one's argument.

shoo   Next, develop that.

ten   At the point where this development is finished, turn the idea to a subtheme where there is a connection, but not a directly connected association [to the major theme]

ketsu   Last, bring all of this together and reach a conclusion.

(Hinds 1983b: 80)

Hinds (1983a) took several articles from a newspaper representing this style, and created both Japanese and English versions of them. Readers of both languages were asked to rate the different passages on a scale representing the categories of Unity, Focus, and Coherence within the passages. The native speakers of English rated the texts lower on each category across all of the passages than did the Japanese speakers. This provides some indirect evidence that this rhetorical pattern might cause problems for a native English speaker reading Japanese texts of this sort.

Hinds (1987) proposed that Japanese writing demands more of the reader, in terms of coherence, whereas the rhetorical form preferred in the West places the burden of exposition on the writer more than does Japanese. He notes that there is a strong sense of responsibility in English speakers to make 'clear and well-organized statements. If there is a breakdown in communication ... it is because the speaker/writer has not been clear enough, not because the listener/reader has not exerted enough effort in an attempt to understand' (143). In Japanese, on the other hand, he asserts that the reader is expected to connect the sections of the text together with fewer cohesion markers than are required in English. This reflects what some see as a difference in the degree to which a particular culture assumes an internal order of the text to be general-to-specific (GS), involving a general statement followed by specifics, or specific-to-general (SG), involving a text that begins with specifics that lead to a general statement (Connor 1996; Hinds 1987; Kobayashi 1984). English academic writing tends to follow the GS pattern while Japanese tends to follow the SG order. Kobayashi (1984) found that US students frequently chose the GS pattern while Japanese speakers chose to write in the SG pattern.

In a second study, Hinds (1983b) again examines the *ki-shoo-ten-ketsu* structure to investigate this expectation that the reader carries the burden in text comprehension. His example is a text about throwaway chopsticks that appeared in a Japanese newspaper. The text begins with a questioning of whether the use of disposable chopsticks is a good practice (*ki*). Then the passage presents the context of using these chopsticks in restaurants and the amount of wood wasted (*shoo*). At this point the article begins to state that Japan is not the only chopstick culture (*ten*), and discusses the materials that chopsticks are made of (*ten*), how some chopsticks were invented out of red Japanese cedar (*ten*), how the Japanese do not like others to use their chopsticks and how in ancient times people believed that the spirits of the person who owned the chopsticks resided in the chopsticks (*ten*), how it is now the heyday of throwaway chopsticks made of silver firs, birches, and Japanese lindens (*ten*). Then the article returns to the issue of wastefulness in throwing away the chopsticks (*ketsu*). Hinds contends that Japanese readers are required to construct transitions themselves while reading this type of essay. Non-native speakers of Japanese reading such a text could feel that the essay is rambling and poorly written. Here is a mismatch in formal schema regarding text structuring.

Chu, Swaffar, and Charney (2002) examined the Chinese *qi-cheng-zhuan-he* style. University-level Taiwanese English language majors in their freshman and senior years were presented with versions of English language texts that were written to reflect either the Chinese *qi-cheng-zhuan-he* rhetorical structure or Western rhetorical conventions. Corresponding passages had very similar readability scores. On both immediate- and delayed-recall measures, the students performed significantly better on the English texts reflecting the Chinese rhetorical conventions. These findings indicate a strong influence of a familiar rhetorical style over an unfamiliar rhetorical convention on foreign language comprehension. However, the findings also indicated that on the immediate-recall test there was a passage by convention interaction, and although recall was greater for the Chinese rhetorical versions of all of the texts, only half of the differences between the two versions were statistically significant. This last finding indicates that additional factors such as text difficulty or ease may moderate the strength of the influence exerted by familiarity with text structure. That is, first language rhetorical forms and processing strategies, while influential in second language reading, are only contributing factors that shape the reader's processing, certainly not purely deterministic factors in reading success.

There is some indication in Japanese text that the inductive structure of moving from supporting idea and ending with a general statement of conclusion may in part be due to the type of information that is being presented. Maynard (1996) examined the argument structure of opinion pieces from a Japanese newspaper. She found results consistent with Hinds (1983). There was a tendency for an inductive organization with the initial paragraphs presenting specifics and concluding with a generalizing state- ment. However, Fukuoka and Sypridakis (1999) looked at texts from three different journals containing different types of information. One journal was a business journal, one a general scientific journal, and one contained both general and specific scientific information. They determined whether the general statement in each article came at the beginning of the text or at the end. Their findings indicated that when the authors of the text were presenting their interpretation of the facts, the general statements appeared very late in the articles. However, when the texts were presenting factual and expository information without the author's interpretations, then the general statement appeared near the beginning. Thus, whether the texts are developed inductively or deductively may be a reflection of what role the author assumes regarding whether he or she is primarily a presenter of facts or an interpreter of the information.

Differences in textual representation across languages have their structural aspects as with the Japanese, Korean, and Chinese four unit rhetorical patterns of the *ki-shoo-ten-ketsu, ki-sung-chon-kyul,* or *qi-cheng-zhuan-he* style. However, differences also reflect more subtle social aspects of text representation. Additional research in Korean, Chinese, German, and Hindi has also shown different text-structure characteristics that can lead to a sense of indirectness or affect perceptions about the target text (Eggington 1987, Cai 1999). Although the analyses frequently tend to be based on English compositions as reflections of the first language text structure, they lend some support for the effect of first language text-structure preferences. Bouton (1995) examined letters of reference written by referees from the US, and by referees from India, Japan, Korea, Taiwan, and China. His analysis indicated that the letters differed systematically in terms of whether the recommendation moves were located in the introduction, body, or concluding segments of the letter. Similarly, Precht (1998) examined letters of recommendation from the US, the UK, Germany, and Eastern Europe. She found cross-cultural differences in whether the letters were organized topically or chronologically. These differences can be important if one culture expects recommendations to be stated clearly and explicitly while another culture expects the letter to be a detailed list of accomplishments from which the reader is to infer the writer's intention. This set of different expectations is reflected in the structure of the text.

Zhu (1997, 2000) has examined the structure of Chinese sales letters and has contrasted them with English sales letters. Her analysis notes many similarities in the letters of both language groups. This is in large part due to the fact that the letters of both groups have essentially the same function. They offer a product and wish to develop sufficient interest via the letter that they sell the product. However, there are differences. First, the English sales letters tended to contain a headline at the beginning of the letter such as 'The Latest Appliance on up to 18 Months Interest Free Credit—For One Very Special Night Only!' (482), whereas the Chinese letters did not contain this move. Likewise, the English letters frequently included a postscript, a PS notation about a free gift, for example, but the Chinese letters did not. In contrast, the Chinese business letters tended to include greetings such as 'How are you?', while the English business letters did not contain this move. Following the greeting, the Chinese letters also tended to include an introductory move such as 'In order to offer you better services, (we) would like to report our company's sales to you. (We) hope that you will give us your full support'. The English business letters tended not to include this move, which Zhu sees as a move to establish long-term relationships. The English sales letters provided more extensive detail than did the Chinese letters, and the details that did appear in the Chinese letters tended to focus around relationship building. In short, although there are a large number of similarities between the two letter families, both languages tended to include features that the other did not.

Languages have also been shown to differ in the way digressive propositions are viewed and interpreted. Clyne (1987) examined the differences in academic texts composed by German native speakers and texts by English native speakers. He noted that one feature of German academic discourse is digressiveness. This is characterized as the *Exkurs* within a text, a formal feature which provides more general or peripheral information on the topic which allows writers to work their way toward conclusions. He notes that the *Exkurs* necessarily have to be followed by repetition of the primary line of argument to provide logical progression of the text. Clyne (1987) examined 52 academic texts, 26 written by German native speakers and 26 written by English native speakers. In the articles that were examined, 57 per cent of the texts by English native speakers were linear with 43 per cent having some digressions, while only 23 per cent of the German native speakers' articles were clearly linear with 77 per cent of the total containing some digression. The primary function of digression in the German texts was to provide theory, ideology, qualification, or additional information. He also noted a greater tendency toward asymmetry in the German texts, where asymmetry is indicated by some sections of the paper being much longer than others or presenting a difference in length of related propositions. Texts by English speakers were more likely than those of German-educated writers to use advance organizers to explain the organization of the paper, and these organizers tend to be placed at the beginning of the paper. Other textual differences involved the English texts including more definitions than the German texts and the English texts being less likely to include discontinuity in which an argument is abandoned in 'mid-air' and a new argument initiated. These differences across the two languages could affect comprehension by readers of the second language. If a linear text is expected, then the English first language reader reading a German text may attempt to find some linear rationale for the *Exkurs*, for example.

Academic texts from different traditions are structured in different ways. Duszak (1994) and Golebiowski (1998) both discuss how Polish articles in academic publications lack divisions into sections such as Introduction, Methods, Results, Conclusion, Discussion, but rather feature unsegmented and continuous text. Golebiowski found material normally contained in the introduction section of English articles to be distributed throughout the Polish texts that were examined. The Polish texts, like Clyne's (1987) German texts, indicated frequent digressions. The digressions were employed to: present background information, review previous research, consider theoretical and philosophical issues, develop and clarify concepts, explain terminology, and justify research or methodology. Return to the main research line after digressions was frequently followed by recapitulations. Golebiowski claims that Polish writers usually introduce their research by 'presenting a very broad view of the area and gradually narrowing it down, building up their argument through multiple digressions' (83).

Conceptions of acceptable and unacceptable digression within text can affect text processing. Kachru (1988) describes the differing rhetorical structure for literary criticism and technical writing in Hindi and in English. She points out that within Hindi texts unity of a topic is not a requirement for a paragraph, and that Hindi paragraphs tolerate a great deal of digression. There are examples where an author introduces a digression after two sentences in a paragraph, and then gives his judgments about the digression before resuming the central discussion. Also, in Hindi paragraphs there is no need for an explicit topic sentence. Her example texts show that the presentation of a claim and the justification for that claim can be separated over several paragraphs. In some cases the main topic of the essay does not appear until the sixth paragraph of the essay. A reader from a more Western tradition of writing may have difficulty with these texts.

Mauranen (1993) describes how Finnish writers use metatext, text orienting readers to the text, much less than do Anglo-American writers of economics texts. This relative lack of orienting text and a generally more impersonal style of writing contribute to what Mauranen terms a more 'implicit' rhetorical style than that normally found in English by Anglo-American writers. Metatext assists in organizing the propositional content of a text and to comment upon it with such statements as '*The paper concludes by contrasting the findings with x …*'. While metatext is seen as an asset by some English authors (Crismore and Farnsworth 1990), Finnish textbooks on writing advise writers to avoid its use (Rainio 1988). According to Mauranen:

> The function of metatext is, then, to organise and comment on the discourse, particularly the propositional content that is being conveyed. Through metatext, the writer steps in explicitly to make his or her presence felt in the text.
>
> *(Mauranen 1993: 9)*

In her comparison of English economics texts written by a native English writer and a native Finnish writer, Mauranen found that 54.2 per cent of the English writer's sentences contained metatextual elements while only 22.6 per cent of the Finnish writer's text contained metatextual elements. She notes that Finnish discourse does not explicitly prepare the reader for what to expect by indicating what the text is going to do while native speakers of English employ mechanisms that anticipate what is to follow and how the various parts of the text relate to one another. English writers tend to write deductively while the Finnish writers write more inductively, frequently leaving the main point unsaid. Readers familiar with either of these traditions will have differing expectations about how to proceed in constructing meaning, and this can affect how they interpret the information in the text. The two rhetorical styles place different demands on the reader.

Obviously there are tremendous similarities across languages in terms of their organization of text, and comparison of the structure of similar scientific genres shows a great deal of similarity in the surface text. Additionally, although genres emerge from highly conventionalized social actions, there will be a great deal of variability within the different genres of a language. There are both similarities within genres and differences in text organization across languages that may affect the reading process. Knowledge of the formal schemata of how texts are organized is an important tool for any reader to possess. An important consideration, then, is how pedagogy can utilize knowledge about genres and contrastive rhetoric to improve reading instruction.

Whether or not to explicitly address genres in first language and second language instruction is a contested issue in both reading and writing instruction. In first language instruction there has been an influential child-centered view that children should learn the world through their own words, not through externally determined structures (Berkenkotter and Huckin 1995). Similarly, in recent second language instruction, composition instruction in particular, a focus on process learning has promoted a reticence to focus on such conventional structures as cause-and-effect and comparison and contrast. Additionally, constructivist concerns that tying students to prescriptive models perpetuates existing power relationships within educational institutions have been put forth as arguments against genre instruction (Benesch 2001; Pennycook 2001). However, others argue that failing to teach the genres of education and work disenfranchises non-mainstream students, whether they are racial, ethnic, or economic minorities (Berkenkotter and Huckin 1995; Christie 1985; Kress 1993). Research has shown that minority and economically challenged children overly rely on the narrative and produce 'blurred genres' in their writing when teachers ignore explicit teaching of other genres (Christie 1985). The position taken here is a rather agnostic one. The decision of whether or not to teach genres rests with whether the student will be advantaged in knowing about the characteristics of the genre. It is analogous to deciding whether or not to teach fronted conditionals of the form 'Had I known Ms. Astor was present, I should have stayed at home.' It is rather an affectation, but useful for certain registers. That stated, the remainder of the chapter will address genre instruction.

Instructional approaches in genre and contrastive rhetoric

As noted above, genre instruction has typically been the purview of composition studies. However, instruction in genre composition provides the writer with a critical point of view for thinking like a reader. Most composition approaches that adopt genre studies work with written texts in some form as models for analysis. In fact, genre literacy is a product of both reading and writing, particularly in academic and professional settings. As a consequence, several of the studies and approaches to genre study discussed below will attend to composition as well as the model texts and purposes that are analyzed in the study of genres.

One large-scale application of genre pedagogy has been that utilized in the Adult Migrant English Program (AMEP) in Australia implemented the late 1980s and 1990s (Feez 2002). The program involved systemic functional linguists and teachers working together to develop a syllabus that linked context with language use. Researchers examined extensive samples of primary-school student writing and identified distinctive patterns of lexical, grammatical, and cohesive choices that create the stages of different genres. The pedagogy that was developed strove to integrate learning about language into the teaching of literacy and writing across the curriculum. The approach takes the view that through making the literacy practices and demands of different genres more visible, the values and worldviews embodied in the texts become more visible and available to the learner, and thus more open to discussion, criticism, negotiation, and challenge (Feez 2002). As the learner moves from low-level proficiency to higher levels of proficiency, he or she moves from general learning text genres to more specialized contexts of work, study, or community life. There is a set of 'can do' statements (for example 'can demonstrate understanding of a spoken information text') for different stages across the ability scale used. The syllabus is a text-based syllabus in which the organizing principle is the study of whole texts in their context. Teachers customize course content to the learners in their classes through needs analysis. The learning cycle consists of: 1) building the context; 2) modeling and deconstructing the text; 3) joint construction of the text; 4) independent construction of the text; and 5) linking related texts. Teachers appreciated the relative stability of the curriculum based on genre pedagogy (Feez 2002). Basically this approach attempts to contextualize the texts, but it includes explicit modeling and discussion of the texts.

Not all genre-based instructional units need to be as comprehensive as that presented by Feez (2002). Henry and Roseberry (1998) used the genre of brief tourist information at the University of Brunei Darussalam Faculty of Management. The instructional objective was to have the students produce their own tourist information texts. The experimental group of students was presented with six example authentic texts and then identified the rhetorical moves. They determined which of the moves were obligatory and which were optional. The students then had two tasks. The first task was to look at an existing text that was missing two of the mandatory rhetorical moves and to rewrite it correctly. The second task involved the students in generating their own tourist destination promotions. The control group worked with a set of non-genre materials, and was encouraged to use the six example texts as models. The results indicated that the genre group had higher motivation and also had better control of cohesive devices. They also tended to produce texts that conformed to the generic move structure more than the control group. For this relatively narrow genre type, and over a short treatment period, the genre instruction appeared to work fairly well.

Hyon (2002) describes a genre-based reading program of instruction for university students whose first language is other than English. It utilized explicit discussion, modeling and analysis of genres. The units of instruction involved tasks that elicited students' observations about text features. Students would analyze text segments in class and reconstruct texts that had been cut up into isolated segments. The discussions served as metacognitive tools for raising students' awareness of the formal and functional features of written text. The program involved the genres of a hard news story, a magazine feature article, a textbook, and a research article. Discussions focused around the text content, structure, language style, and purpose. An exam was given at the end of 12 weeks of instruction in which the students worked with texts of the same types as those used in the instructional sessions. Results indicated that the students could recognize and describe the genre types as well as discuss the structure and language style found in the texts. Fewer of the students described the purpose of the texts, perhaps because purpose had not been emphasized in the course as much as the other elements. From the previous discussion of genre, it seems clear that more emphasis should have been placed on discussions of purpose and how purpose relates to rhetorical moves. A year after the course, Hyon (2001) followed up with eight of the original 11 students in the study. They were again shown example texts of the four genres used in the instruction. Most of the students used the terminology from the course when discussing the academic genres of research article and textbook. However, they merely described the hard news story and feature article. Most likely, this is in part because they were in an academic context. Thus, it is difficult to determine whether genre knowledge was a result of the previous instruction or a result of continued focus on these particular genres in their academic environment over the time period between instruction and follow-up.

Reppen (1995) piloted a genre-based unit with fifth-grade public school students in a low socioeconomic area school. English was a second language for approximately 75 per cent of the students in the class. The class was a regular social studies unit that had explorers as the content and the treatment covered 15 45-minute classes. The teacher modeled the new rhetorical patterns for the students to practice. The genre forms included narrative, descriptive, persuasive, and expository. The rationale for this order was:

> After the explorers returned, they would have told their stories (narrative).
> Second, they would have given detailed descriptions of the places and

people that they had seen (descriptive). Explorers would have had to persuade crew members to accompany them, and royalty or other affluent people to fund their expeditions (persuasive). Finally, explorers would have had to provide reports about their explorations (expository).

(Reppen 1995: 33)

The students discussed the attributes of each genre and contrasted them. They learned point of view and audience. Reppen found that the students improved in their understanding of the different genre forms, and began to utilize the narrative as the default genre for all writing. These learners developed some initial understanding of the genres that are valued at their level of education, both in reading and writing. On a very positive cautionary note, Reppen argues against turning genre instruction into a formulaic type of structure learning and manipulation. Rather, instruction should focus on the informational and organizational demands of the context.

In general, genre instruction has shown some effectiveness in some contexts. As noted in the last chapter, instruction is useful in teaching readers the structural characteristics of texts. Teaching genres is more complex and involves a more social look at how the reader interacts with the context of the text. However, those programs that have been successful indicate that genre instruction should include specific components in order to be effective. Instruction should include: 1) consciousness raising about the reader-writer relationship; 2) recognition of discourse communities and their expecta-tions; 3) examination of prototypical rhetorical structure and its moves, variability in prototypical structure, and why that variability may be employed; 4) exploration of author's purpose in producing the text; 5) formality versus informality of the register; 6) particular grammatical and lexical features associated with the genre; 7) cross-cultural comparisons; and 8) relations of genre and text type (for example newspapers, textbooks, research articles, grant applications, etc.). Genre instruction is viewed as being much more complex now than when instructional textbooks were written to provide models organized around such chapter headings as *special organization, classification, contrast, chronological order, process*, and other purely structural designations. It needs to teach the reader to situate the text in a purposeful context.

Summary and conclusions

Genre is a central concept in understanding how text is organized and what purpose motivates the text's existence. Genres represent the functions of a text as they are intended to affect others. In many ways genres are a conundrum in that we can see a text structure explicitly, but have to infer the genre as being a reflection of that structure. Genres are both highly conventionalized and variable. It is often the very conventionalized nature of the genre that allows creative variability to effectively communicate the message. For example, parody depends crucially on the conventional nature of the object of parody. Furthermore, genres are closely linked to the discourse communities they are a part of. Their success is linked to how the discourse community accepts and interprets them. These discourse communities can be large or small, very conventional or flexible and open. However, they always exert a pull on the construction of their texts.

Genres, being social inventions, vary in their representations across cultures. Differing cultural emphases, assumptions, and linguistic forms can create different textual structures designed to represent the same genre. Readers from different languages and cultures need to recognize and be open to the potential differences in order to become accomplished readers. Instruction designed to achieve this cognizance should engage the learner in examining the text and its purposes, focusing more broadly than on the text structure.

Discussion and study questions

1 In your view, are genres and discourse communities real, or are they simply useful heuristics for description and instruction?
2 Swales (1990) discusses a study that determined that two senior college Chemistry classes and Engineering classes comprised different and distinct communities, different in the issues they engaged and the social purposes in their writing, and in that they assumed different audience roles. What implications would this finding have for generalizing to genres in different scientific classes? Different social science classes?
3 Swales defines genre as a class of communicative events, 'the members of which share some set of communicative purposes (58)'. Further, he provides five criterial observations about genres. These are:
   A A genre is a class of communicative events.
   B The principal criterial feature that turns a collection of communicative events into a genre is some shared set of communicative purposes.
   C Exemplars of genres vary in their prototypicality.
   D The rationale behind a genre establishes constraints on allowable contributions in terms of their content, positioning and form.
   E A discourse community's nomenclature for genres is an important source of insight.
   Why does he consider each of these to be criterial? How do these relate to the six defining characteristics that he sees as necessary and sufficient for identifying people as members of discourse communities?

4 Some authors take a structural (linguistic) approach to genre, while others take a functional (social) approach. What are advantages and disadvantages of both approaches? Which view do you tend toward?

5 Find a text for a genre analysis. The text should be at least 200–300 words in length. Look at each move in the text and determine how it fits with the moves identified by Swales and others in the preceding chapter.

A What genre did you assign the text to?

B What subject matter is the text concerned with?

C What audience is the text aiming at?

D What assumptions does the text make in terms of what other texts the audience is familiar with?

E What genre conventions do you find in the text?

F Does the text assume the audience is aligned with its point of view or against its point of view?

G To what extent does the text appear to go beyond the genre's conventions?

H Assume an audience of students. Describe them and outline a process you would use to raise their awareness of the genre.

9 VOCABULARY IN SECOND LANGUAGE READING

Introduction

Language is formed of words. Words allow us to talk about objects as diverse as helicopters and penguins. The language learner learns words before acquiring syntax or conventional discourse patterns. The learner's vocabulary is key in language and its acquisition. Over time the learner learns lexical meaning, syntax, and morphology. The learner learns how to use morphology to create new words and meanings, such as *nation*, *national*, *nationalize*, and *nationalization*. Vocabulary size continues to grow throughout a learner's life. The centrality of vocabulary was indicated by Krashen (in Lewis 1993: iii) when he noted that language learners do not carry around grammar books, they carry around dictionaries.

Vocabulary has been seen as a primary factor in verbal comprehension throughout much of the history of modern psychological and educational research. In fact, measures of verbal reasoning such as analogy tests inherently value vocabulary control as essential to the trait itself. Likewise, the close relationship between reading comprehension and vocabulary knowledge has long been recognized. Measures of lexical knowledge are among the best predictors of reading comprehension ability (Sternberg 1987). The research on reading skills by Davis (1972), Thorndike (1973), and others discussed in Chapter 4 indicated that vocabulary is a considerable factor in reading ability. Consequently, it appears that a large vocabulary can facilitate reading comprehension. But, how large is large? Bryson (1990) notes that *Webster's Third New International Dictionary* and the revised *Oxford English Dictionary* list 450,000 and 625,000 words respectively. Adding all the additional scientific and technical words in English would add millions more. Luckily, it is not necessary for readers to know all the words in a language. There are about 200,000 English words in common use (Bryson 1990), and most first language readers have acquired a vocabulary of approximately 40,000 to 50,000 words, or 20,000 word families, by the time they reach college (Just and Carpenter 1987; Nation 2001). So, we have to address the question, 'How much vocabulary does a second language reader need to know?'

The question posed at the end of the last paragraph uses *vocabulary* rather than *words* for a reason that is specific to how reading vocabulary will be addressed in this chapter. Nation (2001) has shown that there is a large overlap across the various word frequency lists, and that the most frequent 2,000 words account for approximately 80 per cent or more of the words in most fiction, newspaper, or academic texts. For those lexical items, it makes a great deal of sense to talk in terms of words in that they are essential for reading success. But it is also necessary to think of vocabulary beyond numbers of words because of lexical structures such as phrasal verbs (for example *take out*), compound nouns (for example *dishwashing soap*), and idioms (for example *in black and white*). Additionally, many of the most frequent words are used in combinations and have several meanings. For example, in the Thorndike-Lorge (Thorndike and Lorge 1944) word list of the most frequent words, there are large numbers of words like *bill, cost, eye, face, hand*, etc., that have multiple meanings and can represent different parts of speech. Consider the many dictionary entries for the word *give*. Its meanings include such phrases as: 1) the doctor gave her a shot of penicillin; 2) he gave his last breath; 3) you gave a valid argument; 4) they gave a concert; 5) he gave you a cold; 6) they gave their all for the cause; 7) I give you my word; 8) the floor gave under him as he walked; 9) she gave him a push; 10) the priest gave him the last rites; 11) he gave a nod; and 12) frankly, my dear, I didn't give a damn. So being able to easily read the most frequent 2,000 words means knowing many more than 2,000 meanings.

One problem in studying individual reader differences in vocabulary is that each individual's vocabulary knowledge is so idiosyncratic. 'High frequency' and 'low frequency' are inexact indicators because people confront so many different words in different contexts. Haggard (1982) reported that an entire cohort of high-school students began using the word *behooves* after hearing an assistant principal use it in a speech at a school assembly. The students began to use the word actively and in many contexts. Apparently most directives produced by the students began to incorporate the term. *Behooves* is an extremely low-frequency lexical item. In fact, the Francis and Kučera (1982) word frequency list indicates that *behooves* appears only eight times in 50,406 word types. Yet, one chance utterance by an assistant principal, and peer pressure, made the word salient enough to become a productive vocabulary item for these adolescents. Inadvertent salient encounters of relatively infrequent words are not rare.

A second problem in conceptualizing differences in vocabulary knowledge relates to the interaction of vocabulary and world knowledge. Knowledge of vocabulary goes well beyond a mere recognition of a particular orthographic representation. It also involves a semantic representation incorporating a wide range of meanings. There is a close relation between lexical knowledge and world knowledge, but theoretically it is possible to distinguish between them. Absence of a vocabulary item does not necessarily imply an absence of the concept, particularly with second language readers who may not know the word *bicycle* in English, but have no problem with the concept. However, often the two go together. An untrained person trying to read an oceanography text coming across the term *eustatic change* (a worldwide change in sea level due to an increase or decrease in the amount of seawater) may be facing lack of familiarity with an essential concept as well as lacking knowledge of a particular vocabulary term.

What does it mean to know a word?

It is almost axiomatic now that vocabulary develops incrementally and that knowing a word is not a dichotomous distinction. Rather, there is a continuum from not knowing a word at all, to recognizing a word, to some knowledge of the word, to full control of the word in all general contexts. Various aspects of a word are learned and it is generally the case that this learning initially develops into a receptive vocabulary and that over time much of that receptive vocabulary used in listening and reading becomes productive vocabulary for speech and writing. This is not to argue that a word does not appear in productive vocabulary until all facets of the word are learned. For example, someone may learn the term *bachelor* as an unmarried male (Katz and Fodor 1963). However, there are a number of other features that may not be known at the early stages of acquisition, such as that in the unmarked case a bachelor is usually assumed not to have been married and divorced, is generally not assumed to be elderly, but is assumed to be an adult. It would seem odd to refer to Bart Simpson as a bachelor. These nuanced aspects of word knowledge may develop more slowly as understanding of the word becomes more robust. Such word knowledge is particularly important in vocabulary learning in foreign language contexts where words have local or dialectical connotations that are not readily apparent from dictionary entries. For example, the dictionary definition of the term *hillbilly* 'a person from a backwoods area' (Webster 1980: 536) in no way represents the connotative semantic attributes that have attached to the term within the US. Consequently, it is important to examine both breadth and depth of word knowledge. Measuring both of these is essential, though difficult (Laufer et al. 2004).

Breadth of word knowledge

Breadth of word knowledge is generally estimated based on word frequency lists. The concern is essentially 'How many words should a reader know in a second language in order to read an authentic text?' So, a baseline of candidate words is needed, with the assumption that the more frequently a word appears the more likely the reader is to have learned it. Tied to this is the notion that if a reader knows a less frequent word, the probability is higher that he or she will know words that are more frequent than that word.

Basically, in some form or another, the words are ranked according to frequency and the learner is given a test to determine at what band of vocabulary he or she demonstrates control. There are many word frequency lists that are useful for different cohorts of language learners depending upon their goals. Because they are frequently referenced in the literature, and represent somewhat different approaches to vocabulary identification, some of the better-known lists are described below.

The Teacher's Word Book of 30,000 Words (Thorndike and Lorge 1944), better known as the Thorndike-Lorge List, samples English words from juvenile literature, the Bible, newspapers, private and business correspondence, and factual texts such as farm almanacs, the US postal regulations, and material on sewing, cooking, and dressmaking. Words are listed in alphabetical order with columns indicating their frequency of occurrence per million words of text, and additionally indicating such frequencies as magazine counts and juvenile literature counts. One obvious drawback of the work is its age. Some of the counts were done as part of a federal works project during the Depression of the 1930s. For example, it has an entry for *crinoline*, but not for *computer*.

A General Service List of English Words (West 1953) provides a set of 2,000 words selected to be of assistance to learners of English as a foreign language. The list, like the Thorndike and Lorge List, is dated, having been originally published in 1936. The headwords representing a language family are listed in alphabetical order. Each word is listed with its frequency out of five million words. A useful feature is that a percentage is given for the proportion of use of each meaning of a word. For example, the word *enter* occurred 1,118 times in five million words. Fifty per cent of the time it was used as in 'enter the room', six per cent of the time it was used as in 'enter Macbeth, left', 16 per cent as in 'enter the army, a profession, the church, a school', four per cent as in 'enter into a partnership, treaty', two per cent as in 'enter an item in the accounts', and a few less easily classified meanings. This feature might be useful in teaching or preparing materials.

Computational Analysis of Present-Day American English (Kučera and Francis 1967) presents words both in frequency rank order and alphabetical order. The corpus consists of one million words of American English texts in print in 1961. The texts for the corpus were sampled from 15 different text genres, such as press reportage, press editorials, religion, skills and hobbies, *belles lettres*, learned and scientific writings, adventure, western fiction, and humor. The 100 most frequent word-types are also presented by genre, though the fact that most of these entries are function words such as articles, prepositions, pronouns, conjunctions, forms of the verb *be*, numbers, or modals limits the usefulness of this feature.

The American Heritage Intermediate Corpus (Carroll, Davies, and Richman 1971) was designed to examine the word frequencies for materials that might be encountered by students in grades 3 through 9. It lists the 86,741 word types found in 5,088,721 words of running text from over 1,000 different publications across 17 topics. The sampled texts included textbooks, periodicals, encyclopedias, novels, student workbooks, and kits of various types. The words are listed in alphabetical order and by rank. In the alphabetical order, the frequencies are broken down by grade and topic. Again, this frequency list is now fairly dated, and the particular topics may be somewhat biased against adult learners.

A University Word List (Xue and Nation 1984) focuses on the vocabulary of university study. It first took a word list developed by Campion and Elley (1971) based on 301,800 words from textbooks, published lectures, and a selection of university examination papers in 19 academic disciplines. It then took the 272,466-word *American University Word List* (Praninskas 1972) that had been developed from basic university-level textbooks. The first few thousand words in Thorndike and Lorge's (1944) list and West's (1953) list were excluded since those words represented basic vocabulary that was considered already mastered by students ready to study in a university. The two lists were then compared to two other lists that were developed by noting words that foreign students wrote annotations about and words that students had identified as difficult. The final list is comprised of 737 base words. These words were then divided into ten sublists from most frequent to least frequent. This word list has been used as one of the advanced levels in Nation's Vocabulary Levels Test (Nation 1983, 1990).

The Academic Word List (AWL) also focused on the vocabulary of academic texts (Coxhead 2000). The corpus from which the list was derived contained 414 academic texts by more than 400 authors, containing approximately 3,500,000 words, from diverse academic sources. The texts were divided into the four general academic areas of arts, commerce, law, and science. In order for an item to be retained in the file it had to meet three criteria: 1) occur in word families outside West's 2,000 most frequent words; 2) occur at least ten times in each of the academic areas; and 3) occur at least 100 times in the total corpus. The AWL matches about 10 per cent of the total tokens in the corpus. It should be noted that this is more than twice the 4.3 per cent covered by the third 1,000 words of West's General Service List. Thus, the first 2,000 words of the GSL plus the AWL account for about 86 per cent of all tokens in the corpus. This list, then, would appear to be more helpful in developing vocabulary lists for targeted instruction in academic settings than the General Service List.

These lists may be used in assessing the size and breadth of a reader's vocabulary. For example, Nation (1983) developed the Vocabulary Levels Test based on West's (1953) General Service List. The test is designed to measure five different vocabulary size levels, the 2,000-, 3,000-, 5,000- word level, what is termed the *university word level*, and the 10,000-word level. The 2,000- and

3,000-word levels contain high-frequency words. The university word level builds on the General Service List, but is designed to represent academic vocabulary. The 5,000-word level is at the edge of high- and low-frequency words, and the 10,000-word level is comprised of low-frequency words. Each level is represented by six items made up of two lists. The first list contains six words and the second list contains three definitions that the examinee is to match to three of the six words. An example from Nation (1990) is presented below:

1 apply
2 elect   _____ choose by voting
3 jump   _____ become like water
4 manufacture _____ make
5 melt
6 threaten

Each of the lists is used in assessment and teaching to determine the reader's vocabulary level. For instance, as noted above, there is general agreement that the 2,000 most frequently occurring words cover about 80 per cent of the vocabulary that a reader will encounter. So, if a reader knows all those words, he or she will still encounter difficulty with about 20 per cent of the words read, one out of every five words, or approximately two words per line of text. Therefore, the reader will still experience extensive difficulty and frustration. Laufer (1989) estimates that a reader should know about 95 per cent of the words encountered, somewhere around the 5,000 most frequent words, in order to read successfully. In a later study of second language lexical knowledge and general academic ability, Laufer (1992) found that with a vocabulary size of fewer than 3,000 words, no amount of general ability will allow the learner to read academic material well; a vocabulary size of about 8,000 words will allow satisfactory reading regardless of general ability; and with vocabulary size of between 5,000 and 6,500 words the reading may or may not be affected by general academic ability. Hirsh and Nation (1992) also estimate that a vocabulary size of around 5,000 word families is needed to read unsimplified novels for pleasure. Laufer (1992, 1996) has found correlations ranging from about .50 to .75 between measures of vocabulary size and reading comprehension. Hazenberg and Hulstijn (1996) conclude that the minimal vocabulary size for second language readers in Dutch university studies is 10,000 base words. Carver (1994), on the other hand, found that for successful reading when the material that is read is easy, 0 per cent of the vocabulary will be unknown basic words, and when the material is relatively hard, two per cent of the vocabulary is unknown. From that perspective, at least 98 per cent of the vocabulary should be known. However, many of the tests designed to measure size of vocabulary do not reflect depth of vocabulary. In many cases it is necessary to know more than the number of words a learner has. It is necessary to know the depth of knowledge of the vocabulary.

Depth of word knowledge

Depth of word knowledge refers to a learner's knowledge of the different aspects of a given word. This knowledge has to do with extent of knowledge of the following categories: 1) pronunciation and orthography; 2) morphological properties; 3) syntactic properties and collocations; 4) meaning (including connotations, polysemy, antonymy, and synonymy); 5) register; and 6) frequency (Qian 1999). Thus, for reading comprehension and use of any particular word, depth of knowledge relates to the following aspects of word knowledge:

- recognizing the word in speech or print
- recognizing its morphology
- knowing and recognizing multiple meanings and functions of a word
- knowing and selecting the word for the particular meaning associated with the word in the given context, and recognizing inappropriate use
- knowing the concept behind the meaning of the word
- knowing and activating collocations
- knowing and activating the syntactic placement of the word in a sentence
- being able to recognize and activate synonyms and antonyms
- recognizing and using the word in an original context
- recognizing and activating the correct word for the appropriate formality.

A key concept in this notion of vocabulary depth is that, as the word is known in a deeper manner, then the more words that are associated with that word are also known. It is also congruent with the view that lexical depth is incremental and there are degrees of word knowing. Knowledge of vocabulary is multidimensional, encompassing various types of knowledge. The relationships between words are connected on different dimensions. Words may be related thematically (book–journal–manuscript), phonologically (rock–sock–wok), morphologically (indemnification–notification–intensification), conceptually (pan–pot–steamer), and sociolinguistically (dude–man–chap), among others (Vermeer 2001). The number of relations that are established between words is in part a function of the number of exposures to a word providing a variety of information about the item (Nagy and Herman 1987). Understanding the richness of these connections represents the depth of knowledge of a particular word.

Much of the research recognizing the incremental nature of second language vocabulary knowledge employs one of two elicitation techniques that represent partial stages of knowledge. The first approach (Read 1993, 2000) uses a stimulus adjective and two boxes, each of which contains four words. The first box contains four adjectives, any one of which can be synonymous with the meaning of the word or an aspect of its meaning (for example stimulus = *sudden* and four responses = *beautiful, surprising, quick, thirsty*). The second box contains nouns that may collocate with the stimulus (for example stimulus = *sudden* and four options = *change, doctor, noise, school*) (Read 2000). The learner's task is to identify the related words, or *word associates* (Read 1993). Each word associate represents one of three types of semantic relationship to the stimulus word: 1) paradigmatic, where the two words are similar in meaning or one is more general than the other (for example edit–revise, team–group); 2) syntagmatic, where the two words are collocates that frequently occur together (for example edit–film, team–scientists); and 3) analytic, where the associated word represents one aspect of the stimulus word, and is likely to be part of its dictionary definition (for example edit–publishing, team–together). The approach focuses on depth of knowledge by examining a number of different associations with each of the words on the test.

The second common approach to examining depth of knowledge is the Vocabulary Knowledge Scale (VKS) which has been developed and used to assess vocabulary ability in academic settings (Paribakht and Wesche 1993, 1997; Wesche and Paribakht 1996). The VKS uses a scale with both self-report and demonstrated knowledge items to determine depth of knowledge and level of lexical access. The scale ranges from complete unfamiliarity to the ability to use the word with grammatical and semantic accuracy. The scale is presented in Table 9.1 below:

There is a very high correlation (r=.92 to .97) between the self-report scores and the scores on the demonstrated knowledge section of the test. Although it presents a picture of depth of vocabulary knowledge, the VKS is not intended to tap knowledge of broad word meanings or reflect paradigmatic, syntagmatic, or analytic relationships such as those addressed in Read's scale (1993, 2000). The VKS, then, attempts to present a picture of the learner's depth of knowledge across a set of selected lexical items. In the case of Paribakht and Wesche (1993), the vocabulary was taken from the instructional themes of media, family custody, and fitness. Variations could be made for local instructional settings or based on one of the breadth word lists discussed above.

I   I don't remember having seen this word before.
II   I have seen this word before, but I don't know what it means.
III   I have seen this word before, and I think it means _____ (synonym or translation)
IV   I know this word. It means _____. (synonym or translation)
V   I can use this word in a sentence: _____. (If you do this section, please also do Section IV.)

(from Wesche and Paribakht (1996))

Table 9.1: *The VKS elicitation scale self-report categories*

Relationships of breadth and depth

Most likely the breadth and depth dimensions of vocabulary knowledge interact and operate interdependently. The larger the vocabulary size the more likely it is that the reader will know words in more depth and will be aware of collocations and potential synonyms.

Qian (1999) investigated the relationships between breadth of vocabulary knowledge, depth of vocabulary knowledge, and reading comprehension for Korean (n=41) and Chinese (n=33) speakers studying English in two intensive academic institutions in Canada. Subjects had demonstrated that they were at the 3,000 word-family or better, the level estimated to be at the threshold level for academic reading (Laufer 1997), prior to engaging in the study. The study involved four language tests and a background questionnaire. The first test, a breadth test, was Nation's (1990) Vocabulary Levels Test. The second test was a pre-1995 modified version of the TOEFL reading comprehension test. The test had four reading passages with associated multiple-choice reading comprehension items. The third test was Read's word associates (1993, 2000) depth-of-vocabulary-knowledge test. The fourth test was a morphological knowledge test, designed to examine the role that morphology plays in reading comprehension. It measured each subject's knowledge of affixes and part-of-speech identification. The results of multiple-regression analysis indicated that the breadth of vocabulary test and the depth of vocabulary knowledge tests both significantly predicted scores on the reading comprehension test. They correlated with each other at r=.82. Together they produced an r^2=.71. When the breadth of knowledge test was entered first, it explained 60 per cent of the variability in the reading comprehension score and when depth of knowledge was entered first it explained 68 per cent of the variability in the reading comprehension score. Thus, there was overlap in what each test was measuring. The morphology test had no significant contribution to prediction of reading comprehension. Unfortunately, these findings really do not provide a clear picture of the relative contributions of these two tests because the reading comprehension test turned out to be relatively easy for this group of subjects, with a mean score of 15.89 (SD=2.62) out of a possible score of 20, and to have a low split-half reliability of .64. Thus, there was very little variation at the upper end of the distribution. It could be the case that if the score distribution were broader, the contribution of either the breadth or depth measures would show differences. However, the study does show that both breadth and depth of vocabulary knowledge are important and that the two are highly correlated.

In a follow-up study, Qian (2002) examined vocabulary breadth, depth, and reading comprehension with 217 subjects from some 19 different language backgrounds. Additionally, the subjects were given a form of the TOEFL reading comprehension and vocabulary test as the comprehension measure.

He again administered Nation's (1983) Vocabulary Levels Test as a measure of vocabulary size (vs) and Read's (1993, 2000) word associates test as a measure of depth of vocabulary knowledge (DVK). This time, the reliability measures of all the tests ranged from .80 to .91. The results indicated that DVK and vs both contributed statistically significant unique predictive power to the TOEFL comprehension score. The vs and TOEFL vocabulary test performed about equivalently in predicting reading comprehension. Additionally, the DVK and vs correlated at r=.70, indicating that they share about 49 per cent of their total variance. Thus, although depth and breadth share a great deal in common, they also each contribute to the role of vocabulary in reading comprehension.

Vermeer (2001) presented a study examining the relationship between depth and breadth from the perspective that they should be closely related because depth and breadth both affect the language user's ability to provide detailed definitions. In the study, vocabulary breadth was measured using a receptive vocabulary task in which the subjects, either Dutch first language or Dutch second language kindergarteners, were asked to identify the correct picture for an orally presented word, and were also asked to explain or describe the meaning of words presented to them. To measure depth of vocabulary, ten words were presented and subjects described them in detail. Their knowledge of the words as well as the number of different characteristics they mentioned about the word were scored. This last measure of the number of different characteristics mentioned turned out not to be a suitable measure since it actually came to be more an indication of individual talkativeness than of vocabulary control. The breadth of vocabulary measures and the depth measures of word knowledge all had inter-correlations of over r=.82, the same as that in Qian's (1999) study. These findings indicate a very strong relationship between breadth and depth of vocabulary, supporting the view that the two reflect the process of vocabulary growth.

Reading and first language vocabulary learning

It was noted earlier that by the time a reader is ready to exit high school he or she knows somewhere around 20,000 words. A basic question is how someone goes from zero words to 20,000 words. That is over a thousand words a year, about three new words per day. For decades it has been assumed that these words are learned implicitly through the contexts of listening or reading without awareness, and generally incidentally without intention. The argument in part has been that there is no way that parents or teachers could provide enough explicit instruction to push the learner as far as needed in acquiring an appropriate vocabulary.

In incidental learning contexts, the reader's primary motivation is not to learn words. In many respects, the assumption that learners learn vocabulary in context is a logical default position since research has shown that even though there is a paucity of direct vocabulary instruction in schools (Durkin 1979), learners have vocabularies that continue to grow. Several first language reading studies of incidental learning have been carried out over the past decades examining the effectiveness of incidental learning vocabulary in context (Swanborn and de Glopper 1999). Some of the studies produced strong effects for incidental learning of vocabulary while other studies were less successful in demonstrating that vocabulary could be learned through natural reading of texts with no explicit focus on vocabulary learning. Additionally, some studies have examined the task of *deriving* words from context, an activity in which the reader is asked to try to determine meanings of words that are highlighted or enhanced in some manner. While this may be a successful instructional approach, it is not clear that it provides direct explanatory relevance to the issue of what the reader does in a natural reading context in which he or she is expected to determine and remember unfamiliar vocabulary items while reading. The issue of whether reading is the source of large vocabulary gains over a student's career is apparently not a simple yes or no answer. Several variables enter into the equation, variables such as text type, level of reading ability, age, and extent to which the reader is expected to have complete control and knowledge of word-meaning depth. Additionally, the salience of clues to any particular unknown lexical item varies considerably across texts. Although in some texts there may be a definition through an APPOSITIVE, in most cases the word clues related to only a single aspect of a word's meaning. Many encounters may be necessary to develop complete information about a word.

An additional concern in explanations of incidental vocabulary learning relates to depth of processing of language. Craik and Lockhart (1972) have proposed a Levels of Processing framework which asserts that information can be encoded in multiple forms, such as semantic or phonemic features, verbal associates, images, etc. They indicate that 'memory trace persistence is a function of depth of analysis, with deeper levels of analysis associated with more elaborate, longer lasting, and strong traces' (675). Deep processing in which semantic associations are accessed and elaborated leads to longer retention than does shallow processing. However, in the reading process, the reader may simply comprehend the meaning of the word because the context makes it clear and the reader has no need to process the word with very much depth. Actually, successfully learning the word is a function of two assumptions (Craik and Tulving 1975): 1) when readers have to infer the word to successfully comprehend, they will invest more mental effort than if merely given the meaning by a teacher or text; and 2) information that is gained through mental effort will be better remembered than information gained with little effort. Thus, incidental learning does not automatically take place when an unknown word is encountered. Whether or not the word is learned will depend upon a variety of variables such as the number of encounters the reader has with the word, the reader's attention level, the task that is being performed, and other factors. In short, we need to identify what variables create the conditions for deep processing.

Sternberg and Powell (1983) proposed a theoretic framework for how learning vocabulary from context takes place that focuses on *contextual cues* and *mediating variables*. The approach distinguishes between those aspects of vocabulary that lie outside the learner, the contextual cues, and those aspects that exist at least partially within the learner, mediating variables. The contextual cues are:

1 temporal cues—cues relating to the duration or frequency of the unknown word, or regarding when it can occur
2 spatial cues—cues regarding the general or specific physical location or the possible locations in which the word can be found
3 value cues—cues about the desirability of the word or regarding the affect elicited by the word
4 stative descriptive cues—cues regarding physical characteristics such as the size or shape of the word
5 functional descriptive cues—cues regarding the capacities, uses, or purposes of the word
6 causal/enablement cues—cues regarding the possible causes or necessary conditions for the word
7 class membership cues—cues regarding one or more classes in which the word is a member
8 equivalence cues—cues regarding the meaning of the word or contrasts to the meaning of the word (for example antonymy).

Sternberg and Powell (1983) acknowledge that there may be a great deal of overlap in the functioning of these cues, and that not every cue will be useful in every context. Further, the usefulness of these cues will be affected by mediating variables which specify relations between the unknown word and the passage in which it is found. The mediating variables they propose are:

1 the number of occurrences of the unknown word
2 the variability of contexts in which multiple occurrences of the unknown word appear
3 the density of the unknown words
4 the importance of the unknown word to understanding the surrounding context
5 the perceived helpfulness of the surrounding context in understanding the meaning of the unknown word
6 the concreteness of the unknown word and the surrounding context
7 the usefulness of prior knowledge in cue utilization.

A number of studies have examined such areas as the extent to which contextual vocabulary learning takes place, how many and what types of exposures are needed, the importance of word frequency, the role of content-based instruction, the effect of word features such as concreteness, and whether different writing systems affect how vocabulary might be learned in context. There are often conflicting conclusions in the studies, in part as a result of focusing on different age groups and using different types of instrumentation. Some of these studies are summarized below.

An early study which supported the role of incidental indirect vocabulary learning is that of Saragi, Nation, and Meister (1978). Although this study is frequently discussed in second language reading and vocabulary literature, the subjects of the study were in fact English first language readers. Saragi et al. examined how readers learned the vocabulary in the novel *A Clockwork Orange* by Anthony Burgess (1963) through reading for comprehension. This futuristic novel contains many non-English words that would not be known by native English speakers on their first encounter with the text. The words in the argot that Burgess created were called *nadsat*. The text is English with a mixture of slang terms and jargon thrown in. The source for most of the *nadsat* words is Russian, though many other languages are also represented. For example, the following are *nadsat* terms and their English synonyms (Burgess, 1963):

Nadsat	English	Nadsat	English	Nadsat	English
Bezoomny	Mad	Dama	Lady	Droog	Friend
Biblio	Library	Ded	Old man	Mersky	Filthy
Cantora	Office	Golly	Money unit	Pogly	Frightened
Chest	To wash	Drat	Fight		

According to Saragi et al. (1978) there are 241 different *nadsat* terms in the book, and they are repeated an average of 15 times each, with a range of from one to 209 times. In this study, 90 of the *nadsat* words were selected for a multiple-choice test. Each item consisted of a *nadsat* word and four English options. Twenty native English speakers who were working at various educational projects in Indonesia were given the book with the glossary removed and told that they would be given a comprehension test after completing it. Within a few days of reading the book, the subjects were given the vocabulary test. The results found a correlation of 0.34 for the number of times each word occurred and the number of people who answered the item correctly. Further, the range of test scores was from 50 per cent to 96 per cent with an average of 76 per cent and a median of 77 per cent. These findings indicate that word frequency is one of the variables involved in whether a word is learned, but they also show that incidental vocabulary learning can be an important contributor to a reader's vocabulary size.

Nagy, Herman, and Anderson (1985) also represents one of the early empirical studies concluding that learners did indeed learn new vocabulary incidentally.

The study involved the results of 57 eighth graders who read either a spy narrative or an expository passage about river systems. The students were given ten minutes to read one of the passages, and then took a multiple-choice vocabulary test and a word-knowledge oral interview to determine depth of understanding of the vocabulary. Both of these measures were designed to reflect any partial knowledge of the target lexical item. Some of the students went from no knowledge to partial knowledge and others went from scant knowledge to fuller knowledge of the words. The results showed that each of the subjects performed significantly better on the vocabulary of the passage they read than on the passage they did not read. There was a slight tendency for the more able students to perform better than the less able students, but unfortunately the students were fairly homogeneous in their reading ability to begin with and this similarity might have affected the lack of significant results. Additionally, the subjects showed a significantly better gain on the words that they had no knowledge of before the study than on those they had partial knowledge of at the beginning. They found that the probability of learning an unknown word from an exposure in context was about ten per cent. The findings reflect part of the perplexing nature of vocabulary learning from context that many researchers have tried to address. That is, while it is fairly consistently found that incidental learning of vocabulary takes place, it usually is a relatively small amount.

The original Nagy et al. (1985) study involved only one grade level with one narrative text and one expository text with a limited interval between reading the passage and testing for word meaning. In order to expand their findings, Nagy, Anderson, and Herman (1987) carried out a second study that spanned three grade levels, third (n=129), fifth (n=85), and seventh (n=138), and employed 12 texts with testing taking place after an interval of six days. Easier and more difficult narrative and expository texts at each grade level were selected. Prior to reading, students completed a vocabulary checklist with approximately 200 words that came from the following five categories: target text words, decoding distracter words (for example *cobe*, *robbit*), morphologically possible pseudo-derivatives (*bonely*, *earthous*), and non-words that look like English words but are not (for example *sprale*, *shumet*), along with general vocabulary items not in the texts. Each student read two narratives or two expository passages. One week after this session, students were given a multiple-choice test unannounced. Because the researchers were interested in what particular variables might account for successful or unsuccessful incidental word learning, each text was coded for number of occurrences of each word, length of each target word in syllables, part of speech, morphological transparency, conceptual difficulty, word familiarity and item difficulty. Additionally, each text was examined in terms of contextual support for each word, readability, and density of difficult words. The results confirmed that a small but significant number of words were learned from context; the scores were higher for texts that had been judged to be easy than for texts judged to be hard. The scores for narratives were higher than for expository texts, and higher for words that the subjects had indicated on the vocabulary checklist that they already knew. The only word property that had an affect on incidental learning from context was conceptual difficulty. Although there was no effect for the length of the target word in syllables on contextual learning, there was an effect for average length of target words in a particular text. That is, the longer the average length of target words in a text, the less likely any target word in the passage was learned.

In discussing the finding that conceptual difficulty of individual target words significantly affected learning from context, Nagy et al. note that the property that distinguished the conceptually difficult target words from the other target words was that they had to be learned as part of a system of concepts. Since word familiarity and word difficulty had no effect on learning from context, they argue that:

> the relevant measure of text difficulty is not the *volume* of new information in the text, but the *type* of learning that the text requires. The presence of unfamiliar words alone did not diminish learning from context; the obstacle posed by conceptual difficulty is the need to acquire new *systems* of concepts.

> *(Nagy et al. 1987: 264–5)*

They found virtually no incidental vocabulary learning from context with concepts at the highest complexity. These findings help to broaden the understanding of what factors affect incidental learning in a way not clear in prior studies. Vocabulary learning was hindered when the text as a whole was conceptually difficult, regardless of how much of the vocabulary the readers already knew.

Schwanenflugel, Stahl, and McFalls (1997) examined the effects of text reading on the growth of word knowledge for partially known and unknown words. They also examined the effects of word features such as concreteness and part of speech as well as text features such as contextual support, number of repetitions in the text, and importance. Their subjects were 43 fourth graders who participated in four experimental sessions. Prior to any treatment, the subjects were given a vocabulary checklist made up of words they were likely to know, pseudo-words that were phonologically regular (for example *jabit*), non-words that were phonologically irregular (for example *itflm*), difficult words not from the target passages, and difficult words from the target passages. The subjects were asked to provide definitions to the words, then go back through the list and put a check mark next to the items they could not define but that looked familiar to them, and finally to circle any item that they had not seen before but which they thought might be a real word. One week later, each subject read two of the possible four stories a day apart. Immediately after reading each story, they were asked to write a summary of the story. Finally, three days after reading the last story, they were given a multiple-choice test containing the target items.

The findings agree with much of the previous research in that although the subjects learned vocabulary through reading the passages, the growth was fairly small. However, they found that both unknown words and partially known words increased at about the same rate even though the partially known words were somewhat familiar to the subjects while the unknown words were not. Additionally, their results indicated that subjects learned concrete words better than more abstract terms, and nouns were acquired less well than other parts of speech for partially known words. Interestingly, they did not find that contextual support or the importance of the sentence in which the word was embedded were significant predictors of vocabulary learning. However, this may be because of the tremendous variation in texts and text structure. It must be kept in mind that a reader interacting with a text is attending to many different textual aspects. Text structure and organization may affect comprehension yet play little role in vocabulary acquisition as long as the text is co-operative in general. The crucial variable may just be the factor of having sufficient context for the word.

All of the research discussed so far has looked at students learning to read English. Shu, Anderson, and Zhang (1995) were interested in the extent to which the incidental vocabulary findings were consistent across languages, specifically what contrasts would be found between first language students reading English texts and first language students reading Chinese texts. They note that there had been no research indicating whether or not readers with writing systems different from English were able to learn vocabulary incidentally from text while reading. They examined learner characteristics such as grade level, verbal ability, and prior knowledge of a particular word. They also looked at vocabulary characteristics, such as how morphologically *transparent* or *opaque* the words were. In English, the meanings of some words, like the word *indecision*, can be determined based on the morphological components of the word without needing to rely on context if the reader knows the function of the prefix *in-* and the meaning of the word *decision*, while others have morphology that does not help in determining meaning at all. These two types of words are termed transparent or opaque here. Most words lie somewhere in between the two extremes. Shu et al. note that Chinese characters employ concrete visual representations of words in which each character is related to its meaning, and that the structure of the character generally provides clues to meaning. Chinese characters include a meaning-based radical and a component that offers a phonetic clue 80 per cent to 90 per cent of the time. The radical in the character indicates a semantic category, such as *female*, although it is not possible to get the meaning of the word only on the basis of the character's radical. Also, there are irregular characters which have a radical not related to the semantic category. They hypothesized that since morphology can affect vocabulary learning through reading, the different types of morphology between English (affixes and roots) and Chinese (semantic meaning carrying radicals) might lead readers to develop different and language specific strategies.

The study involved 146 American and 301 Chinese third- and fifth-grade students studying at schools in their native countries. Two grade-level narrative texts were selected for each grade from American and Chinese textbooks. The English texts were translated into Chinese and the Chinese texts were translated into English. They assumed that the students would be unfamiliar with the knowledge necessary to understand the text from the other language. Teachers from each language selected words they felt would be difficult for the readers. Each student completed a checklist containing the target words as well as non-words, pseudo-words, non-target words, and general words one week prior to the study to determine whether they knew the word or not. After reading, the subjects were given multiple-choice tests to measure their word knowledge, with each word tested in both a difficult context and an easy context. Each target word was categorized for morphological transparency, concept difficulty, and contextual support similar to the coding in Nagy et al (1987) and later in Schwanenflugel et al. (1997). The students were matched for verbal ability and divided into two groups. One group read an American story and the other read a Chinese story.

The American students showed a significant gain in the words they encountered in the text over words from the text they did not read, indicating that they did in fact learn words from context. Further, there was no interaction of ability and learning from context, indicating that subjects at all ability levels were able to learn from context. Scores were also higher for the easier word context than for the difficult word context, indicating a sensitivity in the test to partial knowledge. There was no interaction of knowing words from context and morphological transparency, indicating that the American students were not using word structure to learn meanings from context more effectively, as had been found in Nagy et al. (1987). They also found results similar to Nagy et al. in that the conceptual difficulty of the word affected learning of the word. Finally, they found that the probability of incidentally learning a word was larger for words with strong contextual support than words with weak contextual support, but that they learned fairly well regardless of contextual support if they had reported prior knowledge of the word.

With the Chinese subjects, they also found significant learning from context, as with the American subjects. For the American subjects, there was no interaction of ability with learning from context, so readers at all ability levels learned some words. However, they found that with the Chinese readers there was a significant interaction of learning from context with prior knowledge, indicating that they were more likely to learn words they had checked as unknown than words they had checked as known. This had not been the case with the American subjects. Additionally, there was a significant interaction of learning from context and morphological transparency with the fifth-grade students. Morphologically transparent words were learned better than morphologically opaque words. This had not been the case with the American subjects. The Chinese third graders also learned more words that were associated with easy concepts than difficult concepts. Finally, they found that contextual clues helped in learning the words. The study, then, indicates that Chinese learners acquire vocabulary from context, and that the patterns of their results are very similar to the American subjects. They hypothesize, then, that learning incidental vocabulary from context may be a universal in written vocabulary acquisition. The study found that three factors of interest here affected learning from context: 1) conceptual difficulty of the unfamiliar word; 2) strength of contextual support; and 3) morphological transparency.

The various first language studies have produced differential results depending upon the types of tests and reading materials used. Swanborn and de Glopper (1999) conducted a meta-analysis across 20 different first language experiments of incidental word learning during normal reading. Their results indicate that subjects learn about 15 per cent of the unknown words that they encounter. They found that several factors affected the learner's ability to learn from context while reading. Pre-test sensitization, grade, level of reading ability, assessment methods that were sensitive to partial word knowledge, and text-to-target word ratio all affected the probability that word learning while reading would take place. Studies that utilized assessment methods sensitive to partial word knowledge demonstrated higher amounts of incidental word learning, reflecting the incremental nature of vocabulary acquisition. Basically, one of the primary reasons for many of the conflicting findings regarding the effectiveness of incidental learning in context resides with the absence of a clear standard for context. Some context will provide rich sources of information allowing inferencing of meanings, while other contexts will not. Additionally, some words are narrow enough in meaning that they may be learned in one or two encounters. Others have broad meanings and will need a substantial number of encounters regardless of the textual richness.

Finally, it is important to keep the findings regarding first language incidental vocabulary learning in context. Sternberg (1987) notes that finding that learning takes place incidentally does not imply that learning from context is the fastest or most efficient way to learn vocabulary. Although it is a natural and typical way of learning, naturalness and typicality are not necessarily the same as optimality. There may very well be direct conscious approaches to learning vocabulary that are more effective than incidental learning; they are just not generally applied as spontaneously as incidental learning.

Reading and second language vocabulary learning

The factors that have emerged in the literature on first language as central to vocabulary also have a key place in understanding second language lexical learning. There is general agreement that much second language vocabulary learning occurs incidentally through extensive reading, rather than through explicit vocabulary instruction. There are three primary advantages to incidental vocabulary learning: 1) the vocabulary is contextualized, giving a richer meaning to each word; 2) it is pedagogically efficient in that it allows both reading and vocabulary learning to occur at the same time; and 3) it is more individualized because the vocabulary that is learned is learner based (Huckin and Coady 1999). However, incidental learning is still ill understood. We do not know exactly how it occurs, and we are left with such questions as: How many exposures are necessary? Does it work in tandem with explicit vocabulary instruction? How dependent is it on the type of text that is read? What role does glossing play? What vocabulary strategies do learners adopt?

Much of the second language research on incidental learning focuses on the guessing and inferencing-from-context processes of the reader confronting text. Additionally, much of the second language interest in incidental vocabulary learning is directed at determining the best pedagogical approach for presenting vocabulary. While most first language researchers such as Nagy and Herman (1987) eschew explicit vocabulary instruction because they see it as ineffective, many involved in second language see a role for such instruction. Approaches range from a focus on: 1) non-intervention; 2) incorporating marginal glosses for target words; 3) second language/first language translation paired associates; 4) keyword techniques; 5) elaborating the text surrounding a target lexical item; and 6) teaching lists of words out of context. A lot of the concern is with the realization that learning vocabulary from context is a complex, untidy, and lengthy process. Consequently, a great deal of the second language vocabulary research focuses on ways to speed up the process. Likewise, as with reading skills in the previous chapter, there is an interest in identifying word-learning strategies and in the effectiveness of teaching those strategies.

The development of a large vocabulary through incidental learning is one of the effects of extensive reading, according to its proponents. Day and Bamford (1998) see the development of a large sight vocabulary to be a process of over-learning words to the point that they become automatically recognizable in text. The reliance in extensive reading programs on large amounts of text with assumed multiple encounters with vocabulary items is seen as a basis for incidental vocabulary learning.

In order to confirm that second language as well as first language readers could acquire vocabulary incidentally from reading in a manner similar to that discussed above (Saragi et al. 1978), Pitts et al. (1989) asked 51 non-native speakers of English to read the first two chapters of *A Clockwork Orange*. Thirty *nadsat* words with a frequency of from 1 to 27 were selected for a multiple-choice post-test. The experimental subjects read the selection of approximately 6,700 words containing 123 *nadsat* words and took the post-test. A control group of 23 subjects did not read the passage, but took the post-test. The subjects who read the text scored significantly higher than the control group, but only scored about seven per cent on the test. Thus, they learned a fairly modest number of the tested words, especially in comparison with the readers in Saragi et al. (1978). However, they read a much smaller portion of the text than the subjects in the previous study, and only 30 of the 123 *nadsat* words in the selection were tested. That is, while Saragi et al. (1978) tested 37 per cent of the *nadsat* words, Pitts et al. (1989) tested only 16 per cent of the words. However, it may be that the *nadsat* words are not the best example to use for looking at incidental vocabulary since Burgess intentionally meant the meanings of the words to be learnable. That is a different type of context from that which most readers face.

Bensoussan and Laufer (1984) examined the effect of context, word *guessability* (the extent to which contextualized words or word categories are more easily guessed than others), and proficiency level on vocabulary learning. Sixty students in an EFL course were given a list of 70 vocabulary items and asked to translate them into their native language. After one week, the subjects were again given the list, but also asked to read a 574-word text containing the vocabulary items and answer comprehension questions. The passage and comprehension test were also given to a control group that had not seen the words previously. There was no difference between the scores of the two groups, indicating that presenting the words ahead of time had not affected their comprehension. Thus, Bensoussan and Laufer reasoned, any change in vocabulary knowledge would be due to learning from the context of the passage. Of the 70 words, 41 had contextual clues to the meaning. The results indicated that for 17 of these 41 words, the number of subjects who did not know the word in isolation but did in context was greater than the number of subjects who did not know the word on either occasion. Further, the findings indicate that the most frequent types of errors in definitions were related to applying the wrong meaning of a word given the context, and mistranslation of a 'morphological troublemaker' (for example translating *outline* as *out of line*), mistranslation of an idiom, confusion of a word that looks similar (for example *uniquely* and *unequally*), and use of a false cognate. Bensoussan and Laufer consider this to be evidence that in guessing the meaning of the unknown word, the readers applied some 'preconceived notions' about what they thought a word meant. In other words, they used context to disambiguate the meaning only after they had checked a word against what they already believed they knew. The results also indicated, predictably, that the less able students got fewer definitions correct than the more able group, but that the two groups did not differ in the types of errors made. Although Bensousssan and Laufer were disappointed in the small number of words learned by their subjects, it does represent a gain of about 25 per cent of the unknown vocabulary. If second language readers can learn 17 new words in passages approximately 600 words in length, they should be able to develop a sizeable vocabulary through extended reading.

Hulstijn (1992) conducted a series of experiments to test the mental-effort hypothesis, which holds that the retention of inferred meaning will be better than the retention of word meaning for words that are given a definition by a text or teacher. This is a variation of the deep processing model (Craik and Lockhart 1972; Craik and Tulving 1975). The studies involved variations of providing readers with different types of meaning cues about Dutch low-frequency words or pseudo-words. The cues were: 1) a translation of the word in the margin of the text; 2) a concise simple sentence providing inferable meanings for the word; 3) a set of multiple-choice options from which the reader had to select the meaning that fit the context; or 4) no cue as to the meaning at all. The results indicate that if second language readers read a text for comprehension of its content, they are more likely to learn a word if it is inferred by themselves than if the meaning of the word has been given to them. These results reflect a contrast between high and low mental effort conditions. However, the results also indicate that learners are more likely to infer an incorrect meaning of an unknown lexical item when they have not been given a cue to the meaning. In the case of these studies, then, there is caution about the role that lexical inferencing may play in vocabulary learning. While incidental vocabulary learning can be effective, it can also lead to inferencing an incorrect meaning.

Rott (1999) addressed the issue of the number of exposures required in second language to learn a word meaning in incidental learning. In her study, 67 fourth-semester college German students whose first language was English were presented with half of a set of 12 target words. The subjects had been tested to ensure that they did not know the target words prior to the study. Each of the words was embedded in six separate passages, each of which presented the word in a different context. The subjects were divided into two treatment groups, one for each half of the target word set. This enabled one of the groups to act as the control group for the set of words they did not encounter. Each treatment group was further divided into three groups of two, four, or six exposures to the target words. The entire study lasted 13 weeks. During each treatment session, the subjects read six passages. After reading the passages they recalled as much of the passage as they could. After week two, week four, and week six of the treatment, the subjects took two vocabulary tests: one in which they supplied definitions for words in a decontextualized word list to test for productive word learning, and a multiple-choice test which asked the readers to select the best definition of each word. Retention tests were given one week and one month after the last day of treatment. The findings showed that the amount of vocabulary gained varied as a function of exposure frequency and as a function of time of vocabulary measurement for both the supply and select definition tests. After two, four, and six exposures the subjects gained more word knowledge for both the immediate and the retention tests than the subjects who had not encountered the words. Thus, the finding that second language learners learned incidentally confirmed other findings, supporting the importance of normal reading for second language vocabulary acquisition. Further, four exposures did not significantly improve productive or receptive word knowledge over two exposures, but six exposures did produce significantly higher scores than two exposures. Retention for all exposure rates dropped significantly from the immediate tests, but remained higher than that for zero exposures. The learning was stronger, however, for the receptive word-knowledge group than the productive knowledge group.

Nasaji (2003) explored the strategies and knowledge sources used in second language lexical inferencing using introspective reports. His results indicated that the intermediate-level learners in the study were not very successful at inferring word meanings. Learners were completely wrong in their inferences 55.8 per cent of the time. They were only completely successful 25.6 per cent of the time. When the learners used morphology to infer meaning, they were successful 57.1 per cent of the time, but the analysis indicated no significant differences between use of morphological, grammatical, first language, discourse, or world knowledge. Of the strategies used, the most successful were repeating the section of the text surrounding the word, verifying the inferred meaning with surrounding context, self-inquiry about the text, words or meaning inferred, and consciously monitoring the vocabulary problem. Thus, the most productive strategies involved more global types of metacognitive strategy use, rather than more local strategies of repeating words, use of local grammatical information, or translating the word into the first language.

Zahar, Cobb, and Spada (2001) addressed the issue of whether level of proficiency is a factor in the number of exposures needed to learn vocabulary. Their subjects were 144 male Canadian seventh-grade ESL students, predominately francophones, who had been placed into four different levels of English language proficiency. Thirty words were taken from the selected text passage and developed into a pre-test in a format similar to that of Nation's Levels Test (1983) discussed earlier. The test showed the groups to be different in their pre-test knowledge of the words selected. Approximately two weeks after the pre-test, the subjects listened to the story on a cassette tape as they followed along reading the written text. After the tape was finished, they were allowed to reread the text for the remainder of the class period. Two days later, the subjects were given a post-test that was identical to the pre-test. There was a positive gain in the scores of each group with an average gain of about 2.16 of the 30 selected words. Thus, the results are consistent with other findings that second language learners learn a modest number of words incidentally from reading. The research further found that the frequency of times that each word occurred was correlated with the proportion of learners who learned the word. However, most of this effect was for the lowest ability level group. In fact, regression analysis showed the effect of frequency to be three to four times more facilitative for lower-level readers, the group that learned the fewest new words in the study, than for more advanced readers. In part, this may be explained by the fact that the learners possessing the fewest words to begin with need more exposures before they make a connection to the word meaning. The study also examined the role of contextual richness for the words that were most and least acquired. That is, it looked at the types of contextual support the surrounding text provided for inferring a meaning. Although somewhat inconclusive, the results indicated that frequency of occurrence is a more important factor than contextual support in learning new vocabulary.

Research into incidental learning indicates that it is effective in vocabulary gains even though it is a long and slow process. However, for the lower proficiency level reader it appears to be a bit of a catch-22 in that struggling readers do not read well enough to make breadth and depth reading an option. To acquire words requires decoding skills, the ability to recognize an unknown word, and the ability to use context. However, the struggling reader cannot do this easily. So, incidental implicit learning from reading alone may not be an optimal approach in early second language reading. Several forms of reading intervention have been proposed. They involve such aids as dictionaries, marginal glosses, meaning-in-context activities, simplified texts, and others. These will be addressed below.

Second language vocabulary and pedagogy

Dictionary use

The role of dictionaries, of either the bilingual or monolingual variety, is a topic that can bring out passion in even the most soft-spoken teacher. Views vary from those that see dictionaries as a crutch that slows the reading and learning process, some form of narcotic smuggled surreptitiously into the classroom as contraband, to those that place dictionaries as the single most important language learning nutrient. Unfortunately, the views taken are rarely based upon research findings. The findings of such research indicate that a view somewhere between the two just mentioned is probably most warranted. As with the research in other areas of reading, whether dictionaries are effective depends upon the context of the learner, the learner's ability vis-à-vis the language threshold, the type of word that is looked up, and the importance of the word for text comprehension. Some of the relevant research studies are discussed below.

Several researchers view dictionaries as essential to efficient vocabulary learning. Hulstijn (1993) noted that some reading instruction that encourages inferring meaning in context often leads learners into three pitfalls. It 1) may entice the reader to believe that the meaning of all unknown words may be inferred from context when in fact they cannot; 2) encourages an uncritical impulsive guessing behavior on the part of the reader as inferences are made; and 3) fails to encourage readers to check the correctness of their inferences if they are in doubt. Sound reading instructional materials, on the other hand, not only provide the learner with tools for inferencing meaning from context, but also sensitize him or her to the need to verify tenuous inferences by consulting a dictionary. Hulstijn's study examined the types of unknown words in a text that prompted learners to use a dictionary. The research predicted that subjects were more likely to look up relevant words than irrelevant words, and would look up words that could not be inferred from context more than words that could be inferred. Forty-four Dutch subjects read a chapter of a spy novel and were asked to answer eight comprehension questions. In the text, eight words were replaced with pseudo-words in such a way that it was not possible to correctly answer the comprehension questions without knowing the meaning of the pseudo-words. Eight additional words throughout the text were also pseudo-words unrelated to the comprehension questions. The first eight words were labeled in the study as plus relevant and the second set of eight was labeled minus relevant. Further, four of the plus relevant words and four of the minus relevant words could be inferred from context while the other eight words could not. Thus, a word like *gaired* was placed in a context where it could be inferred to mean *lit*, but no question was asked about it. Thus, it was plus inferable but minus relevant. Likewise, a word like *buls* was put in a context in which it could be inferred to have a meaning of *account*, and it was essential to one of the comprehension questions. It was plus inferable and plus relevant. Subjects read the story on a computer and had access to an online dictionary. The results showed a significant effect for both relevance and inferability, but no inferability by relevance interaction effect. Thus, the study shows clear evidence that relevant words were more often consulted than irrelevant words. However, the study had predicted that inferable words would be looked up less frequently than non-inferable words only if the words were relevant. This turned out not to be the case. Inferable words were looked up whether they were tied to the comprehension questions or not. Apparently, these readers felt the need to look up most unknown words, regardless of whether they were relevant. This may be related to the fact that the readers were relatively advanced and thus knew a lot of the vocabulary they confronted in the text. Lower-ability students may not have the luxury of looking up all unknown words.

The positive role of dictionary use was further supported by Luppescu and Day (1993) who found that Japanese first language subjects reading English as a foreign language performed better on a vocabulary test when they were allowed to use a dictionary than those who were not. In fact, their probability of getting an item correct was almost two times (1.86) better than those without dictionaries. However, it was also found that the gain due to dictionary use was not universal across all lexical items. Some items appeared more difficult for the dictionary-using readers. It is hypothesized that this is because use of a dictionary was confusing or misleading if the reader was not able to find the correct choice out of several possible definitions in the dictionary. This effect appeared to be primarily for items that contained several entries in the dictionary definitions.

Knight (1994) found that English first language students studying Spanish as a second language who used a dictionary while reading Spanish texts recalled more vocabulary than students not using a dictionary. In this study, 105 second-year Spanish students were divided into high verbal and low verbal ability groups based on their American College Test (ACT), a national standardized test used by many universities as an admissions criterion. Four authentic Spanish texts, each containing approximately 12 unknown words, were divided into two sets of two readings each. Subjects were randomly assigned to one of the text-sets. Two weeks prior to reading the texts, all subjects were given a yes/no vocabulary-knowledge checklist in order to ensure that the target words were unknown. Subsequently they were given two vocabulary tests on the target words from the texts that they were not going to read. The subjects were assigned to a dictionary group or a non-dictionary group and read the assigned text-set on a computer. After reading the text, they wrote recalls of the texts in English of everything they could remember, and were then given unannounced vocabulary tests. Two weeks later, the subjects were given delayed vocabulary tests on their target words. One of the tests asked them to supply a definition and the other was a four-option multiple-choice test. Knight found that both the immediate and delayed vocabulary test scores were significantly greater than the no-exposure pretests. Additionally, the dictionary use group scored higher than the non-dictionary group and the high verbal ability group identified more meanings than the low verbal ability group. The low verbal ability group particularly benefited from dictionary use. Finally, the dictionary group scored significantly higher on the recall comprehension measure. The study shows that there was modest gain in vocabulary on the supply definition test (mean = 14 per cent) with a somewhat higher mean on the multiple-choice definition test (mean = 48 per cent). This higher mean on the select definition test reflects the previously mentioned concern regarding how vocabulary knowledge is measured. In this case, being greater than the chance score of 25 per cent, it indicates a growth in sight vocabulary recognition. The study indicates that dictionary use can be effective in promoting vocabulary growth.

Marginal glosses

Attention has also been given to the role that textual glosses have on increasing comprehension and vocabulary acquisition. Such glosses are typically definitions or explanations of a word and are located in the side or bottom margins of the text. Although glosses are fairly standard in language teaching textbooks, little empirical research has been published on the effectiveness of the glossing technique. Johnson (1982) investigated the effects on reading comprehension of building background knowledge. She prepared a reading selection about Halloween with familiar and unfamiliar information sections. The subjects were 72 ESL advanced level readers. They were assigned to one of four groups: 1) read the passage without a vocabulary list (control group); 2) study the definitions of the target words prior to reading but do not look at the list while reading; 3) read the passage with the target words glossed; and 4) study the target vocabulary before reading with the definitions of the target words glossed in the passage. Subjects provided a recall of idea units for both the familiar and unfamiliar sections of the text after reading the passage and completed a cloze test. The results showed little effect for exposure to difficult words in the passage. The only significant contrast found in relation to group membership was that group 2 scored higher than group 4 on the recall of the familiar section of the passage. The possible explanation offered by Johnson is that perhaps seeing the words prior to reading and having the glosses present while reading led the readers to over-emphasize vocabulary at the expense of comprehension. The approach apparently provided a false garden path effect leading the readers to focus on vocabulary.

In contrast to Johnson (1982), Davis (1989) examined whether or not marginal glosses would improve comprehension of a complete and authentic foreign language text. A literary text of approximately 1,000 words in French was selected. To assess comprehension, the subjects completed a recall protocol in their first language, English, immediately after reading the text. The subjects were 71 third-semester French students in the US. The text was presented in three versions: 1) without aids; 2) with questions and comments that guided the reader along the story, and some vocabulary definitions presented prior to the story; and 3) the same information as in 2 but with a glossed format. The number of idea units recalled was calculated for each subject. The results indicated that the first group scored significantly lower than the other two groups. The second and third groups were not significantly different. Thus, the subjects who received the vocabulary guide in either form recalled significantly more than the control group that had no assistance. In contrast to Johnson (1982), glosses in this study were more effective than reading alone.

The Johnson (1982) and Davis (1989) studies looked at the effect of glosses on text recall. Watanabe (1992, 1997) examined glossing in the context of text enhancements and augmentation as they might enhance vocabulary learning. For the final analysis, 231 undergraduates in Japan were randomly assigned to one of five conditions. Subjects saw the text with one of the following modification options in combination with one of the two possible tasks: 1) original unmodified text; 2) text modified to include appositives next to the target words; 3) text modified to include a marginal gloss; 4) text modified to include multiple-choice glosses (two alternatives for the word meaning); and 5) a different text entirely to act as a control for any pre-test/post-test learning effects. Sixteen target words from a 500-word text were selected. The subjects first took a vocabulary pre-test in which they wrote the meaning of each word in Japanese and filled out background questionnaires, read the passage, took a cloze proficiency test, and then took a vocabulary test identical to the pre-test. The vocabulary test included the 16 target words and 16 words from the control passage. A week after the treatment, the subjects took two unexpected delayed post-tests, one with the target words in isolation and one with the target words in context. The analysis indicates no significant difference between the gloss and multiple-choice conditions, but indicates that these conditions produced significantly higher scores than the appositives, the original, and the control. The appositive group was not significantly different from the original group. This pattern was similar in the delayed post-test. Additionally, the groups receiving the gloss conditions performed better than the other groups on the comprehension measure. Thus, Watanabe found glosses to be an effective aid for vocabulary learning.

Jacobs, Dufon, and Hong (1994) expanded somewhat their focus on the role played by glosses. They were interested not only in whether glosses were more effective than the absence of glosses, but also whether the language of the gloss had an effect and whether students prefer glosses or not. The text was a 613-word text containing 32 target words. Subjects in the experimental study were 85 students in the fourth semester of Spanish in a US university who were randomly assigned within regular classes to one of three conditions; 1) no glosses—the control group; 2) English glosses; and 3) Spanish glosses. The subjects read the passage, returned it to the teacher, wrote a recall of as much as they could remember, and translated the words into English. Four weeks later, a subset of the subjects was given the word-translation test again. The results indicated that while there was no significant difference between the three conditions on the recall test, glossing was associated with a greater recall for those subjects whose proficiency level, as measured by course grade, was 0.8 standard deviations above the mean. For this group the two gloss groups performed significantly better than the control group on the first vocabulary test. There were also no significant differences on the delayed vocabulary test, though each group had a small sample size of only eight or nine. There were no significant differences between the scores of the English gloss or Spanish gloss groups. The results, again, appear mixed for the effectiveness of glossing. However, the fact that the above average subjects were able to benefit from the glosses on their recall of the text indicates that there may be an effect for text difficulty.

Hulstijn, Hollander, and Greidanus (1996) looked at the role of marginal glosses and dictionary accessibility in the incidental learning of vocabulary. They present some of the contexts in which readers fail to learn vocabulary incidentally during reading for meaning. These are: 1) the reader either fails to notice the unknown word or believes he or she knows it when that is not the case; 2) the reader simply decides to ignore the unknown word; 3) the context may be so redundant that it is not necessary to expend energy on the unknown word; 4) there is not enough context to infer the meaning; and 5) a single encounter with a word is insufficient to learn it. The study examined whether multiple exposures to unknown words in conjunction with glosses would increase the likelihood that incidental learning would take place. The 78 Dutch students of French read a text under one of three conditions. A marginal gloss group read the text with first language translations of targeted words, a dictionary group was free to use a dictionary as they read, and a control group read with neither glossed text nor a dictionary. The subjects read a short story three pages in length containing 16 target words, half of which occurred one time in the text and half of which occurred three times in the text. Three vocabulary post-tests were given. The first involved a list of 32 words, half of which had appeared in the text and half of which had not. Subjects were asked to indicate whether each word had appeared in the text and to provide a definition in either French or Dutch. Second, the subjects were presented with the target words and asked whether they had been familiar with each word prior to reading the text. Third, the subjects were shown the 16 target words in the context of a few lines taken from the original text, and were asked to provide meanings for the words.

The results showed that the subjects, regardless of group, recognized the target words that had appeared three times or more in the text than those that had appeared only once. The test of pre-knowledge indicated that the subjects had known hardly any of the target words prior to the study. Subjects with the marginal glosses had the highest scores for both the words occurring only once and those occurring three times. However, there was no significant difference between the control group and the dictionary group. In part, this is due to the fact that the dictionary group seldom actually looked up any words in the dictionary. However, when the dictionary group did look up words in the dictionary, their retention was greater than that of the marginal gloss group. There was also a significant effect for frequency of occurrence in that the words occurring three times were retained better than those occurring only once. The results on the third test on the target words in context paralleled the results on the first test of decontextualized word knowledge. Thus, the study indicated that marginal glosses were more effective than only a dictionary or context alone. However, there is also some indication that when actually used, the dictionary may be more effective than glosses, a finding indicating the need to teach effective dictionary use skills.

In the end, there is likely to be no single answer such that we can definitively say that glossing is either effective or is not effective. If there is no reason to use the glosses because the words are already known, or there is no way the glosses will help because the text is too difficult, then glosses may be of little value.

Meaning-in-context vocabulary learning strategies

The strategies employed by second language readers as they cope with vocabulary problems while reading vary widely. Some of the strategies vary by language ability while others appear to represent idiosyncratic preferences. It is useful to look at the words readers have identified as difficult in order to determine how successfully they have inferred word meanings, and to understand what specific factors seem to have led to misinterpretation. For example, knowledge of morphology is frequently mentioned as an aid in the inferencing of unfamiliar words. If the reader knows the meaning of *contextualized* then inferencing the meaning of *decontextualized* should be relatively easy. However, knowing the word *diction* will not aid substantially in inferring the meaning of *dictionary*. In many instances, case studies provide insight into reader strategy differences and the processes that are used. The focus in this section will be on how strategies appear to interact with comprehension as well as vocabulary retention. However, the discussion will be limited to the strategies employed while reading, not vocabulary learning more generally, such as list learning or flash-card use.

Parry (1991, 1997) has carried out qualitative studies into the vocabulary processing of four second language readers. These learners were taking an anthropology class at Hunter College in New York City. They were asked to keep a log of their reading assignments and to keep lists of difficult words that caused them problems. They were also asked to write down their guessed meanings of these words and to write down the dictionary meanings they found if they resorted to dictionary use. They were encouraged to express their guessed meanings as precisely as possible, using their first language if that helped. In the case of two of the subjects, Parry was able to conduct think-aloud protocols as they generated the lists and to have them to provide a translation of a part of the textbook they were using. Parry found different students using different strategies, using them differently, and achieving different results. One of the subjects read through the whole passage rapidly, marked words, then read again, and then looked words up in a dictionary. Another read through the passage only once, stopped at each word that was problematic, and deliberated. For most of the students, infrequent words caused the most problems. Though they were all reading texts relating to anthropology, they all identified different vocabulary items. This again indicates the idiosyncratic nature of vocabulary knowledge.

There was a wide range across the readers in the number of words that were identified as problematic—from approximately 0.12 per cent of all words read to 1.60 per cent of all words read. Many of the words identified were bridging vocabulary, not technical vocabulary from anthropology. Further, it was possible to see the processes of inference generation as the readers read in the think-aloud process. The strategies involved attempting to generate a meaning from the immediate context, using knowledge of English morphology, or putting an unknown word into a buffer until a second reading. One finding that is important to any evaluation of the effectiveness of guessing words from context was that of the 58 incorrect guesses that one of the subjects made, the vast majority actually do make sense in the passage context. For example, in a sentence that read '… must be *substantiated* …' the subject guessed *examined*. In another case, '*circuitous* route' was guessed as *special*. The interpretation of vocabulary with only partial word knowledge can affect reading comprehension severely. That the guessed words make sense, but provide a restricted or slightly oblique relationship to the original word, again points to the need to emphasize that readers need to confirm their guesses with a dictionary or other authoritative source.

Grabe and Stoller (1997) provide a very detailed example of how one reader applied lexical learning strategies consciously. The overall case study was designed to: 1) analyze the development of a learner's reading abilities in a second language; 2) consider the relationship between reading development and vocabulary acquisition; 3) explore the relationship between reading development and general comprehension processing; and 4) examine the relationship between reading development and overall second language acquisition.

The case study involves Grabe's own reading development during a five-month stay in Brazil. He arrived in Brazil as a true beginner in Portuguese. One of the interesting parts of this study is that Grabe adopted several conscious and explicit strategies for vocabulary learning. He read the *Journal do Brasil* newspaper daily and followed the regimen below:

1 selecting the most interesting articles
2 underlining unknown words on the first page
3 looking up all the underlined words in a bilingual dictionary
4 rereading the articles for comprehension
5 writing down all looked-up words on a pad
6 stopping writing when the page was full
7 reading the rest of the newspaper without writing anything down.

He also read Portuguese comic books, a Portuguese grammar book, a weekly newsmagazine, and occasionally other magazines and newspapers. He also maintained a journal in which he recorded his daily use of the language and his observations about the language learning process. This set of strategies was part of a decision to have a regular procedure for focused vocabulary learning each day. These global strategies were much more systematic than those observed in Parry's (1991, 1997) subjects.

Grabe evaluated his vocabulary learning in several ways. First, he took vocabulary tests written by university faculty members at one-month intervals from the end of the second month until the end of his stay. Each of the tests comprised 200 words from a word list of 800 words selected from a Portuguese junior high school text, and Grabe was asked to supply an English synonym for each one that he knew. These tests indicated that his vocabulary doubled from months 2 to 5, going from scores of about 25 per cent to scores of 50 per cent. A second form of evaluation was an examination of Grabe's vocabulary lists. These indicated that he mostly looked up nouns and verbs, and that he looked up about 19 per cent of the words multiple times. Finally, Grabe kept a learning journal. The journal entries indicate that he felt his reading was enhanced when he could:

1 recognize conjugated forms of verbs
2 distinguish nouns and verbs from transition words
3 identify the word root meaning
4 identify cognates and differences in meaning that some cognates have.

Grabe also commented that guessing from context was frustrating because it was difficult to know when he was right or not. The study points out the usefulness of a bilingual dictionary for learning vocabulary, at least for this learner. It is also of interest that Grabe looked up many words multiple times, sometimes as many as six times. Further, Grabe and Stoller (1997) note that these were not always words with several meanings, they were just words that he found difficult to remember. In sum, Grabe developed very clear strategies for learning that appear to have helped him increase his vocabulary. Additionally, he took reading comprehension tests in the form of translations from Portuguese into English. His scores went from 30 per cent accuracy for the first month's translation to 90 per cent on the final month's translation. Evaluators from the university noted that his translations went from sentence-level translations with many errors to a translation that captured the essence and reflected the original author's style. All of this shows how his word-learning strategies affected his comprehension and vocabulary size.

Coady (1979) hypothesized that in the development of reading skills, second language learners begin by attending to more form-oriented process strategies such as phoneme–grapheme correspondences and grapheme–morpheme information, gradually shifting to the use of more meaning-oriented strategies involving context and lexis. Field (1985) however, argued, from her experiences in China, that Chinese learners have difficulty employing the more meaning-level strategies even when they have reached relatively advanced levels of proficiency. Her Chinese informants indicated that they had too little language proficiency to take advantage of contextual meaning, and Field claimed that traditional teaching approaches have discouraged the transfer of contextual use in Chinese reading to application in English second language reading. Consequently, she proposed, Chinese students' reading strategies are shaped by cultural assumptions and by their lack of background knowledge to such an extent that they will adhere to the concrete strategies of syllable-morpheme, syntactic and lexical reliance.

Chern (1993) examined the word-solving strategies used by Chinese students while reading English specifically to examine the claims of Coady and Field. Using a case-study approach, Chern's subjects were asked to first skim a short 239-word passage and then go back through the passage providing a think-aloud report as they proceeded through the second reading. They also gave a definition or synonym for each of the target words and summarized the passage. The passage was a modified cloze in that rather than the traditional blank spaces the text contained underlined nonsense words. The underlined words were located such that they allowed a comparison of global versus local context strategy use. The words were classified into four categories with three words each: 1) parallelism—sensitivity to grammatical relations and semantic similarity between words is necessary to understand the word; 2) sentence-bound cues—these words can be understood with information in the sentence that contains it; 3) forward cues—it is necessary to read beyond the words in order to get more information before the word meaning can be successfully inferred; and 4) backward cues—referring back or remembering previously encountered cues is necessary. The subjects were 20 recently arrived Chinese students at a US university. The subjects were divided into a higher-ability group and a lower-ability group on the basis of test scores. Subjects in the higher group appeared to use all four of the strategies while those in the lower group tended not to use the forward cues strategy. Also, the higher-ability group showed greater use of backward cues and forward cues, both of which are global cue types. The study found that there was a hierarchy of the skill use from reliance on lexical to reliance on contextual information as the subjects' proficiency increased. This finding supports Coady's (1979) view of strategy development rather than that of Field (1985).

Huckin and Bloch (1997) focused on the strategies used in inferring the meaning of unknown words in context by second language readers, on how context serves to assist that inferring process, and on how second language readers often fail to take full advantage of available context. They employed think-aloud procedures with three Chinese graduate students in the US at an intermediate level of English proficiency. The reading materials included two English texts, one from a textbook and one from a journal. A total of 27 difficult words from the passages were identified. The subjects were given a pre-test, wrote a translation in Chinese while thinking aloud, and were given a post-test. The subjects indicated on the pre-test that they knew 46 per cent of the words. Of the remaining words, they correctly guessed 57 per cent. Most of those successful guesses were based on context clues. The unsuccessful guesses were generally as a result of not using context clues, for instance mistaking one word for another (for example *pillars* for *appliers*). In several of the cases, the subjects failed to make a guess at all. In general, all three of the subjects followed a similar pattern. They would first simply try to use their existing vocabulary store, and if they thought they knew the word they would stick to that meaning and try to make it fit in a coherent manner, without checking any additional context clues. Although this worked well for the words they did know prior to the study, it did not work for those words they thought they knew but did not. Second, they would try to use their knowledge of morphology to find a meaning and then check that with surrounding context clues. Finally, if they did not recognize the word or its stem they would use the context clues that were available. The clues they sought were local linguistic units, global text representation, and world knowledge. In general, when they recognized that they did not know a word, the subjects first examined the morphology to see if they knew any of its parts to aid in providing information regarding the meaning. If they could use the morphology, they would hypothesize a meaning and use context, such as collocations in the immediate environment. If they could not find a clue, they attempted to see if they could get by without knowing the meaning of the word. Context helped to evaluate the guesses they made. The biggest problem they had with words they did not know was when they incorrectly thought they did know the word, as with the Hulstijn (1992) study. Again, it appears to be clear that vocabulary instruction needs to acknowledge the confirmation stage in guessing vocabulary in context.

In an attempt to better understand how incidental learning of vocabulary takes place, Paribakht and Wesche (1999) employed an introspective study of lexical inferencing strategies. They examined how a word may, or may not, be learned in the iterative process of learning vocabulary while attending to text meaning. The study involved data from ten intermediate level students in a university ESL class from a variety of first language backgrounds. Several weeks prior to the study, the subjects were presented with a text on acid rain and were asked to read it and circle all the words that they did not know as a pre-test. The individual introspective sessions lasted up to two hours. Initially, participants were trained in think-aloud procedures. Following the training, think-aloud protocols were collected for all ten students as they carried out two reading comprehension tasks based on the target text, a question task, and a summary task. The question task presented questions for the subjects to answer aloud as they read the text. They were also asked to indicate any unfamiliar words they had encountered and explain how they had dealt with them. The summary task required the subjects to read the text, stopping after each paragraph to summarize the text contexts.

The data analysis involved: 1) identification of the words that learners reported as unknown while carrying out the comprehension tasks; 2) identification of the unknown words that were ignored; 3) identification of the lexical processing strategies used each time the learners decided to deal with an unknown word; and 4) development of a descriptive system for classifying the types of knowledge and information learners used when they attempted to infer word meanings. The results indicated that content words were most often reported as unknown, and the subjects reported problems more during the summary task than the question-answering task. The results for how learners dealt with unknown words differed somewhat from Huckin and Bloch (1997). In both comprehension tasks, the readers ignored approximately half of the words they identified as unknown, a much larger proportion than in the Huckin and Bloch study. The primary reason reported for this was that the words were not seen as necessary. Three strategies were identified for dealing with unknown words when they were addressed. The first was retrieval (repeating the word out loud or rereading several times). The second was appeal for assistance (directly asking the interviewer or verifying with a dictionary). The third was inferencing, which made up approximately 80 per cent of all the strategies. While inferencing, the learners used sentence-level grammatical knowledge (35 per cent), word morphology (15 per cent), punctuation (11 per cent), world knowledge (nine per cent), and what are termed 'minor sources', such as discourse text, homonymy, cognates, and unknown (30 per cent). It is striking, in terms of viewing reading as a source of vocabulary learning, that the subjects ignored about half of the unknown words. Thus, these words were not attended to and hence not really candidates for incidental learning.

Summary and conclusions

There are strong relationships between successful reading and the richness of a reader's vocabulary store. Even though it is a slow and time-consuming process, a lot of vocabulary is learned through context. However, even proficient readers will have failures of strategies for making contextual inferences. This may be due to a lack of context sufficient to provide meaning. Vocabulary learning for many words involves learning different levels and nuances of the word's meaning. Successful reading involves both this depth of knowledge and a breadth of knowledge such that the reader confronts few unfamiliar words while reading.

There has been a great deal of discussion regarding the extent to which learners acquire vocabulary incidentally. In general, it appears that vocabulary can be acquired both incidentally and intentionally as readers process text. However, it is apparent that readers learn little vocabulary incidentally at any one time while reading. Most words take multiple exposures to learn. For most second language readers, other tools such as dictionaries, glosses, and direct instruction are useful.

Learners employ a number of vocabulary learning strategies in the process of becoming accomplished readers. The research reviewed indicates that there are large individual differences in these strategies across learners. More advanced readers are more flexible in their strategy use and are generally more determined to succeed at the task than lower ability level readers. Further, the advanced readers tend to use more strategies than do the lower ability readers.

Discussion and study questions

1 Several of the studies have demonstrated that incidental learning of vocabulary takes place, but that guessing from context can sometimes lead the reader to infer the incorrect meaning. How can this be addressed in instructional contexts?
2 What are the advantages and disadvantages of dictionary use? How can learners be taught to utilize the dictionary effectively? When, if ever, should a learner rely on a monolingual dictionary?
3 To what extent does attention to explicit or implicit vocabulary learning differ depending upon whether the learner is a beginning-level learner or an advanced-level learner?
4 Grabe reflected on his vocabulary learning abilities and strategies. In your own language learning situation, how did you learn vocabulary? Did you work at it explicitly and systematically?

10 READING AND WRITING RELATIONSHIPS

Introduction

A theme from previous chapters has been the need for context and purpose in reading. This need reflects a view that interaction and context are essential features in literacy learning. In many ways, it also reflects a view that there are important relationships between reading and writing. Traditionally, the two skills of reading and writing have been seen as distinct, and have generally been taught separately. However, more recently, attention has come to be placed on the relationships between the two skills. The distinctiveness of the relationships between reading and writing emerge in part from the particular literacy tasks in which the language learner engages. At one extreme we can see the activity of pleasantly reading a novel, reading the morning newspaper, or reading a magazine on the bus, activities not apparently related to writing. The goal is diversion, appreciation, escape, or keeping up on current events. It is generally the case that we read a great deal more than we write. At the other extreme, we have school writing of a report, a thesis, a dissertation, email discussions, or blogs, activities which inherently involve both comprehension and composition.

Arguments have been presented that the underlying cognitive processes of regulating and framing that are involved in conversational discourse production and comprehension are not so distant from the frame constructing and inference regulation that is involved in written text production and comprehension (Bracewell, Frederiksen, and Frederiksen 1982). From this perspective, although the processes involved in discourse comprehension and discourse production differ in many clearly identifiable ways, there are many parallels from the standpoint of cognitive processing and social interaction. Such perspectives view readers and texts as interlocutors. As Salvatori (1996) states, 'Expert readers and writers have developed a kind of introspective reading that allows them to decide—as they read and as they write—when to pursue, when to revise, when to abandon a line of argument, and when to start afresh' (446). This chapter will examine the views and implications for reading and writing relationships, as they are important for second language reading research and pedagogy. It focuses on broadening the views of reading to incorporate writing, and indeed a view of literacy that is broader than just the ability to read and write decontextually.

Views of reading and writing relationships

Viewing reading and writing as separate skills or processes is a tradition that goes back to American colonial schools (Nelson and Calfee 1998), or even further to the Middle Ages when the printing press eliminated the need to handwrite every book (Hout 1988). Kucer (1985) notes that traditionally there has been little interaction between reading researchers and writing researchers. Professional divisions between reading and writing educators have developed as the two groups joined different professional organizations, attended different conferences and colloquia, and read different journals. Each group focused on its own particular domain with little investigation of the psychological, linguistic, and contextual connections between the two areas of literacy. The two processes were seen as complementary activities that were mirror images of each other. The process was viewed as the message → encoder → channel → decoder → message relationship mentioned in Chapter 1. However, over the past two decades the reader has come to be seen as being much more active in searching for meaning. The separation of the cognitive mechanisms in reading and writing was challenged by van Dijk and Kintsch (1983), who posited that cognitive efficiency would require some sharing of processes in the two skills. They saw readers as engaged in cyclical processing of selecting micropropositions and reconciling these propositions with prior knowledge in the creation of an internal text, a creation not unlike the creation of text by writers. There has been a growing awareness that an examination of cognitive processes at a deeper level than surface behaviors indicates shared goals and strategies.

Models that view reading and writing as interactive and knowledge-driven processes speculate on the bases of the interrelationships. As noted in Chapter 2, Tierney and Pearson (1983, 1985) and Pearson and Tierney (1984) proposed a close connection between the two, indeed, they proposed a composing model of reading in which readers construct meaning through an ongoing dialogue with themselves in the same way that writers compose to represent their meaning. They see reading and writing as essentially similar processes of meaning construction and both are acts of composing. Here, reading and writing are connected because they rely on identical or very similar knowledge representation processes. The reader creates meaning as background experiences are linked with the writer's cues in understanding what the writer is attempting to convey and what the reader is interested in generating for her/himself. The writer, on the other hand, is engaged in trying to convey a message in a considerate manner for the anticipated reader. Thus, 'both reader and writer must adapt to their perceptions about their partner in negotiating what a text means' (Tierney and Pearson 1983: 568). They break apart the composing process into the five characteristics of *planning, drafting, aligning, revising,* and *monitoring.* As described in Chapter 2, their comparisons between reading and writing are:

Planning: both readers and writers have procedural, substantive, and intentional goals (How do I approach writing this topic?—I want to get sense out of this text; I want to say something about how this works—I need to find out about this relationship; I want to convince people about this—I wonder what the author is trying to say.) The writer plans what to write given the constraints. The reader alters goals depending upon background knowledge of the topic and how learning of the topic is desired.

Drafting: Both writers and readers need a first draft. The writer reaches for a pen and the reader opens the text. The writer searches for a lead statement and the reader scans the first lines in search of what the general idea is about. The writer proceeds to develop the ideas and the reader reconstructs/deconstructs the text. The commonality between reading and writing is the goal of making ideas cohere.

Aligning: Both writers and readers adjust their roles with regard to the audience (writer) or author (reader). These stances can be intimate, sympathetic, challenging and critical, or neutral. The author assumes a stance and a generic role of relative authority. The reader determines a relationship with the author and topic.

Revising: The writer examines what has been written to discover and clarify ideas, repeatedly rereading, re-examining, deleting, shaping and correcting. The successful reader examines developing interpretations and views the constructed meaning as subject to revision.

Monitoring: Both readers and writers distance themselves from what they have created and evaluate the product. As noted previously, this metacognitive monitoring tracks and controls the process, indicating when a good job has been done and when success is lacking. This monitoring involves an inner dialogue that critically evaluates the adequacy of the message.

Several approaches have been proposed identifying the commonalities between reading and writing. Wittrock (1983) sums up the common relationships between the two skills when he posits that 'good reading, like effective writing, involves generative processes that create meaning by building relations between the text and what we know, believe, and experience' (600). Although it has long been accepted that writing is a generative activity, Wittrock brings reading into generative processing as well. While reading for comprehension, meaning is generated by relating segments of text together and to background knowledge and memories. Effective writing involves generating meaning by relating knowledge and experience to the text. Both skills involve generating relations among the text segments—words to sentences, sentences to paragraphs, paragraphs to larger texts—as well as generating relationships between knowledge and experience and the text. Squire (1983), on the other hand, sees the commonality between composing and comprehending as being that both are process-oriented interrelated thinking skills. In this view both comprehending and composing are basic reflections of the same cognitive process. Comprehending requires the learner to reconstruct the structure and meaning of the writer's ideas and composing engages the writer in constructing meaning and developing, relating, and expressing ideas (Squire 1983). The focus here is on the iterative processes of construction in both reading and writing.

Kucer (1985), in a view very much influenced by schema theory, posits reading and writing universals that represent cognitive basics in both literacy events. He initially established the role of long-term memory and schemata as the building blocks of what he terms 'text worlds'. In both reading and writing, schemata are activated, constrained both by the availability to locate content schemata and by the reader's familiarity with the act of reading or writing. The appropriateness of the information brought to bear is evaluated by the reader for its support of a plausible interpretation of the message encountered, and by the writer as representations of information appropriate for expressing the intended message. Throughout the process, the language user is incrementally developing the message, whether reading or writing. The activity does not begin with a full formulation of the message, but rather emerges from initially rather vague intentions and predictions. Connections are made to new or newly realized information, and the language user adapts to this, as reading and writing to learn are central to the acts of literacy. That is, in most cases the pre-established background knowledge structure of the reader or writer will not be an adequate fit to the new situation, and the language user will have to adapt or build new knowledge structures.

Kucer (1985, 2001) also proposes that one of the cognitive fundamentals is the contextual dependency of both reading and writing. Text comprehension and production do not exist within a vacuum outside situational factors, but rather take place through interactions and transactions with context. Kucer (2001) provides five aspects that connect reading and writing: knowledge search, context, goals and plans, strategies, and evolving text.

The *knowledge search* is initiated in reading as the reader searches for schemata stored in long-term memory. In that search process, the reader evaluates the schemata for their relevance and appropriateness, examining the extent to which the background knowledge supports the construction of a plausible interpretation of the incoming print message. The schemata provide a basis for comprehension, and are elaborated and refined as the new information is constructed. Likewise, when writing is begun, the writer initiates a search for and evaluation of relevant background knowledge. Just as the reader takes the available schemata and uses them to create new information, the writer takes available schemata and rearranges, organizes, and refines them through planning, writing, and revising.

The *context* that readers and writers encounter involves the gamut from personal attitudes, subject matter, and interlocutors, to the social role of the communication. There is a clear relationship between context and the language user's knowledge. Thus, the language user is not sampling background knowledge randomly. Rather, the reader or writer is sampling based on knowledge of context and audience. What the reader remembers from a text varies as a result of the context in which the reading takes place. Acts of reading and writing are functionally based and emerge from a transaction between a language user and the context. Through this context, the reader and writer are also dealing with universals of goals and plans. The context exists and the language user instigates plans and goals within that context. Not all texts are read or written for the same purpose, and the reader or writer constructs an evolving set of plans to carry out the goal. The context in which a text is written will affect its content and form. Both the reader and writer consider the purpose and role of the text within the situation, one asking what the text is supposed to elicit and the other asking how the text will elicit what is desired.

Kucer's (2001) view of *goals and plans* supports the view of both reading and writing being intentional acts that are goal directed. Texts are read to accomplish a variety of goals, so the reader establishes plans to reach the established goals. The reader's interactions with the text are altered based on his or her intentions, such as whether the goal is to find a particular piece of information, to get just a taste of the text, or to read for depth. As with reading, the writer generates intentions through goals and plans. Writers take their plans and generate text that is designed to be coherent and tailored to those goals.

Kucer (1985, 2001) offers a set of universal reading and writing *strategies*. Strategies are information-processing procedures that operate within short-term memory. The strategies, seen as common to both reading and writing, are viewed in the context of propositional theory. The language user is involved in generation of macropropositions and micropropositions. This is the generation of what are often termed main ideas and supporting details in the reading literature. These are generated in both reading and writing processes. The language user is also involved in macro-integrating and micro-integrating strategies that create a more global meaning for the text. Some common strategies between reading and writing are: 1) generating and organizing major ideas and concepts; 2) developing and expanding generalizations and concepts with details and particulars; 3) organizing or integrating meaning across the text into a logical and coherent whole; 4) using a variety of linguistic cues in generating meaning; 5) utilizing a variety of text aids (for example charts and graphs); 6) using relevant linguistic and conceptual background knowledge; and 7) making meaningful predictions based on text available. The strategy of selecting is applied in the schema-generating process, operating in parallel to the generating and integrating strategies, and assists in revising the comprehended or produced emerging propositions, similar to the process proposed by Tierney and Pearson (1983). Thus, Kucer claims there to be a set of important commonalities between reading and writing as literacy acts.

Finally, Kucer (2001) notes that both the reader and writer are continually engaged in an *evolving cognitive text* as they work to control the ideas that create meaning. This is the process of continually revising the message to refine the intended meaning. This evolving world of meaning serves to support both the reader as text is sampled and the writer as new text is generated. The language user moves away from a close interaction with the print itself into an interaction with how to employ that print to comply with the meaning that is being constructed. The interactions of this evolving text world are, in essence, the executive control mechanisms that monitor the comprehension and production process.

However, there are differences between reading and writing as well, and studies on the relationship typically have correlations in the .20–.30 range (Fitzgerald and Shanahan 2000). There is not a one-to-one transfer from one skill to the other, and both must be taught. It is necessary to provide separate instruction and experiences for each of the skills, though there can be combinations of ways in which those experiences can be viewed. According to Fitzgerald and Shanahan:

> Reading and writing encourage different enough cognitive operations that they offer alternate perspectives that can give rise to new learning or appreciation. Writing about a text, for example, leads to different types of rethinking than rereading alone provides. If reading and writing were identical, this would not be the case, and if they were very separate, they may not be so mutually supportive.
>
> *(Fitzgerald and Shanahan 2000: 43)*

Some of the approaches and combinations are discussed below as *read-to-write*, *write-to-read*, and *reading and writing and knowing*. The distinctions are not always mutually exclusive, but they are used here to indicate the relative emphasis each focus has placed on the relationships between the two skills.

The first language literacy skills of reading and writing

Read-to-write

Smith (1983) focuses on the reading-to-write relationship by claiming that it is the only way to explain how anyone learns to write. In effect, his argument mirrors the arguments relating to the incidental learning of vocabulary while reading discussed in Chapter 9. Simply put, there is no other way to explain how people learn such a complex activity as writing. He notes how little writing anyone actually does in school, and how little feedback is received. 'No one writes enough to learn more than a small part of what writers have to know' (560). The reader must learn how to write from what others have written. The ability does not come through deliberate formal analyses because what is learned is much too intricate and subtle. There is not enough time to learn the complexities of register, genre, spelling, form, appropriateness, etc. through direct and deliberate study. He points to the necessity of learning to write from what is read in an unconscious, incidental, and collaborative manner. In short, readers must read like writers in order to write like writers. The reader engages with the author, anticipating what the author will write next.

Spivey and King (1989) adopt a constructivist view of readers who make meaning by integrating content from source texts with previously acquired knowledge from both reading to understand and reading to write. This meaning making on the part of readers is one predictor of the writer's success in composing from text. The readers *select* from available content, *organize* as they construct a mental representation of the text, and *connect* the content to discourse structures. Research has shown that in studies of recall and summarizing, developmental maturity, as indicated by grade level and reading ability, is associated with awareness of textual importance (McGee 1982; Brown and Smiley 1978). Spivey and King note also that in several studies of synthesizing multiple texts on similar topics, proficient readers performed more successfully than less skilled readers. The proficient readers were generally more successful at selecting relevant source text material, better able to organize the compositions, and more successful at producing text that was reader friendly (Spivey 1984, 1988). Spivey and King (1989) examined the performance of younger students on discourse synthesis in order to see how developmental differences were manifested across the sixth-, eighth-, and tenth-grade levels. There were 20 subjects in each grade, half of whom were accomplished readers at their grade level and half of whom were less accomplished readers. The subjects were given three texts on a topic entitled *Rodeo*. The results of the study indicated that the more accomplished readers produced compositions showing better organization and extensiveness in their writing. Moreover, the older students produced texts with more, and more important, content from the source texts than did the younger students. In general, reading ability was more closely related to synthesis performance than was grade level. The better readers produced texts with more local and global coherence than the less able readers. Thus, in their study, Spivey and King conclude that reading ability can assist writing ability in text-based writing tasks.

Kennedy (1985) studied three fluent and three less fluent college students as they constructed an objective essay based on three assigned articles. She was interested in answering three questions: 1) how do readers who are about to become writers behave? 2) do subjects writing from sources proceed in a linear fashion from pre-reading, reading, post-reading/pre-writing, or do they behave in a less predictable recursive manner? and 3) is there an association between reading fluency and the number and type of reading/composing strategies that writers use? The subjects in the study read three articles on the topic of communication and wrote an essay based on the material contained in the articles. The first finding was that the six subjects did not approach the task of writing from sources in the same way. Second, although all of the subjects referred to the reading sources as they wrote, they consulted them at different points in the reading–writing process. They differed in how they orchestrated the activities involved in writing the multiple-source essay. As with Spivey and King (1989), the fluent and less fluent students differed in their ability to utilize sources. The more fluent readers employed a larger number of strategies and activities in synthesizing the information from the assigned source texts. They were more actively involved in the task, reading and writing with a purpose, using notes, revising, and including important quotations in integrating the content from the articles with their own ideas. The fluent readers engaged in more high-level processing and used a richer variety of study-type strategies than the less proficient readers. The not-so-fluent readers, on the other hand, tended not to utilize the strategies used by the more fluent readers and frequently simply inserted large segments of text from the source materials into their essays. Third, the truly fluent readers generally engaged in more planning than the less fluent readers, particularly during the post-reading and pre-writing phase. The not-so-fluent readers did little initial planning, and planned only moderately during the composition activity itself. The more able readers did most of their text manipulation prior to the composition phase while the less fluent readers manipulated the text rarely prior to composition, extensively relying on quotes from the texts during their composing process, frequently selecting a direct quote and working it into the essay.

McGinley (1992) examined composing from multiple sources through a series of case studies of readers involved in the process of creating text on the basis of multiple texts. McGinley involved seven college undergraduates of junior or senior standing with grades ranging from 4.2 to 4.7 on a five-point scale. The study included analysis of transcripts of think-aloud protocols, examination of videotapes of student writing sessions, evaluation of students' written products, analysis of information collected during debriefing interviews, and examination of researcher notes and observations. The subjects were provided with two reading passages on the topic of mandatory drug testing in the workplace, and were asked to write a persuasive essay on the topic. The results indicated that the composing process was not a linear one. While students spent much of their time reading the articles at the beginning of the task, they also continued to return to the text and reread the texts throughout the composing process. Likewise, the reasoning processes employed were not strictly linear. Although questioning and hypothesizing decreased over time, these operations demonstrated continued importance throughout the task. Similarly, these writers engaged in using schemata and metacomments relatively equally across the time they were writing. These findings indicate a recursive process in which writing, reading, and reasoning are intertwined. Further, the debriefing interviews showed some of the ways in which subjects employed various reading and writing activities across the writing and restructuring process. The subjects reported that reading the source texts functioned primarily to help them acquire new information about the topic, while writing notes served as an intermediate text that they used to plan and organize their arguments. However, they also reported that almost all of the reading and writing activities functioned as vehicles for reshaping their ideas and refining their arguments. The reading and writing activities influenced and were influenced by one another, and indicated that the subjects adopted different roles throughout the composing process. The roles included a reader of the source articles, a writer, a reader, a note-taker, and a note reader, much as in Tierney and Pearson's (1983) proposal of reading and writing roles.

Greene (1992) discusses the reading-to-write process through the metaphor of *mining* a text: 'reconstructing context, inferring or imposing structure, and seeing choices in language' (1). He notes that reading has long played an important role in writing instruction through a widely held view that students can learn about writing through examination and imitation of well-written prose models. The assumption here is that students will internalize the style, structure and correctness in such exemplary works. More recently, this view has been challenged among composition researchers, even though it is strongly held within academic content disciplines.

An alternative explanation for reading-based approaches to writing is that the student is immersed in a literate environment in which a disciplinary community affects text construction and reading/writing judgments. This is consistent with Swales' (1990) discussion of discourse communities discussed in Chapter 8. For Greene (1992) the metaphor of *mining* provides a means for understanding how writers read consciously to gain discourse knowledge that can be applied while writing. Reading from a writer's perspective involves imposing or inferring a structure as well as examining possible options and choices in the way language can be deployed. Writers can embellish what they read with examples, thinking critically about what they read given their goals, and structure information in order to construct coherent text representations. However, Greene (1992) notes that this *mining* as a writer is more than traditional critical reading in that it involves important differences. First, the mining of texts involves inquiry that informs not only about the texts writers have read, but also the types of texts that they themselves can produce over time. As such, it is not concerned with the decomposition of a particular text so much as a sampling across several texts that may provide approaches for carrying out the reader's own rhetorical intentions. Finally, the text mining activity is not focused merely on knowledge of discourse conventions, but on the appropriate uses of strategies in different settings. In short, the writer as reader reads for knowledge about how to utilize particular strategies in appropriate contexts given the writer's goals as well as for the text information itself.

Summarizing a text, like synthesizing from sources, has been a frequently studied read-to-write activity. Winograd (1984) examined the effects of the presence or absence of strategic skills on summarization by 80 eighth-grade students and 40 adults associated with a university as students or recent graduates. The study focused on three aspects of strategy use: 1) awareness of the task demands involved in producing summaries; 2) the ability to identify important elements in the text; and 3) the ability to transform and reduce the full meaning of the text into its gist. Good and poor eighth-grade readers were presented with measures of reading speed, written interview questions, and an intelligence test. Then, six times, they read a passage, answered comprehension questions about the passage, wrote a 60-word summary of the text, rated the importance of each sentence in the passage, and selected the five most important sentences. A subset of the subjects took a delayed measure six months after the initial study phase. The results indicated that the good readers and adults were better judges of the importance of the passage content than were the poor readers. The results also indicated some consistency across the poor readers in their ratings of importance, indicating that their judgments were not idiosyncratic. The poor readers appeared to find sentences full of rich visual detail to be important more than the good readers, who related importance to textual salience. The results also indicated that the good readers and adults tended to put the information that they considered important into their summaries to a much greater degree than the poor readers. This indicates that the good readers were more attuned to the relationship between the text that was read and the task of summarizing. That is, the poor readers appeared to be using two unrelated strategies, one for deciding what was important and one for deciding what to include in the summary. The good readers and adult readers, on the other hand, were using their evaluation of importance across both the selection task and the summary construction task. Finally, the results indicated that the ability to identify important elements in a text was a significant factor in both comprehension and summarization scores, providing evidence that the ability to identify important elements in a text is a strong strategic component in both reading comprehension and summarization. Such a finding appears to promote the view that there are common cognitive factors in both reading and writing, at least as far as summarization represents one aspect of writing.

There are arguments in the literature regarding the extent to which some of the reading/writing tasks, such as summarizing, are predominately reading or writing activities. Hare (1992) addresses this issue within the task of summarizing text. There is general agreement that summarizers begin the process by constructing a macrostructure that exemplifies the relationships between individual propositions in the text. However, there are differing views as to whether this summarizing takes place during the comprehending process or after comprehension has occurred. If the summarizing takes place during the reading process, it is argued that summarizing is primarily a reading task, whereas if it takes place after comprehension then it may be considered primarily a writing task. Hare notes that van Dijk and Kintsch (1978, 1983) found summarizing to be primarily a reading task in which their subjects abstracted higher-level summary statements when asked to summarize. In this case, the reader produces the macrostructure from memory, recalling the important propositions from the text that has been read. That is, information has been retained and reproduced based on the macrorules which identify important information. Summarizing is just reproducing the structure stored in memory.

On the other hand, researchers such as Brown and Day (1983) and Johnson (1983) view the retrieval of the propositions as the precursor to the two primary summarizing activities of selecting important ideas and condensing them into a suitable summary. Summarizing involves more than simply identifying important ideas and reproducing them. It crucially involves selecting and condensing those ideas in a structure recognized as the summary genre. Hare (1992) indicates that in truth the summarizing activity may lie somewhere between being either a reading or a writing activity. Summarizing is a recursive activity that begins with encoding what may be a recounting of the comprehended passage (a reading activity) which is then edited through selection and condensation (a writing activity). The iterative nature of the summary construction process involves both reading and writing throughout. Further, the processes will be affected by other mediating variables. The person variables of view of the task and level of content knowledge will affect the process and product. Individuals have varying mental representations of what it means to summarize a text. Some have only a vague idea that it means to shorten the original while others have very proscriptive views involving length in relation to the original and whether verbatim text from the original text may be used. Further, knowledge of the topic will affect whether the summarizing process is primarily a reading task or a writing task. If the person is unfamiliar with the topic, then the summary can only be accomplished after comprehension of the new information has taken place, and will more closely reflect a writing task. Selecting and condensing are not possible while comprehending because the information is not available. On the other hand, if the content is fairly familiar to the reader, then the task becomes more of a writing task taking place while the text is being processed.

Write-to-read

Although most research has examined the reading-to-write relationship, a modest amount of research has also examined the writing-to-read relationship. This approach typically sees writing prior to reading as an avenue to activating information that is already known to the potential reader and to prompting expectations about the possible content of the upcoming text. However, it also frequently mirrors McGinley (1992), discussed above, in seeing that the processes of writing and reading are not linear. Hefflin and Hartman (2002) point out the difficulty of determining precisely where writing and reading begin and end. They contend that a writer reads while writing, and a reader thinks like a writer while reading. They raise a chicken-and-egg issue in noting that writing can lead to reading which leads to more writing which leads to more reading, and on and on. Filling out a job application might result from writing a letter to a prospective employer. Filling out the application involves reading the application, writing answers, perhaps then reading information about conditions of employment, writing a letter of acceptance, and so on. This view takes a very broad temporal view of the literacy activity involving both reading and writing.

McGinley and Tierney (1989) focus on the connection between reading and writing not so much from a cognitive relationship as from the two skills being two different conceptual 'lenses' through which critical literacy is applied. For them, the arguments that see the relationship between reading and writing as textual-world production reinforce the active and productive nature of both reading and writing in engendering learning. They propose a metaphor for critical literacy 'in which various forms of reading and writing are understood as different ways of knowing or criss-crossing a conceptual landscape' (250). In this view, a topic of study is represented as a landscape and different forms of reading and writing are routes for traversing the landscape from multiple perspectives. They note that Marshall's (1987) research demonstrated how students engaged in reacting to literature through writing were more engaged in thinking about what they were reading than readers who only read, or read and only worked with work-sheets. Such an activity is seen as comprising a complex traversal of the literacy landscape. When students engaged in formal writing, rather than fragmented activities such as note-taking or answering study questions related to the reading content, they were more involved in extensive thought, planning, generating, and goal setting.

Crowhurst (1991) examined the effects of reading on writing and writing on reading within the mode of persuasive texts. The subjects were 100 sixth-grade students classified as high, medium, and low ability based on reading comprehension scores who were assigned to one of four groups twice a week over five weeks: writing, reading, control, and single-lesson-model. The members of the writing group were shown a chart outlining the structure of persuasive texts and were presented with a persuasive text. Then they themselves wrote and revised four persuasive texts. The members of the reading group received the same initial instruction in persuasive text structure as the writing group, received guided instruction in reading persuasive texts, and shared opinions on the topics. The control group members read novels and wrote book reports. The single-lesson-model group received the same type of instruction as the control group except for one lesson in the last week that was identical to the common lesson for the reading and writing groups. All subjects were given two reading tests involving writing a recall protocol of an assigned text, and pre- and post-writing tests involving the writing of two persuasive compositions.

The results of Crowhurst's study showed that both the writing and the reading groups improved significantly in the quality of their writing from the pre-test to the post-test, and both groups scored significantly higher on the post-test than the control group. Scores for the single-lesson-model group did not increase significantly between the pre-test and the post-test. Both the writing and reading groups wrote longer compositions than the control group on the post-test, used more conclusions and text markers, elaborated more, and wrote compositions that were better organized than the control group. The reading group showed significant improvement in the writing quality of their persuasive texts, indicating that reading was a factor in writing ability for these subjects. The reading of persuasive texts apparently played a role in the writing improvement of the reading group, helping to build a schema for how persuasive texts are structured and argued. However, although the writing group showed gains between the reading pre-test and post-test, gains higher than any of the other groups, the gains were not statistically significant. In fact, the reading group failed to show significant gains in reading ability between the two tests as well. These results may be a result of the reading tests not being sensitive to the relatively small gains that one would expect over five weeks in the ability of sixth-grade students to recall text propositions and holistic ratings of the recall protocol quality which were made on a rather narrow four-point scale.

Lenski and Johns (1997) examined how the pattern of reading multiple-source texts during a read-to-write research activity affected the style of a subsequent written research report. They note that in the researching task, the processes of searching, reading, and writing must be integrated, and that when the three processes are combined, each individual process alters the others in very complex ways. Although the writing task drives the other processes, researching is not a linear step-by-step process. It involves using strategies to advance the inquiry process through revising the research question, further searching of source texts, or writing. Lenski and Johns followed six middle-school students through the research–reading–writing process over seven class sessions as they wrote a paper stating what historical figure they would want as a personal mentor. The research indicated that the six subjects employed three basic researching patterns. The first pattern was sequential in which one of the subjects carried out a search, read source material, and then wrote the paper from notes. The second pattern was a spiral pattern in which four of the subjects researched, took notes, wrote, and then began the process again as they noted a need for more information. The third pattern was a recursive pattern in which one of the students began by writing what she already knew about the topic and then engaged in more searching and reading in order to complement what was already written. The results of the study indicated that the research patterns were consistent in the way the subjects organized their writing. The five subjects who viewed the process as sequential or spiral wrote papers that followed a generally chronological discussion of the selected person with separate application sections explaining why the person would be a good mentor. The subject that used a recursive pattern had a much more integrated paper by weaving her reasons throughout the description of the person's life. The study indicates how integrally related reading and writing can be when literacy tasks are being conducted. All six papers received a grade of A, though the papers differed in their structure. However, the structure of the writing and the structure of the researching and reading process are intertwined. Reading may shape the writing product, and writing may shape the form that the reading process takes.

Langer and Applebee (1987) carried out a study over more than three years investigating writing, thinking skills, and the teaching of writing and thinking skills in high school content areas. They conducted a series of studies involving 23 teachers and their students with reference to how writing was used to foster learning in academic courses. They also carried out a series of studies of learning in which they examined the effects of different types of writing tasks on academic learning. It is not possible to go into depth regarding the quantitative and qualitative study of over 900 students here. However, certain strong trends did emerge. Across all of the studies, there was clear evidence that writing leads to learning better than those activities that involved reading and studying alone. Further, they found that different writing tasks provided the readers with different kinds of information, and helped them to think about information in different ways. Short-answer questions lead students to focus on particular items of information located or implied in the text, involving little rethinking of the material. Such questions, however, did lead to substantial short-term recall of textual information. Analytic writing leads to more concentration on a narrow focus of information, focusing in complex ways on a small number of ideas.

Information is retained longer. Summary writing tasks and note-taking, on the other hand, focused the participants on the whole reading passage itself in less depth than the analytical writing. There appear to be indications, then, that writing provides a strong venue for learning from text, and specific types of writing affect the types of understanding readers take from text. Writing in conjunction with reading directs the reading and learning process in goal-oriented way.

There are limitations to the implications of this study, however. Because of the relatively artificial setting of the study, there are problems with generalizability. Additionally, the subjects were examined over a short period of time. Longer exposure to the treatments may have produced different results. The findings may be limited because of the particular passages and topics chosen. Finally, the self-report data must be critically evaluated.

Reading and writing and knowing

Fitzgerald and Shanahan (2000) reiterate that reading and writing rely on analogous mental processes. Through these processes, learning takes place and the two skills reinforce themselves and each other recursively. These processes are interactive and interrelated, not unidirectional (Shanahan and Lomax 1986). Fitzgerald and Shanahan (2000) note that both reading and writing involve four categories of knowledge throughout literacy acquisition: 1) metaknowledge (knowing about functions and purposes of reading and writing, knowing that readers and writers interact, monitoring one's own knowledge); 2) domain knowledge about substance and content (vocabulary meaning, meaning through context of connected text); 3) knowledge about universal text attributes (phonological awareness, grapheme awareness, morphology, syntax of sentences, text organization); and 4) procedural knowledge and skill to negotiate reading and writing (knowing how to access, use, and generate knowledge in any of the previous areas, instantiating smooth integration of various processes). Each of these categories is involved in learning and knowing through text. Comprehension and composing together and separately in a concerted task reconcile new and borrowed information in newly produced knowledge (Ackerman 1991).

Greene (1993) examined how two different writing tasks influenced students' thinking in reading and writing. The two tasks involved either writing a historical account or a problem-based essay, and required synthesis of information from six different source texts and background knowledge in the composing process. These tasks involved integrating source knowledge from texts on the one hand and defining a problem and speculating about alternative behaviors on the other. These two tasks involved substantially different types of composition on the part of the reader. The assumption is that as the readers perform different writing tasks, they construct different representations of meaning because the tasks elicit different types of organization, selection, and connections of the information. In turn, these different goals create different knowledge configurations. Fifteen college juniors and seniors were enrolled in a history course entitled *European Lifestyle and Culture*. The subjects were given ten days to read the source texts and write a three-page report or problem-based essay. They were given a measure of topic knowledge as a pre-test, after completing the essay, and three weeks after the assignment. After receiving the assigned task, the subjects provided ten-minute think-aloud protocols outside of class in order to provide their initial impressions of the task and to identify how they clarified the task to themselves. Additionally, as they began the writing assignment during the ten-day completion period they provided an additional ten-minute think-aloud outside of class. After they finished the writing task, they again provided a think-aloud outside of class, this time in 15 minutes. Their internalized writing task interpretation, either text (they appeared to rely on the texts assigned as the only source of information) or *text* × *self* (they indicated they would also rely on their background knowledge) was determined from the think-aloud protocols. The essays were analyzed in terms of the organization that framed the essay, whether the information was borrowed from the texts or elaborated by background knowledge, and uses of citations to appeal to authority.

The results from the think-aloud protocols indicated that the two groups of subjects differed in the way they interpreted the tasks. Those writing the report appeared to believe they were primarily limited to information from the source texts while the problem-based writers felt that they should integrate prior knowledge with the source information. In terms of essay organization, the subjects writing the reports organized their essays around sets of descriptions grouped around particular issues, while the subjects writing the problem-based essays organized their writing in a problem/solution pattern in which ideas were organized in a cause-and-effect manner. For the most part, the two groups of writers used the same pattern of primarily using information from the sources. Further, there was little difference in the functions of text citations used by the two groups. Both tended to use citations as sources of information rather than as resources for supporting an argument, a result not expected for the problem-based writers. Finally, the post-test results on the knowledge measures did not indicate that task affected the amount of knowledge gained from the assignment. Thus, engagement in either task appears to have brought about a slight gain in knowledge. However, the instruments used for measuring gains in knowledge were not sensitive to differences in the way knowledge was internalized by the readers or how their thinking about the information may have been influenced by task structure.

Newell and Winograd (1995) also focused on how students of differing academic abilities use writing to learn the content of the subject area of history. The study involved 15 11th-grade students in an academic class and seven students in a general class who read, wrote about, and took a series of tests on prose passages excerpted from US history textbooks. The academic class students were at an advanced academic ability level, while the general class students were of approximately average ability. The study involved three study conditions: review without writing, restricted writing (responding with short answers to 20 study questions), and extended writing (analytic essay writing). The subjects received treatment six times over a two-week period. The results will be discussed in terms of trends since the sample of subjects was so small that the statistical tests could be misleading. The results not surprisingly indicated that the students did more writing in the essay condition than in the study question condition. Also, the academic students wrote more than the general students. Essay writing led to more complex syntax than the study questions. This indicates that the essays involved more integration of information and completeness. Answers to the study questions contained substantially more textual-content units than the essay answers did. The study questions allowed the students to spread their attention over a wider selection of passage content, while the essay writing focused the writing over a narrower topic area. On the follow-up tests of concept application, the essay task elicited higher scores than did the study question or review only conditions, and scores for study question writing were about the same as those for the review only condition. Further, students who answered the study questions recalled a higher percentage of content units than either of the other two conditions. However, the essay condition produced better recall of content units that had appeared in the subjects' previous writing sample than the study condition. This held for both the analytic essay and study question conditions. Thus, the type of condition affects recall in two different ways. The large number of study questions caused the subjects to focus on a greater number of text areas than the essay. This apparently created better overall recall of content units. However, the content units included in the essays became more salient and were, hence, recalled more. These results reflect how type of writing task affects the way reading takes place.

Second language reading and writing connections

Although there have been discussions for some time about the relationships between reading and writing, there is much less empirical work in the second language literature than the first language literature. Further, the literature that does exist, with some exceptions, is generally linked to academic settings. Basically, academic settings involve completion of tasks that require reading and writing in interaction rather ubiquitously. Second language reading and writing relationships are more complex, and inherently more difficult to disentangle, than those examined thus far in this chapter. Those models that we have been looking at in first language assume a generally fully formed speaking ability prior to both reading and writing (Eisterhold 1990). Second language learners generally do not have such an initial highly developed control of oral language. Further, as noted earlier, the second language language user frequently already has literacy skills developed from the first language experience. Despite the literacy issues unique to second language readers, there is extensive interest in reading-writing connections. Indeed, Zamel (1992) notes, 'In order to give students experiences with reading that demonstrate the ways in which readers engage, contribute to, and make connections with texts, writing needs to be fully integrated with reading' (463). Additionally, anthologies on the topic of reading and writing relationships, Carson and Leki (1993) and Belcher and Hirvela (2001), focus on the need to connect reading and writing. Studies have shown that linking reading and writing activities thematically may lead to better performance than when reading and writing tasks are not thematically related (Esmaeili 2002).

As a consequence of the second language learner's frequent existing first language literacy ability, the issue of transfer of literacy skills from first language to second language is an important one. There are a number of relationships for the second language language user, those between first language reading and first language writing, first language reading and second language reading, first language writing and second language writing, and second language reading and second language writing. Carson et al. (1990) demonstrated that these are less than clear-cut relationships, and that they appear to differ across first language language groups. In their research, they indicated that for both their Japanese and Chinese subjects there was a moderate correlation between first language and second language reading (r=.509 and .366 respectively). Additionally, there were moderate relationships between first language writing and first language reading (r=.493 and .271 respectively), as well as between second language reading and second language writing (r=.271 and .494 respectively). However, they found very little relationship between first language writing and second language writing (r=.230 and -.019 respectively). Thus, first language writing skill does not appear to transfer easily to second language composition. Moreover, for the Chinese, the study found that the amount of first language education affected the scores much more than first language education affected the scores of the Japanese subjects. Basically, the reading and writing relationships for second language language users appear to reflect variation due to both first language language and second language ability.

In academic contexts, second language readers/writers deal with both language and what the academy expects regarding how writers work with and incorporate information from the texts they read. Newell, Garriga, and Peterson (2001) looked at reading-writing relationships in case studies of three ESL undergraduate students as they constructed analytic essays over a ten-week term. The students wrote three out-of-class essays. The first involved reading a newspaper article that was accompanied by two reaction letters and the author's reply to the letters. The second essay was a comparison and contrast in relation to autobiographical writings concerning the lives of young adults. The third essay reflected reactions to a 35-page short story by Doris Lessing. The essays were examined for line of reasoning, level of abstractions, and hierarchical organization. One of the interesting areas of the study is how it shows that learning the conventions of writing from sources is an extended process taking a lot of time and effort. For the lines of reasoning analysis, all essays considered the authors' intentions and the validity of the criticisms, and they attempted to interpret the motives of the character in the story. However, the less successful of the three readers remained tied to the text, addressing questions in the essays of the type 'What is x?'. Further, the analysis of level of abstraction indicated that while authors might begin with a solid thesis statement, they would often fall back on a summary of the target text. Although the analyses of the target essays points out the slow and deliberate nature of writing development, their writing did become progressively more elaborate as they analyzed the readings, reacted to the readings, and then created text about those reactions. In this instance, the reading-writing connection was an integral part of the literacy acts in which the authors engaged. The study points out how it is impossible to separate reading from writing in this type of activity.

Just as there is a language threshold or thresholds necessary for reading literacy to be developed in the target language or transferred from the first language, there is also apparently a linguistic threshold that is at work with composition such that the reading-writing relationships are not activated until it is reached. Carrell and Conner (1991) studied the relationship between reading and writing of descriptive and persuasive texts by undergraduate and graduate students. They found a correlation between reading recall and holistic scoring of compositions on the two genres to be .45 for descriptive texts and .48 for persuasive texts. However, they found that for writing scores alone, language proficiency was significant while genre type was not. For the reading scores, they found a significant effect for genre, ability, and an interaction between genre and ability. This means that while the descriptive texts were easier than the persuasive texts, the higher-ability readers did not score significantly higher on the descriptive text than the lower-ability students, only higher on the persuasive texts. Thus, these subjects had not reached a threshold of ability to the level at which difference in genre difficulty alone manifested itself in writing. However, the results can be interpreted in terms of whether the glass is half full or half empty. True, the lower-ability readers did not perform as well as the higher-level readers on the persuasive text reading. Yet they did perform as well as the higher-level readers on the descriptive text. This reinforces the notion of there being moveable thresholds for second language reading.

Connecting reading and writing can assist in deeper reading processing (Craik and Lockhart 1972), and hence better comprehension. Oded and Walters (2002) conducted a study with low-ability EFL readers in Israel. The subjects were given two passages from *Scientific American* magazine and either wrote a summary of the article or listed the examples used by the writer of the article for support. After completing the summary of the list, the subjects took a reading comprehension test. The scores across both passages were higher for the summary group than for the listing group. In this case, the deeper processing called for in producing a summary led the readers to deeper comprehension.

An area of the second language reading-writing relationship that has received some interest is the potential interaction between the amount of pleasure reading that is done and composition ability. Elley and Mangubhai (1983) in their *book flood* study mentioned briefly that they found that readers who read more also had better composition ability than other second language readers. Janopoulos (1986) followed up on this potential role of pleasure reading with 79 foreign college students in the US. In this study, the subjects who reported the most pleasure reading in English tended to be more proficient writers. Flahive and Bailey (1993) examined a number of first language and second language reading-writing variables in order to examine whether it was the case that better readers tended to be better writers. Their study involved 40 university-level non-native English speakers from 12 different language backgrounds. No relationship was found between the amount of time the subjects reported reading for pleasure and scores on a writing test. There was, however, a correlation of approximately .50 between reported pleasure reading time and a test of reading comprehension, indicating that the self-reported pleasure reading questionnaire held some validity. Further, there was only a modest correlation (.35) between scores on a reading comprehension test and the writing scores. Although the results appear to indicate no clear linear relationship between reading ability and writing ability, there were relationships between the skills for two-thirds of the subjects in the study. This indicates that the relationship may be very idiosyncratic, subject to individual variation, and only one of the many variables that affect writing ability in the second language. However, in neither case is it clear that amount of pleasure reading is a causal factor of second language composition ability rather than both variables being due to some third variable such as second language reading ability.

There is, however, some evidence that second language reading can affect second language writing ability (Flahive and Bailey 1993). Tsang (1996) examined three different instructional programs across four school grade levels in Hong Kong over 24 weeks. Students were randomly assigned to one of three groups. In one group, the students were required to read eight books and complete eight reviews of the books. Students in the second group were given eight essay-writing tasks over the course of the study, but were given minimal feedback on the essays they wrote. The third group acted as the control group, receiving additional mathematics enrichment during the course of the study. On post-test descriptive essays the reading group showed significant gains in ratings of essay content, language use, and overall improvement of writing quality. However, they showed no gains in essay organization, vocabulary, or mechanics. Neither the group that received mathematics nor the essay-writing treatment showed gains in essay content, while the reading group did. Further, the reading group demonstrated significantly greater gain in language use than the other two groups. The study demonstrates that extensive reading can affect writing quality, and also indicates that writing alone in second language without feedback is of limited benefit. It is a bit surprising that the reading group showed no gain on vocabulary, but that may have been due to the fact that a program of 24 weeks is too short for wide vocabulary gains to evidence themselves in the productive task of essay writing.

Although the relationships between reading and writing are less clear-cut in the second language context than in the first language context, there does appear to be a relationship such that incorporating both skills together has promise. One of the problems with interpreting the second language research into this area is that the many studies do not take the effects of a language threshold into account. Whether or not the subjects in a study have reached the ability threshold relevant to the language task involved in the study has often not been addressed. However, the language threshold is a continual factor in second language considerations to a much larger extent than it is in first language studies of reading and writing. The studies have tended to indicate that integrating writing with reading improves reading on subsequent reading comprehension measures. However, there is less evidence that reading assists in writing development in the sense of improving grammatical and rhetorical features.

Instructional bases of reading and writing

The views of reading-writing relationships have emerged as forceful bases for curriculum. Nelson and Calfee (1998) discuss the five movements that they believe have fostered connections between reading and writing within schools since the 1970s. These are: the reader response movement, the process writing movement, the whole language movement, the comprehension-as-construction movement, and the discourse community movement. The first three of these will be loosely grouped together here as the 'progressive educational' movements, while the last two will be grouped as the 'social construction of knowledge' movements.

The progressive movements share the themes of learner growth, experience, and self-expression (Nelson and Calfee 1998). The *reader response movement* focused on the reader and the reader's internal and subjective reactions to text. The focus was on student growth, experience, and self-expression. Judith Langer (1992) discussed stances that readers can take in response to literature and encouraged the writing of logs and journals. The *process writing movement* focused on the recursive nature rather than the linear nature of writing. This recursiveness employs both reading and writing as the composition is refined. Input and responses from peers and peer groups during the writing process almost necessarily involve the writer in close reading of composition drafts. Students move back and forth between reader and writer perspectives (Flower and Hayes 1981). Associated with process writing is the writing across the curriculum movement, in which writing is embedded in the coursework of content courses and the reading associated with them. The *whole language movement* emphasizes holistic aspects of the language and language learning. The basic view is that all language skill modalities develop in conjunction with one another. Learning is most effective when moving from whole to part. A focus is generally on authentic and naturally occurring text which provides models for learners. Reading and writing are frequently studied together.

The social construction of knowledge groups emphasize how both reading and writing are situated in the social context of the reader or writer. The *comprehension-as-construction* movement comes from the recognition that the reader brings large amounts of information to the text, and does not simply extract meaning. Rather, the reader constructs a meaning. This focus on constructing meaning has formed connections between reading and writing since writing is so clearly a constructive process. Conceptual links between reading and writing have been made from this perspective, such as the parallels noted by Pearson and Tierney (1984). Summarization in which a text is reduced, critiques in which a work is closely commented on, and synthesis in which multiple texts are used, value the socially acquired knowledge readers and writers have gained. The *discourse community* movement places emphasis on the social construction of meanings, genres, and conventions. As discussed previously, members adopt the conventions that their community has socially developed historically. The community idea has pushed the unity of reading, writing and oral use of language with respect to disciplinary discourse. Frank Smith has talked about the 'literacy club'.

Swales has talked about his stamp-collecting community. University students learn a genre as they research and produce research papers. Writing across multiple texts requires organization and strategic thinking in order to form an appropriate text type.

Shanahan (1990) argues for combining reading and writing in instructional settings by arguing that the two skills are tools for learning and thinking. By combining the skills, readers are encouraged to use them in concert in order to accomplish goals and solve their own problems. For him, the combination of reading and writing in the classroom goes beyond the notion that the two skills simply reinforce learning that has taken place through reading. Rather, the foundation of reading and writing is that they take advantage of similar cognitive strategies, and hence can be combined to improve the learning of both. For example, both reading and writing utilize discourse structure, and a focus on these structures can improve both composition and comprehension. The reading-writing relationship goes beyond simply capitalizing on gains in efficiency in the classroom by the combination. It creates a more complete view of literacy in capturing the learning potential of carrying out literacy acts.

A collaboration of these different views is part of the basis for the writing-across-the-curriculum (WAC) movement that began in the late 1970s and 1980s and is prevalent among many universities as well as some primary and secondary schools. Such programs 'promote general literacy, critical thinking, improved writing, and active learning' among students (Fulwiler and Young 1990: 1). These programs have many forms, but most take philosophical and pedagogical positions that language is central to writing, that writing is central to disciplined thinking, and that writing is central to teaching and learning. Writing is not seen as isolated from reading course materials or listening to lectures. Writing is seen as an interrelated language process with reading. Both processes are seen as essential to focuses on the critical thinking necessary for effective learning.

An approach from second language instruction that lends itself to an instructional focus on reading and writing is content-based instruction (Snow and Brinton 1997). The primary purpose of instruction within a content-based approach is to teach some content or information using the language that the students are also learning. The students are simultaneously language students and students of whatever content is being taught. The subject matter is primary, and language learning occurs incidentally to the content learning to the extent that language learning per se is not the primary focus of the learner. The content teaching is not organized around the language teaching, but vice versa. There are strong forms of this approach which focus solely on content, and weak forms of the approach which use the texts as vehicles for language teaching. Most implementations are somewhere in between. An example of content-based language teaching is a science class taught in the language the students need or want to learn, possibly with linguistic adjustment to make the science more comprehensible.

The adjunct model is one example of how reading and writing can be combined (Brinton, Snow, and Wesche 1989; Shih 1986; Carson 2000). One early example of the adjunct model initially took place at UCLA in the 1980s. Undergraduate students deemed to be 'at risk' as a result of being in minority groups, or being ESL students, or through other socioeconomic factors attended a summer term prior to their freshman year as a bridge between high school and college. Each of them took a university breadth requirement such as political science, history, psychology, or sociology, along with their freshman composition course, or the equivalent esl composition course for non-native speakers of English. The composition courses utilized the reading materials from the content course and integrated them into the composition course. Content faculty were consulted regarding their grading criteria for written work. Research assignments and content course writing assignments were incorporated into English language instruction. Snow and Brinton (1988a, b) found that over 80 per cent of all students in the program reported that they were better writers as a result of the program. Additionally, they were found to perform as well as students who had not taken the program but who had significantly higher initial ESL placement scores.

Summary and conclusions

Across the perspectives on reading and writing relationships there is a common thread that views concentrating on the similarities between reading and writing as more productive than focusing on the differences. It promotes a broader perspective on reading. By combining reading and writing into literacy instruction it is possible to avoid the inefficiencies and arbitrary distinctions that persist when instruction in the two is separated. It provides for more focused teaching and learning with cross-learning opportunities. Focusing on the unity of purpose in the two skills situates both and helps to develop critical thinking. Engagement with multiple texts can capitalize on content-based reading and writing, and provide for the deeper knowledge processing promoted by Craik and Lockhart (1972).

In second language contexts, the combination of reading and writing can provide alternatives to traditional skill-based approaches. By contextualizing the reading/writing task, the learner is able to refine his or her views of task expectations. Writing can be used as a rich product for examining comprehension and using knowledge. It is true that developing composition skills that are commensurate with reading ability is a long, slow, and deliberate process. However, with extensive examples of texts across relevant genres, the learner is at least exposed to working with rich input with which to experiment.

Discussion and study questions

1 The chapter has made a strong case for the effectiveness of reading–writing interactions in learning. To what degree do you find the discussion convincing? Think of teaching contexts you have been engaged with. How could you include both reading and writing?

2 One potential problem with read-to-write courses is that the learner may not get a broad coverage of either reading or writing activities and texts. How do you think this can be improved?

3 If it is true that certain literacy acts inherently involve both reading and writing to the same degree, how would you evaluate them? For example, how would you evaluate a summary of an academic article that a student produced? A synthesis of two articles and a lecture? How would you report the results?

4 What types of contexts lend themselves to content-based instruction and what types do not?

5 What effects do the studies reported generally indicate that writing has on reading? That reading has on writing?

11 WRAP-UP OF SECOND LANGUAGE READING: TEACHING ISSUES

Issues covered

Complexity of the issue

Chapter 1 presented an overview of issues that recur throughout discussions of second language reading and its instruction. It presented an argument for considering reading instruction that engages a large number of reading formats, tasks, and goals. Additionally, it strove to present an overview of the areas within the reading literature that have been the key features of discussions about reading and literacy. Reading is a complex activity that involves combinations of factors such as: grapheme recognition, phonological representation (perhaps), syntactic structure, background knowledge, processing strategies, text structure understanding, vocabulary (mixed with background knowledge?), and the context of the reading act. The factors vary in their relative importance depending upon the particular reading context. There are contexts in which basic grammatical parsing is of primary concern, while in others the reader's knowledge of the world factors heavily. The chapter noted the need to distinguish between what Gough (1995) terms literacy[1] and literacy[2]. The first refers to the ability to read and write, while the second refers to the contextual application of that ability, in the sense of a person being educated and being a part of the literacy community that produced the text. We will also see that the two concepts are not always mutually exclusive or clearly dichotomous. In general, the complexity of the relationships among variables in reading performance makes any strong statements of relative importance outside of context appear simplistic. Second language reading instruction needs to take this complexity into account.

First and second language theories of reading

Chapters 2 and 3 examined theoretical and conceptual issues in first and second language reading. In first language reading discussions, the various models are endeavors to capture important aspects of the reading process. Some models focus primarily on the cognitive-processing needed to turn images on a page into some basic meaning. Others take a broader view of the importance of reading as an applied ability in culture and society. Some of the models assert reading to be a linear process while others view it as involving parallel processing. Some of the models, such as those of Just and Carpenter (1980, 1987) and Rayner and Pollatsek (1989) place most emphasis on the observable psychological aspects of reading, such as eye fixation, while others, such as Rumelhart (1975, 1977) or Anderson and Pearson (1984) focus primarily on factors that affect comprehension or miscomprehension.

The discussions of second language reading models emphasized that while the first language reading models are useful, there are fundamental differences between a first language reader and a second language reader. These differences come into play when we attempt to account for such variables as age, first language literacy, reading purpose, and second language proficiency, among many other factors that are important in understanding the various facets of second language reading and learning. Throughout the studies of the relationship between first language reading ability, second language proficiency, and second language reading performance, there has been a general trend that indicates that there are interrelationships between all three. Further, there has tended to be a finding that second language proficiency plays a greater role than does first language reading ability. Yet there also are results that indicate that this relationship may depend upon the reader's level of second language proficiency and upon what particular reading task is involved. The roles played by reading task and text type have yet to be thoroughly researched in second language studies. More research is needed in the area, research which attempts to include subjects who represent variability in both first language reading ability and second language proficiency, and which uses a range of authentic materials and tasks that can inform us regarding the nature and uniformity of the threshold across different types of reading. Some of this research could be undertaken in action research studies carried out by second language reading teachers.

The research findings that overall second language ability is a more important variable for reading success at lower levels of second language proficiency than at higher levels is consistent with what Perfetti (1985, 1988) has termed the Verbal Efficiency Model. The lower-level language learner has automated very few of the local textual-processing skills. As a result, most of the reader's effort and attention are devoted to the processes of lexical access and elementary propositional encoding. Basically, those activities drain the reader's working memory of all of its capacity. Readers at this level have not yet sufficiently automated such features as syntactic function words, morphology and vocabulary. Mastery of these features releases attention to the work of encoding propositions within and across sentences, inferencing requiring memory searches, and the interpretive and critical comprehension of text. As noted, the extent to which attention is allocated systematically to local text processes will, in part, be due to similarities between the first language and the second language in terms of orthographic systems, language family memberships, cognate size, and other features that distinguish the languages.

An implication of the cognitive-processing results for reading instruction is that the processing load of second language reading at early levels of proficiency must be addressed in some way. The research is fairly consistent in showing that learners with very little exposure to the second language have difficulty in reading that language. Thus second language reading instruction must find ways to avoid continually frustrating the reader. This can be accomplished through the use of graded readers to fit readers' ability levels (Day and Bamford 1998), or through identifying tasks whose difficulty matches the reader's ability. Both of these approaches have positive and negative aspects. Graded readers may become a crutch that gives the reading learner a false sense of his or her reading level, or may not truly engage the reader in the types of reading processes that need to be mastered. On the other hand, identifying actual real-world texts and tasks that can be tailored to the readers' levels may become very time-consuming for the teacher and materials developer, or may provide the learner with material that is boring or irrelevant.

Reading skills

Chapter 4 examined the role of traditionally defined reading skills. In general, both the first language and second language literature related to reading skills do not support the existence of strictly hierarchically ordered reading skills. Rather, skills appear to be activated throughout the reading process, and represent a range of task difficulties. Additionally, skills appear to group in broad categories, such as word-attack skills, comprehension skills, fluency skills, and critical reading skills. They do not appear to represent a detailed list of numerous discrete reading skills. Factors such as text, purpose, and content appear to affect the application of the skills that have been identified. Although detailed lists of skills may be of some utility in curriculum and materials development, the actual development of activities that clearly isolate simple unitary skills is problematic. Reading acts and literacy events are sufficiently complex that they involve multiple skills and skills that are not unitary in their structure.

Identifying discrete skills in practice is an area that needs to be addressed in reading instruction. Many of the reading materials that teachers are provided with represent a synthetic type of syllabus in which the learner is presented with discrete bits of the language with the assumption that that information will be taken in, synthesized, and acquired. However, the research that has been addressed in this text emphasizes the need to focus on more complex tasks that allow opportunities for the learner to notice areas of need. Gordon's (1982) distinctions may offer insight here. That research indicated that 'there are three distinct sets of competencies that a student must develop in order to become an effective reader: reading skills development, reading comprehension, and reading research and study skills' (41). Here, 'reading skills development' is viewed as separate from 'reading comprehension development'. The first includes such reading prerequisites as names of letters, consonants, plurals, root words, and vowels, while the second includes issues of reading engagement such as categorizing, reading for facts, making inferences, evaluating source material, and drawing factual conclusions. In some ways, this is consistent with the findings that second language proficiency affects second language reading much more at low levels of proficiency than at higher levels of proficiency. It indicates that 'reading skills development' must be addressed early, but that at higher-ability levels the learners can be much more engaged in 'reading comprehension development'.

Again, we are left with determining how the reading threshold interacts with the task. Once learners have moved past the very early recognition skills, they can be presented with more complex literacy tasks in order to push them into engaging more of the reading skills that affect comprehension. The literature is clear that it is not likely to be productive to isolate the skills to be taught and focus on them until they are learned. The level to which they will be learned is directly involved with the purpose learners have in engaging the skill.

Strategies and metacognitive skills

The discussion in the Chapter 5 addressed the difficulties with distinguishing between reading skills and strategies solely by seeing skills as subconscious and strategies as conscious activities. The same activity can represent skill application in some contexts and strategic moves at other times. In discussing reading strategies, we need to recognize that they represent not only repair actions, but also a repertoire that is of importance in strategy marshaling, monitoring, and regulation throughout the reading process. This is particularly pertinent in that strategies are applied in support of the reader's primary purpose for reading, the literacy act in which he or she is engaged. Further, there do not appear to be sets of strategies that are uniquely used by proficient readers and sets of strategies that are uniquely used by poor readers. The same skills are often employed by both good and poor readers. The primary difference is that they are employed with differing levels of success. Of further interest is that the types of strategies that a reader applies are often somewhat idiosyncratic in that the particular strategies that are used differ across individuals. However, more able readers tend to use more strategies than less successful readers. Apparently, metacognitive strategies play an increasing role in distinguishing good readers from poor readers as the reader progresses (Shoonen, Hulstijn, and Bossers 1998).

Of particular importance is that the research appears to support the contention that direct training in strategies and metacognitive skills is both possible and productive. It is also important to examine the successful strategy-training programs actually involved. Successful training programs tended to provide models and demonstrations of strategy use. It was not effective to present the strategies as lists and then ask the learners to practice them on texts that are of little interest or for purposes that are not embedded in their own lives. Additionally, successful instruction needs to be sustained in nature. It is important that the strategies be modeled in a sustained manner and applied across a number of different text and task types.

Content schema and background knowledge in second language comprehension

Chapter 6 investigated how reading comprehension is related to background knowledge and content schemata. On a very basic level, it is clear that knowledge of any text topic is essential for successful comprehension regardless of the language of the text being processed. Without basic knowledge it would be impossible to even approximate a writer's intended message. However, the exact nature of the interaction is not clear. Throughout this text it has been emphasized that there are effects due to the linguistic threshold, and that there are questions about how that linguistic threshold affects a reader's ability to access background knowledge in order to facilitate comprehension.

There are certainly questions about the extent to which content schemata are utilized by less proficient readers in comparison with how they are used by more proficient readers. Some researchers have argued that it is the less proficient reader who relies most strongly on background knowledge in an attempt to compensate for reading difficulties. However, others argue that the lower ability prevents any application of the background knowledge. Still others argue that the relative role played by content schemata may depend upon idiosyncratic or cultural factors, factors which value or devalue reservedness or impetuousness in relying on inferences. These personal or cultural factors have apparently led to many of the conflicting research findings on second language readers' use of schemata. Carrell (1983) and Carrell and Wallace (1983) indicate that second language readers may not effectively utilize knowledge-based processes or the contextual information they are supplied with to facilitate comprehension. Second language readers who do not utilize such processes or information appear to engage almost exclusively in text-based processing rather than applying background knowledge in the comprehension process. Other research (Block 1986) has found that readers often rely too heavily on top-down background knowledge processes and content schemata. Some readers are reluctant risk takers, sticking closely to the printed word, while others are much more impetuous in their knowledge-based processing.

Still, considerations of background knowledge cannot be ignored when attempting to understand second language reading comprehension in instruction. It is not simply an issue of the quantity of prior knowledge, but is also an issue of the quality of the background knowledge. How the content schema is organized affects the depth and flexibility of its use. Such factors support sustained involvement with particular content topics, such as the prolonged engagement with topics content-based education. An additional implication is that encountering the concepts through a number of different task types may assist in developing more depth of knowledge. Thus, with some learners reading instruction that includes schema activation prior to reading may be very useful, while at other times schema building may be necessary through content input, perhaps through information presented in different modalities. Some information may be presented through a lecture or film clip while other information is presented through text.

Formal schemata and second language reading

Chapter 7 addressed the role that formal schema knowledge plays in first language and second language reading performance. Language learners have default concepts of how script functions, how syntax operates, what creates a cohesive text, and how text is structured. These views strongly influence how readers attempt to process text. The second language reader needs to master these aspects of text processing at some threshold level. As such, instruction will need to address these issues. Some of these types of knowledge may be less problematic than others for the language learner. For example, the alphabetic script employed in English will be less of a problem for a Spanish first language learner than for a Chinese first language learner.

There is support for the view that language learners can be taught formal schematic concepts of text structure, and can use that knowledge in the recall and comprehension of text. Carrell (1985) reported results indicating that explicit text-structure training enabled learners to recognize and use expository structures such as *comparison, problem/solution, causation*, and *collection of descriptions*. The results also indicated that the effects of instruction remained effective weeks after the instruction. This work indicated that direct instruction in text structure can facilitate the reading recall of second language readers, just as it was shown to facilitate comprehension by first language readers of English. Davis, Lange, and Samuels (1988) also showed an effect for training in text structure, even relatively weak instruction. Lee and Riley (1990) showed that providing text structure prior to reading can assist foreign language learners with certain text types but not with others. Thus, the instruction that is developed will need to take into account the different extents to which the text structure is salient. Teachers and materials developers need to view the effects of formal schema instruction within the overall function of the reader's purpose. That is, some tasks, such as writing a summary, may require the reader to internalize the particular text structure, while other tasks, such as scanning for a particular date, may not need as rich a text representation.

Genre and contrastive rhetoric

Chapter 8 examined the effects of text genre as well as what role can be played by contrastive rhetoric. Recognition of genre is very important in understanding how text is organized and what are the purposes behind that organization. This goes beyond structural text organization. Genres represent the functions of a text as they are intended to affect others. Moreover, genres are closely linked to the discourse communities of which they are a part. Their success is linked to how the discourse community accepts and interprets them. These discourse communities can be large or small, very conventional or flexible and open. However, they always exert a pull on the construction of their texts. As noted before, genres are both highly conventionalized and variable. The conventionalized nature of a genre, ironically, can be utilized to change the purpose of the text. For example, J.P. Donleavy (1975) utilized a common social experience with books of etiquette when he wrote *The Unexpurgated Code: A Complete Manual for Survival and Manners*. He provides example rules for behavior in a chapter on 'Social Climbing' when the reader is 'Associating with the Bootless and Unhorsed' as follows:

> Be civil and tolerant when dismounting among this swarming caste who, already totally submerged by about two new generations of go-getters, nevertheless still bravely play their isolated solitary roles in failure. When confronting them suddenly on the boulevard, do not immediately suggest a handout or job opportunity. Some of these fellows may still have their pride left. Let their "they haven't beaten me yet" spirit come to the fore. Other types of course will push their open palms out. And tell you to cough up with a giant elbow bending gratuity before they shout two miles all over the street what a big phony upstart you've now become. Guys like this might have made good top business executives.

> But under no circumstances invite either gent back to the house.

> *(Donleavy 1975: 38)*

Donleavy depends upon the conventionalized form of social advice being presented in the popular press designed to help avoid social blunders. It is precisely because of this socially familiar genre that his parody works. Throughout his book, he is parodying an existing genre, that of admonitions by Miss Manners. The structure itself is part and parcel of the genre he has created.

Being social inventions, genres vary in their representations across cultures. Differing cultural emphases, assumptions, and linguistic forms can create different textual structures designed to represent the same genre. Readers from different languages and cultures need to recognize and be open to the potential differences in order to become accomplished readers. Instruction designed to achieve this cognizance should engage the learner in examining the text and its purposes, focusing more broadly than on the text structure. Bringing in an original genre and then a parody of that structure can be an effective type of reading instruction at higher levels of language ability.

Vocabulary in second language reading

Chapter 9 addressed the role of vocabulary in second language reading and instruction. It was noted that there are strong relationships between successful reading and the richness of a reader's vocabulary knowledge. The research has shown that a great deal of vocabulary is learned through the context of the reading process. Thus, even though it is a slow and time-consuming process, a lot of vocabulary is learned in this way. However, even proficient readers will have failures of strategies for making contextual inferences. This may be due to a lack of context sufficient to provide meaning. Vocabulary learning for many words involves learning different levels and nuances of the word's meaning. Successful reading involves both this depth of knowledge and a breadth of knowledge such that the reader confronts few unfamiliar words while reading.

There has been a great deal of discussion regarding the extent to which learners acquire vocabulary incidentally. In general, it appears that vocabulary can be acquired both incidentally and intentionally as readers process text. However, it is apparent that readers learn little vocabulary incidentally at any one time while reading. Most words take multiple exposures to learn. For most second language readers, other tools such as dictionaries, glosses, and direct instruction are useful.

Learners employ a number of vocabulary learning strategies in the process of becoming accomplished readers. The research reviewed indicates that there are large individual differences in these strategies across learners. More advanced readers are more flexible in their strategy use and are generally more determined to succeed at the task than lower-ability readers. Further, the advanced readers tend to use more strategies than do the lower-ability readers.

Reading and writing relationships

Finally, Chapter 10 discussed the relationships between reading and writing. Across the perspectives on these relationships there is a common thread that approaches which concentrate on the similarities between reading and writing are more productive than those which focus on the differences. They promote a broader perspective on reading. By combining reading and writing into literacy instruction it is possible to avoid the inefficiencies and arbitrary distinctions that persist when instruction in the two is separated. This provides for more focused teaching and learning with cross-learning opportunities. Focusing on the unity of purpose in the two skills situates both and helps to develop critical thinking. Engagement with multiple texts can capitalize on content-based reading and writing, and provide for the deeper knowledge processing promoted by Craik and Lockhart (1972).

In second language contexts, the combination of reading and writing can provide alternatives to traditional skill-based approaches. By contextualizing the reading/writing task, the learner is able to refine his or her views of task expectations. Writing can be used as a rich product for examining comprehension and using knowledge. It is true that developing composition skills that are commensurate with reading ability is a long, slow, and deliberate process. However, with extensive examples of texts across relevant genres, the learner is at least exposed to working with rich input with which to experiment.

Summary

In the end, we are left knowing that there is no magic bullet, no single explanation for what teachers can do to ensure that their students learn to read a second or foreign language. Nor is there a single explanation for why students do not learn to read. Learners vary widely as do the contexts in which they study and learn.

However, we do have a great deal to give hope and support for the teaching enterprise. First, reading is one activity that learners can practice on their own. Second, it is clear that motivation to learn is extremely important. Third, the learner's reading threshold varies with the task and type of reading purpose. As noted in the first chapter, we need to take all of the following into account: grapheme recognition, phonological representation, syntactic structure, background knowledge, processing strategies, text-structure understanding, vocabulary, and context of the reading act. These are all factors that teachers can look for when assisting their students in the pursuit of written second language processing.

GLOSSARY

Only those items that have a special or technical meaning in first or second language reading have been included here. Terms that have an accessible dictionary definition are not included. The definitions that are provided reflect their usage within the present text. Some of the terms may be used in other ways by other authors.

ANOVA: This is an acronym for *analysis of variance*. ANOVA is a statistical test to find significant differences between the means of different groups. (*See* SIGNIFICANCE LEVEL)

Appositive: An appositive is a noun phrase, usually a reduced relative clause that generally follows another noun phrase and renames or describes it. An example is, 'Mary Ames' new desk, the Unisteel 9000 wood on metal issue, is already covered with papers.' The appositive can often replace the word next to it.

Autonomous reader: The notion of an autonomous reader is that the reader is entirely self-directed in his or her reading. It may also be used to indicate that reading is a single independent ability that exists outside a social or cultural context.

Automaticity: This is a general term that refers to any skilled and complex behavior that can be performed rather easily with little attention, effort, or conscious awareness. Such skills become automatic after extensive practice.

Balanced bilingual: The term *balanced bilingual* refers to someone who is equally fluent in two languages in the skills of reading, writing, listening, and speaking.

Channel: The way in which information is transmitted from one person to another, usually speech or writing.

Cloze: A method of assessment in which words (for example every seventh, eighth, or ninth word, or every verb, etc.) are systematically eliminated from a reading passage. The examinee then uses the context of the passage to determine the appropriate word for the blank.

Comprehension strategies: Comprehension strategies are the plans or steps that readers use to make sense of text. Some strategies are productive, such as skimming the text before careful reading, while others may be less successful, such as concentrating on each and every word in a text.

Decoding skills: The ability to analyze graphic symbols to determine the intended meaning of individual words. It involves using knowledge of the conventions of spelling-sound relationships and knowledge about pronunciation of irregular words to produce a recognition of written words.

Diacritics: A diacritic is a mark placed above, through, or below a letter or character, in order to indicate a sound different from that indicated by the letter without the diacritic. Some languages have fairly elaborate diacritic systems (for example Arabic) while others do not (for example English).

Expository: Expository text is text written to explain and convey information about a specific topic. It explains an event, concept, or idea using facts and examples. (*See* NARRATIVE)

Function word: A word that does not have lexical meaning, but which primarily serves to express a grammatical relation (for example AND, OF, OR, THE).

Garden path effect: Garden path can refer to types of sentences that are difficult to parse or to the creation of inaccurate expectations in instruction. The first might be seen with the sentence, 'The horse raced past the barn fell'. The sentence might appear ungrammatical unless the reader interprets 'raced' to be adjectival in the sense of identifying a horse that had been raced past the barn and noting that the horse fell. In the second type, students might be engaged in predicting what a passage might be about based on the title, but they predict wrongly and hence have difficulty reading the passage.

Genre: A type or category of text marked by conventions of style, format, and/or content. Genres include narrative, exposition, poetry, science fiction, etc.

Gricean maxims: These are conversational maxims proposed by the philosopher Paul Grice. They are seen to reflect pragmatic assumptions that regulate expectations. The four maxims are: 1) Maxim of Quality (Truth): Do not say what you believe to be false. Do not say that for which you lack adequate evidence. 2) Maxim of Quantity (Information): Make your contribution as informative as is required for the current purposes of the exchange. Do not make your contribution more informative than is required. 3) Maxim of Relation (Relevance): Be relevant. And 4) Maxim of Manner (Clarity): Avoid obscurity of expression. Avoid ambiguity. Be brief (avoid unnecessary prolixity). Be orderly.

Intersentential processing: Reading often requires that the reader process text across sentences within paragraphs. This type of processing is noted as intersentential processing, involving the use of either adjacent or distant sentences in comprehending the text message.

Lexical: The words or the vocabulary of a language in contrast to syntactic or phonological aspects.

Lexicon: the knowledge that a reader has about individual words. It addresses both breadth and depth of word knowledge.

Logographic system: A writing system, such as that used in Chinese, wherein each spoken word in the language is represented by a unique symbol. It contrasts with an alphabetic system.

Metacognition: Metacognition is the activity of 'thinking about thinking.' Readers reflect on how they comprehend and recognize what is successful and what is not successful.

Modality: In the present use this indicates whether the language study is in the receptive mode or productive mode. This may reflect whether one form of assessment (for example multiple-choice) is acceptable or whether another form is needed (for example written essay).

Morphology: The structure and the study of word structure. A morphological analysis of the word *unbendable* would recognize the prefix 'un', the stem or root 'bend' and the suffix 'able'. It would recognize the three different morphemes.

Narrative text: Narrative text conveys a story or relates temporal events or dialog. (*See* EXPOSITORY)

Orthography: The complete writing system used by a language or set of languages. Orthographies include the alphabetic or logographic system used as well as the punctuation.

Phoneme–grapheme correspondence: This is the relationship between a letter's graphical form and the sound that corresponds to it. In English this would be noting the relationship between the 'S' grapheme, and the different sounds it represents in 'simple', 'division', 'ship', or 'dogs'. Many educators who support phonics see the mastery of phoneme–grapheme correspondences as essential to reading success.

Phonological control: This is the control of phoneme–grapheme relationships in the target language.

Prototypicality: This refers to the extent to which different text types have a prototypical form or structure. For example, many research articles have the format: Introduction to the problem, Methods (subjects, materials, procedures, design), Results, Conclusions. This is the prototypic structure, though some articles might vary somewhat.

Radicals: Radicals are stroke patterns whose locations within characters, such as Chinese written characters, signal text characteristics. These patterns can cue the phonology of a character (phonetic radicals) or they may cue semantic relationships (semantic radicals).

Recursive reading strategies: This refers to the reading processes in which the reader reads the text in a linear fashion for a period of time, regresses to a prior location in the text to re-read some text, and then moves ahead again. Reading is not a clear and constant linear activity.

Schema: The reader's background knowledge on which the interpretation of a text depends. Plural = schemata or schemas.

Statistical significance level: The statistical significance of a result is a measure of the degree to which it is correct. The value, often called the *p-level*, represents an index of the reliability of a result. The *p-level* represents the probability of error resulting from accepting the observed result as being representative of the population. For example, a *p-level* of .05 means that there is a five per cent probability that the results are due to chance alone and are accidental. There is a *p-level* associated with each contrast that is made. Hence, if many contrasts are made then the overall level must be adjusted.

Story or text structure: The conventions that govern different kinds of texts such as characters, plot, settings, or, in an informational text, cause-and-effect or comparison and contrast.

Summarizing: Summarizing is a process in which a reader includes only the important ideas in a text, eliminating minor details.

Synthesis: Synthesizing involves taking important information from different texts and creating a new text reflecting the information in each of the previous texts.

BIBLIOGRAPHY

1961. *Webster's Third New International Dictionary*. Springfield, MA: Merriam-Webster, Inc.

1980. *Webster's Collegiate Dictionary*. Springfield, MA: Merriam-Webster, Inc.

1989. *Oxford English Dictionary, 2nd edition*. Oxford: Oxford University Press.

Aaron, I. V., A. Artley, K. Goodman, W. Jenkins, J. Manning, M. Monroe, W. A. Pyle, H. Robinson, A. Schiller, M. Smith, L. Sullivan, S. Weintraub, and J. Wepman. 1976. *Reading Unlimited: Scott Foresman Systems, revised.* Glenview, IL: Scott Foresman and Co.

Abu-Rabia, S. 1996. 'The influence of culture and attitudes on reading comprehension in SL: the case of Jews learning English and Arabs learning Hebrew.' *Reading Psychology: an International Quarterly* 17: 253–71.

Ackerman, J. M. 1991. 'Reading, writing, and knowing: the role of disciplinary knowledge in comprehension and composing.' *Research in the Teaching of English* 25/2: 133–77.

Adler, M. J. 1940. *How to Read a Book: The Art of Getting a Liberal Education.* New York: Simon and Schuster.

Afflerbach, P. 1990. 'The influence of prior knowledge on expert readers' main idea construction strategies.' *Reading Research Quarterly* 25/1: 31–46.

Akamatsu, N. 1999. 'The effects of first language orthographic features on word recognition processing in English as a second language.' *Reading and Writing: An Interdisciplinary Journal* 11: 381–403.

Akamatsu, N. 2003. 'The effects of first language orthographic features in second language reading in text.' *Language Learning* 53/2: 207–31.

Alderson, J. C. 1984. 'Reading in a foreign language: a reading problem or a language problem?' in J.C. Alderson and A.H. Urquhart (eds.): *Reading in a Foreign Language*. London: Longman. pp. 1–27.

Alderson, J. C. 1990. 'Testing reading comprehension skills (part one).' *Reading in a Foreign Language* 6: 425–38.

Alderson, J. C. 1993. 'The relationship between grammar and reading in an English for academic purposes test battery' in D. Douglas and C. Chapelle (eds.): *A New Decade of Language Testing Research*. Alexandria, VA: Teachers of English to Speakers of Other Languages, Inc. pp. 203–19.

Alderson, J. C., S. Bastien, and **A. M. Madrazo.** 1977. 'A comparison of reading comprehension in English and Spanish'. Research and Development Unit Report No. 9, UNAM. Mexico City.

Alderson, J. C. and **Y. Lukmani.** 1989. 'Cognition and reading: cognitive levels as embodied in test questions.' *Reading and Writing: An Interdisciplinary Journal* 5: 253–70.

Al-Jarf, R. S. 2001. 'Processing of cohesive ties by EFFL Arab college students.' *Foreign Language Annals* 34/2: 141–51.

Alverman, D. E., L. C. Smith, and **J. E. Readence.** 1985. 'Prior knowledge activation and the comprehension of compatible and incompatible text.' *Reading Research Quarterly* 20: 420–36.

Amer, A. A. 1992. 'The effect of story grammar instruction on EFL students' comprehension of a narrative text.' *Reading in a Foreign Language* 8: 711–20.

Anderson, J. R. 1975. *Cognitive Psychology: The Study of Knowing, Learning, and Thinking*. New York: Academic Press.

Anderson, J. R. 1990. *The Adaptive Character of Thought*. Hillsdale, N.J.: Lawrence Erlbaum Associates.

Anderson, N. 1991. 'Individual differences in strategy use in second language reading and testing.' *Modern Language Journal* 75: 460–72.

Anderson, R. C. and **P. Freebody.** 1981. 'Vocabulary knowledge' in J. T. Guthrie (ed.): *Comprehension and Teaching*. Newark, DE: International Reading Association. pp. 77–118.

Anderson, R. C. and **P. D. Pearson.** 1984. 'A schema-theoretic view of basic processes in reading' in P. D. Pearson, M. Kamil, R. Barr, and P. Mosenthal (eds.). pp. 255–91.

Anderson, R. C., R. E. Reynolds, D. L. Schallert, and **E. T. Goetz.** 1977. 'Frameworks for comprehending discourse.' *American Educational Research Journal* 14: 367–82.

Anthony, L. 1999. 'Writing research article introductions in software engineering: how accurate is a standard model?' *IEEE Transactions on Professional Communication* 42/1: 38–46.

Armbruster, B. B., C. Echols, and **A. L. Brown.** (1983). 'The role of metacognition in reading to learn: A developmental perspective.' *Volta Review*, 84, 45–56.

Aronson-Berman, R. 1981. 'How hard is it to read? Syntactic complexity as a cause of reading difficulty.' *Cahiers Linguistiques d'Ottawa* 8: 265–282.

Auden, W. S. 1967. 'Afterward' in G. Macdonald (ed.): *The Golden Key*. New York: Farrar, Straus, and Giroux. pp. 81–6.

Auerbach, E. R. and **D. Paxton.** 1997. '"It's not the English thing:" bringing reading research into the ESL classroom.' *TESOL Quarterly* 31: 237–61.

August, D., J. H. Flavell, and **R. Clift.** 1984. 'Comparison of comprehension monitoring of skilled and less skilled readers.' *Reading Research Quarterly* 20/1: 39–53.

Baker, L. 1985. 'How do we know when we don't understand?' in D. L. Forrest-Pressley, G. E. MacKinnon, and T. G. Waller (eds.): *Metacognition, Cognition, and Human Performance. Volume 1: Theoretical Perspectives*. New York: Academic Press. pp. 155–206.

Baker, L. 1989. 'Metacognition, comprehension monitoring, and the adult reader.' *Educational Psychology Review* 1: 3–38.

Baker, L. 1994. 'Fostering metacognitive development.' *Advances in Child Development and Behavior* 25: 201–39.

Baker, L. 2002. 'Metacognition in comprehension instruction' in C. C. Block and M. Pressley (eds.): *Comprehension Instruction: Research-based Practices*. New York: Guilford Press. pp. 77–95.

Baker, L. and **A. L. Brown.** 1984. 'Metacognitive skills in reading' in P. D. Pearson, M. Kamil, R. Barr, and P. Mosenthal (eds.). pp. 353–94.

Barnett, M. A. 1986. 'Syntactic and lexical/semantic skill in foreign language reading: importance and interaction.' *The Modern Language Journal* 70: 343–9.

Barnett, M. A. 1988. 'Reading through context: how real and perceived strategy use affects L2 comprehension.' *The Modern Language Journal* 72: 150–62.

Barnett, M. A. 1989. *More than Meets the Eye: Foreign Language Reading Theory and Practice*. Englewood Cliffs, N.J.: Center for Applied Linguistics and Prentice-Hall, Inc.

Barr, R., M. L. Kamil, P. Mosenthal, and **P. D. Pearson** (eds.). 1991. *Handbook of Reading Research (Vol. II)*. Mahwah, N.J.: Lawrence Erlbaum Associates.

Barrett, T. C. (N.D.). *Taxonomy of Cognitive and Affective Dimensions of Reading Comprehension*. Referenced in T. Clymer, (1968).

Barry, S. and **A. A. Lazarte.** 1995. 'Embedded clause effects on recall: does high prior knowledge of content domain overcome syntactic complexity in students of Spanish?' *The Modern Language Journal* 79/4: 491–504.

Barry, S. and **A. A. Lazarte.** 1998. 'Evidence for mental models: how do prior knowledge, syntactic complexity, and reading topic affect inference generation in a recall task for non native readers of Spanish.' *The Modern Language Journal* 82: 176–93.

Bartholomae, D. and **A. R. Petrosky.** 1986. 'Facts, artifacts and counterfacts: a basic reading and writing course for the college curriculum' in D. Bartholomae and A. R. Petrosky (eds.): *Facts, Artifacts and Counterfacts: Theory and Method for a Reading and Writing Course.* Upper Montclair, N.J.: Boynton/Cook Publishers, Inc. pp. 3–43.

Bartlett, F. C. 1932. *Remembering: A Study in Experimental and Social Psychology.* London: Cambridge University Press.

Bauman, J. F. 1984. 'The effectiveness of a direct instruction paradigm for teaching main idea comprehension.' *Reading Research Quarterly* 20: 93–117.

Bauman, J. F. 1986. 'Effect of rewritten content textbook passages on middle grade students' comprehension of main ideas: making the inconsiderate considerate.' *Journal of Reading Behavior* 18: 1–21.

Bazerman, C. 1997. 'The life of genre, the life of the classroom' in W. Bishop and H. Ostrom (eds.): *Genre and Writing: Issues, Arguments, Alternatives.* Portsmouth, N.H.: Boynton/Cook Heineman. pp. 19–26.

Beck, I. L. and **P. A. Carpenter.** 1986. 'Cognitive approaches to understanding reading: implications for instructional practice.' *American Psychologist* 41: 1098–1105.

Beck, I. L., M. G. McKeown, R. C. Omanson, and **M. T. Pople.** 1984. 'Improving the comprehensibility of stories: the effects of revisions that improve coherence.' *Reading Research Quarterly* 19/3: 263–76.

Beck, I. L., M. G. McKeown, G. M. Sinatra, and **J. A. Loxterman.** 1991. 'Revising social studies text from a text-processing perspective: evidence of improved comprehensibility.' *Reading Research Quarterly* 26/3: 251–76.

Belcher, D. and **A. Hirvela** (eds.). 2001. *Linking Literacies: Perspectives on L2 Reading-Writing connections.* Ann Arbor: The University of Michigan Press.

Benedetto, R. A. 1986. 'First and second language ability and the use of top-level organizational structures' in J. A. Niles and R. V. Lalik (eds.): *Solving Problems in Literacy: Learners, Teachers, and Researchers.* Rochester, New York: The National Reading Conference. pp. 199–203.

Benesch, S. 2001. *Critical English for Academic Purposes: Theory, Politics, and Practice.* Mahwah, N.J.: Lawrence Erlbaum Associates.

Bensoussan, M. and **B. Laufer.** 1984. 'Lexical guessing in context in EFL reading comprehension.' *Journal of Research in Reading* 7: 15–32.

Bereiter, C. and **M. Bird.** 1985. 'Use of think aloud in identification and teaching of reading comprehension strategies.' *Cognition and Instruction* 2: 131–56.

Berkenkotter, C. and **T. N. Huckin.** 1995. *Genre Knowledge in Disciplinary Communication: Cognition, Culture, Power.* Hillsdale, N.J.: Lawrence Erlbaum Associates.

Berkmire, D. P. 1985. 'Text processing: the influence of text structure, background knowledge, and purpose.' *Reading Research Quarterly* 20: 314–26.

Berkowitz, S. J. 1986. 'Effects of instruction in text organization on sixth-grade students' memory for expository reading.' *Reading Research Quarterly* 21: 161–78.

Bhatia, V. K. 1993. *Analysing Genre: Language Use in Professional Settings.* Harlow, Essex: Longman Group UK Ltd.

Bhatia, V. K. 1999. 'Integrating products, processes, purposes and participants in professional writing' in C. N. Candlin and K. Hyland (eds.): *Writing: Texts, Processes, and Practices.* London: Longman. pp. 21–39.

Birch, B. M. 2002. *English L2 Reading: Getting to the Bottom.* Mahwah, N.J.: Lawrence Erlbaum Associates.

Blau, E. K. 1982. 'The effect of syntax on readability for ESL students in Puerto Rico.' *TESOL Quarterly* 16: 517–28.

Block, E. 1986. 'The comprehension strategies of second language readers.' *TESOL Quarterly* 20/3: 463–94.

Block, E. 1992. 'See how they read: comprehension monitoring of L1 and L2 readers.' *TESOL Quarterly* 26: 319–43.

Bloom, B. S. 1956. *Taxonomy of Educational Objectives: The Classification of Educational Goals. Handbook 1: Cognitive Domain.* New York: David McKay Company, Inc.

Bloome, D. 1993. 'Necessary indeterminacy and the microethnographic study of reading as a social process.' *Journal of Research in Reading* 16/2: 98–111.

Bossers, B. 1991. 'On thresholds, ceilings and short-circuits: the relation between L1 reading, L2 reading and L2 knowledge.' *AILA Review* 8: 45–60.

Bouton, L. F. 1995. 'A cross-cultural analysis of the structure and content of letters of reference.' *Studies in Second Language Acquisition* 17: 211–44.

Bracewell, R. J., C. H. Frederiksen, and **J. D. Frederiksen.** 1982. 'Cognitive processes in composing and comprehending discourse.' *Educational Psychologist* 17/3: 146–64.

Bransford, J. D. and **M. K. Johnson.** 1972. 'Contextual prerequisites for understanding: some investigations of comprehension and recall.' *Journal of Verbal Learning and Verbal Behavior* 11: 717–26.

Bransford, J. D. and **M. K. Johnson.** 1973. 'Considerations of some problems of comprehension' in W. G. Chase (ed.): *Visual Information Processing.* New York: Academic Press. pp. 383–438.

Brett, P. 1994. 'A genre analysis of the results section of sociology articles.' *English for Specific Purposes* 13/1: 47–59.

Brinton, D. M., M. A. Snow, and **M. Wesche.** 1989. *Content-based Second Language Instruction*. Boston: Heinle and Heinle.

Brown, A. 1982. 'Learning to learn how to read' in J. A. Langer and T. Smith-Burke (eds.): *Reader Meets Author, Bridging the Gap: A Psycholinguistic and Social Linguistic Perspective*. Newark, DE: International Reading Association.

Brown, A. 1987. 'Metacognition, executive control, self-regulated and other more mysterious mechanisms' in F. Weinert and R. Kluwe (eds.): *Metacognition, Motivation, and Understanding*. Hillsdale, N.J.: Lawrence Erlbaum Associates. pp. 65–116.

Brown, A. L., B. B. Armbruster, and **L. Baker.** 1986. 'The role of metacognition in reading and studying' in J. Orasanu (ed.): *Reading Comprehension: From Research to Practice*. Hillsdale, N.J.: Lawrence Erlbaum Associates. pp. 49–75.

Brown, A. L. and **J. D. Day.** 1983. 'Macrorules for summarizing texts: the development of expertise.' *Child Development* 54: 968–79.

Brown, A. L. and **A. S. Palincsar.** 1989. 'Guided cooperative learning and individual knowledge acquisition' in L. B. Resnick (ed.): *Knowing, Learning, and Instruction: Essays in Honor of Robert Glaser*. Hillsdale, N.J.: Lawrence Erlbaum Associates. pp. 393–451.

Brown, A. L. and **S. S. Smiley.** 1978. 'The development of strategies for studying texts.' *Child Development* 49: 1076–88.

Brown, R., M. Pressley, P. V. Meter, and **T. Schuder.** 1996. 'A quasi-experimental validation of transactional strategies instruction with low-achieving second-grade readers.' *Journal of Educational Psychology* 88: 18–37.

Brown, T. L. and **M. Haynes.** 1985. 'Literacy background and reading development in a second language' in T. H. Carr (ed.): *The Development of Reading Skills. New Directions for Child Development, no. 27*. San Francisco: Jossey-Bass, Inc.: pp.19–34.

Bruck, M. and **G. S. Waters.** 1990. 'An analysis of the component spelling and reading skills of good readers—good spellers, good readers—poor spellers, and poor readers—poor spellers' in T. H. Carr (ed.): *Reading and its Development: Component Skills Approaches*. San Diego, CA: Academic Press, Inc. pp. 161–206.

Bryson, B. 1990. *The Mother Tongue: English and How it Got That Way*. New York: William Morrow and Company.

Burgess, A. 1963. *A Clockwork Orange*. New York: W.W. Norton.

Byrnes, H. and **M. Canale** (eds.). 1987. *Defining and Developing Proficiency: Guidelines, Implementations and Concepts.* Lincolnwood, IL: National Textbook Company.

Cai, G. 1999. 'Texts in contexts: understanding Chinese students' compositions' in C. R. Cooper and L. Odell (eds.): *Evaluating Writing: The Role of Teacher's Knowledge about Text, Learning, and Culture.* Urbana, IL: National Council of Teachers of English. pp. 279–97.

Calero-Breckheimer, A. and **E. T. Goetz.** 1993. 'Reading strategies of biliterate children for English and Spanish texts.' *Reading Psychology: An International Quarterly* 14: 177–204.

Calfee, R. C. and **R. Curley.** 1984. 'Structure of prose in content areas' in J. Flood (ed.): *Understanding Reading Comprehension: Cognition, Language, and the Structure of Prose.* Newark, DE: International Reading Association. pp. 161–80.

Campbell, K. S. 1995. *Coherence, Continuity, and Cohesion: Theoretical Foundations for Document Design.* Hillsdale, N.J.: Lawrence Erlbaum Associates.

Campion, M. E. and **W. B. Elley.** 1971. *An Academic Vocabulary List.* Wellington, NZ: New Zealand Council for Educational Research.

Carpenter, P. A. and **M. A. Just.** 1977. 'Integrative processes in comprehension' in D. LaBerge and S. J. Samuels (eds.): *Basic Processes in Reading: Perception and Comprehension.* Hillsdale, N.J., Lawrence Erlbaum Associates. pp. 217–41.

Carr, T. H. 1982. 'What's in a model: reading theory and reading instruction' in M. H. Singer (ed.): *Competent Reader, Disabled Reader: Research and Application.* Hillsdale, N.J.: Lawrence Erlbaum Associates. pp. 119–40.

Carr, T. H., T. L. Brown, L. G. Vavrus, and **M. A. Evans.** 1990. 'Cognitive maps and cognitive skill profiles: componential analysis of individual differences in children's reading efficiency' in T. H. Carr and B. A. Levy (eds.): *Reading and its Development: Component Skills Approaches.* San Diego, CA: Academic Press, Inc. pp. 1–55.

Carrell, P. L. 1982. 'Cohesion is not coherence.' *TESOL Quarterly* 16: 479–88.

Carrell, P. L. 1983. 'Three components of background knowledge in reading comprehension.' *Language Learning* 33: 183–207.

Carrell, P. L. 1984a. 'Evidence of a formal schema in second language comprehension.' *Language Learning* 34: 87–112.

Carrell, P. L. 1984b. 'The effects of rhetorical organization on ESL readers.' *TESOL Quarterly* 18/3: 441–69.

Carrell, P. L. 1985. 'Facilitating ESL reading by text structure.' *TESOL Quarterly* 19: 727–52.

Carrell, P. L. 1987. 'Content and formal schemata in ESL reading.' *TESOL Quarterly* 21/3: 461–81.

Carrell, P. L. 1988. 'Some causes of text-boundedness and schema interference in ESL reading' in P. L. Carrell, J. Devine, and D. E. Eskey (eds.): *Interactive Approaches to Second Language Reading*. Cambridge: Cambridge University Press. pp. 101–13.

Carrell, P. L. 1989. 'Metacognitive awareness and second language reading.' *The Modern Language Journal* 73: 121–34.

Carrell, P. L. 1991a. 'Second language reading: reading ability or language proficiency.' *Applied Linguistics* 12: 158–79.

Carrell, P. L. 1991b. 'Strategic reading' in J. E. Alatis (ed.): *Georgetown University Round Table on Languages and Linguistics 1991: Linguistics and Language Pedagogy: The State of the Art*. Washington, D.C.: Georgetown University Press. pp. 167–178.

Carrell, P. L. 1992. 'Awareness of text structure: effects on recall.' *Language Learning* 42: 1–20.

Carrell, P. L. and U. Conner. 1991. 'Reading and writing descriptive texts.' *Modern Language Journal* 75/3: 314–24.

Carrell, P. L. and B. Wallace. 1983. 'Background knowledge: context and familiarity in reading comprehension' in M. Clarke and J. Handscombe (eds.): *On TESOL '82*. Washington, D.C.: Teachers of English to Speakers of Other Languages. pp. 295–308.

Carroll, J., P. Davies and B. Richman. 1971. *The American Heritage Word Frequency Book*. New York: American Heritage.

Carroll, J. B. 1964. *Language and Thought*. Englewood Cliffs, N.J.: Prentice-Hall, Inc.

Carson, J. E., P. L. Carrell, S. Silberstein, B. Kroll, and P. A. Kuehn. 1990. 'Reading-writing relationships in first and second language.' *TESOL Quarterly* 24: 245–66.

Carson, J. G. 2000. 'Reading and writing for academic purposes' in M. Pally (ed.): *Sustained Content Teaching in Academic ESL/EFL*. Boston: Houghton Mifflin Co. pp. 19–34.

Carson, J. G. and I. Leki (eds.). 1993. *Reading in the Composition Classroom: Second Language Perspectives*. Boston: Heinle and Heinle.

Carver, R. P. 1994. 'Percentage of unknown vocabulary words in text as a function of the relative difficulty of the text: implications for instruction.' *Journal of Reading Behavior* 26: 413–37.

Celce-Murcia, M. and **E. Olshtain.** 2000. *Discourse and Context in Language Teaching.* Cambridge: Cambridge University Press.

Chandler, D. (1997). 'An introduction to genre theory.' Retrieved June 2000, from http://www.aber.ac.uk/media/Documents/intgenre/intgenre.html.

Charrow, V. 1988. 'Readability vs. comprehensibility: a case study in improving a real document' in A. Davidson and G. M. Green (eds.): *Linguistic Complexity and Text Comprehension.* Hillsdale, N.J.: Lawrence Erlbaum Associates. pp. 85–114.

Chen, Q. and **J. Donin.** 1997. 'Discourse processing of first and second language biology texts: effects of language proficiency and domain-specific knowledge.' *The Modern Language Journal* 81/2: 209–27.

Chern, C. L. 1993. 'Chinese students' word-solving strategies in reading in English' in T. N. Huckin, M. Haynes, and J. Coady (eds.): *Second Language Reading and Vocabulary Learning.* Norwood, N.J.: Ablex. pp. 67–85.

Chikamatsu, N. 1996. 'The effects of L1 orthography on L2 word recognition: a study of American and Chinese learners of Japanese.' *Studies in Second Language Acquisition* 18/4: 403–32.

Chitiri, H.-F., Y. Sun, D. M. Willows, and **I. Taylor.** 1992. 'Word recognition in second-language reading' in R. J. Harris (ed.): *Cognitive Processing in Bilinguals.* Amsterdam, The Netherlands: Elsevier Science Publishers B.V. pp. 283–97.

Christie, F. 1985. 'Language and schooling' in S. Tchudi (ed.): *Language, Schooling, and Society.* Upper Montclair, N.J.: Boynton/Cook. pp. 21–40.

Chu, H.-C. J., J. Swffar, and **D. H. Charney.** 2002. 'Cultural representations of rhetorical conventions: the effects on reading recall.' *TESOL Quarterly* 36/4: 511–41.

Chung, J. S. L. 2000. 'Signals and reading comprehension – theory and practice.' *System* 28: 247–59.

Clark, H. H. 1998. 'Communal lexicons' in K. Malmkjaer and J. Williams (eds.): *Context in Language Learning and Language Understanding.* Cambridge: Cambridge University Press. pp. 63–87.

Clark, J. L. D. and **R. Clifford.** 1987. 'The FSI/ILR/ACTFL proficiency scales and testing techniques: development, current status, and needed research' in A. Valdman (ed.): *Proceedings of the Symposium on the Evaluation of Foreign Language Proficiency.* Indiana University, Bloomington. pp. 1–18.

Clarke, M. A. 1978. 'Reading in Spanish and English: evidence from adult ESL students.' *Language Learning* 29: 121–51.

Clarke, M. A. 1980. 'The short circuit hypothesis of ESL reading—or when language competence interferes with reading performance.' *The Modern Language Journal* 64: 203–9.

Clymer, T. 1968. 'What is "reading"?: some current concepts' in H. M. Robinson (ed.): *Innovation and Change in Reading Instruction*. Chicago: The National Society for the Study of Education. pp. 7–29.

Clyne, M. 1987. 'Cultural differences in the organization of academic texts.' *Journal of Pragmatics* 11: 211–47.

Coady, J. 1979. 'A psycholinguistic model of the ESL reader' in R. Mackay, B. Barkman, and R. Jordan (eds.): *Reading in a Second Language*. Rowley, MA: Newbury House Publisher. pp. 5–12.

Collins, N. D. 1994. 'The nature of metacognition: metacognition and reading to learn.' (ERIC Document Reproduction Service. No. ED-CS-94-09). June 1994.

Connor, U. 1996. *Contrastive Rhetoric: Cross-cultural Aspects of Second-language Writing*. Cambridge: Cambridge University Press.

Cook, V. J. 1992. 'Evidence for multicompetence.' *Language Learning* 42/4: 557–91.

Cooper, M. 1984. 'Linguistic competence of practised and unpractised non-native readers of English' in J. C. Alderson and A. H. Urquhart (eds.): *Reading in a Foreign Language*. London: Longman. pp. 122–35.

Coxhead, A. 2000. 'A new academic word list.' *TESOL Quarterly* 34: 213–38.

Craik, F. I. M. and **R. S. Lockhart.** 1972. 'Levels of processing: a framework for memory research.' *Journal of Verbal Learning and Verbal Behavior* 11: 671–84.

Craik, F. I. M. and **E. Tulving.** 1975. 'Depth of processing and the retention of words in episodic memory.' *Journal of Experimental Psychology: General* 25: 314–38.

Crismore, A. and **R. Farnsworth.** 1990. 'Metadiscourse in popular and professional science discourse' in W. Nash (ed.): *The Writing Scholar*. Newbury Park, CA.: Sage. pp. 118–36.

Crookes, G. 1986. 'Towards a validated analysis of scientific text structure.' *Applied Linguistics* 7/1: 57–70.

Crowhurst, M. 1991. 'Interrelationships between reading and writing persuasive discourse *Research in the Teaching of English* 25/3: 314–38.

Crowley, K., J. Shrager, and **R. S. Siegler.** 1997. 'Strategy discovery as a competitive negotiation between metacognitive and associative mechanisms.' *Developmental Review* 17: 462–89.

Cummins, J. 1981. *Bilingualism and Minority Language Children*. Toronto: OISE Press.

Davis, F. B. 1944. 'Fundamental factors of comprehension in reading.' *Psychometrika* 9: 185–97.

Davis, F. B. 1968. 'Research in comprehension in reading.' *Reading Research Quarterly* 3: 499–545.

Davis, F. B. 1972. 'Psychometric research on comprehension in reading.' *Reading Research Quarterly* 7: 629–78.

Davis, J. N. 1989. 'Facilitating effects of marginal glosses on foreign language reading.' *The Modern Language Journal* 73: 41–8.

Davis, J. N., D. L. Lange, and **S. J. Samuels.** 1988. 'Effects of text structure instruction on foreign language readers' recall of a scientific journal article.' *Journal of Reading Behavior* 20: 203–14.

Day, R. R. and **J. Bamford.** 1998. *Extensive Reading in the Second Language Classroom.* Cambridge: Cambridge University Press.

DeFrancis, J. 1989. *Visible Speech: The Diverse Oneness of Writing Systems.* Honolulu: University of Hawai'i Press.

Degand, L. and **T. Sanders.** 2002. 'The impact of relational markers on expository text comprehension in L1 and L2.' *Reading and Writing* 15/7–8: 739–57.

Devine, J. 1984. 'ESL readers internalized models of the reading process' in J. Handscombe, R. Orem, and B. Taylor (eds.): *On TESOL '83. The Question of Control. Selected Papers from the Annual Convention of Teachers of English to Speakers of Other Languages, Toronto.* Washington, D.C.: Teachers of English to Speakers of Other Languages. 95–108.

Dochy, F. J. R. C. 1994. 'Prior knowledge and learning' in T. N. Postlethwaite (ed.): *International Encyclopedia of Education (Second edition).* Oxford/New York: Pergamon Press. pp. 4698–702.

Doctor, E. A. and **M. Coltheart.** 1980. 'Children's use of phonological encoding when reading for meaning.' *Memory and Cognition* 8: 195–209.

Dole, J. A., K. J. Brown, and **W. Trathen.** 1996. 'The effects of strategy instruction on the comprehension performance of at-risk students.' *Reading Research Quarterly* 31: 62–88.

Donin, J. and **M. Silva.** 1993. 'The relationship between first- and second-language comprehension of occupation-specific texts.' *Language Learning* 43: 373–401.

Donleavy, J. P. 1975. *The Unexpurgated Code: A Complete Manual of Survival and Manners.* New York: Delacorte Press/Seymour Lawrence.

Dudley-Evans, T. 1994. 'Genre analysis: an approach to text analysis for ESP' in M. Coulthard (ed.): *Advances in Written Text Analysis.* London: Routledge. pp. 219–28.

Duffy, G. G. and **L. R. Roehler.** 1989. 'Why strategy instruction is so difficult and what we need to do about it' in C. B. McCormick, G. E. Miller, and M. Pressley (eds.): *Cognitive Strategy Research: From Basic Research to Educational Applications.* New York: Springer-Verlag. pp. 133–54.

Durkin, D. 1979. 'What classroom observations reveal about reading comprehension instruction.' *Reading Research Quarterly* 14: 481–533.

Duszak, A. 1994. 'Academic discourse and intellectual styles.' *Journal of Pragmatics* 21: 291–313.

Dyer, M. G. 1983. *In-depth Understanding: A Computer Model of Integrated Processing for Narrative Comprehension.* Cambridge, MA: MIT Press.

Eggington, W. G. 1987. 'Written academic discourse in Korean: implications for effective communication' in U. Connor and R. B. Kaplan (eds.): *Writing across Languages: Analysis of L2 Text.* Reading, MA: Addison-Wesley. pp. 153–68.

Ehri, L. C. 1991. 'Development of the ability to read words' in R. Barr, M. Kamil, P. Mosenthal, and P. D. Pearson (eds.). pp. 383–417.

Ehri, L. C. 1995. 'Phases of develpment in learning to read words by sight.' *Journal of Research in Reading* 18: 116–25.

Eisterhold, J. C. 1990. 'Reading-writing connections: toward a description for second language learners' in B. Kroll (ed.): *Second Language Writing: Research Insights for the Classroom.* Cambridge: Cambridge University Press. pp. 88–101.

Elley, W. B. and **F. Mangubhai.** 1983. 'Interactive models for second language reading: perspectives on instruction.' in P. L. Carrell, J. Devine, and D. E. Eskey (eds.):.' *Reading Research Quarterly* 19: 53–67.

Eskey, D. E. and **W. Grabe.** 1988. 'Interactive models for second language reading: perspectives on instruction' in P. L. Carrell, J. Devine, and D. E. Eskey (eds.): *Interactive Approaches to Second Language Reading.* Cambridge: Cambridge University Press. pp. 223–38.

Esmaeili, H. 2002. 'Integrated reading and writing tasks and ESL students' reading and writing performance in an English language test.' *The Canadian Modern Language Review / La Revue Canadienne des Langues Vivantes* 58/4: 599–622.

ETS 1980. *Achievement Test: French Reading. Form M-XAC.* Princeton, N. J., Educational Testing Service.

Fairclough, N. 1995. *Media Discourse.* London: Edward Arnold.

Fecteau, M. L. 1999. 'First- and second- language reading comprehension of literary texts.' *The Modern Language Journal* 83/4: 475–93.

Feez, S. 2002. 'Heritage and innovation in second language education' in A. M. Johns (ed.): *Genre in the Classroom: Multiple Perspectives.* Mahwah, N.J.: Lawrence Erlbaum Associates. pp. 43–69.

Feldman, J. 1975. 'Bad-mouthing frames' in R. Shank and B. L. Nash-Webber (eds.): *Tinlap Conference Proceedings.* Cambridge, MA.: The MIT Press. pp. 92–3.

Ferdman, B. M. and **R. Weber.** 1994. 'Literacy across languages and cultures' in B. M. Ferdman and R. Weber (eds.): *Literacy across Languages and Cultures*. Albany, New York: State University of New York Press. 3–29.

Ferreiro, E. 2002. 'The distinction between graphic system and orthographic system and their pertinence for understanding the acquisition or orthography' in J. Brockmeier, M. Wang, and D. R. Olson (eds.): *Literacy, Narrative and Culture*. Richmond, Surrey: Curzon Press. 215–28.

Field, M. L. 1985. 'A psycholinguistic model of the Chinese ESL reader' in P. Larson, E. L. Judd, and D. S. Messerschmitt (eds.): *On TESOL '84. A Brave New World for TESOL*. Washington, D.C.: Teachers of English to Speakers of Other Languages. 171–82.

Fillmore, C. J. 1976. 'Frame semantics and the nature of language.' *Annals of the New York Academy of Sciences: Conference on the Origin and Development of Language and Speech* 280: 20–32.

Fincher-Kiefer, R. 1992. 'The role of prior knowledge in inferential processing.' *Journal of Research in Reading* 15: 12–27.

Fitzgerald, J. 1984. 'The relationship between reading ability and expectations for story structures.' *Discourse Processes* 7/1: 21–41.

Fitzgerald, J. and **T. Shanahan.** 2000. 'Reading and writing relations and their development.' *Educational Psychologist* 35: 39–50.

Flahive, D. E. and **N. H. Bailey.** 1993. 'Exploring reading/writing relationships in adult second language learners' in J. E. Carson and I. Leki (eds.): *Reading in the Composition Classroom: Second Language Perspectives*. Boston, MA: Heinle and Heinle. 128–40.

Flavell, J. H. 1982. 'On cognitive development.' *Child Development* 53: 1–10.

Flavell, J. H., P. H. Miller, and **S. A. Miller.** 2002. *Cognitive Development*. (4th edn.) Upper Saddle River, N.J.: Prentice-Hall.

Flower, L. 1990. 'Introduction: studying cognition in context' in L. Flower, V. Stein, J. M. Ackerman M. J. Kantz, K. M. McCormick, and W. C. Peck (eds.): *Reading-to-write: Exploring a Cognitive and Social Process*. Oxford: Oxford University Press. pp. 3–32.

Flower, L. and **J. R. Hayes.** 1981. 'A cognitive process theory of writing.' *College Composition and Communication* 32: 365–87.

Francis, W. N. and **H. Kucera.** 1982. *Frequency Analysis of English Usage, Lexicon and Grammar*. Boston: Houghton Mifflin Co.

Frederiksen, C. H. 1977. 'Structure and process in discourse production and comprehension' in P. A. Carpenter and M. A. Just (eds.): *Cognitive Processes in Comprehension*. Hillsdale, N.J.: Lawrence Erlbaum Associates. pp. 313–22.

Freebody, P. and **J. R. Anderson.** 1981. 'Effects of vocabulary difficulty, text cohesion, and schema availability on reading comprehension.' Technical Report No. 225. University of Illinois, Center for the Study of Reading.

Freedman, A. and **P. Medway.** 1994. 'Introduction: new views of genre and their implications for education' in A. Freedman and P. Medway (eds.): *Learning and Teaching Genre*. Portsmouth, N.H.: Boynton/Cook Publishers, Inc. pp. 1–22.

Friere, P. 1982. *Education for a Critical Consciousness*. New York: Continuum Publishing.

Friere, P. and **D. Macedo.** 1987. *Literacy: Reading the Word and the World*. Cambridge, MA: Bergin and Garvey.

Fukuoka, W. and **J. H. Spyridakis.** 1999. 'The organization of Japanese expository passages.' *IEEE Transactions on Professional Communication* 42/3: 166–74.

Fulwiler, T. and **A. Young** (eds.). 1990. *Programs that Work: Models and Methods for Writing across the Curriculum*. Portsmouth, N.H.:, Boynton/Cook Publishers.

Garner, R. 1990a. 'When children and adults do not use strategies: toward a theory of settings.' *Review of Educational Research* 60: 517–29.

Garner, R. 1990b. 'Children's use of strategies in reading' in D. F. Bjorklund (ed.): *Children's Strategies: Contemporary Views of Cognitive Development*. Hillsdale, N.J.: Lawrence Erlbaum Associates. pp. 245–68.

Garner, R. and **R. Reis.** 1981. 'Monitoring and resolving comprehension obstacles: an investigation of spontaneous text lookbacks among upper-grade good and poor readers' comprehension.' *Reading Research Quarterly* 16: 569–82.

Gaskins, R. W. 1996. '"That's just how it was": the effect of issue-related emotional involvement on reading comprehension.' *Reading Research Quarterly* 31: 386–405.

Gibson, E. J. and **H. Levin.** 1975. *The Psychology of Reading*. Cambridge, MA: The MIT Press.

Golebiowski, Z. 1998. 'Rhetorical approaches to scientific writing: an English-Polish contrastive study.' *Text* 18/1: 67–102.

Goodman, K. S. 1968. 'The psycholinguistic nature of the reading process' in K. S. Goodman (ed.): *The Psycholinguistic Nature of the Reading Process*. Detroit, MI: Wayne State University Press. pp.15–26.

Goodman, K. S. 1976. 'Reading: a psycholinguistic guessing game' in H. Singer and R. B. Rudell (eds.): *Theoretical Models and Processes of Reading*. Newark, DE: International Reading Association. pp. 497–508.

Goodman, K. S. 1984. 'Unity in reading' in A. C. Purves and O. Niles (eds.): *Becoming Readers in a Complex Society. Eighty-third Yearbook of the National Society for the Study of Education: Part I.* Chicago: University of Chicago Press. pp. 79–114.

Goodman, K. S. and **Y. M. Goodman.** 1978. 'Reading of American children whose language is a stable rural dialect of English or a language other than English.' NIE-C-00-3-0087, U.S. Department of Health, Education, and Welfare. (ERIC Document Reproduction Service ED 173; 754; 670p). Washington, D.C.

Gordon, W. M. 1982. *The Reading Curriculum: A Reference Guide to Criterion-based Skill Development in Grades k–8.* New York: Praeger Publishers.

Gough, P. B. 1972. 'One second of reading' in F. Kavanaugh and I. G. Mattingly (eds.): *Language by Ear and by Eye: The Relationship Between Speech and Reading.* Cambridge, MA: The MIT Press. pp. 331–58.

Gough, P. B. 1995. 'The new literacy: caveat emptor.' *Journal of Research in Reading* 18: 79–86.

Gourgey, A. F. 1998. 'Metacognition in basic skills instruction.' *Instructional Science* 26: 81–96.

Grabe, W. 1991. 'Current developments in second language reading research.' *TESOL Quarterly* 25/3: 375–406.

Grabe, W. and **R. B. Kaplan.** 1996. *Theory and Practice of Writing.* London: Longman.

Grabe, W. and **F. L. Stoller.** 1997. 'Reading and vocabulary development in a second language: a case study' in J. Coady and T. N. Huckin (eds.): *Second Language Vocabulary Acquisition.* Cambridge: Cambridge University Press. pp. 98–122.

Graesser, A. C. 1978. 'How to catch a fish: the memory and representation of common procedures.' *Discourse Processes* 1: 72–89.

Graesser, A. C. 1981. *Prose Comprehension Beyond the Word.* New York: Springer-Verlag.

Graesser, A. C. and **L. F. Clark.** 1985. *Structures and Procedures of Implicit Knowledge.* Norwood, N.J.: Ablex.

Graesser, A. C., J. M. Golding, and **D. L. Long.** 1996. 'Narrative representation and comprehension' in R. Barr, M. Kamil, P. Mosenthal, and P. D. Pearson (eds.). pp. 171–205.

Greene, S. 1992. 'Mining texts in reading to write.' *Journal of Advanced Composition* 21: 151–67.

Greene, S. 1993. 'The role of task in the development of academic thinking through reading and writing in a college history course.' *Research in the Teaching of English* 27: 46–75.

Grimes, J. E. 1975. *The Thread of Discourse*. The Hague, the Netherlands: Mouton.

Hacker, D. J. 1998. 'Self-regulated comprehension during normal reading' in D. J. Hacker, J. Dunlosky, and A. C. Graesser (eds.): *Metacognition in Educational Theory and Practice*. Mahwah, N.J.: Lawrence Erlbaum Associates. pp. 165–91.

Haggard, M. R. 1982. 'The vocabulary self-collection: an active approach to word learning.' *Journal of Reading* 27: 203–7.

Halliday, M. A. K. and **R. Hasan.** 1976. *Cohesion in English*. London: Longman.

Hammadou, J. 1991. 'Interrelationships among prior knowledge, inference, and language proficiency in foreign language reading.' *The Modern Language Journal* 75: 27–38.

Hammond, J., A. Burns, H. Joyce, D. Brosnan, and **L. Gerot.** 1992. *English for Social Purposes: A Handbook for Teachers of Adult Literacy*. Sydney: National Centre for English Language Teaching and Research, Macquarie University.

Hamp-Lyons, L. 1985. 'Two approaches to reading: a classroom-based study.' *Reading in a Foreign Language* 3: 363–73.

Hansen, J. 1981. 'The effects of inference training and practice on young children's reading comprehension.' *Reading Research Quarterly* 16: 391–417.

Hansen, J. and **P. D. Pearson.** 1983. 'An instructional study: Improving the inferential comprehension of fourth grade good and poor readers.' *Journal of Educational Psychology* 75/6: 821–29.

Hare, V. C. 1992. 'Summarizing text' in J. W. Irwin and M. A. Doyle (eds.): *Reading/writing Connections: Learning from Research*. Newark, DE: International Reading Association. pp. 96–118.

Harris, L. A. and **C. B. Smith.** 1976. *Reading Instruction*. New York: Holt, Rinehart, and Winston.

Harris, T. L. and **R. E. Hodges** (eds.). 1981. *A Dictionary of Reading and Related Terms*. Newark, DE: International Reading Association.

Hasan, R. 1984. 'Coherence and cohesive harmony' in J. Flood (ed.): *Understanding Reading Comprehension*. Newark, DE: The International Reading Association. pp. 181–219.

Hatch, E., P. Polin, and **S. Part.** 1974. 'Acoustic scanning or syntactic processing.' *Journal of Reading Behavior* 6: 275–85.

Haviland, S. E. and **H. H. Clark.** 1974. 'What's new? Acquiring new information as a process in comprehension.' *Journal of Verbal Learning and Verbal Behavior* 13: 512–21.

Haynes, M. and **T. H. Carr.** 1990. 'Writing system background and second language reading: a component skills analysis of English reading by native-speakers of Chinese' in T. H. Carr and B. A. Levy (eds.): *Reading and Its Development: Component Skills Approaches.* San Diego, CA: Academic Press, Inc. pp. 375–421.

Hazenberg, S. and **J. H. Hulstijn.** 1996. 'Defining a minimal receptive second-language vocabulary for non-native university students.' *Applied Linguistics* 17/2: 145–63.

Heath, S. B. 1983. *Ways with Words: Language, Life, and Work in Communities and Classrooms.* Cambridge: Cambridge University Press.

Hefflin, B. R. and **D. K. Hartman.** 2002. 'Using writing to improve comprehension' in C. C. Block, L. B. Gambrell, and M. Pressley (eds.): *Improving Comprehension Instruction: Rethinking Research, Theory, and Classroom Practice.* San Francisco: Jossey-Bass. pp. 199–228.

Henderson, L. 1982. *Orthography and Word Recognition.* London: Academic Press.

Henry, A. and **R. L. Roseberry.** 1998. 'An evaluation of a genre-based approach to the teaching of EAP/ESP writing.' *TESOL Quarterly* 32/1: 147–56.

Higgs, T. V. (ed.): 1984. *Teaching for Proficiency, the Organizing Principle.* Lincolnwood, IL: National Textbook Company.

Hinchley, J. and **B. A. Levy.** 1988. 'Developmental and individual differences in reading comprehension.' *Cognition and Instruction* 5/1: 3–47.

Hinds, J. 1983a. 'Contrastive rhetoric: Japanese and English.' *Text*/3: 183–95.

Hinds, J. 1983b. 'Linguistics and written discourse in English and Japanese: a contrastive study.' *Annual Review of Applied Linguistics* 3: 78–84.

Hinds, J. 1987. 'Reader versus writer responsibility: a new typology' in U. Connor and R. B. Kaplan (eds.): *Writing Across Languages: Analysis.* Reading, MA: Addison-Wesley. pp.141–52.

Hirsh, D. and **P. Nation.** 1992. 'What vocabulary size is needed to read unsimplified texts for pleasure?' *Reading in a Foreign Language* 8: 689–96.

Holmes, R. 1997. 'Genre analysis, and the social sciences: an investigation of the structure of research article discussion sections in three disciplines.' *English for Specific Purposes* 16/4: 321–37.

Hoover, W. A. and **W. E. Tunmer.** 1993. 'The components of reading' in G. B. Thompson, W. E. Tunmer, and T. Nicholson (eds.): *Reading Acquisition Processes.* Clevedon: Multilingual Matters. pp. 1–19.

Hopkins, A. and **T. Dudley-Evans.** 1988. 'A genre-based investigation of the discussion sections in articles and dissertations.' *English for Specific Purposes* 7: 113–21.

Horiba, Y. 1993. 'The role of causal reasoning and language competence in narrative comprehension.' *Studies in Second Language Acquisition* 15/1: 49–81.

Horiba, Y. 1996. 'Comprehension processes in L2 reading: language competence, textual coherence, and inferences.' *Studies in Second Language Acquisition* 18/4: 433–73.

Horiba, Y., P. W. van den Broek, and **C. R. Fletcher.** 1993. 'Second language reader's memory for narrative texts: evidence for structure-preserving top-down processing.' *Language Learning* 43/3: 345–72.

Hosenfeld, C. 1977. 'A preliminary investigation of the reading strategies of successful and nonsuccessful second language readers.' *System* 5: 110–23.

Hout, B. 1988. 'Reading/writing connections on the college level.' *Teaching English in the Two-year College* 15/2: 90–8.

Huckin, T. and **J. Coady.** 1999. 'Incidental vocabulary acquisition in a second language: a review.' *Studies in Second Language Acquisition* 21/2: 181–93.

Huckin, T. N. and **J. Bloch.** 1997. 'Strategies for inferring word-meanings in context: a cognitive model' in T. N. Huckin, M. Haynes, and J. Coady (eds.): *Second Language Reading and Vocabulary Learning.* Norwood, NJ: Ablex Publishing Corporation. pp.153–76.

Hudson, T. 1982. 'The effects of induced schemata on the "short circuit" in L2 reading: non-decoding factors in L2 reading performance.' *Language Learning* 32/1: 1–31.

Hudson, T. 1991. 'A content comprehension approach to reading English for science and technology.' *TESOL Quarterly* 25/1: 77–104.

Hudson, T. 1993. 'Testing the specificity of ESP reading skills' in D. Douglas and C. Chapelle (eds.): *A New Decade of Language Testing.* Alexandria, VA: TESOL. pp. 58–82.

Huey, E. B. 1908. *The Psychology and Pedagogy of Reading.* New York: The Macmillan Company.

Hulstijn, J. H. 1991. 'Guest-editor's preface: how is reading in a second language related to reading in a first language?' *AILA Review* 8: 5–14.

Hulstijn, J. H. 1992. 'Retention of inferred and given word meanings: experiments in incidental vocabulary learning' in P. J. L. Arnaud and H. Béjoint (eds.): *Vocabulary and Applied Linguistics.* London: Macmillan Academic and Professional, Ltd. pp. 113–25.

Hulstijn, J. H. 1993. 'When do foreign-language readers look up the meaning of unfamiliar words? The influence of task and learner variables.' *The Modern Language Journal* 77: 139–47.

Hulstijn, J. H., M. Hollander, and **T. Greidanus.** 1996. 'Incidental vocabulary learning by advanced foreign language students: the influence of marginal glosses, dictionary use, and reoccurence of unknown words.' *The Modern Language Journal* 80: 327–39.

Hyland, K. 2000. *Disciplinary Discourses: Social Interactions in Academic Writing.* Harlow, England: Longman.

Hyland, K. 2002. 'Genre: language, context, and literacy.' *Annual Review of Applied Linguistics* 22: 113–35.

Hyon, S. 1996. 'Genres in three traditions: implications for ESL.' *TESOL Quarterly* 30: 693–722.

Hyon, S. 2001. 'Long term effects of genre-based instruction: a follow-up study of an EAP reading course.' *English for Specific Purposes* 20/1: 417–38.

Hyon, S. 2002. 'Genre in ESL reading: a classroom study' in A. M. Johns (ed.): *Genre in the Classroom: Multiple Perspectives.* Mahwah, NJ: Lawrence Erlbaum Associates. pp. 121–41.

Irwin, J. W. 1986. 'Cohesion and comprehension: a research review' in J. W. Irwin (ed.): *Understanding and Teaching Cohesion Comprehension.* Newark, DE: International Reading Association. 31–43.

Jacobs, G., P. Dufon, and **F. C. Hong.** 1994. 'L1 and L2 vocabulary glosses in L2 reading passages: their effectiveness for increasing comprehension and vocabulary knowledge.' *Journal of Reading Research* 17: 19–28.

James, C. J., (ed.): 1985. *Foreign Language Proficiency in the Classroom and Beyond.* Lincolnwood, IL.: National Textbook Company.

Janopoulos, M. 1986. 'The relationship of pleasure reading and second language writing proficiency.' *TESOL Quarterly* 20/4: 763–68.

Janzen, J. 2003. 'Developing strategic readers in elementary school.' *Reading Psychology: an International Quarterly* 24: 25–55.

Janzen, J. and **F. L. Stoller.** 1998. 'Integrating strategic reading in L2 instruction.' *Reading in a Foreign Language* 12/1: 251–69.

Jiménez, R. T. 1997. 'The strategic reading abilities and potential of five low-literacy Latina/o readers in middle school.' *Reading Research Quarterly* 32/3: 224–43.

Jiménez, R. T., G. E. García, and **P. D. Pearson.** 1996. 'The reading strategies of bilingual Latina/o students who are successful English readers: opportunities and obstacles.' *Reading Research Quarterly* 31/1: 90–112.

Johns, A. M. 1980. 'Cohesion in written business discourse: some contrasts.' *The ESP Journal* 1: 35–44.

Johns, A. M. 1997. *Text, Role, and Context: Developing Academic Literacies.* Cambridge: Cambridge University Press.

Johns, A. M. 2002. 'Introduction: genre in the classroom' in A. M. Johns (ed.): *Genre in the Classroom: Multiple Perspectives.* Mahwah, NJ: Lawrence Erlbaum Associates. pp. 3–13.

Johnson, N. S. 1983. 'What do you do if you can't tell the whole story? The development of summarization skills' in K. E. Nelson (ed.): *Children's Language.* (Volume 4). Hillsdale, NJ: Lawrence Erlbaum. Associates. pp. 315–83.

Johnson, N. S. and **J. M. Mandler.** 1980. 'A tale of two structures: underlying and surface forms in stories.' *Poetics* 9: 51–86.

Johnson, P. 1981. 'Effects on reading comprehension of language complexity and cultural background of a text.' *TESOL Quarterly* 15: 169–81.

Johnson, P. 1982. 'Effects on reading comprehension of building background knowledge.' *TESOL Quarterly* 16/4: 503–16.

Jolly, D. 1978. 'The establishment of a self-access scheme for intensive reading.' Paper presented at the Goethe Institute, British Council Colloquium on Reading, Paris, October 1978.

Just, M. A. and **P. A. Carpenter.** 1980. 'A theory of reading: from eye fixations to comprehension.' *Psychological Review* 87: 329–54.

Just, M. A. and **P. A. Carpenter.** 1987. *The Psychology of Reading and Language Comprehension.* Boston: Allyn and Bacon, Inc.

Kachru, Y. 1988. 'Writers in Hindi and English' in A. C. Purves (ed.): *Writing Across Languages and Cultures: Issues in Contrastive Rhetoric.* Newbury Park, CA: Sage Publications. pp. 109–37.

Kant, E. 1963. *Critique of Pure Reason.* (1st edition, 1972, translated by N. K. Smith). New York: The Humanities Press.

Kaplan, R. B. 1966. 'Cultural thought patterns in intercultural education.' *Language Learning* 16: 1–20.

Kaplan, R. B. 1987. 'Chapter 1: Cultural thought patterns revisited' in U. Connor and R. B. Kaplan (eds.): *Writing Across Languages: Analyses of L2 Texts.* Reading, MA: Addison-Wesley. 9–21.

Kaplan, R. B. 2000. 'Contrastive rhetoric and discourse analysis: who writes to whom? when? in what circumstances?' in S. Sarangi and M. Coulthard (eds.): *Discourse and Social Life.* Harlow, England: Longman. pp. 82–101.

Katz, J. and **J. Fodor.** 1963. 'The structure of semantic theory.' *Language* 39: 170–210.

Kemper, M. (2004). 'Personal ad leaving newspaper classified.' Retrieved July 2004, from http://www.communitypapers.com/ANAGRAMS/myarticles.asp?S=409&PubID=2713&P=367986.

Kennedy, M. L. 1985. 'The composing processes of college students writing from sources.' *Written Communication* 2: 434–56.

Kern, R. G. 1989. 'Second language reading strategy instruction: its effects on comprehension and word inference ability.' *The Modern Language Journal* 73: 135–49.

Kern, R. G. 1994. 'The role of mental translation in second language reading.' *Studies in Second Language Acquisition* 16/4: 441–61.

Kern, R. G. 1997. 'L2 reading strategy training: a critical perspective.' Paper presented at the AAAL Conference, Orlando, Florida, March 10, 1997.

Kintsch, W. 1982. 'Text representations' in W. Otto and S. White (eds.): *Reading Expository Material.* New York: Academic Press. pp. 87–101.

Kintsch, W. 1988. 'The role of knowledge in discourse comprehension: a construction-integration model.' *Psychological Review* 92: 163–82.

Kintsch, W. 1998. *Comprehension: A Paradigm for Cognition.* Cambridge: Cambridge University Press.

Kintsch, W., E. Kozminsky, W. J. Streby, G. McKoon, and **J. M. Keenan.** 1975. 'Comprehension and recall of texts as a function of content variables.' *Journal of Verbal Learning and Verbal Behavior* 14: 196–214.

Kintsch, W. and **T. van Dijk.** 1978. 'Toward a model of text comprehension and production.' *Psychological Review* 85: 363–94.

Kintsch, W. and **C. Yarbrough.** 1982. 'Role of rhetorical structure in text comprehension.' *Journal of Educational Psychology* 74: 828–34.

Knight, S. 1994. 'Dictionary use while reading: the effects on comprehension and vocabulary acquisition for students of different verbal abilities.' *The Modern Language Journal* 78: 285–99.

Knight, S., Y. Padron, and **H. C. Waxman.** 1985. 'The cognitive reading strategies of ESL students.' *TESOL Quarterly* 19: 789–92.

Kobayashi, H. 1984. 'Rhetorical patterns in English and Japanese.' *TESOL Quarterly* 18: 737–38.

Koda, K. 1987. 'Cognitive strategy transfer in second language reading' in J. Devine and P. L. Carrell (eds.): *Research in Reading in English as a Second Language.* Washington, D.C.: Teachers of English to Speakers of Other Languages. pp. 125–44.

Koda, K. 1989. 'Effects of L1 orthographic representation on L2 phonological coding strategies.' *Journal of Psycholinguistic Research* 18/2: 201–22.

Koda, K. 1990. 'The use of L1 reading strategies in L2: effects of L1 orthographic structures on L2 phonological recoding strategies.' *Studies in Second Language Acquisition* 12: 393–410.

Koda, K. 1992. 'The effects of lower-level processing skills on FL reading performance: implications for instruction.' *The Modern Language Journal* 76: 502–12.

Koda, K. 1995. 'Cognitive consequences of L1 and L2 orthographies' in I. Taylor and D. R. Olson (eds.): *Scripts and Literacy: Reading and Learning to Read Alphabets, Syllabaries and Characters.* Dordrecht: Kluwer Academic Publishers. pp. 311–26.

Koda, K. 1997. 'Orthographic knowledge in L2 lexical processing: a cross-linguistic perspective' in J. Coady and T. N. Huckin (eds.): *Second Language Vocabulary Acquisition.* Cambridge: Cambridge University Press. pp. 35–52.

Koda, K. 2005. *Insights into Second Language Reading: A Cross-linguistic Approach.* Cambridge: Cambridge University Press.

Kress, G. 1993. 'Genre as social process' in B. Cope and M. Kalantzis (eds.): *The Power of Literacy: A Genre Approach to Teaching Writing.* Pittsburgh: University of Pittsburgh Press. pp. 22–37.

Kucer, S. B. 1985. 'The making of meaning: reading and writing as parallel processes.' *Written Communication* 2: 317–36.

Kucer, S. B. 2001. *Dimensions of Literacy: A Conceptual Base for Teaching Reading and Writing in School Settings.* Mahwah, N.J.: Lawrence Erlbaum Associates.

Kucera, H. and **W. N. Francis.** 1967. *Computational Analysis of Present-day American English.* Providence, RI: Brown University Press.

LaBerge, D. and **S. J. Samuels.** 1974. 'Toward a theory of automatic information processing in reading.' *Cognitive Psychology* 6: 293–323.

Langacker, R. W. 1972. *Fundamentals of Linguistic Analysis.* New York: Harcourt Brace Jovanovich, Inc.

Langer, J. A. 1992. 'Rethinking literature instruction' in J. A. Langer (ed.): *Literature instruction: A Focus on Student Responses.* Urbana, IL.: National Council of Teachers of English. pp. 35–53.

Langer, J. A. and **A. N. Applebee.** 1987. *How Writing Shapes Thinking: A Study of Teaching and Learning.* Urbana, IL: National Council of Teachers of English.

Laufer, B. 1989. 'What percentage of text-lexis is essential for comprehension?' in C. Laurén and M. Nordman (eds.): *Special Language: From Humans Thinking to Thinking Machines.* Clevedon, Great Britain: Multilingual Matters. pp. 316–23.

Laufer, B. 1992. 'Reading in a foreign language: how does L2 lexical knowledge interact with the reader's general academic ability?' *Journal of Research in Reading* 15: 95–103.

Laufer, B. 1996. 'The lexical threshold of second language reading comprehension: what it is and how it relates to L1 reading ability' in K. Sajavaara and C. Fairweather (eds.): *Approaches to Second Language Acquisition*. Jyväskylä, Finland: University of Jyväskylä. pp. 55–62.

Laufer, B. 1997. 'The lexical plight in second language reading: words you don't know, words you think you know, and words you can't guess' in J. Coady and T. N. Huckin (eds.): *Second Language Vocabulary Acquisition*. Cambridge: Cambridge University Press. pp. 20–34.

Laufer, B., C. Elder, K. Hill, and **P. Congdon.** 2004. 'Size and strength: do we need both to measure vocabulary knowledge?' *Language Testing* 21/2: 202–26.

Lee, J. F. 1986. 'Background knowledge and reading.' *The Modern Language Journal* 70: 350–54.

Lee, J. F. and **G. L. Riley.** 1990. 'The effect of prereading, rhetorically-oriented frameworks on the recall of two structurally different expository texts.' *Studies in Second Language Acquisition* 12/1: 25–41.

Lee, J.-W. and **D. L. Schallert.** 1997. 'The relative contribution of L2 language proficiency and L1 reading ability to L2 reading performance: a text of the threshold hypothesis in an EFL context.' *TESOL Quarterly* 31: 713–49.

Lehnert, W. G. 1981. 'Plot units and narrative summarization.' *Cognitive Science* 5: 293–331.

Lennon, R. T. 1962. 'What can be measured?' *The Reading Teacher* 15: 326–37.

Lenski, S. D. and **J. L. Johns.** 1997. 'Patterns in reading-to-write.' *Reading Research Instruction* 37/1: 15–39.

Leow, R. P. 1993. 'To simplify or not to simplify: a look at intake.' *Studies in Second Language Acquisition* 15/3: 333–55.

Levy, B. A. and **J. Hinchley.** 1990. 'Individual developmental differences in the acquisition of reading skills' in T. H. Carr and B. A. Levy (eds.): *Reading and Its Development: Component Skills Approaches*. San Diego, CA: Academic Press, Inc. pp. 81–128.

Lewis, M. 1993. *The Lexical Approach: The State of ELT and a Way Forward*. London: Language Teaching Publications.

Linderholm, T., M. G. Everson, P. W. van den Broek, M. Mischiniski, A. Crittenden, and **S. J. Samuels.** 2000. 'Effects of causal text revisions on more- and less-skilled readers' comprehension of easy and difficult texts.' *Cognition and Instruction* 18/4: 525–56.

Lipson, M. Y. 1982. 'Learning new information from text: the role of prior knowledge and reading ability.' *Journal of Reading Behavior* 14/3: 243–61.

Lipson, M. Y. 1983. 'The influence of religious affiliation on children's memory for text information.' *Reading Research Quarterly* 19: 448–57.

Liskin-Gasparro, J. E. 1984. 'The ACTFL Proficiency Guidelines: a historical perspective' in T. V. Higgs (ed.): *Teaching for Proficiency, the Organizing Principle.* Lincolnwood, IL: National Textbook Company. pp. 11–42.

Logan, G. 1979. 'On the use of a concurrent memory load to measure attention and automaticity.' *Journal of Experimental Psychology: Human Perception and Performance* 5: 189–207.

Lovett, S. B. and **J. H. Flavell.** 1990. 'Understanding and remembering: children's knowledge about the differential effects of strategy and task variables on comprehension and memorization.' *Child Development* 61/6: 1842–58.

Lunzer, E., M. Waite, and **T. Dolan.** 1979. 'Comprehension and comprehension tests' in E. Lunzer and K. Gardner (eds.): *The Effective Use of Reading.* London: Heinemann Educational Books. pp. 37–71.

Luppescu, S. and **R. R. Day.** 1993. 'Reading, dictionaries, and vocabulary learning.' *Language Learning* 43: 263–87.

Malik, A. A. 1990. 'A psycholinguistic analysis of the reading behavior of EFL-proficient readers using culturally familiar and culturally nonfamiliar expository texts.' *American Educational Research Journal* 27: 205–23.

Mandler, J. M. 1978. 'A code in the node: the use of a story schema in retrieval.' *Discourse Processes* 1: 14–35.

Mandler, J. M. 1984. *Stories, Scripts, and Scenes: Aspects of Schema Theory.* Hillsdale, N.J.: Lawrence Erlbaum Associates.

Mandler, J. M. 1987. 'On the psychological reality of story structure.' *Discourse Processes* 10: 1–29.

Mandler, J. M. and **M. DeForest.** 1979. 'Is there more than one way to recall a story?' *Child Development* 50: 886–9.

Mandler, J. M. and **N. S. Johnson.** 1977. 'Remembrance of things parsed: story structure and recall.' *Cognitive Psychology* 9: 111–51.

Mannes, S. M. and **W. Kintsch.** 1987. 'Knowledge organization and text organization.' *Cognition and Instruction* 4: 91–115.

Marr, M. B. and **K. Gormley.** 1982. 'Children's recall of familiar and unfamiliar text.' *Reading Research Quarterly* 18/1: 89–104.

Marshall, J. D. 1987. 'The effects of writing on students' understanding of literary text.' *Research in the Teaching of English* 21: 31–63.

Marshall, N. and **M. D. Glock.** 1978. 'Comprehension of connected discourse: a study into the relationships between the structure of text and information recalled.' *Reading Research Quarterly* 14: 10–56.

Mathewson, G. C. 1976. 'The function of attitude in the reading process' in H. Singer and R. B. Rudell (eds.): *Theoretical Models and Processes of Reading.* (2nd edn.). Newark, DE: International Reading Association. pp. 655–76.

Mathewson, G. C. 1985. 'Toward a comprehensive model of affect in the reading process' in H. Singer and R. B. Ruddell (eds.): *Theoretical Models and Processes of Reading.* (3rd edn.). Newark, DE: International Reading Association. pp. 841–56.

Mathewson, G. C. 1994. 'Model of attitude influence upon reading and learning to read' in R. B. Ruddell, M. P. Ruddell, and H. Singer (eds.): *Theoretical Models and Processes of Reading.* (4th edn). Newark, DE: International Reading Association. pp. 1131–61.

Mauranen, A. 1993. 'Contrastive ESP rhetoric: metatext in Finnish-English texts.' *English for Specific Purposes* 12/1: 3–22.

Maybin, J. and **G. Moss.** 1993. 'Talk about texts: reading as a social event.' *Journal of Research in Reading* 16/2: 138–47.

Maynard, S. K. 1996. 'Presentation of one's view in Japanese newspaper column: commentary strategies and sequencing.' *Text* 16/2: 391–421.

McClelland, J. L., D. E. Rumelhart, and **G. E. Hinton.** 1986. 'The appeal of parallel distributed processing' in D. E. Rumelhart, J. L. McClelland, and T. P. R. Group (eds.): *Parallel Distributed Processing: Explorations in the Microstructure of Cognition.* Volume 1: Foundations. Cambridge: MA: The MIT Press. pp. 3–44.

McConkie, G. W. and **K. Rayner.** 1975. 'The span of the effective stimulus during a fixation in reading.' *Perception and Psychophysics* 17: 578–86.

McCormick, S. 1994. 'A nonreader becomes a reader: a case study of literacy acquisition by a severely disabled reader.' *Reading Research Quarterly* 29/2: 156–76.

McGee, L. M. 1982. 'Awareness of text structure: effects on children's recall of expository text.' *Reading Research Quarterly* 17: 581–90.

McGinley, W. 1992. 'The role of reading and writing while composing from sources.' *Reading Research Quarterly* 27: 227–48.

McGinley, W. and **R. J. Tierney.** 1989. 'Traversing the topical landscape: reading and writing as ways of knowing.' *Written Communication* 6: 243–69.

McKeown, M. G., I. L. Beck, G. M. Sinatra, and **J. A. Loxterman.** 1992. 'The contribution of prior knowledge and coherent text to comprehension.' *Reading Research Quarterly* 27/1: 79–93.

Mecartty, F. H. 1998. 'The effects of proficiency level and passage content on reading skills assessment.' *Foreign Language Annals* 31: 517–34.

Meyer, B. J. F. 1975. *The Organization of Prose and Its Effects on Memory.* Amsterdam: North-Holland Publishing Company.

Meyer, B. J. F. 1977. 'The structure of prose: effects on learning and memory and implications for educational practice' in R. C. Anderson, R. J. Spiro, and W. E. Montague (eds.): *Schooling and the Acquisition of Knowledge.* Hillsdale, N.J.: Lawrence Erlbaum Associates. pp. 179–208.

Meyer, B. J. F. 1985. 'Prose analysis: purposes, procedures, and problems' in B. Britton and J. Black (eds.): *Understanding Expository Text.* Hillsdale, N.J.: Lawrence Erlbaum Associates. pp. 11–64.

Meyer, B. J. F. 1999. 'Importance of text structure in everyday reading' in A. Ram and K. Moorman (eds.): *Understanding Language Understanding: Computational Models of Reading.* Cambridge, MA: The MIT Press. pp. 227–52.

Meyer, B. J. F., D. M. Brandt, and **G. J. Bluth.** 1980. 'Use of top-level structure in text: key for reading comprehension of ninth-grade students.' *Reading Research Quarterly* 16: 72–103.

Meyer, B. J. F. and **R. O. Freedle.** 1984. 'Effects of discourse type on recall.' *American Educational Research Journal* 21: 121–43.

Meyer, B. J. F. and **L. W. Poon.** 2001. 'Effects of structure training and signaling on recall of text.' *Journal of Educational Psychology* 93/1: 141–59.

Meyer, B. J. F. and **G. E. Rice.** 1984. 'The structure of text' in P. D. Pearson, R. Barr, M. Kamil, and P. Mosenthal (eds.). pp. 319-51.

Mitchell, R. and **F. Myles.** 1998. *Second Language Learning Theories.* London: Arnold.

Moe, A. J. and **J. W. Irwin.** 1986. 'Cohesion, coherence, and comprehension' in J. W. Irwin (ed.): *Understanding and Teaching Cohesion Comprehension.* Newark, DE: International Reading Association. pp. 3–8.

Mori, Y. 1998. 'Effects of first language and phonological accessibility on Kanji recognition.' *British Journal of Psychology* 55: 165–80.

Morton, J. A. 1964. 'The effects of context on the visual duration threshold for words.' *British Journal of Psychology* 55: 165–80.

Mulcahy, P. I. and **S. J. Samuels.** 1987. 'Problem-solving schemata for text types: a comparison of narrative and expository text structures.' *Reading Psychology: An International Quarterly* 8: 247–56.

Munby, J. 1978. *Communicative Syllabus Design.* Cambridge: Cambridge University Press.

Myers, G. 1991. 'Lexical cohesion and specialized knowledge in science and popular science texts.' *Discourse Processes* 14: 1–26.

Nagy, W. E., R. C. Anderson, and P. A. Herman. 1987. 'Learning word meanings from context during normal reading.' *American Educational Research Journal* 24: 237–70.

Nagy, W. E. and P. A. Herman. 1987. 'Breadth and depth of vocabulary knowledge: implications for acquisition and instruction' in M. G. McKeown and M. E. Curtis (eds.): *The Nature of Vocabulary Acquisition.* Hillsdale, N.J.: Lawrence Erlbaum Associates. pp. 19–35.

Nagy, W. E., P. A. Herman, and R. C. Anderson. 1985. 'Learning words from context.' *Reading Research Quarterly* 20: 233–53.

Nanri, K. 2001. 'Logical structures of Japanese texts.' *Text* 21/3: 373–409.

Nassaji, H. 2002. 'Schema theory and knowledge-based processes in second language reading comprehension: a need for alternative perspectives.' *Language Learning* 52/2: 439–82.

Nassaji, H. 2003. 'L2 vocabulary learning from context: strategies, knowledge sources, and their relationship with success in L2 lexical inferencing.' *TESOL Quarterly* 37/4: 645–70.

Nation, I. S. P. 1983. 'Testing and teaching vocabulary.' *Guidelines* 5: 12–25.

Nation, I. S. P. 1990. *Teaching and Learning Vocabulary.* New York: Newbury House Publishers.

Nation, I. S. P. 2001. *Learning Vocabulary in Another Language.* Cambridge: Cambridge University Press.

National Assessment of Educational Progress 1973. 'Reading: Summary (Report 02-R-00).' U.S. Government Printing Office. Washington, D.C.

Nelson, G. L. 1987. 'Culture's role in reading comprehension: a schema theoretical approach.' *Journal of Reading* 30: 424–29.

Nelson, N. and R. C. Calfee. 1998. 'The reading-writing connection viewed historically' in N. Nelson and R. C. Calfee (eds.): *The Reading-writing Connection: Ninety-seventh Yearbook of the National Society for the Study of Education – Part II.* Chicago: The University of Chicago Press. pp. 1–52.

Newell, G. E., M. C. Garriga, and S. S. Peterson. 2001. 'Learning to assume the role of author: a study of reading-to-write in an undergraduate ESL composition course' in D. Belcher and A. Hirvela (eds.): *Linking Literacies: Perspectives on L2 Reading-writing Connections.* Ann Arbor, MI: The University of Michigan Press. pp. 164–85.

Newell, G. E. and P. Winograd. 1995. 'Writing about and learning from history texts: the effects of task and academic ability.' *Research in the Teaching of English* 29: 133–63.

Nicholson, T. 1993. 'The case against context' in G. B. Thompson, W. E. Tunmer, and T. Nicholson (eds.): *Reading Acquisition Processes*. Clevedon: Multilingual Matters. pp. 91–104.

North, B. 2000. *The Development of a Common Framework Scale of Language Proficiency*. New York: Peter Lang.

Oded, B. and **J. Walters.** 2002. 'Deeper processing for better EFL reading comprehension.' *System* 29/3: 357–70.

Oh, S.-Y. 2001. 'Two types of input modification and EFL reading comprehension: simplification versus elaboration.' *TESOL Quarterly* 35/1: 69–96.

O'Malley, J. and **A. U. Chamot.** 1990. *Language Learning Strategies*. Cambridge: Cambridge University Press.

Otto, W. and **E. Askov.** 1974. *Rationale and Guidelines: The Wisconsin Design for Reading Skill Development*. Minneapolis, MN: National Computer Systems.

Oxford, R. 1990. *Language Learning Strategies: What Every Teacher Should Know*. New York: Newbury House Publishers.

Padron, Y., S. L. Knight, and **H. C. Waxman.** 1986. 'Analyzing bilingual and monolingual students' perceptions of their reading strategies.' *The Reading Teacher* 39: 430–33.

Padron, Y. and **H. C. Waxman.** 1988. 'The effect of ESL students' perceptions of their cognitive strategies on reading achievement.' *TESOL Quarterly* 22: 146–50.

Palincsar, A. S. 1986. 'Metacognitive strategy instruction.' *Exceptional Children* 53/2: 118–24.

Palincsar, A. S. and **A. L. Brown.** 1984. 'Reciprocal teaching of comprehension-fostering and comprehension-monitoring activities.' *Cognition and Instruction* 2: 117–75.

Paltridge, B. 1996. 'Genre, text type, and the language learning classroom.' *ELT Journal* 50: 237–43.

Paltridge, B. 1997. *Genre, Frames and Writing in Research Settings*. Amsterdam: John Benjamins Publishing Co.

Paribakht, T. and **M. Wesche.** 1993. 'The relationship between reading comprehension and second language development in a comprehension-based ESL program.' *TESL Canada Journal* 11: 9–29.

Paribakht, T. and **M. Wesche.** 1997. 'Vocabulary enhancement activities and reading for meaning in second language vocabulary acquisition' in J. Coady and T. N. Huckin (eds.): *Second Language Vocabulary Acquisition*. Cambridge: Cambridge University Press. pp. 174–200.

Paribakht, T. and **M. Wesche.** 1999. 'Reading and "incidental" L2 vocabulary acquisition: an introspective study of lexical inferencing.' *Studies in Second Language Acquisition* 21: 195–224.

Paris, S. G., M. Y. Lipson, and **K. K. Wixon.** 1983. 'Become a strategic reader.' *Contemporary Educational Psychology* 8: 293–316.

Paris, S. G., B. A. Wasik, and **J. C. Turner.** 1996. 'The development of strategic readers' in R. Barr, M. Kamil, P. Mosenthal, and P. D. Pearson (eds.). pp. 609–40.

Parry, K. 1991. 'Building a vocabulary through academic reading.' *TESOL Quarterly* 24: 629–52.

Parry, K. 1993. 'The social construction of reading strategies: new directions for research.' *Journal of Research in Reading* 16/2: 148–58.

Parry, K. 1997. 'Too many words: learning the vocabulary of an academic subject' in T. N. Huckin, M. Haynes, and J. Coady (eds.): *Second Language Reading and Vocabulary Learning*. Norwood, N.J.: Ablex Publishing Corp.: pp. 109–26.

Pearson, P. D., L. R. Roehler, J. A. Dole, and **G. G. Duffy.** 1992. 'Developing expertise in reading comprehension' in S. J. Samuels and A. E. Farstrup (eds.): *What Research Has to Say About Reading Instruction.* (2nd edn.). Newark, DE: International Reading Association. pp. 145–99.

Pearson, P. D. and **R. J. Tierney.** 1984. 'On becoming a thoughtful reader' in A. C. Purves and O. Niles (eds.): *Becoming Readers in a Complex Society.* Chicago: National Society for the Study of Education. pp. 143–73.

Pearson, P. D., M. Kamil, R. Barr, and **P. Mosenthal.** (eds.): *Handbook of Reading Research (Vol. 1).* New York: Longman.

Pennycook, A. 2001. *Critical Applied Linguistics: A Critical Introduction.* Mahwah, N.J.: Lawrence Erlbaum Associates.

Perfetti, C. A. 1977. 'Language comprehension and fast decoding: some psycholinguistic prerequisites for skilled reading comprehension' in J. T. Guthrie (ed.): *Cognition, Curriculum and Comprehension.* Newark, DE: International Reading Association. pp. 20–41.

Perfetti, C. A. 1985. *Reading Ability.* New York: Oxford University Press.

Perfetti, C. A. 1988. 'Verbal efficiency in reading ability' in M. Daneman, G. E. MacKinnon, and T. G. Waller (eds.): *Reading Research: Advances in Theory and Practice. (Volume 6).* New York: Academic Press. pp. 109–43.

Perfetti, C. A. 1991. 'Representations and awareness in the acquisition of reading competence' in L. Rieben and C. A. Perfetti (eds.): *Learning to Read.* Hillsdale, N.J.: Lawrence Erlbaum Associates. pp. 33–44.

Perfetti, C. A. 1995. 'Cognitive research can inform reading education.' *Journal of Research in Reading* 18: 106–15.

Perkins, K., S. R. Brutten, and **J. T. Pohlmann.** 1989. 'First and second language reading comprehension.' *RELC Journal* 20: 1–9.

Phakiti, A. 2003. *An empirical investigation into the relationships of state-trait strategy use to EFL reading comprehension test performance: A structural equation modeling approach.* Unpublished dissertation. University of Melbourne, Australia.

Pitts, M., H. White, and **S. Krashen.** 1989. 'Acquiring second language vocabulary through reading: a replication of the *Clockwork Orange* study using second language acquirers.' *Reading in a Foreign Language* 5: 271–75.

Praninskas, J. 1972. *American University Word List.* London: Longman.

Precht, K. 1998. 'A cross-cultural comparison of letters of recommendation.' *English for Specific Purposes* 17/3: 241–65.

Pressley, M. and **P. Afflerbach.** 1995. *Verbal Protocols of Reading: The Nature of Constructively Responsive Reading.* Hillsdale, N.J.: Lawrence Erlbaum Associates.

Pritchard, R. 1990. 'The effects of cultural schemata on reading processing strategies.' *Reading Research Quarterly* 25: 273–95.

Proctor, R. W. and **A. Dutta.** 1995. *Skill Acquisition and Human Performance.* Thousand Oaks, CA: Sage Publications.

Qian, D. D. 1999. 'Assessing the roles of depth and breadth of vocabulary knowledge in reading comprehension.' *The Canadian Modern Language Review/La Revue canadienne des langues vivantes* 56: 282–308.

Qian, D. D. 2002. 'Investigating the relationship between vocabulary knowledge and academic reading performance: an assessment perspective.' *Language Learning* 52: 513–36.

Rafoth, B. A. 1990. 'The concept of discourse community: descriptive and explanatory adequacy' in G. Kirsch and D. H. Roen (eds.): *A Sense of Audience in Written Communication.* Newbury Park, CA: Sage Publications. pp. 140–51.

Rahman, T. and **G. L. Bisanz.** 1986. 'Reading ability and use of story schema in recalling and reconstructing information.' *Journal of Educational Psychology* 78/5: 232–333.

Rainio, R. 1988. *Asiatyyli ja viestintä [Prose style and communication].* (8th edn). Helsinki: Suomalaisen kirjallisuuden seura.

Raymond, P. M. 1993. 'The effects of structure strategy training on recall of expository prose for university students reading French as a second language.' *The Modern Language Journal* 77: 445–58.

Rayner, K. 1978. 'Eye movements in reading and information processing.' *Cognitive Psychology* 85: 618–60.

Rayner, K. and **A. Pollatsek.** 1989. *The Psychology of Reading.* Englewood Cliffs, N.J.: Prentice Hall.

Read, J. 1993. 'The development of a new measure of L2 vocabulary knowledge.' *Language Testing* 10: 355–71.

Read, J. 2000. *Assessing Vocabulary.* Cambridge: Cambridge University Press.

Read, S. J. and **M. B. Rosson.** 1982. 'Rewriting history: the biasing effects of beliefs on memory.' *Journal of Social Cognition* 1: 240–55.

Recht, D. R. and **L. Leslie.** 1988. 'Effect of prior knowledge on good and poor readers' memory of text.' *Journal of Educational Psychology* 80/1: 16–20.

Reder, S. 1994. 'Practice-engagement theory: a sociocultural approach to literacy across languages and cultures' in B. M. Ferdman, R.-M. Weber, and A. G. Ramirez (eds.): *Literacy Across Languages and Cultures.* Albany, New York: State University of New York Press. pp. 33–74.

Reppen, R. 1995. 'A genre-based approach to content writing instruction.' *TESOL Journal* 4/2: 32–35.

Reutzel, D. R. and **P. M. Hollingsworth.** 1991. 'Investigating topic-related attitude: effect on reading and remembering text.' *Journal of Educational Research* 84: 334–44.

Reynolds, R. E., M. A. Taylor, M. S. Steffensen, L. L. Shirey, and **R. C. Anderson.** 1982. 'Cultural schemata and reading comprehension.' *Reading Research Quarterly* 17: 353–66.

Rhoder, C. 2002. 'Mindful reading: strategy training that facilitates transfer.' *Journal of Adolescent and Adult Literacy* 45/6: 498–512.

Richards, J. C., J. Platt, and **H. Weber.** 1985. *Longman Dictionary of Applied Linguistics.* London: Longman.

Riley, G. L. 1993. 'A story structure approach to narrative text comprehension.' *The Modern Language Journal* 77/4: 417–32.

Roller, C. M. 1990. 'Commentary: the interaction of knowledge and structure variables in the processing of expository prose.' *Reading Research Quarterly* 25/2: 79–89.

Roller, C. M. and **A. R. Matambo.** 1992. 'Bilingual readers' use of background knowledge in learning from text.' *TESOL Quarterly* 26: 129–41.

Rosenshine, B. V. 1980. 'Skill hierarchies in reading comprehension' in R. J. Spiro, B. C. Bruce, and W. F. Brewer (eds.): *Theoretical Issues in Reading Comprehension: Perspectives from Cognitive Psychology, Linguistics, Artificial Intelligence, and Education.* Hillsdale, N.J.: Lawrence Erlbaum Associates. pp. 535–54.

Rosenshine, B. V. and **C. Meister.** 1994. 'Reciprocal teaching: a review of the research.' *Review of Educational Research* 64: 479–530.

Rott, S. 1999. 'The effect of exposure frequency on intermediate language learners' incidental vocabulary acquisition and retention through reading.' *Studies in Second Language Acquisition* 21: 589–619.

Rumelhart, D. E. 1975. 'Notes on a schema for stories' in D. G. Bobrow and A. Collins (eds.): *Representation and Understanding: Studies in Cognitive Science.* New York: Academic Press. pp. 211–36.

Rumelhart, D. E. 1977. 'Understanding and summarizing stories' in D. LaBerge and S. J. Samuels (eds.): *Basic Processes in Reading: Perception and Comprehension.* Hillsdale, N.J.: Lawrence Erlbaum Associates. pp. 265–303.

Rumelhart, D.E., P. Smolensky, J.L. McClelland, and **G.E. Hinton.** 1986. 'Schemata and sequential thought processes in PDP models' in J.L. McClelland, D.E. Rumelhart, and the PDP Research Group. (eds.): *Parallel Distributed Processing: Explorations in the Microstructure of Cognition. Volume 2: Psychological and Biological Models.* Cambridge, MA: The MIT Press. pp. 7-57.

Ryan, E. B. 1981. 'Identifying and remediating failures in reading comprehension: toward an instructional approach for poor comprehenders' in T. G. Waller and G. E. MacKinnon (eds.): *Reading Research: Advances in Theory and Practice.* New York: Academic Press. pp. 224–57.

Sadoski, M. 1999. 'Essay book reviews: comprehending comprehension.' *Reading Research Quarterly* 34/4: 493–500.

Salager-Meyer, F. 1990. 'Discoursal flaws in medical English abstracts: a genre analysis per research and text-type.' *Text* 10/4: 365–84.

Salvatori, M. 1996. 'Conversations with texts: reading in the teaching of composition.' *College English* 58: 440–54.

Samuels, S. J. and **M. L. Kamil.** 1984. 'Models of the reading process' in P. D. Pearson, R. Barr, M. Kamil, and P. Mosenthal (eds.). pp. 85–224.

Saragi, T., I. S. P. Nation, and **G. F. Meister.** 1978. 'Vocabulary learning and reading.' *System* 6: 70–8.

Sarig, G. 1987. 'High-level reading in the first and in the foreign language: some comparative process data' in J. Devine, P. L. Carrell, and D. E. Eskey (eds.): *Research in Reading in English as a Second Language.* Washington, D.C.: Teachers of English to Speakers of Other Languages. pp. 105–23.

Scherr, G. H. 1986. *The Journal of Irreproducible Results* (3rd edn.). New York: Dorset Press.

Schneider, W., J. Körkel, and **F. Weinert.** 1989. 'Domain-specific knowledge and memory performance: a comparison of high- and low-aptitude children.' *Journal of Educational Psychology* 81/3: 306–12.

Schoonen, R., J. H. Hulstijn, and **B. Bossers.** 1998. 'Metacognitive and language-specific knowledge in native and foreign language reading comprehension: an empirical study among Dutch students in grades 6, 8, and 10.' *Language Learning* 48: 71–106.

Schraw, G. 1998. 'On the development of adult metacognition' in M. C. Smith and T. Pourchot (eds.): *Adult Learning and Development: Perspectives from Developmental Psychology.* Mahwah, N.J.: Lawrence Erlbaum Associates. pp. 89–106.

Schraw, G. and **D. Moshman.** 1995. 'Metacognitive theories.' *Educational Psychology Review* 7: 351–73.

Schwanenflugel, P. J., S. A. Stahl, and **E. L. McFalls.** 1997. 'Partial word knowledge and vocabulary growth during reading comprehension.' *Journal of Literacy Research* 29: 531–53.

Scollon, R. 1997. 'Contrastive rhetoric, contrastive poetics, or perhaps something else?' *TESOL Quarterly* 31/2: 352–58.

Shanahan, T. 1990. 'Reading and writing together: what does it really mean?' in T. Shanahan (ed.): *Reading and Writing Together: New Perspectives for the Classroom.* Norwood, MA: Christopher-Gordon Publishers, Inc.: pp. 1–18.

Shanahan, T. and **R. G. Lomax.** 1986. 'An analysis and comparison of theoretical models of the reading-writing relationship.' *Journal of Educational Psychology* 78: 116–123.

Shank, R. C. and **R. P. Ableson.** 1977. *Scripts, Plans, Goals, and Understanding.* Hillsdale, N.J.: Lawrence Erlbaum Associates.

Sheorey, R. and **K. Mokhtari.** 2001. 'Differences in the metacognitive awareness of reading strategies among native and non-native readers.' *System* 29/4: 431–49.

Shih, M. 1986. 'Content-based approaches to teaching academic writing.' *TESOL Quarterly* 20/4: 617–48.

Shu, H., R. C. Anderson, and **H. Zhang.** 1995. 'Incidental learning of word meanings while reading: a Chinese and American cross-cultural study.' *Reading Research Quarterly* 30: 76–95.

Shub, A., R. Friedman, J. P. Kaplan, J. Katien, and **J. L. Scroggin.** 1973. *Diagnosis: An Instructional Aid.* Palo Alto, CA: Science Research Associates, Inc.

Singer, H. and **D. Donlan.** 1982. 'Active comprehension: problem-solving schema with question generation for comprehension of complex short stories.' *Reading Research Quarterly* 17: 166–86.

Singhal, M. (2001). 'Reading proficiency, reading strategies, metacognitive awareness, and L2 readers.' Volume 1(1). Retrieved 8/12/02, from www.readingmatrix.com/articles/singhal/index.html.

Slater, W. H., M. F. Graves, and **G. L. Piché.** 1985. 'Effects of structural organizers on ninth-grade students' comprehension and recall of four patterns of expository text.' *Reading Research Quarterly* 20: 189–202.

Smith, F. 1971. *Understanding Reading: A Psycholinguistic Analysis of Reading and Learning to Read.* New York: Holt, Rinehart and Winston.

Smith, F. 1983.' Reading like a writer.' *Language Arts* 60/5: 558–67.

Smith, F. 1988. *Joining the Literacy Club.* Portsmouth, N.H.: Heinemann Educational Books, Inc.

Smith, F. 1994. *Understanding Reading: A Psycholinguistic Analysis of Reading and Learning to Read.* (5th edn.) Hillsdale, N.J.: Lawrence Erlbaum Associates.

Snow, M. A. and **D. M. Brinton.** 1988a. 'The adjunct model of language instruction' in S. Benesch (ed.): *Ending Remediation: Linking ESL and Content in Higher Education.* Washington, D.C.: Teachers of English to Speakers of Other Languages. pp. 33–52.

Snow, M. A. and **D. M. Brinton.** 1988b. 'Content-based language instruction: Investigating the effectiveness of the adjunct model.' *TESOL Quarterly* 22/4: 553–74.

Snow, M. A. and **D. M. Brinton.** (eds.): 1997. *The Content-based Classroom: Perspectives on Integrating Language and Content.* White Plains, New York: Addison Wesley Longman Publishing Company.

Spearritt, D. 1972. 'Identification of subskills of reading comprehension by maximum likelihood factor analysis.' *Reading Research Quarterly* 8: 92–111.

Sperber, D. and **D. Wilson.** 1988. *Relevance: Communication and Cognition.* Cambridge, MA: Harvard University Press.

Spilich, G. J., G. T. Vesonder, H. L. Chiesi, and **J. F. Voss.** 1979. 'Text processing of domain-related information for individuals with high and low domain knowledge.' *Journal of Verbal Learning and Verbal Behavior* 19: 275–90.

Spivey, N. N. 1984. 'Discourse synthesis: Constructing texts in reading and writing'. (Outstanding Dissertation Monograph Series). Newark, DE: International Reading Association.

Spivey, N. N. 1988. *Discourse Synthesis: Constructing Texts in Reading and Writing.* Newark, DE: International Reading Association.

Spivey, N. N. and **J. R. King.** 1989. 'Readers as writers composing from sources.' *Reading Research Quarterly* 24: 7–26.

Squire, J. R. 1983. 'Composing and comprehending: two sides of the same basic process.' *Language Arts* 60/5: 581–89.

Stahl, S. A. and **D. Hayes.** 1997. *Instructional Models in Reading.* Mahwah, N.J.: Lawrence Erlbaum Associates.

Stanovich, K. E. 1980. 'Toward an interactive-compensatory model of individual differences in the development of reading fluency.' *Reading Research Quarterly* 16: 32–71.

Stanovich, K. E. 1986. 'Mathew effects in reading: some consequences of individual differences in the acquisition of literacy.' *Reading Research Quarterly* 21: 360–406.

Stanovich, K. E. 1991. 'Changing models of reading and acquisition' in L. Rieben and C. A. Perfetti (eds.): *Learning to Read*. Hillsdale, N.J.: Lawrence Erlbaum Associates. pp. 19–32.

Stanovich, K. E. 2000. *Progress in Understanding Reading: Scientific Foundations and New Frontiers*. New York: Guilford Press.

Stanovich, K. E. and P. J. Stanovich. 1995. 'How research might inform the debate about early reading acquisition.' *Journal of Research in Reading* 18: 87–105.

Steffensen, M. S., C. Joag-Dev, and R. C. Anderson. 1979. 'A cross-cultural perspective on reading comprehension.' *Reading Research Quarterly* 15: 10–29.

Stein, N. L. and C. G. Glenn. 1979. 'An analysis of story comprehension in elementary school children' in R. O. Freedle (ed.): *Advances in Discourse Processes, Vol. II: New Directions in Discourse Processing*. Norwood, N.J.: Ablex. pp. 53–120.

Sternberg, R. J. 1987. 'Most vocabulary is learned from context' in M. McKeown and M. E. Curtis (eds.): *The Nature of Vocabulary Acquisition*. Hillsdale, N.J.: Lawrence Erlbaum Associates. pp. 89–105.

Sternberg, R. J. and J. S. Powell. 1983. 'Comprehending verbal comprehension.' *American Psychologist* 38: 878–93.

Strain, L. B. 1976. *Accountability in Reading Instruction*. Columbus, OH: Charles E. Merrill Publishing Co.

Street, B. V. 1993a. 'The new literacy studies.' *Journal of Research in Reading* 16: 81–97.

Street, B. V. 1993b. ' Introduction: the new literacy studies' in B. V. Street (ed.): *Cross-cultural Approaches to Literacy*. Cambridge: Cambridge University Press. pp. 1–21.

Street, B. V. 1997. 'The implications of the "new literacy studies" for literacy education.' *English in Education* 31/3: 45–59.

Street, B. V. 1999. 'New literacies in theory and practice: what are the implications for language in education?' *Linguistics and Education* 10/1: 1–24.

Street, B. V. 2003. What's "new" in new literacy studies? Critical approaches to literacy in theory and practice. *Current Issues in Comparative Education* 5/2: 1–14.

Strother, J. B. and **J. M. Ulijn.** 1987. 'Does syntactic rewriting affect English for science and technology text comprehension?' in J. Devine, P. L. Carrell, and D. E. Eskey (eds.): *Research in Reading in a Second Language.* Washington, D.C.: Teachers of English to Speakers of Other Languages. pp. 91–101.

Swales, J. M. 1981. *Aspects of Article Introductions.* Birmingham: University of Aston.

Swales, J. M. 1990. *Genre Analysis: English in Academic and Research Settings.* Cambridge: Cambridge University Press.

Swales, J. M. 2004. *Research Genres: Explorations and Applications.* Cambridge: Cambridge University Press.

Swanborn, M. S. L. and **K. de Glopper.** 1999. 'Incidental word learning while reading: a meta-analysis.' *Review of Educational Research* 69: 261–85.

Taillefer, G. F. 1996. 'L2 reading ability: further insight into the short-circuit hypothesis.' *The Modern Language Journal* 80: 461–77.

Taylor, B. M. 1979. 'Good and poor readers' recall of familiar and unfamiliar text.' *Journal of Reading Behavior* 11: 375–80.

Taylor, B. M. and **R. W. Beach.** 1984. 'The effects of text structure instruction on middle-grade students' comprehension and production of expository text.' *Reading Research Quarterly* 19/2: 134–46.

Taylor, S. E. 1962. 'An evaluation of forty-one trainees who had recently completed the "Reading Dynamics" program' in E. P. Bliesmur and R. C. Staiger (eds.): *Problems, Programs, and Projects in College Adult Reading.* Eleventh yearbook of the National Reading Conference. Milwaukee, WI: National Reading Conference. pp. 41–56.

Thorndike, E. L. and **I. Lorge.** 1944. *The Teacher's Word Book of 30,000 Words.* New York: Teachers College Press.

Thorndike, R. L. 1973. *Reading Comprehension in Fifteen Countries.* New York, Wiley and Stockholm: Almqvist and Wiksell.

Thorndyke, P. W. 1977. 'Cognitive structures in comprehension and memory of narrative discourse.' *Cognitive Psychology* 9: 77–110.

Tian, G. S. 1990. 'The effects of rhetorical organization in expository prose on ESL readers in Singapore.' *RELC Journal* 21/2: 1–13.

Tierney, R. J. and **J. H. Mosenthal.** 1980. 'Discourse comprehension and production: analyzing text structure and cohesion.' Technical Report No. 152, Center for the Study of Reading. Champaign, IL: University of Illinois.

Tierney, R. J. and **J. H. Mosenthal.** 1981. 'The cohesion concept's relationship to the coherence of text.' Technical Report No. 221, Center for the Study of Reading. Champaign, IL: University of Illinois.

Tierney, R. J. and **P. D. Pearson.** 1983. 'Toward a composing model of reading.' *Language Arts* 60: 568–79.

Tierney, R. J. and **P. D. Pearson.** 1985. 'New priorities for teaching reading.' *Learning* 13/8: 14–8.

Tierney, R. J., A. Soter, J. F. O'Flahavan, and **W. McGinley.** 1989. 'The effects of reading and writing upon thinking critically.' *Reading Research Quarterly* 24: 134–73.

Trabasso, T. and **P. W. van den Broek.** 1985. 'Causal thinking and the representation of narrative events.' *Journal of Memory and Language* 24: 612–30.

Tsang, W. K. 1996. 'Comparing the effects of reading and writing on writing performance.' *Applied Linguistics* 17/2: 210–33.

Tsao, F.-F. 1983. 'Linguistics and written discourse in particular languages: contrastive studies: English and Chinese (Mandarin).' *Annual Review of Applied Linguistics* 3: 99–117.

Tulving, E. and **C. Gold.** 1963. 'Stimulus information and contextual information as determinants of tachistoscopic recognition of words'. *Journal of Experimental Psychology* 66: 319–327.

Ulijn, J. M. 1980. 'Foreign language reading research: recent trends and future projects'. *Journal of Research in Reading* 3: 17–37.

Ulijn, J. M. and **G. A. M. Kempen.** 1976. 'The role of the first language in second language reading comprehension. Some experimental evidence.' in G. Nickel (ed.): Proceedings of the 4th International Congress of Applied Linguistics, Vol. 1. Stuttgart: Hochschulverlag.

Ulijn, J. M. and **J. B. Strother.** 1990. 'The effect of syntactic simplification on reading EST texts as L1 and L2.' *Journal of Research in Reading* 13: 38–54.

Unger, J. M. and **J. DeFrancis.** 1995. 'Logographic and semasiographic writing systems: a critique of Sampson's classification' in I. Taylor and D. R. Olson (eds.): Scripts and Literacy: *Reading and Learning to Read Alphabets, Syllabaries and Characters.* Dordrecht, Netherlands: Kluwer Academic Publishers. pp. 45–58.

Upton, T. A. (1997). 'First and second language use in reading comprehension strategies of Japanese ESL students.' Retrieved 2/19/02, from www-writing.berkeley.edu/TESL-EJ/ej09/a3.html.

Valencia, S. W., A. C. Stallman, M. Commeyras, P. D. Pearson, and **D. K. Hartman.** 1991. 'Four measures of topical knowledge: a study of construct validity.' *Reading Research Quarterly* 26/3: 204–33.

Valle, E. 1997. 'A scientific community and its texts: a historical discourse study' in B.-L. Gunnarson, P. Linell, and B. Nordberg (eds.): *The Construction of Professional Discourse.* London: Longman. pp. 76–98.

van den Broek, P. W. 1988. 'The effects of causal relations and hierarchical position on the importance of story statements.' *Journal of Memory and Language* 27: 1–22.

van Dijk, T. and **W. Kintsch** 1978. 'Cognitive psychology and discourse: recalling and summarizing stories' in W. Dressler (ed.): *Current Trends in Text Linguistics*. Berlin, de Gruyter. pp. 61–80.

van Dijk, T. A. 1977. *Text and Context*. London: Longman.

van Dijk, T. A. and **W. Kintsch.** 1983. *Strategies of Discourse Comprehension*. New York: Academic Press.

Venezky, R. L. 1984. 'The history of reading research' in P. D. Pearson, R. Barr, M. Kamil, and J. H. Mosenthal (eds.). pp. 3–38.

Vermeer, A. 2001. 'Breadth and depth of vocabulary in relation to L1/L2 acquisition and fluency of input.' *Applied Psycholinguistics* 22: 217–34.

Walters, J. and **Y. Wolf.** 1986. 'Language proficiency, text content and order effects in narrative recall.' *Language Learning* 36: 47–64.

Watanabe, Y. (1992). *Effects of increased processing on incidental learning of foreign language vocabulary*. Unpublished MA Thesis University of Hawaii at Manoa.

Watanabe, Y. 1997. 'Input, intake, and retention: effects of increased processing on incidental learning of foreign language vocabulary.' *Studies in Second Language Acquisition* 19: 287–307.

Weaver, C. A., III and **W. Kintsch.** 1996. 'Expository text' in R. Barr, M. Kamil, P. Mosenthal and P. D. Pearson (eds.). pp. 230–45.

Wellman, H. M. 1988. 'The early development of memory strategies' in F. E. Weinert and M. Perlmutter (eds.): *Memory Development: Universal Changes and Individual Differences*. Hillsdale, N.J.: Lawrence Erlbaum Associates. pp. 3–29.

Wesche, M. and **T. Paribakht.** 1996. 'Assessing second language vocabulary knowledge: depth versus breadth.' *The Canadian Modern Language Review/La Revue canadienne des langues vivantes* 53: 13–40.

West, M. 1953. *A General Service List of English Words*. London: Longman.

Wilensky, R. 1982. 'Points: A theory of the structure of stories in memory' in W. G. Lehnert and H. Ringle (eds.): *Strategies for Natural Language Processing*. Hillsdale, N.J.: Lawrence Erlbaum Associates. pp. 345–74.

Wilhelm, J. D. 2001. *Improving Comprehension with Think-aloud Strategies*. New York: Scholastic Professional Books.

Wilkinson, I. A. G., J. Elkins, and **J. D. Bain.** 1995. 'Individual differences in story comprehension and recall of poor readers.' *British Journal of Educational Psychology* 65: 393–407.

Williams, I. A. 1999. 'Results sections of medical research articles: analysis of rhetorical categories for pedagogical purposes.' *English for Specific Purposes* 18/4: 347–66.

Winograd, P. 1984. 'Strategic difficulties in summarizing texts.' *Reading Research Quarterly* 19/4: 404–425.

Wittrock, M. C. 1983. 'Writing and the teaching of reading.' *Language Arts* 60/5: 600–6.

Xue, G.-Y. and **I. S. P. Nation.** 1984. 'A university word list.' *Language Learning and Communication* 3: 215–29.

Yamashita, J. 2002. 'Mutual compensation between L1 reading ability and L2 language proficiency in L2 reading.' *Journal of Research in Reading* 25/1: 81–95.

Yano, Y., M. H. Long, and **S. Ross.** 1994. 'The effects of simplified texts on foreign language reading comprehension.' *Language Learning* 44: 189–219.

Yorio, C. A. 1971. 'Some sources of reading problems for foreign language learners.' *Language Learning* 21: 107–15.

Zahar, R., T. Cobb, and **N. Spada.** 2001. 'Acquiring vocabulary through reading: effects of frequency and contextual richness.' *The Canadian Modern Language Review/La Revue canadienne des langues vivantes* 57/5: 41–72.

Zamel, V. 1992. 'Writing one's way into reading.' *TESOL Quarterly* 26/3: 463–85.

Zhang, L. J. 2001. 'Awareness in reading: EFL students' metacognitive knowledge of reading strategies in an acquisition-poor environment.' *Language Awareness* 10/4: 268–88.

Zhu, Y. 1997. 'An analysis of structural moves in Chinese sales letters.' *Text* 17/4: 543–66.

Zhu, Y. 2000. 'Structural moves reflected in English and Chinese sales letters.' *Discourse Studies* 2: 473–96.

Zinar, S. 2000. 'The relative contributions of word identification skill and comprehension-monitoring behavior to reading comprehension ability.' *Contemporary Educational Psychology* 25: 363–77.

INDEX

Note: References to the Glossary are indicated by 'g' after the page number.